JUDITH HERRIN

Byzantium

The Surprising Life of a Medieval Empire

PENGUIN BOOKS

PENGUIN BOOKS

Published by the Penguin Group
Penguin Books Ltd, 80 Strand, London WC2R ORL, England
Penguin Group (USA) Inc., 375 Hudson Street, New York, New York 10014, USA
Penguin Group ... 'a M4P 2Y3

Penguin Ireland, 25 St Stephen's Green, Dublin 2, Ireland

Penguin ... Australia ... Camberwell Road ... Victoria ... stralia

Penguin Books ... 017, India
Penguin ... nd

Penguin Books (S ... , South Africa

Pen ... d

Typeset by Rowland Phototypesetting Ltd, Bury St Edmunds, Suffolk
Printed in England by Clays Ltd, St Ives plc

978-0-141-03102-6

www.greenpenguin.co.uk

Mixed Sources
Product group from well-managed
forests and other controlled sources
www.fsc.org Cert no. SA-COC-1592
© 1996 Forest Stewardship Council

Penguin Books is committed to a sustainable future
for our business, our readers and our planet.
The book in your hands is made from paper
certified by the Forest Stewardship Council.

For Tamara and Portia,

who also asked,

What is Byzantium?

The cover shows Empress Zoe (*c.* 978–1050) horizontally, as if lying on her back. The mosaic was put up in the south gallery of Hagia Sophia in the eleventh century, probably on the occasion of her first marriage (Plate 17 shows it in full with Zoe and her husband flanking a portrait of Christ). However, she married more than once. As the daughter of Emperor Constantine VIII, she transmitted imperial power in turn to three husbands, marrying the last on 11 June 1042. At that point all three heads in the mosaic were renewed as well as the inscriptions. As her last husband's name, Konstantinos, is longer than his predecessors the extra letters have been squeezed in rather awkwardly above his head and on the scroll Zoe is holding. She was about sixty years old then – but is depicted as a young beauty – and the scroll records the privileges she and her new husband granted to the church.

Zoe would have been able to read the scroll. Imperial and high-ranking women in Byzantium were normally well educated as well as influential. So this image reflects some of the themes of this book: the remarkable literacy of Byzantine society, its powerful sense of tradition, the exceptionally important role of women over imperial authority, the quality of Byzantine art, the self-confidence of its inhabitants, and their capacity for renewal.

As you can see, the lowest levels of gold tesserae from the bottom of the mosaic have been picked off. For centuries, generations of superstitious tourists and travellers took them, whether as a memento or to share in its depiction of piety and good fortune. While the masterpiece in today's Hagia Sophia, the immense cathedral of Byzantine influence, still awaits future visitors, much evidence of Byzantine culture has been lost in this way. Zoe's scroll is also a symbol of the destruction of almost all the written records of the Empire, another theme discussed in the book.

Contents

III
Byzantium Becomes a Medieval State

IV
Varieties of Byzantium

List of Illustrations

Photographic acknowledgements are given in parentheses.

List of Maps

Introduction:
A Different History of Byzantium

One afternoon in 2002, two workmen knocked on my office door in King's College, London. They were doing repairs to the old buildings and had often passed my door with its notice: 'Professor of Byzantine History'. Together they decided to stop by and ask me, 'What is Byzantine history?' They thought that it had something to do with Turkey.

And so I found myself trying to explain briefly what Byzantine history is to two serious builders in hard hats and heavy boots. Many years of teaching had not prepared me for this. I tried to sum up a lifetime of study in a ten-minute visit. They thanked me warmly, said how curious it was, this Byzantium, and asked why didn't I write about it for them? For someone dedicated to publishing on Byzantium I felt like objecting, but of course I knew what they meant. Endless books are written on Byzantine history – too many to count and most too long to read. Often they describe the succession of 90 emperors, and about 125 patriarchs of Constantinople, and innumerable battles, in predictable categories of political, military and religious activity, relentlessly across eleven hundred years. Few are attractive enough to engage the interest of construction workers, or indeed non-specialists of virtually any other kind. So I began to compose an answer to the question: 'What is Byzantine history?'

Immediately I got into difficulties – I made too many assumptions, couldn't resist the abstruse anecdote. But I had always prided myself on being able to make Byzantine history interesting to audiences unfamiliar with it. As I searched for a method, I knew very well that in its long millennium Byzantium had enough colourful, shocking and tragic aspects to attract those who were seeking the sensational. But this reduced its history to dramatic episodes without depth, flattening the whole experience. Byzantium means more than wealth, mastery of the sea and the exercise of imperial power. I wanted them, and you the reader, to sense why Byzantium is also hard to grasp, difficult to place and can be obscure. This difficulty is compounded by contemporary newspapers' use of 'Byzantine' as a term of insult, for example in phrases like 'tax regulations of positively Byzantine complexity' (a recent description of EU negotiations).

Byzantium conjures up an image of opaque duplicity: plots, assassinations and physical mutilation, coupled with excessive wealth, glittering gold and jewels. During the Middle Ages, however, the Byzantines had no monopoly on complexity, treachery, hypocrisy, obscurity or riches. They produced a large number of intelligent leaders, brilliant military generals and innovative theologians, who are much maligned and libelled by such 'Byzantine' stereotypes. They never developed an Inquisition and generally avoided burning people at the stake. But there is a mystery associated with this 'lost' world, which is hard to define, partly because it does not have a modern heir. It remains hidden behind the glories of its medieval art: the gold, mosaics, silks and imperial palaces.

To explain my appreciation of Byzantium, in this book I aim to set out its most significant high points as clearly and compellingly as I can; to reveal the structures and mentalities which sustained it. In this way I want to keep you interested to the end, so that you feel you get to know a new civilization. Crucially, I want you to understand how the modern western world, which developed from Europe, could not have existed had it not been shielded and inspired by what happened further to the east in Byzantium. The Muslim world is also an important element of this history, as is the love–hate relationship between Christendom and Islam.

What are the key features of this important but little-known history? First, Byzantium was a thousand-year-long civilization which influenced all the countries of the eastern Mediterranean, the Balkans and Western Europe throughout the Middle Ages. From the sixth to the fifteenth century, this influence waxed and waned but was a constant. Its civilization drew on pagan, Christian, Greek, Roman, ancient and specifically medieval components. Its cultural and artistic influences are now recognized as a lasting inheritance. But in addition, fundamental aspects of government such as the development of an imperial court with a diplomatic service and civilian bureaucracy, the ceremony of coronation, as well as the female exercise of political power, all developed in Byzantium.

The grandeur of Constantinople, at the centre of a vast empire, with an inherited system of imperial government, and the variety of sources that inspired it, combined to give enormous confidence to both rulers and ruled. It is necessary to emphasize this aspect of Byzantium. By the time of the Emperor Justinian (527–65), the underlying structures of empire were two hundred years old and so firmly embedded that they appeared unchangeable. They had created a deeply rooted culture that sprang from ancient Greek, pre-Christian sources, as well as Roman and Christian ideas, both ideological and practical (for instance, philosophical arguments and military fortifications). The entire system was celebrated in imperial rhetoric and displayed in imperial art intended to elevate it to an everlasting permanency. However vacuous the sentiments expressed, they nonetheless confirmed and further engrained the self-confidence of Byzantine emperors, their courtiers and more humble subjects. They provided the bedrock of Byzantium's exceptional ability to respond to severe challenges in the seventh century, again in the eleventh and most spectacularly in 1204. Each time it was able to adapt and reform by drawing on these deep inherited structures that combined in a rich awareness of traditions.

In this sense, Byzantine culture embodies the French historian Fernand Braudel's notion of the *longue durée*, the long term: that which survives the vicissitudes of changing governments, newfangled fashions or technological improvements, an ongoing inheritance that can both imprison and inspire. While Braudel applied this idea more to the geographical factors that determined the history of the Mediterranean, we can adapt it to distinguish Byzantine culture from those of its neighbours. For in contrast to other medieval societies both in the West and among the Muslims, Byzantium was old, many centuries old by the time of Charlemagne and Harun al-Rashid in AD 800, and the structure of its culture was both a constraint and a source of strength. Indeed, as we will see, it was born old, importing into its capital city at its construction the authority of already antique architecture and statuary. Its established cultural framework, condemned as conservative, praised as traditional, provided a shared sense of belonging, commemorated in distinctive and changing fashions all dedicated to the greater glory of Byzantium. This created a flexible heritage which proved able to respond, often with great determination, to enhance, preserve and sustain the empire through many crises.

Byzantium's imperial identity was strengthened by a linguistic continuity that linked its medieval scholars back to ancient Greek culture, and encouraged them to preserve texts by major philosophers, mathematicians, astronomers, geographers, historians and doctors by copying, editing and commenting on them. Above all, Byzantium cherished the poems of Homer and produced the first critical editions of the *Iliad* and *Odyssey*. Although public performances of theatre died away, the plays of Aeschylus, Sophocles, Euripides and Aristophanes were closely studied and often committed to memory by generations of schoolchildren. They also learnt the speeches of Demosthenes and the dialogues of Plato. A strong element of ancient pagan wisdom was thus incorporated into Byzantium.

This ancient heritage was combined with Christian belief, which gradually replaced the cults of the pagan gods. Byzantium nurtured early Christian monastic traditions on holy mountains like Sinai and Athos, where spiritual teachings still inspire monks and pilgrims. It undertook the conversion of the Bulgarians, Serbs and Russians to Christianity, which is why large parts of the Balkans are still dotted with Orthodox churches decorated with medieval frescoes and icons. And it maintained contact with those Christian centres that passed under Muslim control during the seventh century, supporting the patriarchs of Jerusalem, Alexandria and Antioch, as well as communities even more distant like the churches of Ethiopia and Sudan, Persia, Armenia and Georgia.

Using the inheritance of Roman technology and engineering skill, Byzantium continued to build aqueducts, fortifications, roads and bridges, and huge constructions such as the church of Holy Wisdom, St Sophia in Constantinople, which still displays its massive sixth-century form, complete with the largest dome ever built until St Peter's in Rome a thousand years later. Its Byzantine dome has often been repaired but remains intact, and is copied in numerous smaller versions found in churches all over the Orthodox world. It also inspired the form for covered mosques, constructed when the Arabs moved out of their desert homeland where they worshipped in open courts. The Dome of the Rock in Jerusalem is aptly named to commemorate the Muslim occupation of a holy place cherished by Jews and Christians. Not only its circular roof but also its vivid mosaics display Byzantine origins, since the seventh-century Emperor Justinian II was asked by Caliph 'Abd al-Malik to send Byzantine craftsmen to cut the coloured stone and glass tesserae, which shimmer whenever they catch the light. They may also have set the 240-metre-long inscription from the Qur'an, running round the base of the dome, that Islam is the final revelation of Allah (God) and is superior to all others.

From Rome, Byzantium also inherited a developed legal system and a military tradition. Both supported its long history. In theory, Byzantine society lived by the rule of law; judges were trained, salaried and presided over the resolution of disputes. Throughout the empire people brought their grievances to the courts and accepted their judgments. Although the celebrated Roman legions did not continue beyond the seventh century, fighting forces, both foot and cavalry, were trained according to Roman military manuals. Strategies for fighting on land and at sea, siege weapons, methods of supplying the forces, their armour and protective clothing were all adapted from older practice. The composition of 'Greek fire', a sulphurous substance that burns on water, remained a state secret and we still do not know the precise combination of its components. While a similar weapon was developed by the Arabs, Greek fire terrified those unfamiliar with it both in sea battles and in city sieges.

Byzantium considered itself the centre of the world, and Constantinople as the replacement of Rome. Though Greek-speaking, it saw itself as the Roman Empire and its citizens as Romans. It exercised leadership over the Greek-speaking communities in Sicily and southern Italy which were a product of ancient Greek emigration. It both sheltered and stimulated the growth of Italian coastal cities, such as medieval Amalfi and Venice, which lived off international trade. In due course these centres overtook Byzantium as economic centres in their own right and developed superior naval and mercantile capacity. But their debt to Byzantium is clear. Bronze doors commissioned in Constantinople adorn their cathedrals, which are frequently decorated with marble, mosaic and icons in Byzantine style. Their prosperity was born under the wing of the empire.

Perhaps for us today, the most significant feature of Byzantium lies in its historic role in protecting the Christian West in the early Middle Ages. Until the seventh century, Byzantium was indeed the Roman Empire. It ruled North Africa and Egypt, the granaries that fed both Rome and Constantinople, southern Italy, the Holy Land, Asia Minor as far east as Mount Ararat, all of today's Greece and much of the Balkans. Then the tribes of Arabia inspired by the new religion of Islam conquered most of the eastern Mediterranean. They fought in the name of a revelation that presented itself as the successor to the Jewish and Christian faiths. Byzantium checked their expansion into Asia Minor and prevented them from crossing the Dardanelles and gaining access to the Balkans. Constantinople held out against numerous sieges.

The Muslims' aim of capturing Constantinople, making it their capital and taking over the entire Roman world was more than legitimate. It was also logical. Since Islam claimed to supersede both Judaism and Christianity, its forces would naturally replace Rome and take over the political structures of the ancient world. If one follows the ambitions recorded in the Qur'an, the entire Mediterranean should have been reunited under Muslim control. The Persian world of Zoroastrian beliefs would also succumb to Islam. In extraordinarily swift and successful campaigns between 634 and 644, the Arab tribesmen came close to achieving this goal. They provoked the first major turning point in Byzantine history.

Had Byzantium not halted their expansion in 678, Muslim forces charged by the additional resources of the capital city would have spread Islam throughout the Balkans, into Italy and the West during the seventh century, at a time when political fragmentation reduced the possibility of organized defence. By preventing this potential conquest, Byzantium made Europe possible. It allowed western Christian forces, which were divided into small units, time to develop their own strengths. One hundred years after the death of the Prophet

Muhammad in 632, Charles Martel defeated Muslim invaders from Spain in central France near Poitiers and forced them back over the Pyrenees. The nascent idea of Europe gradually took on a particular form under Charles's grandson and namesake, Charles the Great. Charlemagne and his successors fought their own battles and were responsible for creating their own Europe.

During the Middle Ages, most western clerics and rulers were aware, however dimly, of the Christian civilization of Byzantium in the East. Although Byzantium controlled a much smaller empire than Rome at its height, from the seventh to the fifteenth century this medieval state developed new political and cultural forms. It combined different strands from its past to forge a new medieval civilization, which attracted many non-Christian northern tribes. In turn, the Bulgars, Russians and Serbs adopted Christian faith and elements of Byzantine culture. For about seven hundred years Byzantium remained a beacon of orthodox belief and classical learning.

The period of the crusades put Byzantium at the centre of the Christian effort to win back the Holy Places from Muslim control. From the eleventh century onwards, Byzantium and the West became mutually more familiar, often with very negative results. Despite the success of the First Crusade in establishing the Latin Kingdom of Jerusalem, the Fourth Crusade turned against Constantinople and sacked the city in 1204. This was the second great turning point in Byzantine history. The empire was never able to restore its previous strength or form. Although they regained the capital, Byzantine emperors ruled over what had become in effect a city-state from 1261 to 1453, when Constantinople was finally captured by the Ottoman Turks.

But curiously, Byzantine cultural influence expanded almost in inverse proportion to its political strength. From 1204 when numerous works of art were taken back to Western Europe, Byzantium's contribution to the revival of western art and learning is notable. In the fourteenth century, Byzantine teachers of Greek were appointed to Italian universities and they and their pupils began to translate the writings of Plato. Aristotle's works had already reached the West via the Muslim world, but most of Plato's philosophy remained unknown. During the negotiations in Florence which led to a reunion of the western and eastern churches in 1439, public lectures on Plato by the famous Greek scholar and philosopher George Gemistos Plethon inspired Cosimo de' Medici to establish his Platonic Academy. The Byzantine contribution to the Italian Renaissance thus began much earlier than 1453, when the Turks made Constantinople their own capital. Following the fall of the city, refugees who fled to Italy with their manuscripts strengthened the new learning and new art. And a few decades later, when the Protestant reformers condemned religious art and argued for a more spiritual style of Christian worship, they employed all the biblical and patristic texts collected by Byzantine iconoclasts of the eighth and ninth centuries.

Throughout this book I seek to illuminate what Byzantium was, how it worked and what it stands for. This intensely personal view grew out of my previous research for *The Formation of Christendom* on the significance of religion in early medieval history. Matters of faith were vitally important for people who lived in the Middle Ages in ways which are unfamiliar to most in the modern West, and secular scholarship and popular appreciation of medieval art needs to understand how this was so. In addition to the issues that both united and divided Christians, their religious world was filled by other beliefs: unconverted polytheists, adherents of the eastern cults, followers of Zoroaster and Mani, as well as long-established Jewish communities. Islam made a profound impact throughout this world on all who lived on the eastern and southern shores of the Mediterranean, in Syria and Spain and all regions in between. In the eighth century, the first official destruction of icons (iconoclasm) in Byzantium provoked ordinary people to die for the sake of their religious images. While Islam developed a strict ban on holy images, Rome discovered its allegiance to icons, and Charlemagne's theologians began to doubt theirs. The eighth and ninth centuries were thus critical to the development of three separate but related regions: the Byzantine East, the Islamic South – Egypt, North Africa and Spain – and the Latin West which became Europe. In different forms, this division has lasted until our own time.

A further fascination with this period of history lies in the apparent devotion of women to religious icons in medieval Byzantium, which may be related to the exclusion of women from the official church hierarchy. It also raises questions about the motives of the two female rulers I write about in *Women in Purple*, who restored the veneration of icons in 787 and 843. When Empresses Irene and Theodora reversed the iconoclast policy, introduced and supported by their husbands and more distant male relatives, they seem to me to have acted with all the ruthlessness and guile of men. But in taking these initiatives, they also assumed a political prominence that is unparalleled in other medieval societies. So while chroniclers of the time assume that their love of icons is a feature of feminine weakness, there is clearly more to this link, which I would connect with a Byzantine tradition of female rule, 'the imperial feminine'.

Digging up Byzantium was another way of discovering the Byzantines. On excavations in Greece, Cyprus and at Kalenderhane Camii, a major site in the heart of Constantinople, modern Istanbul, I worked with the material culture on which its civilization was built. Exploring the churches of Crete and Kythera, an island off the south coast of mainland Greece, and recording pottery finds at the medieval manor house of Kouklia in southwest Cyprus, brings you very close to their medieval inhabitants. In my first archaeological season at Paphos, also in Cyprus, we found the remains of a female skeleton in the ruins of the castle of Saranda Kolonnes, with the gold and pearl rings she was wearing when the earthquake of 1222 struck. In Istanbul, workmen investigating a winter leak at the mosque of the Kalendars discovered a hollow behind a wall close to the monumental aqueduct which still dominates the old city. One of these skilled restorers felt round the edge of a panel and identified the tesserae of what turned out to be an early Christian mosaic of the Virgin presenting the Christ Child to Symeon. It had possibly been covered by a wall to protect it from iconoclast destruction. Similarly, an entire chapel with fragmentary frescoes dedicated to St Francis of Assisi had been bricked up in 1261 when the friars fled from Constantinople after the Latin occupation. These two fine works of Christian art, eastern and western, were later restored by Ernest Hawkins and are now on display in the Archaeological Museum in Istanbul.

My understanding of Byzantium was also coloured by far-flung witnesses to its medieval dominance. As a teenager I was taken to

Ravenna in northern Italy and was astounded by the mosaic portraits of the Byzantine Emperor Justinian and his wife, Empress Theodora, the stars in the heavenly firmament of Galla Placidia's tomb, and the processions of saints and flocks of sheep that decorate the city's churches. In 2005, over forty years later, I was privileged to climb into the roof of the church of St Catherine's monastery in the Sinai peninsula, which was built by the same imperial couple, despite the 2,000 miles between the north Adriatic and the Red Sea. There, on what was thought to be the site of the Burning Bush, where Moses was instructed to take off his sandals because the ground was holy, I read the inscriptions that record the patronage of Justinian and Theodora, carved on the original sixth-century beams which survive perfectly in the dry, termite-free conditions of the Egyptian desert. Such physical experiences give immediacy to what Byzantine historians wrote about the emperor and his wife.

In Rome, Sicily, Moscow, and of course most clearly in Constantinople, all over Turkey, Greece and the Balkans, you can see Byzantium preserved. But there is nothing like the amazement of finding Byzantine mosaics in the mihrab of the Mezquita, the Great Mosque of Cordoba, in Spain, which were commissioned by the tenth-century Caliph al-Hakam II; or the surprise of arriving late in the afternoon at Trebizond on the Black Sea after the long journey through the Pontic Alps, and looking up at the palace above the city.

Byzantium also lives on in the experience of witnessing the descent of the Easter fire at the Holy Sepulchre in Jerusalem, when in darkness the metropolitan emerges from the tomb with a lit candle marking the Resurrection of Christ, from which all the faithful light their own. Even in modern Athens today, the crowds descending Mount Lykabettos with their candles after midnight on Easter Sunday are a forceful reminder of the power of ceremonies which have commemorated the event for nearly two millennia.

For reasons that will become apparent in this book, Byzantine objects have been scattered throughout Europe and are preserved in unexpected museums. Coming across the Byzantine silk called the Cloak of Alexander in Bavaria, or finding the tenth-century marriage contract of Theophano and Otto II in Wolfenbüttel, or tenth-century ivories now used as book covers, makes you aware of the craftsmen who produced them and the culture in which such luxuries were made. In the West these have been treasured for centuries, although western medieval scholars and churchmen were also responsible for encouraging many of the misleading stereotypes of what 'Byzantine' means.

Byzantium became more familiar to me every time I prepared courses on its history. I specially want to thank all those students who challenged my views. While it is customary to acknowledge this influence, in my case my appointment to Princeton in 1990 brought an unexpected bonus in the exposure to a particularly brilliant group of graduates attracted by an unrivalled history faculty. Among such stimulating colleagues and intellectually curious students, I was encouraged to try out new ways of communicating my passion for Byzantium. Christine Stansell, one of those colleagues, later visited me in London and asked with sympathy and expectation whether it was not 'time to bring in the harvest'. This book is partly due to her, as well as to my unexpected visitors.

This brings me back to the question of form. In Shakespeare's London, the bezant and caviar were equally familiar: a gold coin named after Byzantium and the fish roe consumed in such quantities by its inhabitants. In such indirect ways, the heritage of Byzantium can be found in unexpected places. This book attempts to show why. Rather than follow the pattern of numerous earlier introductions and studies, I decided to select particular events, monuments and individuals characteristic of Byzantium and to explore them within a framework that observes the basic divisions of Byzantine history. The first seven chapters are devoted to essential subjects such as the city of Constantinople, law or orthodoxy, and range right across the Byzantine millennium. Other chapters overlap if they approach the same events from different perspectives. My chief problem has been one of exclusion, for it is hard to leave out so many rich examples and intriguing details. I can only provide a selection of *meze*, a dish of starters. The recommended further reading at the end of the book may encourage many additional, fuller courses. Here I try to answer the question posed by the builders at King's, and to explain why we should all know more about Byzantine history.

I

Foundations of Byzantium

I

The City of Constantine

Constantine resolved to make the city a home fit for an
emperor . . . He surrounded it with a wall . . . cutting off the
whole isthmus from sea to sea. He built a palace scarcely in-
ferior to the one in Rome. He decorated the Hippodrome most
beautifully, incorporating the temple of the Dioscuri in it.

Zosimus, *New History*, c. 501

Byzantium–Constantinople–Istanbul is one of the most extraordinary
natural sites. Like New York, Sydney and Hong Kong, it is a great
metropolis with a deep-water harbour which brings the sea into the
heart of the city. The proximity of water, the play of sunlight on the
waves and views out towards the horizon create a very special quality
of light. What attracted Constantine when he looked for a new capital
for the Roman Empire in the early fourth century AD was a location
from which he could control land and sea routes between Asia and
Europe. He found a suitable site with a safe harbour on the Golden
Horn, which could be sealed by a chain to keep out enemy ships and
provide security from the dangerous currents of the Bosphoros. The
lighthouse known as the Maiden's Tower was believed to mark the
spot where Leander of Greek myth swam to his beloved Hero (a
confusion between the Bosphoros and the Dardanelles). Now it guides
Russian tankers. But until recently you could rent a small boat and
be rowed across the strait, with a magnificent panorama of Constantinople. And although there are now two bridges joining Asia and
Europe, and modern Istanbul has a population of 12 million, passen-
ger ferries continue to cross the Bosphoros, offering glasses of black

3

tea and *semits*, rings of baked dough coated with sesame. On a fine day it is one of the great pleasures of life in Istanbul to sit on deck and enjoy a splendid view of Constantine's city.

Born in the central Balkans at Niš, Constantine was the son of Emperor Constantius Chlorus, one of the four rulers established by Diocletian (284–305), in an attempt to provide a much-needed element of stability in the vast Roman world. The Tetrarchy, 'rule of four', effectively divided the empire into two halves, ruled by two emperors acting in concert, with two junior colleagues who would succeed to full power on their death. It faltered due to the ambitions of sons of emperors who were denied a role. Constantine manifested this very problem after his father's death at York in 306, when he was acclaimed emperor by his troops. Yet he was not recognized by Licinius, the senior emperor in the East, and a few years later there were three different military leaders each claiming the imperial title in the West. Moving south from England, Constantine fought and defeated the others, and then in 312 confronted Maxentius at the Milvian Bridge just outside Rome. After this decisive victory Constantine entered the eternal city in triumph, where he was acclaimed by the Senate but declined to thank the gods for his success at the Altar of Victory in the expected fashion. Later he said that he had seen a vision of the Cross in the sky, which he interpreted as a sign from the God of the Christians, who promised him victory. He had made himself Emperor of the West by military conquest and now had to negotiate with Licinius, Emperor of the East.

The two rulers met at Milan in 313 and consolidated their joint administration by marriage alliances which united the empire. They also decided to issue an Edict of Toleration, which proclaimed that all religions could be celebrated freely, including Christianity, so long as adherents of every god prayed for the well-being of the Roman Empire and the emperors. Ever since, Christians have prayed for the well-being of their monarchs. Whatever Constantine's personal beliefs (see below), in 313 he had taken a step towards making the faith the official religion of the empire and consistently favoured the Christians. Intense rivalry between the two rulers was only resolved eleven years later when Constantine defeated Licinius at Chrysopolis on the Asiatic side of the Bosphoros. He took his rival prisoner, exiled him to

Thessalonike and treacherously had him assassinated. In this way in 324 Constantine became ruler of the greater, richer and more populated East as well as the West. He had ridden and fought across the length and breadth of the Roman world, which he ruled for another thirteen years until his death in 337.

After his victory over Licinius, Constantine decided that the empire needed a capital in the East, closer to its most serious rival, Persia, which regularly threatened to invade. The ancient city of Troy was considered. Instead, Constantine chose the colony established by Greeks from Megara, supposedly in the seventh century BC, on the European shore of the Bosphoros. From this mythical origin Byzantion had flourished, controlling shipping through the treacherous waters that link the Black Sea with the Sea of Marmara, which in turn flows into the Aegean at the Dardanelles.

Byzantion was built on an elevation and had a well-protected harbour on the Golden Horn. Since the sea bordered it on three sides, to the north (the Golden Horn), the east (Bosphoros) and the south (Sea of Marmara), the only fortification required to enclose the city was a wall in the west. In addition, Byzantion commanded the routes for the lucrative sea-borne transport of amber, furs, metal and wood from the north; oil, grain, papyrus and flax from the Mediterranean; spices imported from the Far East, as well as overland trade between the West and Asia. In the late third century, Emperor Septimius Severus had strengthened its walls, which were always a weak point, and added new monuments.

Constantine transformed Byzantion into a new capital with his own name in the same way that Hadrian founded Hadrianopolis (Adrianople) and Alexander the Great Alexandria. In traditional ceremonies performed in 324, a line was ploughed to mark out the new land walls, which quadrupled the extent of the city and maximized the potential of the site, enclosing an area of approximately eight square kilometres, as Zosimus describes. Gates in the western wall and along the Marmara and Golden Horn were laid out. After six years of intensive construction, the city of Constantine, Constantinople, was inaugurated on 11 May 330 with ceremonies redolent of ancient civic pride and urban festivals. Horse and chariot races, the favourite sport of all Romans, were held in the Hippodrome; the new baths of Zeuxippos were opened for public use; and foodstuffs, clothing and money were distributed to the inhabitants. Those privileged to live in the new capital adopted the name Byzantine, to indicate their affinity with the ancient colony of Byzantion, and to distinguish themselves as its true citizens.

The city of Constantine drew into its centre the great trading routes, both naval and overland, that meet at the deep-water channel separating Europe from Asia. Unlike the Greek colony of Chrysopolis on the Asian side of the Bosphoros, it was protected by its physical setting on an elevated rocky peninsula. One great advantage of being almost surrounded by water was that the western wall stretching across the peninsula enclosed a large amount of land by a relatively short line of fortification. Furthermore, it was harder for the defenders to be taken by surprise by a land attack. It required a regular water supply that was assured by long aqueducts and cisterns for collecting rainwater. With easy access to fertile hinterlands and rich fishing grounds, Constantinople also became a natural fortress exceptionally difficult to storm.

Even with these natural advantages, the decisive element in the city's defence was always its inhabitants, their institutions, culture and organization created within the walls. From the beginning, Constantinople was also called New Rome. In imitation of Old Rome, it was laid out with fourteen regions and seven hills, linked by wide avenues leading from the centre to the gates in the western wall. Its squares were decorated with ancient sculptures collected from all parts of the empire. On its acropolis overlooking the Bosphoros there were two temples dedicated to Rhea, the mother of the gods, and to Fortuna Romae (the Fortune of Rome). In the central Forum of Constantine stood a dramatic porphyry column made of drums of purple stone brought from Egypt. At the top, a pagan statue of Apollo was adapted to represent the emperor. Works of art decorated the porticoes around this circular public space, which had triumphal arches at east and west marking entry to the Mese (the main thoroughfare).

Constantine brought sculptures from all parts of the empire to embellish his new capital, including the Serpent Column dedicated after the Greek victory over the Persians at Plataea (479 BC) from Delphi, and an Egyptian obelisk from Karnak celebrating a much earlier triumph. The Hippodrome became an open-air museum adorned with protecting, symbolic and victorious Greaco-Roman images. Statues of pagan gods (Zeus, Heracles), wild and fantastic animals, and rulers including Alexander the Great, Julius Caesar and Augustus, and of Rome, in the form of the wolf with Romulus and Remus, vied with trophies of military victory. Four ancient bronze horses were set up above the starting gates at the entrance to inspire competitors and spectators alike in the ancient skills of the races (plate 30). With broad thoroughfares linking the regions, each bordered by colonnades in which shopkeepers and craftsmen established their trades, the new capital was constructed to impress.

In his city Constantine minted the solidus (in Greek, *nomisma*), which he had introduced in the West in 309. It was a new type of 24-carat gold coin, which became the most reliable currency of Late Antiquity and the Byzantine world. Until the early eleventh century, all emperors minted gold coins of comparable fineness and quality, maintaining a stable standard for over seven hundred years, an extraordinary achievement (plate 22). Since personifications of Rome and of Victory had often been represented on imperial coins, Constantine adapted this type using the Tyche (Good Luck, Fortuna) of Constantinople. She appears as a woman enthroned, wearing a crown of battlements to represent the city walls, and holding a cornucopia to represent its wealth, an allegory in female form of male power, elucidated by Marina Warner. Imperial coinage minted in Constantinople brought the symbol of the new capital into wide circulation. Gradually the cross became more prominent and replaced ancient symbols, but a portrait of Christ was not used until the late seventh century (plate 11a). After the seventh century, the *nomisma* became the only gold available in the Middle Ages and was highly prized in regions which minted silver. Byzantine gold coins have been excavated in Scandinavia, western Europe, Russia, Persia and Ceylon.

In founding his New Rome, Constantine I brought many of the features of Old Rome on the Tiber to the Bosphoros. He granted land and privileges to senatorial families who agreed to move east and set up a new Senate of Constantinople. Entitlement to a supply of free bread was linked to the construction of new housing. Those who built accommodation in New Rome were granted bread tokens, which allowed them to collect fresh bread daily at points in all the fourteen regions of the city. Grain silos and water cisterns were constructed to ensure the city's supplies. In 359, a prefect was appointed to take charge of the city on the model of Rome, and all imperial administration was concentrated there. Duplicating the Roman pattern of 'bread and circuses' (see chapter 3), Constantine completed construction of the Hippodrome and appointed professional entertainers (the circus factions or demes) to organize the races and spectacles so much enjoyed in ancient times.

From 330 until his death in 337, Constantine continued to campaign against hostile forces in the East, moving from palace to palace, rather than residing permanently in Constantinople. After his initial victory at Rome, he only returned once to the ancient capital, to celebrate the tenth anniversary of his accession (315), when he dedicated the New Basilica and his Victory Arch, which still adorns the Forum. His new foundation grew at the expense of Old Rome and that of other cities previously used as imperial residences: Trier, Nikomedeia, favoured by Diocletian, Sirmium on the Danube or Antioch on the border of modern Turkey and Syria. Although many senatorial families remained in the West, Constantinople attracted craftsmen, architects, merchants and adventurers, while the new court needed educated men to sing the praises of the new Christian emperors as well as to run the administration. Lacking a traditional caste of established families who cherished their genealogies in the Roman style, Constantinople was more open to talent; newcomers who proved successful were rapidly promoted. This social mobility meant that the city experienced a less pronounced divide between aristocrats and plebians, although upstarts were always mocked and slaves continued to be beaten.

The nature and degree of Constantine's commitment to Christianity is disputed: his biographer Eusebius (Bishop of Caesarea, 313–c. 340) emphasizes it above all else, while secular historians record his devotion to the unconquered sun, Sol Invictus, shared with his father. In the late fifth century, Zosimus blames Constantine for all the ills of the Roman Empire, claiming that he abandoned his ancestral religion (of the pagan gods), because 'a certain Egyptian assured him that the Christian religion was able to absolve him from guilt . . .'.

The historian also reports why the emperor felt so guilty: Constantine had killed his son Crispus on suspicion of improper relations with Empress Fausta, his stepmother. Constantine later shut her up in an overheated bath until she died. He was indeed baptized into the new faith but only when he was dying. This was not uncommon as Christians wanted to avoid sinning after baptism, so the ceremony was regularly postponed till the last possible moment.

Different versions of the story of his vision of the Cross before the battle of the Milvian Bridge suggest that it is a myth, although Christian authors later claim it as the moment of his conversion. At Rome during the winter of 312/13, however, Constantine instructed the governor of Carthage to return Christian possessions, which had been confiscated during a recent persecution, to the local bishop and to provide compensation if the objects had been sold or melted down. This implies a definite shift from the previous imperial view of Christianity as a force capable of corrupting military strength, as well as denying due reverence for the ancient gods and emperors.

While Constantine supported Christian leaders and funded the building of Christian churches, his sons also permitted the construction of a temple in Italy dedicated to the cult of the imperial family, complete with priests dedicated to sacrifice in the old pagan style. At the same time, some temples appear to have been forced to give up their statues and any precious metal was stripped from their doors or roofs. The sacrificial element of pagan cult was gradually restricted; the killing of animals was to be replaced by the bloodless sacrifice offered to the Christian God. Since many pagan philosophers had also stressed the need for a spiritual understanding of 'sacrifice', this cannot be considered an exclusively Christian restraint. It indicates nonetheless the gradual demise of animal sacrifice, the central act of pagan cult. So whether he was converted by the vision of 312, or only when he knew that he was dying in 337, Constantine spent most of his adult life as a patron of Christianity, supporting the previously persecuted communities; he endowed their grand new churches with liturgical objects of precious metal set with jewels, and tried to help them define their faith more closely.

It is not clear how many new religious buildings within Constantinople were built by Constantine. He probably planned the church of the Holy Apostles, to which the imperial mausoleum was attached, the cathedral church of St Irene and churches dedicated to the cults of two local martyrs, Mokios and Akakios. Outside his capital Constantine paid particular attention to the sites associated with Christ's life on earth, sending his mother Helena to the Holy Land in 326. In the course of the first imperial pilgrimage, she founded the churches at Bethlehem over the manger of the Nativity and at Jerusalem over the tomb near Golgotha, where she is said to have discovered the True Cross. She also distributed money to the troops, which may have been the primary reason for her journey. Helena set a pattern for later pilgrimage, which was facilitated by building hostels and hospitals. In 335, Constantine himself followed in her steps; he dedicated another shrine to the Saviour and attended a council in Jerusalem, before celebrating the thirtieth anniversary of his rule.

In a decisive shift from the Roman tradition of imperial cremation, however, Constantine was buried according to Christian rites in the mausoleum designed to house relics of the twelve Apostles. The emperor wished to be laid to rest among Christ's chosen disciples; Eusebius describes him as equal to the Apostles and the thirteenth, though the emperor's own perception suggests that he considered himself superior to them. Constantine's son, Constantius II, completed the church of the Holy Apostles and moved what were believed to be the bones of Saints Timothy, Luke and Andrew to the site in 356/7. Subsequent rulers added to an impressive collection of relics: the veil, girdle and shroud of the Virgin deposited in her shrine at Blachernai became particularly important. Emperors paid annual visits to these relics and to the mausoleum where they censed the tombs, lit candles and said prayers for their predecessors. Ceremonies such as these consolidated the notion of an unbroken line of Christian rulers established by Constantine.

Through a naming system which became prevalent in Byzantium and complicates its history, numerous later emperors were also called Constantine, eleven in all. It was common for the first male child of a marriage to be named after his paternal grandfather, which accounts for some of these Constantines. Others were acclaimed as a New Constantine, as if to stress their equality with the founder of Byzantium, or added Constantine to their given name, like Herakleios-

Constantine in the early seventh century. In addition to the eleven Constantines, there are eight emperor Michaels, eight Johns and six Leos. They are listed at the end of this book in an effort to distinguish them by date and achievement. None, however, really challenged the enduring position of the first Constantine.

Gradually, the cult of this great emperor and his pious mother, Helena, developed into a model of Christian rule. Legendary accounts of their devotion effaced Constantine's involvement in the murders of his son and his second wife, and his mother's obscure origins. A key moment occurred in 451 at the Council of Chalcedon, when Marcian and Pulcheria, the ruling emperor and empress, were acclaimed as 'a new Constantine and a new Helena'. Marcian was also compared to Paul and David, while Pulcheria was said to have shown the faith and zeal of Helena. The courtiers and secular officials who stage-managed these acclamations no doubt saw the importance of so elevating their fifth-century masters. In the process they also contributed to the transformation of the founder of Constantinople and his mother into saints of the Christian Church, and this is how they appear in later medieval stories and frescoes, where they are often shown flanking the True Cross.

2

Constantinople, the Largest City in Christendom

O imperial City, City fortified, City of the great king . . . Queen
of the queen of cities, song of songs and splendour of splendours!

Niketas Choniates, early thirteenth century

In the history of Constantinople, a major crisis occurred fifty years after the death of Constantine I, when the Goths inflicted a massive defeat on the Romans at the battle of Adrianople on 9 August 378. Emperor Valens (364–78) had marched out with a great number of troops to drive back the barbarian invaders without waiting for western reinforcements. In the battle he was killed, together with the most experienced eastern commanders and the political class was decapitated. Only two generals escaped to report the disaster to the young western emperor Gratian (375–83), while the Goths ravaged imperial territory up to the walls of the city of Constantine.

In response to this disaster, the empire drew on its traditional skills of diplomacy while the Byzantines shut themselves up behind their fortifications. Gratian, now the only remaining emperor, sent an appeal to Theodosius, who had retired from a military career to his estates in Spain at the far end of the Mediterranean. Initially, this negotiation concerned his appointment to a military command in the East; but since Valens had no successor and the divided empire required two emperors to work together, Theodosius must have appreciated the underlying significance of the invitation. He agreed to head the army in the Balkans and was later acclaimed as emperor by the troops. After several campaigns against the Goths, Theodosius made peace with the invaders and in November 380 entered Constantinople, which he had never previously seen, in triumph. After a two-year interregnum, New Rome had a new ruler and its future was assured.

Theodosius I (379–95) was a strict Christian, who called a council to condemn the Arian definitions of the faith in 381, and issued laws against the public celebration of pagan rites. But he also left his mark on the city of Constantinople in the most traditional fashion. He constructed a new forum, complete with his statue atop a column, and a monumental weathervane, which served as a public clock, in the manner of the Tower of the Winds in Athens. On the central barrier of the Hippodrome, round which the chariots raced, he also put up the Egyptian obelisk from Karnak, commemorating an Egyptian victory of 1440 BC in the oldest and now long-forgotten religion and language of the east Mediterranean. It became another symbol of Roman military triumph. On the base supporting the obelisk Theodosius depicted himself presiding at the races, flanked by his court, with dancing girls and musicians and serried ranks of barbarian peoples bringing their tribute (plate 6). On the north face, carvings document the technique used for raising such a heavy monolith, which is recorded in inscriptions in both Greek and Latin. Although earthquakes frequently caused buildings in Constantinople to collapse and statues to fall off their columns, the obelisk remains where fourth-century engineers placed it in 390, on four corner supports above the base.

Under the new dynasty founded by Theodosius, the Roman world was transformed. Before his death in 395 the emperor divided the empire between his two sons, so that Honorius became Emperor of the West and Arcadius Emperor of the East. During the early fifth century, the western half succumbed to ever-increasing pressure from non-Roman forces such as the Goths, Huns, Vandals and Franks, who gradually established their barbarian rule in different regions. Rome was twice sacked, in 410 and 455, and in 476 Germanic troops commanded by a Hunnic leader, Odovacer, deposed the last Roman emperor in the West. New Rome expanded and prospered at the expense of Old Rome, indeed some barbarian contingents were paid off by the eastern emperors and encouraged to move west, leaving the East undisturbed. Through this long process, the eastern half of the Roman world became what we now call Byzantium (see chapter 3).

Constantinople grew so fast that in 412 new walls were built 1.5 kilometres to the west of the original Constantinian defences. One year later a massive new triple line of fortifications was completed, 6km long with an inner wall 11 metres high and towers every 70–75 metres, a lower outer wall, also with towers, an outer wall and deep moat. Sea walls were also built along the natural barriers of the Golden Horn and the Sea of Marmara. These fortifications would protect the city against all enemies until 1204 and still impress today. The land thus enclosed increased the city by about 5 square km and included the old cemeteries, where builders told frightening tales of disturbing graves and finding funerary statues and bones in tombs. Much of this region was devoted to horticulture, with vineyards, orchards and vegetable gardens, which also extended outside the walls. Under Emperor Anastasius (491–518), the Long Walls were constructed between Selymbria, on the Sea of Marmara, and the Black Sea, a distance of 45km, as an outer ring of Constantinople's defence, although today historians tend to interpret these as a sign of failure, for once the invaders had advanced to the Long Walls they were only 65km west of the capital.

All emperors sought to add their own monuments to the city, such as honorary columns, to improve its markets and harbours, and to build churches, monasteries and extensions to the imperial palace. In the fourth century, Valens is associated with the construction of a major aqueduct, which brought fresh sources of water from Bizye in Thrace, a distance of 120km as the crow flies (plate 5). While this massive engineering project to secure the city's water supply can still be seen striding into the old city above ground, a complex underground drainage system channelled the wastewater out of the city. Water was used for public as well as private baths and fountains, and was stored in vast cisterns lined with water-resistant cement. One of the largest open cisterns for the collection of rainwater was constructed in 421 in the newly enclosed area of Constantinople, probably by Aetios, prefect of the city, with a capacity of 250/300,000 cubic metres. Justinian added a covered cistern at the Basilika, with 336 columns, some raised on antique blocks of statuary, like a colossal head of

Medusa. It could store about 78,000 cubic metres. A visit to this cavernous monument with appropriate *son et lumière* is one of modern Istanbul's tourist attractions. It also transmits a real sense of the city's capacity to withstand siege.

Within its magnificent defences and with developed capacity to store both grain and water, Constantinople resisted numerous attacks, most notably by combined Avar, Slav and Persian forces in 626, and several major sieges. The attack of 626 was brief but very serious because Emperor Herakleios (610–41) was not in the city. He had undertaken a long campaign against the Persians in the east, leaving Constantinople under the leadership of Patriarch Sergios and General Bonos. The Avars and Slavs blockaded the capital by land and cut off its water supply by destroying the aqueduct, while a Persian force arrived on the Asiatic shore of the Bosphoros. Bonos instructed naval forces to prevent the Slavs from ferrying the Persians across the Bosphoros, negotiated with the Avar Chagan and led sorties against the besiegers. Meanwhile, the patriarch organized the entire civilian population in a procession around the walls of the city, carrying their icons of Christ and chanting the Akathistos hymn, which calls on the Mother of God for divine assistance. When the Avars built siege weapons and attacked the walls, eyewitnesses alleged that they had observed a woman leading the defence, who was identified as the Virgin herself. The survival of Constantinople against such fearsome odds perhaps required supernatural powers. Certainly these became a feature of the city, which already claimed the name 'Theotokoupolis', city of the Mother of God, whose relics protected it.

After 626, Arab forces took over the struggle to capture Constantinople, which they intended to make their own capital. Several seventh-century sieges failed. Under Anastasios II (713–15), the Byzantines learned that a major assault was under way, and the emperor ordered every family that could not support itself in foodstuffs for three years to leave the city, a sure sign of preparation for a long siege. Just before the Arab forces arrived (two armies by land and the navy by sea) in the spring of 717, Leo III was sworn in as emperor. He used the same combination of diplomatic and military strategies, persuading the Khazars to harry the Arabs from the rear and directing 'Greek fire' against their ships. After an extremely cold winter in which the besiegers were forced to eat their camels, they resumed the attack. But the following summer the caliph ordered them to withdraw and they suffered further defeats on the way back. Byzantium commemorated the victory of 718 in liturgical services held every year on 15 August, which was also the feast of the Virgin's *Koimesis* (Dormition or falling asleep, known in the West as the Assumption). While the Church ascribed the city's survival to the Virgin's protective powers, Leo III took credit for organizing the defence.

Following internal disputes in the Arab world, the Bulgars took over the attempt to capture Constantinople, making serious challenges in the early ninth century and again in the 920s. But because it was difficult to maintain their long supply lines, they could not plan an extended siege and on both occasions had to withdraw after a few weeks. Later it was the turn of the Russians who sailed across the Black Sea and attacked the city in 860, 941 and 1043. On every occasion, Constantinople resisted successfully. In the early thirteenth century, however, the Latin crusaders' siege of 1204 finally succeeded in forcing an entry – via the Golden Horn – but only thanks to guile, treachery and internal weakness rather than military strength. This sorry story of the Christian attack on Byzantium is told in chapter 24. Despite the devastating sack and the 57-year-long Latin occupation of Constantinople, the city restored its Byzantine character and some of its previous glory from 1261 to 1453. Finally in May 1453, the fifth-century fortifications were no match for Turkish gunpowder and cannon balls.

Throughout its Byzantine history the city's population expanded and contracted under different pressures. Constant growth from the fourth century onwards brought the number of inhabitants to around half a million under Emperor Justinian (527–65). While all population estimates are guesswork, the figure of 500,000 is based on the capacity of the grain fleet which brought the basic foodstuff to the city, as well as government and building activity within it. New Rome attracted inhabitants, making it by far the largest city in the world of Late Antiquity, while Old Rome declined. Then in 541, an outbreak of bubonic plague afflicted the entire empire, leaving innumerable deaths as it moved from region to region, carried by rats on ships and in goods transported overland. When the historian Procopius, who witnessed the horrors, tried to describe them, he adapted Thucydides' famous account of plague in the fifth century BC. To the ancient model Procopius added his own observations, how the living were too few to bury the dead who had to be thrown over the walls and into cisterns. The population must have declined seriously, not only in 541/2, but with recurrent outbreaks of the disease during the seventh and eighth centuries. In addition to this incomprehensible cause of death, a series of earthquakes affected the capital, provoking more terror, destruction and loss of life. In 740, a major tremor reduced the church of St Irene to its foundations and many other buildings collapsed, taking the city's population at a low point.

Constantine V (741–75) reversed this trend by a dedicated plan of rebuilding, starting with St Irene, which was restored to an even more glorious condition. More important for the revival of the city, in 766 he organized the forced immigration of thousands of workers to repair the major aqueduct, cut during the siege of 626. They were recruited in Pontos, Asia, Greece and the Aegean islands, and probably stayed on in the city when the work was finished. Constantine also had a clock in the Great Palace repaired and he sent an organ as a gift to the Franks in an embassy of 767, reflecting his interest in such instruments. They were probably operated by waterpower, like the fountains and mechanical golden decorations of the Byzantine court. New churches like the one near the lighthouse, the Pharos church inside the Great Palace, reflected his ambitious strategy of regeneration, which attracted new inhabitants and merchants to the city. Through internal expansion and the revival of markets, Constantinople regained its position as a hub of international trade.

As the centre of all imperial administration, diplomacy, court patronage and training in skilled craftwork, the city provided opportunities for people from the provinces and farther afield who sought jobs and patrons, as well as mercenaries and spiritual leaders. In the mid-ninth century, a wrestler and horse-breaker named Basil used his talent to make friends with, and eventually to supplant, the emperor Michael III in 867. Even those who had no particular skills sought employment in the great houses and monasteries of the city. Young girls competed for jobs at court, where numerous ladies-in-waiting attended the empress and attracted the attention of potential husbands. Foreigners, identified by nicknames such as 'the Italian' or 'the Slav', rose to leading positions. Close relations with the Caucasus added to this multi-cultural society in which military men regularly made successful careers. Emperors Philippikos (711–13) and Romanos I (920–44), a naval commander, were both from Armenia, while Leo III (717–41) came from a Syrian family that had been moved to Isauria in southern Asia Minor. By the ninth century, Constantinople was once again endowed with numerous villas and palaces constructed by individual patrons, as well as patriarchs, imperial officials and administrators.

During the late eleventh and twelfth centuries, as the Seljuk Turks advanced into Asia Minor (see chapter 21), many refugees fled to Constantinople. Even with a clear increase in population the city seems to have been able to feed everyone, a reflection of the efficient exploitation of estates in the western provinces of the empire, many owned by religious institutions like the monasteries of Mount Athos. By the end of the twelfth century one of the largest, the Great Lavra (see chapter 18), had a small fleet of boats in which it transported the surplus grain from its land outside the Holy Mountain to the capital. Though accurate figures for the population of Constantinople are impossible, visitors from the West were astonished at the numbers and the crowded streets. In his history of the Fourth Crusade, Geoffrey Villehardouin, who died between 1212 and 1218, believed there were 400,000 inhabitants. He made clear his own impression that the city was certainly the largest in Christendom.

Within its walls, Constantinople contained numerous monasteries, churches and shrines, which attracted pilgrims and holy men from all parts of the Christian world. In the fifth century, Daniel, a Syrian monk, mounted his column outside the walls and gave advice from the top, even to emperors. Such ascetics were greatly respected by leading bishops, who administered the Church. The Patriarch of Constantinople directed religious education and collected a great library of theological texts. At the same time there was a serious tradition of secular education, which dated back to earliest times. In 425, Theodosius II strengthened this by establishing thirty-one chairs for teachers of the study of Latin and Greek grammar, rhetoric, philosophy and law in special quarters at the Capitolium. With firm imperial patronage, Constantinople remained the centre of all higher legal studies, as well as the advanced quadrivium of mathematical sciences and philosophy. Meanwhile, Theodosius' older sister Pulcheria encouraged the cult of the Mother of God with special all-night liturgies.

With the support of Empress Verina, wife of Leo I (457–74), this cult was entrenched at two important shrines in Constantinople, at Blachernai at the northwest corner of the walls, and in the copper workers' quarter, Chalkoprateia, near the Great Palace. In addition to the relics of her veil, girdle and shroud, particular icons of the Virgin and Child and the liturgical cycle of her feasts, commemorated in sermons and prayers, enhanced popular devotion to her. Some paintings were said to be the work of St Luke and to date back to her lifetime. Subsequent emperors continued to add to the imperial collection of relics; in the early tenth century, Leo VI installed two particularly important miracle-working icons either side of the main entrance to the cathedral church of Hagia Sophia (see chapter 5). Western visitors from the period of the crusades expressed amazement at the collections of important relics and icons, as well as surprise at the number of court eunuchs (see chapter 15).

Muslim visitors also provide fascinating comments about Constantinople and the Byzantines. In the eleventh century, the diplomat and historian al-Marwazi reports:

The Rum are a great nation. They possess extensive lands, abounding in good things. They are gifted in crafts and skilful in the fabrication of [various] articles, textiles, carpets and vessels.

'Rum' was his approximation of Roman, the term used by the Byzantines to describe themselves. Al-Marwazi believed only the Chinese surpassed them in applied arts, and since he had visited the court of the Great Khan he was in a good position to judge. He also explained the riches of Byzantium, reporting that the empire drew its revenues from 'customs which they collect from the merchants and ships from every region ... and caravans [that] reach them by land ... from Syria, from the Slavs and Rus and other peoples.' To many visitors from the West the wealth of the citizens of Constantinople, who dressed in silk and ate caviar, appeared something fabulous. To educated inhabitants like Niketas Choniates, who recorded the history of Byzantium from 1118 to 1206, Constantinople was indeed 'Queen of the queen of cities', a play on the Greek term *basilissa*, which means imperial, ruling and empress or queen. Its greatness derived from its beauty, marked by monuments and collections of art works, as well as its wealth. This contributed to a western sense of envy, which was fanned by Alexios IV's failure to pay the forces of the Fourth Crusade and led to the sack of the city in April 1204.

Although Constantinople never regained its pre-1204 population level, it retained its leading intellectual position right until its fall to the Turks, continuing to attract merchants, artists and scholars, who patronized new building and the redecoration of churches. Theodore Metochites (1270–1332), the statesman and scholar, restored the ancient foundation of the Chora monastery (Kariye Camii) in the northwestern region of the city with magnificent new mosaics and frescoes (plates 26 and 33). Drawing on the history and strength of imperial culture, architects and craftsmen contributed new forms to Byzantine civilization, for instance in the funerary chapels with tombs for their patrons which were added to many churches. The verdict of Arab visitors was still favourable: in the early thirteenth century, al-Harawi reported that 'Constantinople is a city even greater than its reputation'. He added, 'May God in his grace and generosity deign to make it the capital of Islam.' In the fourteenth, al-Qazwini added, 'Nothing like it was ever built neither before nor after', while the great historian and sociologist Ibn Khaldun (1332–1406) characterized it as 'a magnificent city, seat of the Caesars, containing works famous for their construction and splendour'.

This appreciation contributed to the determination of the Ottoman Turks to make it their capital. After the siege of 1453, Sultan Mehmed II allowed three days of looting and then spent many years rebuilding and repopulating the city. Its domed churches inspired his own foundation, the Mosque of the Conqueror (Fatih Camii), erected on the site of the church of the Holy Apostles to which the imperial mausoleum was attached. Even after its conquest, Constantinople lived on as the capital of the Ottoman Empire. For five hundred years it was known as 'the Sublime Porte', a centre of international diplomacy and Near Eastern policy-making. Constantinople embodied the stimulating combination of overseas trade, local commercial activity, bureaucracy and ceremonial.

Today it is no longer the capital of Turkey and its ancient walls are encircled by new motorways and vast suburbs. Atatürk Boulevard passes below and between the arches of the main aqueduct; the tower built by the Genoese in Galata, the northern suburb across the Golden Horn (also called Pera), stands out among the modern buildings which now surround it, while the domes of St Sophia and the Blue Mosque vie for attention in the old city. Yet Constantine's city is still recognizable with its vistas, public spaces and monuments which continue to evoke the grandeur of seventeen hundred years of history.

3

The East Roman Empire

> Hurl your javelins and arrows against them ... so that they
> know that they are fighting ... with the descendants of the
> Greeks and the Romans.
>
> Emperor Constantine XI Palaiologos addressing his forces
> on 28 May 1453, *Chronicle of Pseudo-Sphrantzes*

The expansion of Rome's empire and the spread of Roman culture to
Britain, North Africa, the Balkans, Egypt, central Europe and the
Near East is still an astonishing phenomenon. With its capacity to
extract taxation from all its provinces to finance further military
activity and to maintain the central bureaucracy, Roman administration achieved a previously unimaginable control over territories of
very different natures. The empire's strength lay in the system which
allowed it to integrate conquered regions so that they added to its
power. It mastered the art of recruiting local talent from the provinces
to its own causes, while reducing the regions to subordinate status.

While Latin was used throughout the West, Greek remained the
lingua franca of all the eastern regions. Until the sixth century, the
Byzantine Empire employed both ancient languages. Administrators
sent from the West to the eastern half of the empire were often issued
with wordbooks giving the Greek equivalent of Latin words and
explaining local terminology. Translation from Greek to Latin was
largely the work of Christian scholars who wanted to make the Scriptures and theological writings available to westerners. Much less Latin
literature was rendered into Greek. Most of Cicero, Ovid, Virgil and
Horace, for instance, remained unknown to monoglot Greek speakers.

Most well-educated men, however, were bilingual. Ammianus Marcellinus (c. 330–92 or later), a native of Antioch who identified himself as a Greek and a soldier, wrote a history of his times in Latin which documents the campaigns of Emperor Julian. He also brilliantly evoked the beauty of ancient sites, such as the temple of Sarapis in Alexandria, levelled by Christians in 391, or the Forum of Trajan in Rome.

While emperors tried to maintain the unity of this vast empire, they recognized the difficulties of imposing a uniform government throughout its far-flung regions. The solution devised by Diocletian (284–305) divided the empire into two halves, each ruled by an emperor and an assistant junior emperor. The two senior emperors were to act in concert, issuing laws to be observed in both halves of the Roman world, while defending their own territories. This 'rule of four' (tetrarchy) was intended to stabilize civilian administration and military defence. It functioned well enough to allow Diocletian and his senior colleague to retire after twenty years of service, when their junior colleagues became emperors. But as we saw in chapter 1, Constantine overturned this system by his determination to become sole ruler, and this restored the monarchy.

Monarchy, however, was no more successful than the tetrarchy in solving the Roman Empire's problems during the fourth century. Constantine's descendants were challenged by two contrasting types of military threat. In the East, the Romans had to contain Persia, always considered the 'other eye' of the face of the known world. In the north and west, Germanic tribes were ever anxious to invade and occupy Roman territory. With no written language, no coinage, no law or recognizable system of government, they were traditionally considered unsophisticated barbarians. Yet Julian (361–3) was obliged to campaign against the Alemanni east of the Rhine before he became emperor, as well as the Persians beyond the Euphrates. No emperor could defend all the borders of this extended empire simultaneously.

In 395, Theodosius I imposed a different solution with the formal division of the empire between his two sons: Honorius was acclaimed emperor in the West and Arcadius in the East. But since both the young emperors needed guardians and advisers, military generals took advantage of the situation. Stilicho (half-Vandal, half-Roman) gained control of the West, while Eutropios, an emancipated slave and eunuch, took charge in the East. They represented the recruitment of non-Roman forces, especially Goths, into the army, which allowed barbarian soldiers to attain the highest military positions. While this process occurred in both halves of the empire, barbarian influence was much more dangerous in the West. A rebellion in Britain forced the withdrawal of imperial troops in 406, which coincided with a major incursion of Vandals, Sueves and Alans across the frozen Rhine, who then advanced through Gaul and into Spain. This marked the beginning of the end of the western half of the Roman Empire.

But the most serious challenge to imperial power came from the Visigoths (West Goths), whose leader Alaric was appointed *magister militum per Illyricum* (master of the soldiers in the eastern province of Illyricum, a large region of the Balkans). By 410 he led the Visigoths into Italy, blockaded Rome and refused the Senate's negotiations and offer of gold. In August of that year Rome, the eternal city, capital of the greatest empire of the ancient world, was sacked by his dissatisfied troops. The disaster prompted St Augustine, Bishop of Hippo in North Africa, to write his *City of God*, to warn Christians in the West of setting any store in earthly glory.

The sack of Rome was followed by increased barbarian conquests, notably by Attila the Hun, the second sack of Rome, by Vandals from North Africa in 455, and the deposition of the last Roman emperor based in Rome itself, Romulus Augustulus, in 476. After this, the western half of the Roman world was divided up among barbarian rulers. Some, like Alaric and Theoderic the Ostrogoth (East Goth), were encouraged by eastern emperors to go west and leave Constantinople in peace. Others, like the Burgundians and Franks, crossed the Rhine to settle in what had been central and northern Gaul. The few officials who represented the remnants of Roman rule fell back on Arles in the south of what is now France and negotiated the best possible arrangements with the newcomers. Many of senatorial status sought refuge in the Church.

The eastern half of the empire, however, did not decline and fall. On the contrary, it survived for over a millennium based in its strong metropolis, Constantinople, and supported by the rich provinces of the Near East. It controlled the eastern basin of the Mediterranean, roughly east of a line passing from Singidunum on the Danube (modern Belgrade), through the Adriatic and south to Cyrene in North Africa (modern Libya) (see map 2). Most of the Balkans, Greece, the Aegean islands and all of modern Turkey, lay within its northern half, and all of Syria, Palestine, Egypt and Libya in the eastern and southern sectors. Across the Black Sea, Roman power retained a small settlement in the Crimea, and navigation across the Euxine or 'friendly' sea continued. In the Mediterranean, Crete, Cyprus and Sicily constituted key points on naval routes, and the ports of Alexandria, Gaza, Caesarea and Antioch maintained their trade under the authority of Constantinople. Until the seventh century, international commerce also extended to western centres like Carthage in North Africa and Cartagena and Seville in southern Spain.

This eastern half of the Roman Empire is Byzantium. That name was not given to it until the sixteenth century, when humanist scholars tried to find a way of identifying what remained after the collapse of Old Rome in the West. Although they coined a term which has been used ever since, it is important to remember that the inhabitants of the empire called themselves Romans (in Greek, *Romaioi*), and saw themselves as such. Their claim on Roman qualities was not a vanity or snobbishness. From 330 to 619 Byzantium enjoyed imperial realities as well as ideology, above all in 'bread and circuses', a shorthand for the principle of providing basic food supplies plus public entertainment free to all the inhabitants of the eastern capital.

As we have seen, Constantine I insisted on the bread dole for all those who built new houses in Constantinople. Organizing sufficient grain imports from Egypt was a major state undertaking, which provided employment for shippers who owned the grain ships, sailors and naval captains who made the annual journey to Alexandria, and hauliers who disembarked the cargo on the island of Tenedos, at the entrance to the Dardanelles, where it was stored in vast silos until favourable winds allowed it to be taken to the capital. There it was distributed to guilds of millers and bakers who made sure that bread was available every day. Those who could document their residence in the city were issued with a bronze token which had to be shown before they could receive their loaf of free bread at distribution points marked by steps. Free bread was not made available on the basis of need; rather it was a privilege for those who could prove they were Byzantines, that is, they lived in the city.

After the Persian occupation of Egypt in 619, the grain fleet no longer arrived, but the provision of bread continued. Alternative sources of grain, primarily from Thrace, ensured supplies which were baked into loaves. But from this date onwards inhabitants had to pay for their bread. Although there were riots whenever the quality declined and the eparch (prefect) of the city was attacked for any shortages, the principle of supplying the most basic foodstuff of antiquity to the leading city of the time was maintained for centuries. Even when the population of Constantinople expanded to its greatest extent, perhaps as high as half a million under Justinian prior to the plague, and around 400,000 in the twelfth century, sufficient bread was baked to satisfy it.

Alongside supplies of bread, the state also guaranteed public entertainment, which took place in the Hippodrome of Constantinople, renovated by Constantine I. This racing arena was constructed on a vast scale, seating senators and dignitaries on the marble seats nearest the track, with the rest of the population on wooden benches above, and even women and children packed into the standing room at the top. The Byzantines were passionate enthusiasts for horse and chariot racing and very partisan in their support for teams identified by colour. The Reds, Whites, Greens and Blues, imported from Rome, were organized by professional corporations. By the sixth century, only the Greens and Blues were significant, but they had become large, powerful bodies with full responsibility not only for racing but also for displays of gymnastics, athletics, boxing, wild animals, pantomime, dancing and singing, which filled the entractes between the races.

Thanks to the history of Procopius we have a detailed description of one famous public entertainer: Theodora, born in about 497. Some historians consider it an unfounded account intended to damn her, but since the emperor had to change the law to make her his wife, she must have come from a family of low status, even if she did not perform in the way Procopius insists. His account reveals something of the way the Greens and Blues organized popular entertainment, documenting the different tasks which their members had to perform: Theodora's father, Akakios, appears as the bear-keeper, who made the bear dance or fight in particular displays; after his death, her mother tried to make a new alliance with the equivalent figure in the Blue faction but without success. She then put her three daughters on the stage and thus got the family re-employed.

Theodora is said to have had no particular skills as a dancer or flute-player (roles depicted on the base of the obelisk in the Hippodrome) but she became a famous circus artist, appreciated for her sexy acts and knock-about comedy. This type of entertainment was quite different from the theatrical dancers who re-created stories from the ancient Greek myths in mime to musical accompaniment. Theodora excelled at a cruder style of entertainment, which may have attracted the emperor's nephew, Justinian, who seems to have shared her taste. Once the law had been changed to allow Justinian to marry her, Theodora became his consort and in due course empress. Later I shall discuss her role and her famous portrait in Ravenna.

The Roman policy of bread and circuses gradually evolved into a Christian one of soup and salvation, as the Church tried to curb popular enthusiasm for racing, betting and what it considered indecent entertainment. Theatrical performances of ancient Greek plays declined and the theatres and odeons, such a prominent feature of ancient cities, became quarries for building material. As they fell into ruins, these sites were often associated with evil spirits; prophetic powers were attributed to certain ancient statues; both were considered dangerous for Christians. In its attacks on urban traditions such as the baths, and rural ones like the celebration of the wine harvest, the Church also tried to check immoral and inappropriate behaviour. But it could never wean the Byzantines from their passion for Hippodrome entertainment.

The Blues and the Greens who organized the races also had more serious duties: they acclaimed the emperor whenever he sat in the imperial box in the Hippodrome, which he could enter directly from within the palace. From this responsibility a political dimension developed, as individuals or groups used the factions to express their anger. Through staged interventions following the obligatory acclamations, the Greens or Blues might chant critical remarks, for example about high prices. In a sixth-century debate, the condemnation of particular practices is recorded, as well as the emperor's response, given via the chief chamberlain (*praipositos*). Some potential for political dissent was brought into the shared space of the Hippodrome, where it could be controlled. Grievances against corrupt officials and excessive taxation could thus be aired. Nevertheless, the Hippodrome did not constitute a space for real deliberation or serious debate, which the autocratic nature of Byzantine rule never admitted.

It did provide a place of exciting public entertainment shared by all classes in Byzantium, including the emperor. On occasions, the ruler even participated in the chariot racing: in the ninth century, the factions were instructed to allow Emperor Theophilos (829–42) wearing the colours of the Blues to win. The factions also provided private entertainment for imperial guests inside the palace, together with the choirs of the city churches. In the tenth century, long banquets were enlivened by dances performed to the sound of organs operated by waterpower. Displays of gymnastics, acrobatics and other circus entertainment, sometimes on camels or high wires suspended above the Hippodrome, which delighted visitors to Constantinople, were also the responsibility of the factions.

The Hippodrome was the place where the Byzantines gathered for ceremonial events such as the commemoration of the city's birthday, always fêted on 11 May; victory celebrations; the death of enemies and condemned criminals; and the birth or crowning of a young co-emperor. The emperor met his people there. In the twelfth century, when the Angelos dynasty decided to celebrate imperial marriages in the privacy of the Blachernai Palace, the populace objected forcefully. Sometimes the circumstances might prove adversarial rather than favourable. Certainly there was plotting and calculating in the subterranean areas of the Hippodrome where Blues and Greens stored their costumes, props and other equipment, while several departments of government functioned in chambers below the seating. The Hippodrome played such a significant role in the life of the city that emperors devoted significant funds to public entertainment.

Imperial ideology sustained all aspects of the Byzantine court with Roman symbols of power and new trappings adopted from Persia. Diocletian was the first emperor to wear a diadem, gold robes and insignia of office – imports from the East – and he expected people to prostrate themselves before him. Fourth-century rulers elaborated these customs from Persia, where the king of kings (Shah an Shah) sat enthroned under golden trees filled with golden birds who could be made to sing, flanked by lions that roared. Theodosius II constructed a polo ground so that Byzantine emperors could play the royal sport, another import from Persia.

In the Byzantine court itself, within the vast palace complex, the symbols and realities of autocratic power met. Imperial authority was demonstrated through technological inventions such as water clocks and astronomical devices. The Byzantines used the principles developed by Hero of Alexandria in the first century AD to develop water-powered automata to impress visitors to the court. In the tenth century, Liutprand of Cremona, sent as an envoy to Constantinople, reported that the immense throne guarded by 'lions that roared' rose high into the air. 'Behold! The man whom just before I had seen sitting on a moderately elevated seat had now changed his raiment and was sitting on the level of the ceiling.' In the imperial baths and outside in the gardens fountains sprayed water into the air while golden birds sang and organs provided musical entertainment. Like the clocks which accurately measured time and astronomical instruments which could predict eclipses, all this symbolized the power of the emperors, their incomparable prestige and ostentatious grandeur.

The architectural setting for this celebration of imperial supremacy was modelled on the palace of Augustus on the Palatine Hill in Old Rome. Septimius Severus (193–211) built the original palace in ancient Byzantion, to which later rulers added until the complex of the Great Palace covered an extensive area in the first of Constantinople's fourteen regions. It contained not only the major reception halls, the living quarters of the imperial family and their servants, numerous churches, baths and garrisons, but also many bureaus of the central administration all linked by corridors, gardens laid out with terraces, and fountains supplied by cisterns (see chapter 16). From its position on the acropolis it had spectacular views out over the Bosphoros. In the late seventh century, Justinian II (685–95 and 705–11) surrounded the area with a wall, thus making it the first of many kremlins. Despite this fortification, numerous rebels and assassins got into the palace, for instance in 820, when they disguised themselves as members of the choir due to sing in the Christmas celebrations, and murdered Leo V.

The palace was always a centre of learning, providing education for the imperial children and maintaining a great library. Most emperors promoted scholarship and patronized individual teachers. Basil I, who deposed Photios from the patriarchate, later brought him back to the palace to teach his sons, Constantine, Leo and Alexander. The second boy, who ruled as Leo VI (886–912), became known as 'Leo the Wise', which may have been partly a tribute to his teacher. The palace library nurtured some intellectual rulers, like Constantine VII (913–59), and maintained scribes who made de luxe copies of manuscripts to be given to foreign rulers. In 827, they copied the writings of Pseudo-Dionysios the Areopagite in a manuscript which was taken to Louis the Pious, and preserved in the monastery of Saint Denis outside Paris (it is now in the Bibliothèque Nationale). And under Romanos II (959–63) they produced an illustrated copy of the medical and pharmacological text by Dioskorides for the caliph of Cordoba in Spain.

In the practical administration of the eastern half of the empire, Roman traditions also persisted, notably in matters of taxation. Officials continued both the census of population and evaluation of land quality in order to tax people, property and landed estates. Tax revenue remained essential to imperial expenditure, and its decline through grants of tax-free land, and the adoption of tax farming in the eleventh century, was to cause a major crisis. In the transition from carved inscription and papyrus documents to written records on parchment, Roman recording practice was sustained, with copies of all imperial decisions kept in triplicate. Monumental inscriptions on stone were used, for example, to date repairs to the walls of Constantinople and to record a victory gained at Nicaea in the early eighth century. Parchment, like papyrus, was prone to destruction by fire and looting, so that only a few traces of this mighty bureaucratic organization have survived, mostly in official correspondence such as that with the bishops of Rome, or imperial donations to monasteries.

In the fundamental procedure of proclaiming a new ruler, Byzantium added a Christian element to its Roman inheritance. Acclamation by the Senate, army and people in the Hippodrome was transformed in 457 by the addition of a coronation performed by the patriarch in Hagia Sophia. Leo I was the first emperor to be sanctioned by this

Christian ritual. Patriarch Anatolius insisted upon it possibly because Leo was an unknown military figure who stepped into the vacuum left by the death of the last representatives of the Theodosian dynasty. Performance of the ceremony and use of a crown became one of the ways pretenders and usurpers would try to increase their power. But more significantly, coronation symbolized the transformation of Roman imperial traditions in Byzantium into Christian ones.

The medieval Byzantine coronation ritual was to be imitated in courts all over Europe. At the elevation of Charlemagne to the position of emperor in AD 800, Pope Leo III had to find a crown to place on his head, because there could be no coronation without a crown. In addition, he anointed him with holy oil, a western innovation in the ritual. In the medieval West, 'unction', as it is called, was normally reserved for bishops and high-ranking clergy. When Leo III used it for the coronation of a monarch, he claimed a vital and superior role for the Church, which popes of Rome, metropolitans of Russia and archbishops of Canterbury became anxious to perpetuate. Napoleon put aside this dependence on the Church when he crowned himself in Paris. Other monarchs in the Old World and the New, however, perpetuated the Byzantine style of coronation and it formed the basis of Queen Elizabeth II's elevation, the first to be televised, in 1953, fifteen hundred years after Leo I was crowned by Anatolius. The crucial moment of unction, as the bishops gathered round the monarch, however, was still regarded as too holy to be shown to viewers.

Though decorated by Christianity, Byzantium maintained the Roman traditions which had made imperial rule famous, not least the imperial ideology, with its ramifications in law, military organization, medicine, administration, taxation and court ceremonial. The emperor remained a god-like figure on earth, even if his undisputed authority was sanctioned by God. He trained and led his troops in battle, though churchmen blessed the campaign and prayed for the victory which was granted by God. The imperial court remained a site of elaborate pomp and lavish display, even though it mirrored the court of heaven. Justice remained the imperial prerogative and duty, and appeals to the emperor from even poor anonymous subjects were given attention. The ancient temples of Constantinople were not demolished or immediately converted: they survived until the sixth century when they were adapted for secular use. Some ancient works of art were appreciated, even though they depicted naked gods and goddesses.

While feats of Roman engineering were visible in the construction of bridges, roads, fortifications and aqueducts, which continued to be built for centuries, the unseen functions of a paid bureaucratic administration were probably more significant in sustaining Byzantium. When incompetent rebels like Phokas (602–10) seized the throne, the official structure of government carried on its work without change. Yet emperors including Alexios I Komnenos (1081–1118) could intervene to reform the system. The need for trained functionaries also helped to maintain high standards of education and raised the general level of literacy. And the bureaucrats themselves developed a sense of their own worth and an esprit de corps which is clear from their letters.

As the eastern half of the Roman Empire transformed itself into Christian Byzantium, new traditions of religious belief were welded to older imperial and classical traditions, including a self-conscious preservation of pre-Christian pagan times. The vitality of Byzantium and its survival owe much to this coexistence of conflicting strands. When Constantine XI Palaiologos urged his subjects to defend their capital against the Ottoman Turks, on the day before the final onslaught on 29 May 1453, he called upon them to demonstrate the spirit and strength of their ancestors, the Greeks and Romans. He himself died in the battle in this spirit, less a Christian martyr than a descendant of Caesar and Augustus, Constantine and Justinian.

4

Greek Orthodoxy

The profession of the divine symbol of faith [the creed], which is made by all, prefigures the mystical thanksgiving of the future age . . . by which we are saved.

St Maximos Confessor, *Mystagogia*, written *c.* 640, quoted by Patriarch Germanos in his *Commentary on the Divine Liturgy* (post-730)

Historians regularly ask why Christianity succeeded, how it won the loyalty of those who previously worshipped many gods, and what factors ensured its permanent presence in the ancient Mediterranean world. As an offshoot from Judaism it inherited the conviction that there was only one creator God, which it universalized by preaching to anyone who would listen. But the old cults had satisfied most needs for centuries. Why did the adherents of Apollo, Isis, Zoroaster, Mithras and other established gods adopt Christianity?

Unlike their contemporaries, the followers of Jesus were confident that death was not the end: they would rise again into a heaven of peace and light. This belief motivated them to behave in a correct Christian fashion, avoiding sin and encouraging faith, hope and charity, so that God would judge them worthy of eternal life in the next world. It set them apart from the Jews, polytheists and members of other cults that flourished in the early centuries AD.

It also prompted some to prefer death to denial of their faith, which the Roman authorities found most extraordinary. From the time of Emperor Nero, who pinned responsibility for the fires that destroyed Rome in AD 64 on the group, 'hated for its abominations', the

Christians opted for martyrdom rather than give up their belief. The slave girl Blandina, who was thrown to the wild beasts with her companions in the Roman arena of Lyons in 180, repeated constantly, 'I am a Christian', nothing else. Numerous public tortures and humiliations followed and she was eventually gored by a bull. 'After six days' exposure to every kind of insult and to the open sky, the martyrs' bodies were finally burnt to ashes and swept by these wicked men into the Rhône ... that not even a trace of them might be seen on earth again.' But those who witnessed the spectacle were amazed and shocked; some may even have been inspired by her courage. Her example was duplicated across the Roman world by Christians of all classes: Lawrence in Rome, Perpetua in Carthage, Duke Artemios of Egypt, and Thekla, alleged companion of St Paul, in Seleukeia. Wherever they could, Christians built shrines over the sites of martyrdom and tombs containing the martyrs' relics.

Martyrdom may not have been the defining feature of early Christianity, but during the third- and early fourth-century persecutions by Emperors Decius and Diocletian, whole communities chose to die rather than burn incense in honour of the Roman rulers. This was because their God forbade the worship of other gods. At Christian celebrations, the bloodless sacrifice of bread and wine, symbolizing the body and blood of Christ, marked the commemoration of his death and replaced all other forms of sacrifice. The resurrection of the Son of God brought the promise of a heavenly afterlife to all who believed. Hence the importance of the creed: 'I believe in one God, maker of heaven and earth . . .', which was recited by the entire congregation at every celebration of the Eucharist.

Through his travels and letters to Christian communities in the eastern Mediterranean, St Paul had documented the early growth of this faith. Later, the Gospel writers collected accounts of the life of Jesus, often in his actual words, such as the Lord's Prayer, the parables and the Sermon on the Mount, and basic instructions about how to be a Christian. As the largely urban groups expanded, they appointed an overseer (in Greek, *episkopos*) as their spokesman. This overseer-bishop gradually became a leader with a staff of officials to assist in the celebration of the liturgy, the instruction of new converts, the care of ill or elderly believers, and the exploitation of lands bequeathed to the Christian community. In Rome, the bishop was considered a direct descendant of St Peter, who had been crucified there. The chains used to restrain him became cherished relics. Since Jesus is reported to have said, 'Thou art Peter and on this rock (*petra*) I will build my church', later Christian bishops in the old pagan capital claimed a unique authority.

So, long before Constantine I's 'conversion', the Christians had created a network of churches throughout the Roman world. Theirs was a small organization, with places of worship less impressive than the temples devoted to the ancient gods, less common than the altars set up to Mithras, the Persian god, and less popular than the cults of Isis and Osiris imported from Egypt. And in the early fourth century, they were profoundly shaken by the 'Great Persecution' instituted by Emperor Diocletian (284–305). Many apostatized, agreed to sacrifice and handed over their sacred books and altar vessels. Others fled into the countryside to hide. The list of martyrs grew longer. Although historians still debate what percentage of the population was Christian at the time of the Edict of Milan in 313, they agree that the churches had been weakened and divided by imperial edicts against the faith.

Undoubtedly, the most significant feature of Constantine's new imperial patronage lay in his decision to summon all the bishops of the Christian world to a meeting held at Nicaea in western Asia Minor in the summer of 325. There is no record of how many there were, though in several cities rival bishops claimed control over the church buildings. The council's tasks were to examine the doctrines propounded by Arius, a deacon of the Church of Alexandria, and to settle the wording of the creed, the statement of basic belief, as well as the method of calculating the date of Easter. The emperor covered all travel and accommodation expenses and presided over the council. Due to the presence of church leaders from all parts of the empire, though very few from the West attended, the council was later given the epithet 'universal' (oecumenical). Subsequent meetings called by emperors to settle the most serious theological problems followed this pattern. Eight were identified as universal (the last, held in 879/80, is not always recognized in the West), and all were summoned by an emperor who often participated in the proceedings. Secular control was therefore built into the organization of the Christian Church from the earliest phase of its incorporation into the Roman Empire.

Earlier, local councils provided a model for resolving divisions within the Church, but Constantine planned something much grander. The twenty disciplinary laws (canons) agreed at Nicaea were intended to legislate for the entire Christian world. Similarly, the council's decision on the views of Arius – who claimed that Jesus, the Son of God, must be subordinate to God the Father and could not be of the same substance – would be universally applied. After discussions, the council defined the Son as consubstantial (*homoousios*) and co-eternal with the Father, sharing the same divine nature. This was vital, because if Christ was not the Incarnate Logos (Word of God) with the same fully divine nature, mere humans could not hope to share in eternal life through salvation. The writings of Arius were condemned and he was exiled. Finally, the council issued a dogmatic definition of Christian belief, the creed, and decided on a method of calculating the date of Easter (to be celebrated on the Sunday after the full moon following the spring equinox). All but two of the bishops present are reported to have signed their agreement.

The condemnation of Arius, the canons, and texts relating to Easter and the creed are the only records that survive from the First Oecumenical Council, as it became known by the late fourth century. The number of bishops who had attended was fixed as being 318, and these became known as the 318 Fathers of the Church. Since no lists of attendance are preserved, they remain an anonymous group, albeit of great authority. The meeting set an important precedent: that the emperor should summon these councils, which represented the entire body of Christians and issued regulations for their correct belief and practice. In practice, they were all held in the East; their discussions were conducted in Greek and often the Bishop of Rome was the sole western representative. The difficulty of travel and greater distance must have deterred western bishops, who learned about conciliar decisions from reports circulated by the pope. Later councils were called to deal with divisions in the Church; they also defined and condemned heretical belief. Their proceedings, which often record every detail of the debates, provide valuable evidence of the growth of Christianity and local variations in belief and practice.

Despite the condemnation of Arius at Nicaea, he was later pardoned and in 335 his theology was rehabilitated. For most of the fourth century Constantine's sons favoured his theological definitions. This had serious consequences both for those who supported the decrees of Nicaea and for the spread of Christianity among non-Roman tribes. During the 340s, Ulfila, a Gothic leader, visited Constantinople and was ordained as bishop by the Arian authorities. He then devised an alphabet to represent spoken Gothic in written form and translated the Gospels into his new script. The Goths were not the only people to embrace Arian definitions of Christianity; almost all the other Germanic tribes adopted them. So when the Roman Empire in the West succumbed to barbarian rule, the Ostrogoths, Visigoths, Sueves, Burgundians and Vandals imported their Arian beliefs, which had repeatedly been condemned by church councils. In this process the newcomers met strenuous opposition from anti-Arian Christians. Theoderic's Ravenna still preserves Arian and Orthodox baptisteries, as well as churches designed to serve the two rival Christian groups. In North Africa, the Vandals were much less tolerant and instituted a serious persecution of anti-Arian Christians. Arianism was only finally rooted out during the sixth century when Justinian's troops imposed orthodox definitions. Gradually the Sueves, Visigoths and Burgundians abandoned their pro-Arian past for the definitions approved by oecumenical councils and a more 'Roman' character.

Although most surviving sources are overwhelmingly Christian in origin, it is clear that the pagan cults did not die out quickly. The schools of philosophy, which sustained higher education in Alexandria, Athens and Antioch, continued to function in a pre-Christian environment. For intelligent young men, this was the only form of advanced instruction available, and four great eastern saints who are recognized as the Greek Fathers of the Church, Basil, Gregory of Nazianzos, Gregory of Nyssa and John Chrysostom, were totally imbued with this culture. Similarly, St Augustine, who became the leading Latin Father of the Church, had followed an entirely pagan curriculum in his education. Basil, who later became Bishop of Caesarea, attended lectures in ancient philosophy by the Platonic expert Prohaeresius at Athens, together with the future emperor Julian. When Julian became emperor in 361 he attempted to reinvigorate worship of the pagan gods, but his premature death only 18 months later removed the leader of this movement, which died with him. Many groups of scholars, however, continued to practise the ancient cults, while rural inhabitants untouched by Christian doctrines lived by their traditional customs, marking the seasons by the rhythms of the sun and moon and cult activities associated with the gods.

Against this persistent substratum of trust in the ancient gods, emperors used universal gatherings of bishops to legislate against both pagan and heretical beliefs, and to establish a fixed Christian hierarchy. Theodosius I (379–95) summoned a council to meet in Constantinople in 381. Under his authority, 150 bishops confirmed the decisions taken at Nicaea, condemned Arianism again, added significant measures against the pagan cults, and clarified the wording of the creed, to be recited by all Christians as their declaration of faith. Theodosius also insisted on the promotion of the sees of Constantinople and Jerusalem to the same patriarchal status as Rome, Alexandria and Antioch, all three of which had been founded by apostles. Jerusalem was honoured as the place of Christ's ministry and death on the Cross, which had been discovered by Helena. Constantinople's claim to prominence was based on the fact that it had become the capital of the Roman Empire, where the emperor resided.

The elevation of Constantinople was of course disputed by Rome. But in 451 at the Council of Chalcedon, when the gathering of 381 was recognized as the Second Oecumenical Council, it was cited as binding. New Rome was thus raised to the same position as Old Rome, even if Old Rome retained the primacy of honour, due to the foundation of its church by St Peter. Old Rome and New Rome were followed by Alexandria, Antioch and Jerusalem; and their bishops were seated in that order of precedence on the emperor's right hand, and signed the acts of the council in the same order. By the end of the fifth century, however, Constantinople was also known as 'New Jerusalem', a clear sign of its claim to superior spiritual power.

These five centres, Rome, Constantinople, Alexandria, Antioch and Jerusalem, each governed by a bishop called patriarch or pope, constituted the pentarchy ('rule of five'), with responsibility for maintaining correct belief and ecclesiastical discipline throughout the Christian universe (*oikoumene*). Gradually they evolved a system of ecclesiastical government based on canons issued by oecumenical councils. Rivalry between Alexandria and Constantinople exacerbated theological differences at the meetings of the Third and Fourth Councils, held at Ephesos in 431 and Chalcedon in 451. Patriarch Nestorios of Constantinople (428–31) caused a major dispute over the role of the Virgin Mary when he preached that she should be considered the mother of Christ (in Greek, *Christotokos*). At Ephesos, however, the assembled bishops insisted that the term Theotokos, she who bore God, was appropriate, and Nestorios was condemned for his stress on the human nature of the Incarnate Christ.

This decision did not prevent further debate over the human and divine elements in Christ, whose dual nature was always a matter of concern. Patriarch Cyril of Alexandria (412–44) elaborated the theology of their union in the person of Christ (using the term *hypostasis* for person). In later developments this hypostatic union, 'the one incarnate nature of God the Word', became confused with definitions of Christ's being (*ousia*) and nature (*physis*). Support for belief in the 'union in one nature' gave rise to a distinct group of Christians later named Monophysite, from the Greek terms for one (*monos*) and nature (*physis*). But at the Fourth Oecumenical Council called to Chalcedon by Emperor Marcian and his wife Pulcheria in 451 to settle the matter, Christ was acknowledged 'in two natures ... perfect in Godhead, perfect in humanity'. Pope Leo I lent his support to this definition in a letter often called the Tome, *tomus*, of Leo. Monophysite refusal to accept it made Chalcedon a permanent symbol of division and led to the growth of separate churches, particularly in Syria and Egypt, where the Coptic Church still sustains belief in the 'union in one nature'.

Because most of this institutional history of Christianity had taken place in the eastern half of the empire and was recorded in Greek, it was directly available to the Byzantines. In contrast, the West had inadequate translations of Greek theological definitions, which did not reflect the subtlety of eastern debate about the divine and human in Christ's nature. In addition to official pronouncements, popular enthusiasm for Christian belief produced unofficial stories and cult activities, often focused on particularly holy people. Belief in the miraculous was widespread – miracles had been an essential feature of Jesus' preaching – and people seeking a cure made special journeys to the shrines of Christian healers. The bones of St Menas, for instance, who died in a Roman arena, became known for their cures, and pilgrims to his tomb to the west of Alexandria often carried home little jars of dust from his shrine. These flasks were decorated with a picture of the saint standing between his two camels with his hands raised (plate 9). They circulated throughout the Christian world and spread the story of his healing powers. While such centres were not confined to the East, many of the stories associated with the early Christian saints were written first in Greek and later translated into Latin.

The most famous example of this new literature was the *Life of Antony*, written by Patriarch Athanasius of Alexandria (328–73), who was also one of the most outspoken opponents of Arius. On several occasions when emperors promoted pro-Arian theology, he was exiled and sought refuge in the desert. There he met Antony. Using oral sources transmitted in the Egyptian spoken by the saint's companions, who had followed him into the desert to learn about his solitary ascetic life, Athanasius wrote the first Christian biography in Greek. It recorded the very long life of a young man who renounced his family and fortune to practise spiritual exercises, night-long vigils, intense prayer and contemplation of God, alone in the desert. This *Life of Antony* established a model of hagiography, writing about saints, which had a dominant influence not only in Byzantine literature but also in the West. Within a few years it was translated into Latin and was read by Augustine, who later became Bishop of Hippo in North Africa. As the author of a very unusual autobiographical work, the *Confessions*, St Augustine's interest in personal formation may well have been influenced by Antony's *Life*. It certainly inspired his self-transformation from a master of ancient rhetoric into an ascetic Christian bishop, who was known throughout the Middle Ages as the founding father of the western Church.

Similar traditions also developed in Syria and Palestine, as holy men left the cities of the Mediterranean world to face the challenge of living in the desert. In the fourth century, St Chariton set up the first *lavra* (a group of cells for individual monks), in the Judaean desert south of Jerusalem; it was a centre for ascetics who came together for their Sunday liturgy but spent the week in their cells, scattered in caves, ancient tombs and remote mountains. At about the same time

Pachom, an Egyptian soldier who died in about 346, wrote down regulations for his followers, which became much-copied monastic rules. Communal living coexisted with isolated hermits and both types of asceticism inspired followers and pilgrims. For Byzantium, St Basil of Caesarea (*c.* 329–79) was perhaps the most influential author. He visited the monastic communities in Syria and Egypt before establishing his own near Caesarea in Cappadocia, central Asia Minor, and wrote Long and Short Rules for monks and nuns, which stressed the importance of life in common, *koinobion*. This Greek term became the word used for monastery, and its derivative, 'coenobite', is often used to mean a monk. Basil also stressed the need to look after the weaker members of society – widows, orphans, the sick, elderly and lepers – in pious foundations devoted to philanthropy.

Some individual holy men stood on the top of columns and were thus known as 'stylites' (from Greek, *stylos*, column), notably St Symeon the Elder and his follower St Symeon the Younger, whose shrines near Antioch attracted numerous pilgrims and performed miraculous cures. Few holy women attained leading positions in desert communities. Susannah, a Desert Mother, was an exception, but stories of holy women like St Mary of Egypt, a reformed prostitute, perpetuated the idea that females could also survive in the desert. Often they had to disguise themselves as eunuchs, which led to some very popular stories. When Marina cut off her hair and put on a man's tunic, she became Marinos and joined a monastery, where she was accused of fathering a child. Excluded from the community, she raised the child without complaint and only when she died did the monks realize that she could never have committed the crime they attributed to her.

Among the earliest monastic centres, the settlement established by the end of the fourth century in the remotest part of the Sinai peninsula became one of the most celebrated. It was built to protect the Burning Bush through which God had spoken to Moses, at the foot of the Holy Mountain where he later received the tablets of the law. These crucial stages in the flight of the Children of Israel out of Egypt on their long journey to the promised land were celebrated by a group of Christian ascetics who constructed a tower near the Burning Bush. When the western pilgrim Egeria visited them in the early 380s, she read aloud the relevant parts of the Book of Exodus recording the story of Moses. In the sixth century, these monks appealed to Emperor Justinian to protect them against local Bedouin raids and he ordered a fortress to be built around the Bush in the rocky wilderness. The historian Procopius describes the region as 'uninhabited . . . a barren land, unwatered and producing neither crops nor any useful thing'.

The garrison sent to guard the monks against attacks by the desert tribes erected enormous fortification walls which have been maintained to this day (plate 2). Using local volcanic rock, an architect named Stephen who came from Aqaba (Eilat) designed the basilica church dedicated to the Mother of God, and on its roof beams recorded the generosity of the emperor and empress (Theodora had recently died in 548), as well as his own name. The original form of the church remains unchanged and the original wooden doors also survive. Some years after the church's dedication, Abbot Longinos commissioned a magnificent mosaic of the Transfiguration to decorate the apse of the church. It commemorates the light which surrounded Christ in the Garden of Gethsemane, as well as Moses and Elijah, the prophets who had witnessed the presence of God on Mount Sinai. Numerous pilgrims had followed Egeria, bringing gifts to the monastery: icons, liturgical objects and donations which enabled the monks to survive in a most inclement environment. Gradually, the community built up the most extraordinary collection of manuscripts in many languages and painted religious images, including the celebrated icons of Christ, the Virgin with the Christ Child and Saints, and St Peter (plate 21).

After the Arab conquests of the seventh century, Sinai passed under Muslim control and became increasingly isolated from other Christians. The monks ensured their independence by forging mutually beneficial relations with local Bedouin tribes, which were enhanced by a document 'signed' by the Prophet Muhammad, who is alleged to have granted the monks permission to remain in Sinai. Whenever Muslim rulers threatened to take over the community, the monks displayed the 'Hand of the Prophet'. A later copy with the image of Muhammad's hand (since he could not write his name) is preserved in the monastery. Throughout the Middle Ages, both the monks and the Arabs of Sinai survived together, assisted by Christian and Muslim pilgrimage to the Holy Mountain, and by the association of

St Catherine of Alexandria and her relics. Now dedicated to her name, the monastery on Mount Sinai represents the earliest traditions of Christian monasticism, a living link with the fourth century AD and beyond that to the Old Testament story of Moses. In 2006, its icons were exhibited in Los Angeles and would later be displayed in London, before returning to their arid fortress.

While the famous desert monasteries of Egypt, Palestine and Syria continued to inspire ascetic practices, hostile invasions, culminating in the Arab conquest of the Near East in the 640s, forced many to seek refuge farther north. Several found their way to Constantinople or Rome and adapted their activity to a more philanthropic role in urban society. At first emperors had banned monks from Constantinople, considering them unsuited to city life, since the ascetic movement was founded on a rejection of the civilized world and flight into desert places. But by the middle of the fifth century, numerous monasteries had been established in cities. Before 454, a senator named Stoudios constructed a basilica church on his property in the southwest corner of Constantinople, where a monastic community cherished its relic, the head of St John the Baptist. This monastery remained a leading one in the capital into the fourteenth century. Other urban monasteries were set up in houses, founded by their owners, such as the two saints Melania. The elder Melania travelled around the Mediterranean and endowed communities in Jerusalem, followed by her granddaughter, the younger, who moved from Italy to the Mount of Olives.

The secular church of bishops and the monastic church of spiritual communities form two branches of Greek Orthodoxy, the Christian world of correct belief as defined in Greek by the oecumenical councils. They were linked by their shared devotion to daily routines of prayer. They also possessed a code of church law, which included all the canons of oecumenical and local councils and additional monastic regulations derived from St Basil and the Cappadocian Church Fathers. By the sixth century, this had been summarized in a distinct system of ecclesiastical law used to regulate spiritual matters, such as the age of entry into monasteries and of ordination to church offices. It coexisted with the civil law and drew on imperial edicts devoted to issues related to Christianity. Although it was not taught in the same systematic way as civil law, canon law provoked commentaries, compendia, treatises on specific problems and collections of judicial decisions which made it practical and useful. In the early thirteenth century, the acts of Archbishop Chomatenos of Ohrid reveal a sophisticated application of Justinianic as well as canon law to resolve problems such as the abduction of a virgin by a married man (as a fornicator he had to pay the girl a monetary compensation or give her half of his property, and the local prelate had to exclude him from communion for seven years).

Similarly, patriarchs of Constantinople presided over a synod or court, which heard cases involving churchmen and gave definitive judgments on issues such as marriage within the prohibited degrees of consanguinity. In 1316, for instance, Patriarch John XIII judged a quarrel over inheritance between the children of a man's first marriage and the daughter from his second union. The following year the synod had to decide who owned an icon of the Virgin and a plot of land, originally given to the Metropolitan of Lakedaimonia by Euphrosyne Marinia, a nun. The property had come into the possession of another bishop and Euphrosyne appealed to have it returned. While many cases concern the wealth of the Church, others reveal clerical misdemeanours, incestuous relations, improper use of magic charms and other superstitious practices, providing fascinating hints about daily life in Byzantium.

While the Church had its own independent administration, the emperor often tried to appoint a particular ally as patriarch. Theoretically, he was limited to choosing one of three candidates whose names were put forward by the clergy of the cathedral church of Constantinople. But on many occasions an outside candidate, the emperor's youngest son, or a favourite monk, might be imposed. Conflicts over these and more serious issues often led to a breakdown in cooperation, and patriarchs might be deposed by imperial power. St John Chrysostom, elected in 398, was one of the first and most famous casualties of this practice. He was exiled to Armenia in 404 because he had denounced Empress Eudoxia for erecting a statue of herself with time-honoured and noisy pagan ceremonies, and died three years later, protesting his innocence in letters to his supporters. In 907, when Leo VI married his fourth wife, the patriarch denied him entry to the church for ten months. Despite such instances of conflict, the cooperation of Empire and Church was one of the great strengths of Christian culture in Byzantium.

It also distinguished Byzantium from the situation in the medieval West, where the leading bishop, the Bishop of Rome, had much less secular support and regularly had to negotiate with invaders. Although Rome was restored to imperial control in the sixth century and remained under nominal Byzantine administration until the eighth, imperial officials and troops often failed to protect the city from attack. The heirs of St Peter, as bishops of Rome considered themselves, stressed their superior moral authority to balance the reality of their political weakness. During the fifth century the term *papa*, which means father, was adopted, and although all Christian priests are regularly addressed as father, bishops of Rome have become distinguished by the title pope. Whether Roman claims to a moral superiority were recognized or not, it became the custom for disaffected eastern clerics or monks, who had been condemned by the emperor or patriarch, to appeal to Rome. In this way they hoped to attract support from Christian authorities outside the empire.

This practice, which set Old Rome against New Rome, can be observed in the appeals by dissidents for support, for example, during the iconoclast controversy (see chapter 10) and when Leo VI was excommunicated by his patriarch for marrying for the fourth time. The emperor appealed to the pope and was pleased to learn that Rome had no objection to his marriage. In 907, this opened a rift between Constantinople and Rome, which was only patched up thirteen years later. Such appeals to the see of St Peter, whether by those in the East who had been condemned and exiled, or by patriarchs who felt they had been unjustly deposed, enhanced the pope's position as the ultimate arbiter of Christian quarrels. In the eyes of eastern Church leaders, who felt uneasy about recognizing papal primacy, they also created a dangerous precedent.

During the reign of Constantine IX Monomachos (1042–55), this latent hostility flared into mutual condemnation. Contacts between Old and New Rome had drawn attention to differences between eastern and western Church practice. Some were fundamental, such as the wording of the creed; what bread to use in the eucharist (leavened with yeast, *zymos*, in the East, unleavened, *azyme*, in the

West); whether priests should marry (celibacy was imposed on all clerics in the West but priests and those in lesser orders were permitted to marry in the East); and the primacy of bishops of Rome. Others were relatively insignificant and had developed over centuries: for instance, in the East cheese (but not meat) was eaten during the week preceding Lent and in the West it was not eaten on certain fast days. But against the background of heightened awareness generated by reformers like Pope Leo IX (1049–54), the West asserted the purity of its traditions. In turn, Byzantium emphasized that the West had added a phrase to the wording of the creed.

The essential theological difference concerned the origin of the Holy Spirit, 'which proceeds from the Father', according to the definition adopted at the Councils of Nicaea and Chalcedon in 325 and 451. Orthodox teaching on the Trinity was clear: the three manifestations of God the Father, God the Son and God the Holy Spirit shared in its uncreated essence and pre-existing substance – in a word they are consubstantial. But each had its own *hypostasis*, a term difficult to translate, which had been rendered in Latin by *natura* (nature) or *substantia* (substance). This was not the same as that pre-existing power which the orthodox identified as the nature or substance, *ousia*, of the Godhead. The complex relationships defined in Greek by early Christian theologians had never been fully reflected in Latin translation, a fact recognized as early as the fifth century by St Augustine.

The relationship of the Son (or *Logos*, the Word) and the Holy Spirit (*Pneuma*) to the Father was not the same, since the Son is generated and the Holy Spirit proceeds from the Father. The Son participates in this process, holding the position of mediator, which gives rise to the formula: 'the Holy Spirit proceeds from the Father through the Son' (*dia tou Hyiou*). This was how Maximos Confessor understood the relationship in the seventh century. Nonetheless, at about this time the clause *and from the Son* (*filioque* in Latin) had been added to the creed in Spain, and with the authority of St Isidore of Seville behind it this wording gradually spread to other churches. Rome did not accept it immediately: in the early ninth century, Pope Leo III erected shields with the traditional wording of the creed in both Greek and Latin at the entrance to St Peter's. In 879/80 at the Council of Constantinople, the western formulation 'the Holy

Spirit proceeds from the Father *and from the Son*' was condemned as heretical, an unauthorized addition to the creed as defined by the Oecumenical Councils of 325 and 451. In the eleventh century, however, Rome adopted the clause and thus endorsed a new interpretation of the Holy Spirit, which was never recognized in the East.

In 1054, Constantine IX invited Pope Leo IX to send a delegation to Constantinople to discuss the possibility of constructing an effective Byzantine-papal alliance against the Normans in southern Italy. The three Roman envoys were all noted for their hostility to Byzantium, although they were polite to the emperor. But their leader, Cardinal Humbert of Silva Candida, clashed immediately with the patriarch, Michael Keroularios. After several stormy meetings, on 16 July he deposited a bull of excommunication on the altar of St Sophia, and Keroularios immediately responded in kind. At the same moment, Pope Leo IX died, leaving the see of Rome vacant and the status of the bull uncertain. This event is sometimes described as the 'Great Schism' between the churches of the East and the West. But the excommunications were considered personal and were rapidly lifted; regular mutual commemoration of the leaders of the Churches of Rome and Constantinople was restored.

When Alexios I Komnenos (1081–1118) asked for evidence of any break in relations between the churches, no document could be found in the patriarch's library. Constantinople and Rome remained in communion and many westerners worshipped in Greek churches and vice versa. Alexios I's appeal to the pope for military aid against the Muslims was based on shared Christian traditions, which resulted in the First Crusade and the recapture of Jerusalem (see chapter 24). With hindsight, however, the split of 1054 assumed larger proportions and was subsequently used by later crusaders to justify their desire to attack Constantinople.

It is hardly surprising that differences had developed between the two major sees of Christendom. Constantinople remained a Greek-speaking city, while Rome used Latin, and translation between the two languages was not always accurate. In contrast to the churches of the medieval West, the lower clergy in the East below the rank of bishop were allowed to marry. Celibacy was required only of eastern bishops, so if a married priest was elected to the episcopacy, he and his wife had to agree to an amicable separation, and she had to enter a nunnery distant from his see. In the West, celibacy slowly became a requirement for all clerics (those who took holy orders). Married men continued to become bishops and to plan for their sons to inherit their churches. In one very visible difference, western churches used an unleavened bread, which has become a wafer, in the Eucharist, while in the East bread raised with yeast, more like a bun, was distributed. Genuflecting was more common in the West than the East, where priests prostrated themselves before the altar at particular moments in the liturgy. Local customs added to the variety, especially in the matter of fasting: meat was eaten on Saturdays in the East but it was prohibited in some churches of the West which prepared for Sunday by fasting.

The churches were nonetheless united in their common zeal to care for Christian souls and to convert those who had not been educated in Christian ways. In Byzantium most people lived in villages, where married priests attended to the needs of their Christian flocks, baptized and married their children, buried their dead and guided their moral lives. In larger towns a bishop and his staff filled this role. In turn, bishops were subordinate to the metropolitan or archbishop who resided in the capital of his archdiocese. This structure is recorded in the hierarchy of ecclesiastical sees, which descend from the Patriarch of Constantinople, through the numbered ranks of metropolitans, down to the bishops. During the late Byzantine period, many sees in the European provinces gained in importance and moved up the list to acquire a higher rank, at the expense of those in Asia Minor, devastated and impoverished by constant warfare.

While Mount Athos became a beacon for ascetic monasticism, local monks and holy men constantly inspired men and women to devote their lives to God and directed their spiritual life. When the young Luke of Steiris (central Greece) left home in the early tenth century, he learned of a stylite at Zemenna in the Peloponnese and begged to be allowed to serve him. For several years he studied ascetic practices with him and then moved to an isolated retreat at Ioannitza as a solitary hermit. Eventually, the disciples who joined him formed a monastery and the local governor, General Krinites, funded its first church, dedicated to St Barbara, a patron of military fighters. The community later erected the church of Hosios Loukas (Holy Luke) over his tomb, and joined it to the church of the Theotokos, thus creating a dual structure at Steiris (plate 31). As the fame of miracles performed at his tomb spread, gifts of property and money allowed the monks to decorate the shrine with exquisite mosaics and frescoes that survive to this day. From donations of this sort, monasteries often became very wealthy and powerful institutions. It is all the more important to recall that their resources were based not only on imperial patronage but also on the faith of peasant families, whose devotion to orthodoxy was typical of Byzantium.

There were, of course, challenges to Christian dominance in society, from intellectuals or heretics such as the philosopher John Italos and Boris the Bogomil (a Bulgarian charismatic leader) in the early twelfth century, or George Gemistos Plethon (who adopted pagan religion as well as philosophy) in the fifteenth. In general though, heresy was less common than in the medieval West. Theological disputes often reveal the characteristic mixture of elements in Byzantine culture. Italos and Plethon represented the philosophical traditions and cults of ancient Greece; Boris, the varieties within medieval religious observance. While Byzantium was the repository of all Christian traditions written in Greek, it also preserved poems and stories about the ancient gods, as well as some of their temples and statues.

I have emphasized the lasting strength which the classical, pagan inheritance gave Byzantium through its educational, administrative and cultural traditions. These were unified by a belief system that was determinedly orthodox – vigorous in its development of Christian definitions that allowed for a variety of different experiences, male and female, solitary and ceremonial. It was through its religion that Byzantium conducted its great arguments, not only with the Muslims, Arab and then Turkish, but also with other Christians, particularly western. Over the centuries these arguments led to the Byzantine refusal to accept subordination to the bishops of Rome. The theological sophistication of this stubborn and persistent Greek Orthodoxy constructed a characteristic belief system and a coherent authority through the combination of emperor and patriarch at its centre. Even if, to the end, emperors fought and died like Greeks and Romans, they wanted to be buried and prayed for as Christians.

5

The Church of Hagia Sophia

Rising above this circle is an enormous spherical dome, which
makes the building exceptionally beautiful. It seems not to be
founded on solid masonry, but to be suspended from heaven
by that golden chain and so to cover the space.

Procopius, *The Buildings*, c. 560

Although Yeats chose the title 'Sailing to Byzantium' for his poem of
1928, he never went to Istanbul, the Turkish name for Constantinople.
He visited Ravenna and saw the Byzantine mosaics there, but did not
experience the thrill of arriving at Byzantium by sea. Approaching
from the Dardanelles through the Sea of Marmara, the first signs of
the old city are eagerly anticipated. Eventually, the land and sea walls
announce the enclosing defences and soon the minarets surrounding
the dome of Hagia Sophia come into view. This is a strangely exciting
moment. It was how I first caught sight of it when I was a student and
the experience remains, despite the skyscrapers that now dominate the
modern quarter. The power of the church's profile dominates the sky-
line, the sheer bulk of the immense structure grows as one approaches
by sea (plate 16). Its great dome is amazing at a distance and becomes
even more striking as the enormous buttresses that support it are
revealed. Beyond it, around Seraglio point and within the harbour of
the Golden Horn, the same church can be seen from the north.

If the exterior of the building amazes, its vast interior is awesome.
Lit by the sun through the windows of the dome and at gallery level,
the distant heights of the church reflect the glowing gold mosaics,
while the lower levels remain darker. Once accustomed to this con-

trast, the multi-coloured marble decoration of the walls and floor can be appreciated, and the finely carved capitals set on magnificent columns carry the eye back up to the dome (plate 18). This monument is the paramount symbol of Byzantium.

For medieval visitors, amazement at the scale of the building and its beauty in Christian use was even more pronounced because they knew few large buildings. It was lit by thousands of candles and lamps hung in front of icons, illuminating the coloured marbles and gold and blue mosaics. From a central ambo, a carved platform like a pulpit, in front of the decorated curtains which separated the main body of the church from the sanctuary around the altar, the deacon read the lessons and the patriarch preached. The ambassadors of Prince Vladimir of Kiev told him:

We knew not whether we were in heaven or on earth. For on earth there is no such splendour or such beauty . . . We only know that God dwells there among men, and their service is fairer than the ceremonies of other nations.

At the time of its consecration on 27 December 537, there was no figural decoration on the walls, apart from the four great seraphim which still peep out from their long wings covering the pendentives. The dominance of gold mosaic in the side aisles and galleries was echoed in the dome decorated with a huge cross in a medallion.

Its form was utterly novel. Most early Christian churches adopted the plan of a basilica, based on imperial reception halls. These long, tall constructions, which survive as St Sabina at Rome and the basilica built by Constantine at Trier (in Germany), were readily adapted for ecclesiastical use with the addition of a raised platform at the east end for the altar. The shrines of martyrs, often constructed round the tomb, prompted an alternative form, with galleries surrounding the central focus, as at St Costanza, Rome. While the dome was known to Roman architects and was used to great effect at the Pantheon, with its oculus open to the sky, there is little evidence of it in the east Mediterranean. Precursors to the dome of Hagia Sophia have been sought in small domed buildings in Isauria, which demonstrate the technical skill required. But no one in the city had ever tried to raise such a vast cupola until Justinian commissioned the new church of Holy Wisdom.

To understand how extraordinary his order was, I will first look at the pre-Christian artistic traditions, which Byzantium used to create its own distinctive styles. The most obvious inheritance of antiquity was imperial art: the depiction of rulers (statues, reliefs, and portraits in mosaics and on coin) and their regalia (jewelled crowns, orbs and sceptres, marriage belts, and costumes made of imperial purple and red boots). Byzantium also adapted for Christian use decorative artistic techniques for sculpting architectural elements such as columns and capitals and reliefs to decorate funerary monuments and sarcophagi. Similarly, Byzantine craftsmen continued ancient skills of working in precious metals, enamel, ivory and rock crystal. They were supremely good at these technical matters: striking coins, carving elephant tusk, cutting different coloured marbles to form polychrome pavements and wall coverings, and weaving complex multi-coloured patterns in silk.

Prior to the sixth century, silk cloth imported from China and Persia was so highly appreciated that it was unravelled to provide thread for Roman and Byzantine looms. According to Theodoretus of Cyrrhus, the 'nimble fingers of women and children' were employed in this activity. When the secret of the silk moth's life cycle was discovered, allegedly by monks who smuggled some silk worms out of China and presented them to Justinian, the planting of mulberry trees to provide their essential foodstuff initiated a new industry in Byzantium. After the Arab conquest of Persia and the Near East in the seventh century, the silk workshops of Tyre and Sidon were moved back behind the Taurus Mountains frontier and later to the capital. Some provincial production was permitted and the making of purple dye from tiny murex shellfish harvested off the coasts of Greece and Asia Minor was encouraged by tax exemptions.

Silk weaving was then concentrated in imperial workshops in Constantinople, where the processes were carefully protected as a state monopoly. Strict controls applied to every stage of production, which was organized by groups of skilled workers. Silks traditionally displayed natural, secular and imperial subjects: pairs of lions, eagles, griffins, hunters, amazons or charioteers, in vivid colours (plate 7). Christian themes, such as scenes from the life of Christ, were much less common. During the seventh and eighth centuries, production within the empire developed so dramatically that bishops of Rome listed gifts of Byzantine silks such as those carried to Rome by Lazaros, the Khazar icon painter, in 857/8. An embassy sent to the western Emperor Louis the Pious in 824 included ten silks of different colours among the diplomatic gifts.

Among other luxury artefacts, enamels and gold jewellery were made, including marriage belts and rings with traditional images of Homonia (Concord), to which images of Christ blessing the married couple were added. Gold filigree and enamel earrings, pendants and bracelets continued the same mixture of ancient and Christian themes. Similar associations of holy authority with secular power are clear on coins and ivories, where Christ crowns the emperor and thus conveys heavenly approval to his worldly representative (plate 14). In the production of manuscripts, dyeing parchment purple and writing on it with silver ink also preserved an ancient practice. Illustrated copies of the *Iliad* and *Odyssey*, usually on papyrus, provided models for the biblical texts illustrated by medieval painters, often using an almost strip-cartoon style.

After an initial emphasis on the symbolic features of Christianity – loaves and fishes, the sign of the cross – artists began to depict its leaders, Christ, His Mother and the martyrs. These Byzantine portraits of holy persons used the technique of painting in encaustic (heated wax coloured with a wide range of tones), which had been employed for Roman funerary portraits. Religious icons are often considered the quintessential feature of Byzantine art. How they became so dominant is much disputed; I discuss the problem in chapter 9. Some of the earliest survive in the monastery of St Catherine at Mount Sinai, which holds three magnificent icons often associated with the emperor's patronage: the celebrated image of Christ Pantokrator (Ruler of All) (plate 21); of the Virgin and Child with military saints and angels; and of St Peter. The icon of Christ was over-painted later and thus not identified as a work of the sixth century until its restoration. It appears to regard the viewer with huge all-seeing eyes differentiated by shape and function: one seems to sternly condemn while the other forgives. The icons of the Virgin and St Peter do not address the viewer so directly. In all three the figures are set against an architectural frame. Such paintings in encaustic are extremely striking, bold and powerful; they are also works produced fast to capture human features, particularly the eyes and flesh tones in lifelike colours. The technique does not appear to have survived into the medieval period, when it was replaced by the use of egg white to fix the colours.

In all these artistic fields, Byzantine craftsmen adapted ancient techniques to new ends. But for the construction of Hagia Sophia they attempted something unheard-of. The context for this novel experiment lies in the early years of Justinian's rule. Justinian became emperor in 527 after the death of his uncle Justin, who had brought him to Constantinople and prepared him for the succession. In contrast to Justin, who was a successful military commander but not an educated man, Justinian had a sure grasp of imperial administration, law, theology and court ceremonial. During his uncle's ten-year rule, he played an influential role and took responsibility for major changes of policy. As we have seen, he insisted on revising the law against senators marrying commoners in order to make Theodora his wife, over the strong disapproval of his aunt Empress Lupicina Euphemia. As soon as he became sole ruler he took initiatives: to reform the law, to enforce higher taxation, to renew warfare with Persia. He appointed generals to fight for the empire and spent most of his life in the capital. Where and how he acquired his passion for building remains unclear.

In 532, the Greens and Blues, the groups responsible for Hippodrome entertainment, organized a serious challenge to the emperor's power. Normally rivals, on this occasion the groups united in their hostility to Justinian's financial policies and proclaimed Hypatius, a nephew of Emperor Anastasius I, as a rival emperor. Over his wife's objections, Hypatius reluctantly served their purposes, and crowds gathered in the Hippodrome to witness his acclamation and robing in the imperial purple. The rebellion was called 'Nika' from the word for 'Conquer', which was chanted by the participants. To heighten the threat, the Greens and Blues set fire to the centre of the city and burned down a large area, including the basilica church of Hagia Sophia. As Procopius recounts the incident, Justinian met with his advisers inside the palace to consider what to do. Within earshot of the chants of the massed crowd, plans for flight on boats from the palace harbour were detailed. Then Empress Theodora – she who had been the master of the crowd and its applause – stepped forward to declare that she was not prepared to leave. 'Purple makes a fine shroud,' she said, quoting ancient authors such as Isocrates: 'I would prefer to die in this imperial cloth.' Inspired by her resolute determination, her husband was, it seems, persuaded to use force rather than negotiate with the rebels or flee. He ordered troops into the Hippodrome and a massacre of unarmed Byzantines followed.

Theodora was not the first but certainly one of the most striking of a series of forceful women who exercised great power in Byzantium. Often they were outsiders speaking for an autocratic power they had bent to their will, and were responsible for great bloodshed. Imperial wives and widows took initiatives unthinkable in other medieval societies. Even if the precise wording of Procopius' account was invented, stories of Theodora's intervention must have circulated within the palace and among the city's residents. Her example is cited as one that other women wanted to follow. Empresses like Irene (780–90, 797–802), Theodora (842–56), Zoe (914–19) and Theophano (963–9), although they were always patronized by men and documented only by male writers, evidently shaped and directed imperial power.

Those like Theodora who married into the ruling dynasty, rapidly learnt to exploit court tensions to their own benefit. Irene's career provides striking evidence of this ability: she cultivated the support of court factions and the Church to rise to the position of emperor, blinding her son Constantine VI and ruling for five years alone (see chapter 10). In contrast, those born into the imperial family, Zoe and her sister Theodora in the eleventh century or Anna Komnene in the twelfth, for example, were trained in ceremonial routines and philanthropic customs from an early age. But they too surprised their contemporaries by taking a much larger role than that allowed to women in general. Zoe and Theodora dominated the period from 1028 to 1056, when they ruled together or alone and promoted five different men to the imperial office. After Zoe's death, Theodora assumed sole control of the empire, which she in turn bequeathed to her husband. The legacy of Justinian's wife can thus be traced down the centuries, reflecting memories of a powerful individual and an unlikely but highly successful marriage.

*

On the burned-out spaces created by the fire in central Constantinople, Justinian envisioned a grand rebuilding plan, laid out around the Augusteum, a large square dedicated to the emperors. To the north he placed both of the most important churches, the cathedral dedicated to Holy Wisdom, Hagia Sophia, commonly called the Great Church, and its neighbour, Holy Peace (Hagia Eirene, St Irene). To the south and west he planned the restored Senate House, parts of the patriarchate, the hospice of Samson (a charitable institution), and the Chalke Gate, which formed the principal entrance of the Great Palace. Close by he rebuilt the public baths, named after Zeuxippos, and the area of colonnaded stoas on either side of the main thoroughfare, the Mese, extending as far as the Forum of Constantine.

In considering the form of the cathedral church, Justinian may have been influenced by the building activity of a wealthy senatorial lady, Juliana Anicia, who had recently completed an extremely grand church dedicated to St Polyeuktos on her property near the aqueduct of Valens. While it is not clear if this church had a dome or a pitched roof, Justinian was determined that the church of St Sophia would be larger and even more beautiful. The emperor spared no expense in the construction, which began immediately after the riot. He commissioned two engineers, Anthemius of Tralles (also known as a mathematician) and Isidore of Miletos, to raise a huge dome, 31m in diameter, over the nave of the church at a height of 55m from the base, a feat never before attempted. In his panegyric for the emperor, *The Buildings*, Procopius described the technique used to construct this unprecedented building, which seems to have been completed within five years of the riot. He was probably one of the congregation who attended the inauguration of the new church just after Christmas 537. But he was at a loss to explain how the structure supported such a broad dome, pierced by forty windows through which the sun filtered into the vast cavern below. He described it as a structure that floats.

While the existence of earlier domes indicates that the necessary engineering skills were familiar, the scale of Hagia Sophia was exceptional. To raise its roof required very substantial structures at each corner of the square base, from which half-diamond-shaped pendentives curved upwards to support the circular base of the dome. To the east and west, semi-domes at a lower level sheltered the apse and covered the double narthex, through which people entered the church through seven doors. The central and largest set of doors was reserved for the patriarch and emperor, who would greet each other here before stepping into the main body of the church. Inside, the multi-coloured marble floor extended to the lower levels of the side walls, and the multitude of coloured columns supported a decorative carved panel which ran all round the building. The capitals preserved the letters of the imperial names, Justinian and Theodora, and the ceilings of the galleries were covered in gold tesserae. When the emperor first saw the finished building he is alleged to have declared, 'Solomon, I have surpassed thee.' Clearly, he wished to be considered in the same category as one of the greatest builders ever known. The result of Anthemius' and Isidore's work is a justly famous architectural innovation that remained unrivalled for about a thousand years.

In the square of the Augusteum, decorated with classical statues of emperors, Justinian erected his own column topped with an equestrian statue. He was shown wearing Persian military uniform, in a reference to Roman victories over Persia achieved by Belisarius. He reconstructed the Senate House, with magnificent white marble columns supporting a portico embellished with coloured marbles, its roof topped by numerous statues. He also commissioned two new hospices, as well as the huge cistern now called Yeri Batan Saray, to the west of Hagia Sophia. By all this rebuilding, Justinian left his mark on the centre of the city of Constantine.

Twenty-one years later, an earthquake caused cracks in the dome. When they were being repaired, the eastern part of the semi-dome over the altar collapsed. With other expert builders, Isidore the Younger, son of the original engineer, decided to secure the dome by raising it by 7 metres, making it narrower and steeper. It was redecorated with the same gold mosaic design of a monumental cross, and the rebuilding was commemorated in a lengthy verse description by Paul, a court official. This gives a sense of the mixture of colours achieved by using varied marbles for the columns: green from Karystos, Lakonia and Thessaly; speckled from Phrygia; white from Prokonnesos in the Sea of Marmara; purple from Egypt; and other imports from Libya and Lydia. Paul documents the use of onyx, of much precious metal and curtains shielding the main body of the church from the area of the apse (*bema*), which were decorated with images of Christ, his Mother and saints. The chancel also had silver discs engraved with similar images, and the ambo was entirely sheathed in silver.

In *The Buildings*, Procopius provides a detailed account of Hagia Sophia and many churches in other cities, fortifications, baths, roads, bridges, and inns at which the imperial post changed horses, all constructed by Justinian. The empire's finances had been improved by Emperor Anastasius, and apparently unlimited resources were available to finance the imperial mania for construction. The army provided engineering techniques and muscle for military constructions, while hundreds of builders and craftsmen must have been engaged for the mosaic and marble decoration that adorned the emperor's numerous churches dedicated to the Mother of God, such as the New Church at Jerusalem. Justinian demanded the best technicians, the most skilled craftsmen, and challenged them to realize his grand ambitions. The cost of all his buildings must have strained imperial finances, although calculating the budget is extremely difficult (see chapter 14). Procopius' account is a eulogy of the emperor, possibly written to gain an imperial position. The same author also recorded the emperor's campaigns against the Persians, the Vandals and the Goths in *The Wars*. Since he accompanied the general Belisarius in a civilian capacity, his eyewitness account of many battles and negotiations forms a remarkable history in the classical style. It is full of detailed information about Justinian's strategy for restoring the Roman Empire. Yet we know very little about the author.

In the *Anecdota*, or *Secret History*, on the other hand, Procopius records what he could not include in his other writings: the empress's origins as a circus performer; her callous treatment of courtiers and determined persecution of religious opponents are related to the emperor's weakness in resisting his wife and to his own devilish practices. Justinian's ability to go without sleep, needing little food, is here related to supernatural powers and a wicked intention of destroying the social fabric of the empire. Both empress and emperor, who came from the lower classes, distrusted the engrained powers of the aristocracy and tried to reduce its traditional superiority. But Procopius' extreme condemnation here stands in marked contrast to his measured account of the military campaigns or the uncritical praise of the buildings. The *Secret History* is so called because it remained unpublished in his lifetime and was only discovered in the seventeenth century in a manuscript in Rome. At first, scholars believed it to be written by another Procopius, but now Averil Cameron has shown that all three works are clearly by the same author. Procopius was evidently a many-layered author and his motives for using such contrasting approaches remain a challenge to modern readers.

During his long rule of nearly forty years, Justinian achieved much, but nothing was more glorious or lasting than Hagia Sophia. On important feasts, when the imperial couple would attend services in the cathedral church, the emperor with the patriarch, the empress seated in the southwest gallery, they could witness the brilliance of the Byzantine liturgy in Hagia Sophia. Unlike other lay people, rulers could also enter the sanctuary reserved to the clergy, for instance when they changed the altar cloth or presented crowns to the church. Descriptions of the church all stress the glittering effect of the light of innumerable lamps, some suspended from the dome, others outlining the structures, which made such an unforgettable impact.

The amazement expressed by later visitors was common among the Byzantines themselves, who wondered how on earth such a structure could have been erected. Arab visitors recorded their admiration for the great clock in Hagia Sophia with twenty-four doors that opened and shut to mark the hours. The monument generated a series of legendary stories which extend from the *Account of the Construction* (probably of the second half of the tenth century), through Russian pilgrim texts and on into modern Greek folklore. The *Account* describes how Justinian planned the monument, using the wood of the Ark of Noah for the doors; how an angel watched over the building to make sure it would not collapse and demanded that the workers construct a triple window in the apse to honour the Trinity. These tales passed into popular memory and resurfaced in different centuries with slight variations and embellishments. Hagia Sophia, for centuries the largest church in Christendom, continued to astonish and to provoke imaginative explanations.

The church of Holy Wisdom also inspired the mosque constructed by Sultan Mehmet II on the site of the imperial mausoleum and church of the Holy Apostles after the occupation of Constantinople in 1453. It was an important symbol of the fundamental change. Yet the new domed mosque, named after the conqueror, celebrated a form of building that was clearly Christian. Similarly, when approaching Istanbul from the sea, the Sultan Ahmet Camii, known as the Blue Mosque from the colour of its tiles, appears to rival Hagia Sophia, yet it was built a thousand years later, and as it is set a little farther down the slope, it lies below its great prototype. After 1453, four minarets added to the corners of Justinian's church marked the conversion of the ancient monument for Islam, but if anything they confirm the strangeness of the mosque named Ayasofya, and the enormous scale of the structure beneath its dome remains a physical symbol of Constantinople's claim to rule the world. While it stands, Byzantium will always be present.

6

The Ravenna Mosaics

In the apse of San Vitale the image of this same Maximin and
of the emperor and empress are beautifully created in mosaic.
Agnellus, *Book of the Pontiffs of the Church of Ravenna*,
early ninth century

The mosaics in Ravenna were my first and most exciting introduction to Byzantine art. During the Second World War they had been damaged by allied bombardment, but after 1945 copies of these sixth-century masterpieces were sent round Europe to raise funds for their restoration. My mother had seen that exhibition and was keen to visit the originals; I was learning Italian at school and we both thought that Ravenna should be the focus of our summer holiday. So off we went from Milan in a rented Fiat Cinquecento to see the mosaic panels that commemorate Justinian and Theodora. Only later did I wonder why portraits of the rulers of Byzantium who never went to Ravenna flanked the approach to the altar in the church of San Vitale. Why are they there?

In 89 BC, Ravenna, a small city on the Adriatic coast of Italy, was conquered by the Romans. Later it became the capital of the Italian province of Flaminia et Picenum. The well-fortified site had a secure harbour at Classis, with important maritime links throughout the Mediterranean, which drew it to the attention of Emperor Honorius (395–423), who ruled the western half of the empire while his brother Arcadius ruled the East (395–408). Like most fourth-century emperors, Honorius did not live in Rome, but had his imperial residence and court at Milan. In 402 he decided to move from Milan to

Ravenna, which could be better protected from barbarian raids. Under imperial patronage Ravenna grew rapidly, expanding in population and in buildings essential for administering the remains of the Roman Empire in the West. It attracted aristocrats from Rome and other centres of the West, traders from all parts of the Mediterranean and embassies from rulers who held power outside the Roman world.

Among those who settled in Ravenna was Galla Placidia, daughter of Theodosius I and younger sister of Arcadius and Honorius. In 423, her son Valentinian III was proclaimed *augustus* (emperor) in the West, when he was only five years old, so Galla assumed power and ruled as Regent for over twenty-five years. She patronized the building of many churches dedicated to the 'orthodox' (anti-Arian) rite while maintaining relations with the pro-Arian Christian faction. Her basilica of St John the Theologian must have been a spectacular monument, which rivalled the city's cathedral dedicated to Apollinaris, the local saint, whose relics were preserved at Classis. It was constructed after she experienced a fierce storm at sea on her return from Constantinople. Praying to St John (a fisherman as well as an evangelist), Galla promised to build him a church if the ship was saved. Details of the story decorated the original church. Galla was also largely successful in protecting her son's imperial claim from ambitious generals. In 437 Valentinian married Eudoxia, daughter of Theodosius II, in a grand ceremony which was also commemorated in mosaics decorating the palace of Ravenna.

Shortly before her death in 450, Galla had prepared her own mausoleum, with Christian mosaics over the three sarcophagi designed to hold her bodily remains and those of her husband and her son. With its fine quartz windows, symbolic scenes of the Good Shepherd, doves and deer drinking at the fountain of life and the starry sky in the central vault, this is an exquisite small burial chamber in the shape of a cross. It was dedicated to the Roman martyr St Lawrence, who is shown beside the fire over which he was tortured on a grill. The mausoleum was probably related to the larger palace complex, where the mosaic floor of a chapel devoted to the cult of the Holy Cross survives. Under Bishop Peter Chrysologus (432–50), Ravenna was endowed with six episcopal sees in Emilia, which had formerly been under the authority of Milan. As it became the undisputed capital of

Italy, it gained additional ecclesiastical power commensurate with its political authority.

In 455, Rome was sacked by Vandals who had occupied North Africa, with a brutality that set a new standard and has coined the modern term 'vandalism'. It never recovered its former status. The political decline of Rome was matched by the rise of Ravenna, which became a truly imperial capital under the Ostrogothic leader Theoderic, who set up his government and court there in 489. He was one of the non-Roman military leaders encouraged by the emperors in Constantinople to go West, to maintain authority among the fractured provinces of Italy. This devious ploy was designed to alleviate pressure on the East, while giving barbarian soldiers an imperial role. It often provoked severe problems for the indigenous authorities, especially bishops of Rome. Theoderic was, however, a different sort of barbarian because he had spent his youth (between *c.* 461 and 470) in Constantinople as a hostage for his father's good behaviour; he was well educated and had absorbed the traditions of the imperial court.

While he claimed the title king of the Goths, and *rex* was commonly used by non-Roman rulers, Theoderic had imperial ambitions. After his arrival in Ravenna with the support of Emperor Zeno (474–91), these hopes are reflected in letters written by his chancellor, the scholarly senator Cassiodorus, in his name. To Emperor Anastasius (491–518) he declared:

Our royalty is an imitation of yours, modelled on your good purpose, a copy of the only empire, and in so far as we follow you do we excel all other nations.

In his building activity, patronage of late antique culture and wearing of purple robes he certainly followed imperial practice. Yet although Theoderic's rule over both Romans and Goths was recognized as superior by his contemporaries in both East and West, Constantinople never granted him the official title *augustus*.

In the first quarter of the sixth century, Theoderic undertook a major programme of building in Ravenna to celebrate the pro-Arian faith of the Goths, with the cathedral dedicated to Christ (now Sant'Apollinare Nuovo), the Arian baptistery and a palace decorated in typical imperial style with scenes of Hippodrome racing. In his church, Theoderic commissioned mosaics of Christ's life and miracles, as well as images of himself leading the Goths in worship, his palace and the harbour city of Classis. In this way, the Arian theology condemned at the First and Second Oecumenical Councils (at Nicaea and Constantinople), but maintained by the Goths and other non-Roman tribes, was enshrined in churches endowed with elegant mosaic decoration. In imitation of Galla Placidia, Theoderic constructed the monument in which he would be buried – the mausoleum still stands with an impressive single block covering the tomb. He also built palaces, fortresses, aqueducts, baths and other public buildings worthy of an imperial patron.

Theoderic visited Rome only once, in 500, when he celebrated his tricennalia (thirty years of rule) in suitably imperial fashion. He seems to have dated his assumption of power from his first military victory in around 470, after the death of his father. Following a ceremonial welcome by Pope Symmachus, the entire Senate and all the people, he prayed at St Peter's, addressed the Senate, gave circus games and increased the *annona*, distribution of bread. For six months he lived on the Palatine in the ancient imperial palace, and promised to maintain the ordinances of previous Roman emperors. He described the ancient capital as a centre of learning: 'All should enjoy Rome, that fertile mother of eloquence, that vast temple of every virtue, that city which cannot be called an alien place.' But Theoderic devoted the next twenty-five years to his own capital in Ravenna, where he ruled over a mixed society of Goths and Romans, pro- and anti-Arian, with considerable skill and tolerance.

This can be seen in numerous letters composed by Cassiodorus that reflect Theoderic's ambitions. In response to an appeal, for instance, he replied: 'I who give thought to justice, even without solicitations, gladly welcome the reasonable petitions of suppliants. For what is more proper than for inviolate equity to preserve my state, even as arms protect it?' Similarly, when the Jews of Genoa asked Theoderic for permission to rebuild their ancient synagogue, he replied that they could re-roof the structure but not enlarge it. 'I grant leave, indeed, but I condemn the prayers of erring men . . . I cannot command your faith for no one is forced to believe against his will.' In this way, Theoderic strengthened the loyalty of his many, varied subjects.

In Ravenna he minted coins in imperial style and issued one medallion with his own distinctive portrait. With the help of Cassiodorus, he ensured efficient administration through records made on papyrus. He commissioned the learned senator to record the history of the Goths, which Cassiodorus did in a twelve-volume work, partly preserved in Jordanes' later version called the *Getica*. Theoderic enhanced the intellectual life of the city and patronized scholars, such as the philosopher Boethius, who was asked to document how to build sundials, water clocks and other technical devices. In about 524, Boethius was accused of treason and wrote his famous *Consolation of Philosophy* in prison before he was put to death, an act which Theoderic later regretted.

While Theoderic maintained his commitment to the Arian definitions of Christ's nature and status, and encouraged neo-Arian scholarship to counter the claims of the orthodox, the two religious communities coexisted peacefully. Under his patronage, de luxe manuscripts of the Gospels in the Gothic translation made by Ulfila were written in silver ink on purple parchment. In terms of language, law and religious definitions, the contrast between Gothic and Roman meant that Ravenna became a key meeting point for the two cultures. Here, non-Roman and Roman beliefs and practices were integrated, an achievement that was crucial for the future history of the West. The process of this confrontation and acculturation is brilliantly displayed in the history of Ravenna, which attracted both Roman and non-Roman groups, and became the new capital of the West.

On his death in 526, Theoderic's daughter Amalasuntha assumed the position of regent for her young son, Athalaric, who was proclaimed king at the age of ten. She had been well educated in the Roman style and was sympathetic to Constantinople, which gradually provoked the hostility of the Gothic courtiers. Although she managed to sustain the regency until 534 when her son died, they forced her to accept her cousin Theodahad as a partner in power. He had her exiled and then strangled, which provoked Justinian to avenge her death. Since the rulers in Constantinople had maintained the fiction that they had ultimate authority over Italy, Justinian justified sending troops against Theodahad because he had usurped the throne. The emperor was already engaged in a campaign to restore his Roman rule in the western provinces overrun by barbarian tribes. In 533 the Byzantine general Belisarius, who had made his name on the eastern front against Persia, achieved a great victory over the Vandals in Africa. Belisarius next advanced to Sicily and from there Justinian ordered him to march north against the Goths, while another general, Mundus, invaded Italy from the north. Faced with these threats, the Goths abandoned Theodahad, and elected another leader, Vitiges. But he proved unequal to the task of defeating Belisarius, who entered Ravenna in 540, captured Vitiges and restored direct imperial rule. The details of these campaigns are recorded by Procopius in his account of *The Wars*.

The defeat of the Goths was the occasion for another great boom in building, mainly organized by bishops of Ravenna with the assistance of a wealthy silver merchant, Julian, who had previously contributed to the pro-Arian basilica of Sant'Apollinare in Classe. He also acted as banker for the church of San Vitale, dedicated to the other patron saint of Ravenna, Vitalis. It had been started by Bishop Ecclesius under Gothic domination, and was only completed by his successor Maximian in 547. In this octagonal building, the mosaic panels of Emperor Justinian and his wife Theodora flanking the approach to the altar counterbalanced earlier portraits of Theoderic and confirmed the return of Ravenna to orthodoxy. Both rulers were shown presenting their gifts to the saint, accompanied by their courtiers (plates 19 and 20).

These mosaics bring the eastern emperor and his wife to the walls of a sixth-century church in Ravenna, although they never went to Italy. Who insisted on setting up the imperial panels in San Vitale? Since Justinian built and adorned so many other churches in different parts of the empire, he could well have financed the final parts of the construction and mosaic decoration. But possibly Julian the silver merchant was responsible, or Bishop Maximian insisted on the inclusion of the imperial couple. Whatever their origin, the panels are unique, the only surviving occasion when these sixth-century Byzantine rulers are depicted within the sanctuary surrounding the altar.

The portrait of Theodora is also much discussed. Here she is shown in her imperial robes, the purple which she claimed to prefer as her shroud rather than flee. On its hem the Magi are pictured bringing their gifts to the Christ Child, while underneath it her white tunic has a deep border of gold, red and green. On her shoulders she carries a broad jewelled collar, and on her head a tall crown with long strings of pearls hanging from the edge over her breast. Unlike her ladies-in-waiting, who wear glorious garments in bright colours, decorated with motifs found on surviving fragments of silk, red shoes, necklaces, earrings and head coverings, Theodora has a monumental rather than human air. Some art historians think she presents her gift, a large bowl of coins, to the fountain in front of a dark space, which represents her death. Whatever the reason, this serious imperial figure captures the supreme authority of Empress Theodora, transformed from her origins as a pantomime artist. She stands facing her husband, who is displayed in full imperial costume, accompanied by Bishop Maximian, members of the clergy and his bodyguard.

The orthodox continued the process of removing all traces of Arianism from Ravenna. In 561, Bishop Agnellus rededicated Theoderic's cathedral, known as the Golden Heaven, to St Martin and the orthodox cult. He replaced the ruler's portrait by golden mosaics of himself with Emperor Justinian. Traces of the original Arian mosaic remain in the palace section, where surviving hands were once connected to saintly bodies. Elsewhere, other images of Theoderic remained in place and continued to make a deep impression. Nearly three centuries later, an ecclesiastical historian praised a mosaic portrait of the Gothic ruler with personifications of Rome and Ravenna, which decorated the palace at Pavia in the 830s. He also recorded that Charlemagne had moved Theoderic's equestrian statue, 'a horse of bronze covered with gleaming gold . . . to his palace which is called Aachen', where it can still be seen.

The final outcome of Justinian's campaigns in the West not only secured the removal of pro-Arian forces, but also brought two large areas of North Africa and Italy back into imperial control. By the end of the sixth century, Constantinople appointed two officials, called exarchs, with extraordinary powers that combined civilian and military authority, to rule from Carthage and Ravenna. This break with the Roman tradition of keeping army and administration separate reflects the importance attached to the reconquered territories. In Africa, the exarch controlled the rich, prosperous coastal region, which continued to export grain and to produce the fine pottery, African redslip ware, found on sites throughout the Mediterranean. From Ravenna, the exarch ruled over northern Italy and as far south as Rome, while the provinces of southern Italy and Sicily were administered by more junior officials appointed from Constantinople. The pre-eminence of Ravenna was thus assured and for nearly two centuries it functioned as the Byzantine capital of the West, the linchpin of imperial contacts between Constantinople and Italy. It remained the major port on the east coast of Italy close to the mouth of the Po, importing rare commodities such as papyrus from Egypt and redistributing them to places farther north and west. It maintained regular naval contact with Constantinople and other parts of the eastern Mediterranean, not only during the summer season, but also in the winter when most captains refused to risk sea travel. It patronized artistic workshops which trained craftsmen in ivory carving, mosaic setting and other skills.

Justinian's ambition of restoring Roman rule in the West was commemorated in the imperial mosaic panels set up in San Vitale. Before the end of the sixth century, however, barbarian forces began their conquest of the north Italian region of Lombardy, and thus became known as Lombards. Once settled in the ancient cities of Pavia and Monza, they directed their forces against Rome and Ravenna. After many attempts the last outpost of Byzantine authority in Italy, defended by the exarch, fell under Lombard control in 751. From Constantinople, Constantine V (741–75) was in no position to send military reinforcements to Rome and Pope Stephen II was forced to seek alternative military protection (see chapter 10). This proved a significant development in the history of Europe, when the Bishop of Rome abandoned the traditional axis of diplomatic loyalty to Constantinople, and made an unprecedented journey over the Alps to Ponthion in northern France to negotiate an alliance with the Frankish leader, Pippin. The Franks agreed to protect Rome from the Lombards and to return to the patrimony of St Peter any Italian territory regained.

In this way, Pippin and Pope Stephen created a new axis linking northern Europe with the centre of western Christendom, one that gradually excluded Byzantium and by-passed Ravenna. Pippin's son,

Charlemagne, later used the city as his administrative base in northern Italy; he also plundered its classical columns and capitals for building material to use in his new capital at Aachen and, as we have seen, removed Theoderic's equestrian statue. But for the Franks and their successors the Carolingians, it was Rome and the relics of St Peter that commanded both their spiritual devotion and military endeavour.

Ravenna declined as its harbour at Classis silted up. From 830 to 846, the priest Andreas Agnellus gave public readings about the history of the city in instalments, which were later collected to form his 'pontifical book' of Ravenna, or lives of its bishops. While the account is dominated by local rivalries and bloody conflicts, Agnellus recorded the inscriptions on monuments and the art works he knew, such as the gold mosaic inscription in hexameters in the bath put up by Bishop Victor, or the verses painted above the four rivers of Paradise at San Zaccaria. He also reported numerous amusing legends, such as the abbot who miraculously flew back from Constantinople to Ravenna when no ship was available, and solemn moments when holy images took the place of written guarantees. In one case, the partners to a commercial loan invoked an icon of St Andrew as their witness and guarantor; similarly, when the Ravenna clergy accused Archbishop Theodore of plundering the wealth of their church, they did so in the presence of images of St Apollinaris.

By the tenth century Ravenna was, literally, a backwater, and it is now several miles from the sea, though three generations of German rulers, Otto I, II and III, knew of its past role and visited it. Its trade with the eastern Mediterranean and connections with Constantinople were inherited by a new community at the head of the Adriatic – Venice. The inhabitants of these Venetian islands scattered across the lagoon concentrated more studiously on shipbuilding, naval warfare and international commerce, and were able to develop different relations with Byzantium, which I shall explain in chapter 19. Fortunately, Ravenna's eclipse preserved its mosaics to recall the days of splendour when Romans, Goths and Byzantines ruled Italy from Ravenna, the Constantinople of the West.

7

Roman Law

> We all recognize law as a general benefactor, saviour, guardian
> of our lives, and so forth, because it does away with vice and
> fosters virtue, and because it makes men think that they ought
> to honour virtue and punish wrongdoers.
>
> Thomas Magistros, *On the Duty of a King*,
> late thirteenth century

The application of written law was fundamental to Byzantium throughout its long history, and ordinary citizens used the courts to secure a binding, legal solution to their inheritance, property and family quarrels. Byzantine law developed from the Roman legal system, which is recognized as one of Rome's great contributions to world civilization, elaborated by jurists between the fifth century BC and the first AD. The innovation of this system was to set up lawcourts and endow trained magistrates with the power to preside over them. These officials could issue a summons, hear the case and order the execution of a sentence, with the possibility of an appeal. The same legal process is still used in all countries governed by a civil code of law. Roman traditions also brought to the eastern Mediterranean a novel emphasis on written law which took several forms: edicts of magistrates, resolutions of the Roman Senate and imperial decrees (constitutions). These different bodies of law were applied in courts based in every major city and all provincial capitals.

Law was also generated by appeals made to the emperor, for instance for a remission of taxes after a bad harvest. Cities and provinces used their best orators for such missions, which often resulted in special constitutions added to imperial decrees. By the mid-second century AD, the emperor was the sole creator of law, but the commentaries of five earlier Roman lawyers, Papinian, Paul, Gaius, Ulpian and Modestus, were recognized as particularly important for the interpretation of past laws. To ensure the correct use of these various collections in Latin, and their interpretation and application, trained experts were necessary, hence the development of law schools and the emergence of a specific class of jurists with practical experience, the *scholastikoi*. Command of rhetoric was an essential feature of courtroom skill. In Late Antiquity, Rome, Alexandria, Athens, Constantinople and Berytus (modern Beirut) emerged as the most important centres of legal training.

As mentioned earlier, Theodosius II established a state-funded law school in the capital in 425. He recognized that it was difficult to use laws which clearly conflicted and decrees which encouraged different interpretations of the same subject. So in 429 he ordered legal experts to compile a law book for the Roman Empire, editing and reforming all the imperial laws issued since the time of Constantine I in a single volume. While earlier collections had been made and were known by the names of their authors, this was the first official codification. The *Codex Theodosianus* was presented to the leading officials of the empire in Constantinople in November 437 and put into force the following New Year's Day. Copies were then transported back to Old Rome and presented to the senators, who arranged for further distribution. The Code contained more than 2,500 edited texts of laws issued between 313 and 437, including laws concerning Christianity in its final section. Contradictions and confusions between different laws had been removed and a simplified system was established. This was to be applied in both halves of the empire and to be taught in law schools, now concentrated in the East.

For many years the Roman colony of Berytus on the coast of Lebanon had excelled in the teaching of law; its fame continued until the destruction of the city by an earthquake in 550/51. The *Life of Severus* (who later became Monophysite Patriarch of Antioch, 512–18) preserves an account of the five years of legal study at Berytus, which included the analysis of particular commentaries. But the author, Zacharias, who also became a lawyer, gives more attention to the Christian students' vivid efforts to uproot magical practices invoking ancient gods, dualist interpretations of the world developed by followers of the third-century Persian prophet Mani, and other illegal beliefs.

Nearly a century after the publication of the *Codex Theodosianus*, Justinian assumed imperial power. He immediately set about a further reform of the law. In 528, he established a commission of ten experienced lawyers under the leadership of Tribonian, the chief legal official (*quaestor*), to sort through all the imperial constitutions of practical value, imposing order and adapting the provisions to sixth-century conditions. As a result, the *Codex Constitutionum* was issued in 529, and all imperial laws not included in it were repealed. This simplified collection does not survive, but it is summarized in the *Corpus Iuris Civilis* – Corpus of Civil Law – which forms the basis of European law still in force today. In this second stage of legal reform, which lasted from 530 to 534, Justinian appointed sixteen lawyers to bring order to the commentaries of leading jurists, which had accumulated into an unwieldy body of contradictory opinions. Their work produced fifty books of approved texts called the *Digest* (or *Pandects*), promulgated in 533, after which all other commentary material was repealed. At the same time, an outline of the elements of Roman law designed to guide students was published in the *Institutes*. Justinian continued to issue many laws, called new laws (*Novels*) to distinguish them from the old ones. The *Code of Civil Law* of 534 thus had four parts: the old constitutions in a revised edition in twelve books identified as the *Codex Justinianus*; the *Digest*; the *Institutes*; and the new laws, to which later emperors added their own promulgations. This was to remain in force in Byzantium until the fall of the empire to the Ottomans nine hundred years later.

In the West, however, the codification of Justinian was never as widespread as that of Theodosius, which influenced both local customary law and the barbarian legal codes used in Visigothic Spain, Francia, Burgundy and Lombard Italy. Knowledge of the *Corpus Iuris Civilis* was virtually lost between the early seventh century and the late eleventh, when a very fine copy of the *Digest*, 'beautiful as a star', was rediscovered. It had probably been made in the sixth century and had survived in southern Italy, where the provinces governed from Constantinople continued to use Roman law. Gradually, the text of the *Insti-*

1. Mount Athos on the Chalkidike peninsula, northern Greece, from the sea, the site of numerous Byzantine monasteries from the ninth century onwards.

2. St Catherine's monastery, Mount Sinai, Egypt, built by Justinian in the mid sixth century. The enclosure protects the Burning Bush, which had attracted Christian monks as early as the fourth century.

3. Land walls of Constantinople, a triple line of defence completed in 413 under Theodosius II, from the west, showing the moat (now filled) and outer wall, the middle wall with towers and the inner wall with taller towers.

4. The walls of the citadel of Thessalonike, probably constructed in the mid fifth century, with over twenty gates and a hundred towers, from the north.

5. The Aqueduct of Valens, inaugurated in 373, central Constantinople (photograph taken in 1966 during the construction of the underpass at Saraçhane).

6. The base of the obelisk of Theodosius I in the Hippodrome, Constantinople, south side, showing the emperor and his sons seated in the imperial box, flanked by senators and soldiers, receiving tribute from kneeling barbarians, erected in 390.

7. Silk roundel (22cm × 19cm), probably from Syria or Egypt, of mounted Amazons hunting leopards, late seventh to eighth century. It reflects the persistence of secular and mythical subjects woven on silks in the Christian world of Byzantium.

8. Lead seal of Synetos and Niketas, general *kommerkiarioi* of Koloneia, Kamacha and Fourth Armenia during the reign of Anastasios II (713–15). The emperor is shown standing on the front (*left*) with the titles of the officials on the back (*right*).

9. Clay pilgrim's flask (ampulla), with St Menas standing between his two camels, probably from Egypt, sixth or seventh century.

10. Frontispiece of the Bible of Leo, made in Constantinople, *c.* 940, showing Leo presenting his Bible to the Virgin, who in turn gestures to the figure of Christ. Leo's beardless face and childish fair hair indicate that he was a eunuch, a fact confirmed by the titles noted in the inscription beside him: *patrikios* (of patrician status), *sakellarios* (treasurer) and *praipositos* (major-domo of the palace). The inscription on the frame is an epigram Leo composed, which compares his humble offering with that of monks who offer their souls to the Virgin.

11. Gold coins all from the mint of Constantinople.

11a. Justinian II (685–95): solidus with a portrait of Christ, bearded and with long hair on the front (*left*), and of the emperor standing and holding a cross on the back (*right*).

11b. Justinian II (second reign, 705–11): solidus with a portrait of the youthful Christ with short curly hair on the front (*left*) and of the emperor and his young son Tiberios holding a cross on the back (*right*).

11c. The Empress Irene (797–802): solidus with her own portrait on both front and back, in marked contrast to normal imperial coins.

11d. Constantine VII (945–59): solidus with a portrait of Christ on the front (*left*) and of the emperor holding an orb and a cross on the back (*right*).

12. Karanlik Kilise, Cappadocia, Turkey, a rock-cut church of the eleventh/twelfth century. The volcanic tufa of this region allows churches, monasteries and houses to be excavated, creating underground structures that are warm in winter and cool in summer.

13. Karanlik Kilise, Cappadocia, Turkey, interior fresco of the Last Supper showing Christ with the Apostles and two-pronged fork, twelfth century.

14. Tenth-century ivory plaque of Christ crowning Otto II and Theophano, to mark their wedding in 972, with inscriptions in Latin and Greek that identify the two figures. The smaller figure kneeling at Christ's feet below Otto's stool is John Philagathos, who begs Christ to help him with the familiar Greek formula, 'Lord help thy servant'. He may have commissioned the plaque.

15. Two miniatures from the Khludov Psalter, mid ninth century, illustrating Psalm 68 (*left*; folio 67r), with Jews at the crucifixion likened to iconoclasts whitewashing an icon of Christ, and Psalm 52 (*right*; folio 51v), with St Peter trampling on Simon Magus, the first heretic, while the iconophile Patriarch Nikephoros tramples on John Grammatikos, the iconoclast heretic. The heretics' love of money is represented by a sack of gold coins.

tutes was identified and teachers in Ravenna, Pavia and above all Bologna began to write glosses on the law and later commentaries. By the middle of the twelfth century, Gratian's collection of canon law, the *Decretum*, of around 1130–40 and Emperor Frederick I Barbarossa's privileges for the students at Bologna (1158) encouraged and expanded knowledge of the ancient sources of both types of law. Whether Byzantine legal codification had a distinct influence on Church–State relations in the West or not, canon law clearly tended to emphasize papal authority, while western emperors used civil law to enhance their own power.

Roman law is characterized by its attention to the law of persons, free and slave, their relations in marriage and divorce; the law of property and possession; violations and contracts; and succession, the whole regulated by the law of procedure, which established the principle of a fair trial before a competent judge, whether in civilian or criminal matters. In addition, by the sixth century a growing body of ecclesiastical regulations existed: canons decreed by oecumenical councils, provincial synods and results of appeals to patriarchs. In both Antioch and Constantinople, collections of this body of material were made in about 580. They were given the title *nomokanon*, that is, a mixture of *nomos*, civil law, and *kanon*, ecclesiastical law or canon. The most significant of these, the *Nomokanon in Fourteen Titles*, was probably put together in the reign of Herakleios (610–41), drawing on the work of sixth-century patriarchs.

A similar process had already taken place in the West, when Pope Hormisdas (514–23) commissioned Dionysius, nicknamed 'the small' (*exiguus*), to make Latin translations of the most significant Greek canons. He included the first fifty of the Apostolic Constitutions (not the remaining thirty-five recognized in the East), the canons of the oecumenical and other councils, and decisions from 38 papal letters dating from 384 to 498, which became known as 'decretals'. The two collections thus had identical conciliar material, but where the eastern collections included the rules of St Basil and laws of Justinian, Dionysius inserted papal rulings which he elevated to canonical status. This additional material formed the basis of subsequent disagreements between the western and eastern churches.

In contrast to the *Code of Theodosius*, Justinian's twelve books of law gave prominence to issues of Christian faith and decisions affecting ecclesiastical, social and economic issues of the sixth century. Some of Justinian's subsequent *Novels* extended Christian morality, for example insisting on the need to protect women dedicated to virginity and to prevent the recruitment of young prostitutes in the country. Civil and ecclesiastical law were gradually harmonized in a dual system of legal administration, which adapted Roman principles to the needs of the Christian empire of Byzantium. After the closure of the Platonic Academy of Athens (529) and a massive earthquake which destroyed Berytus in 550/51, Alexandria in Egypt became the sole centre of legal and philosophical training outside the capital. Its scholars taught a Christianized version of Aristotelian philosophy considered less harmful than the Neoplatonic teaching of Athens. After the Arab conquests of the seventh century, however, all legal and philosophical education was concentrated in Constantinople.

Using the *Institutes* as the basis of legal education, students were expected to master the law in five years of study and had to satisfy their teachers before they could be admitted to the two professional groups of lawyers: advocates (*synegoroi* or *scholastikoi*), and notaries (*taboularioi*). The title *scholastikos* is used by numerous authors up to the seventh century, when it appears to be replaced by *krites*, judge, a title used by the *quaestor*, the eparch (prefect or governor) of Constantinople, and the chief judge of appeals, *epi ton deeseon*, a post established in the seventh century. The eparch headed the city judiciary, controlled the guards and prisons, and was also responsible for ceremonial, commerce and industry in the capital.

In the course of the sixth century, Latin, previously fundamental to all studies of Roman law, was replaced by Greek. The *Corpus Iuris Civilis* issued in November 534 was rapidly translated, and all Justinian's subsequent new laws were issued in Greek only. No longer used, Latin faded away and its teaching ceased. Only in the army and at court, two institutions deeply indebted to Roman traditions, did a few Latin terms survive: the 'Bene, Bene' pronounced as an official welcome at court, and various commands and names for weapons and officers, which were transliterated into Greek but clearly reveal their Latin origin. Nor was Latin literature much read in Byzantium until Maximos Planoudes made translations of Virgil, Ovid, Cicero and Boethius in the late thirteenth century (see chapter 27).

Emperors continued to issue laws reflecting growing Christian influence in matters relating to marriage, for instance in the *Ekloga* of 740. This short law code of Leo III also substitutes physical mutilation for capital punishment. In the late ninth century, the *Basilika* provided a six-volume edition of imperial law in sixty books arranged by subject and in chronological order, with the relevant part of the *Digest* preceding the *Codex Justinianus* and the *Novels*. The new arrangement was ordered by Basil I (867–86) and completed by his son, Leo VI, nicknamed the Wise (886–912), who wrote the Preface. At the same time, Patriarch Photios wrote a new prologue to the second edition of the *Nomokanon* issued in 882/3; it includes all the canons issued since the first edition, and was immediately translated into Slavonic to assist the newly established Bulgarian Church. In both civil and ecclesiastical law, therefore, there is a clear revival of interest, which continued until 1204. Theodore Bestes, a canon lawyer, wrote a third prologue to the *Nomokanon* in 1089/90, and in 1177 a leading ecclesiastic, Theodore Balsamon, composed a fourth and a commentary. In the field of civil law, emperors continued to issue *Novels* on all important issues.

They also took pains to impose the law. Under Theophilos (829–42), an imperial ceremony of riding from the Great Palace to the church of Blachernai and back on Fridays provided opportunities for ordinary citizens to appeal to the emperor. On one of these occasions a widow complained to Theophilos that she had been defrauded of a horse by the city eparch (plate 32). Indeed, she claimed it was the very horse he was riding! He ordered an investigation and discovered that her story was correct: the eparch had taken her horse and given it to the emperor. Theophilos immediately returned the horse to its rightful owner and had the very high-ranking official punished. There being several versions of this tale suggests that it became well known. The practice also continued in thirteenth-century Nicaea and fourteenth-century Constantinople, when it became an official ceremony called *kavalikeuma* (riding out). Then it was accompanied by horns and trumpets,

in order that the advance of the emperor be announced to those who have been treated unjustly, so that those who need help from this source can approach the Imperial Summit.

Within the firm framework of written law, it was possible for particularly intelligent judges to issue minority opinions – evidence of the inner resilience and confidence of Byzantine jurists. In the early eleventh century, Eustathios Romaios, whose grandfather had also been a judge, occupied the highest judicial office, *droungarios tes Vigles* (originally 'commander of the watch', a military office which became a civilian title at this time). As judge of the imperial court until his death in about 1034, he wrote numerous verdicts, opinions and special legal studies, which allow us to see the law as it was applied and interpreted. In one highly disputed case, Eustathios resolved a challenge to a marriage based on the charge of abduction with force. Against the divided opinions of his fellow judges, he pointed out that the original charge had not mentioned the issue of rape, and 'wise women' had later testified to the girl's virginity, so there was no question of rape making the marriage illegitimate. As to the evidence provided by women, which had also been criticized by the plaintiffs, of course it was allowed in court, because in such matters men could not bear witness. Eustathios therefore confirmed that the marriage was perfectly legitimate. His writings were arranged by a fellow judge or student in a textbook, the *Peira* (*Experience*), designed to present simple rules based on his creative interpretation of the laws. It represents a high point in the adaptability and flexibility of the Roman inheritance, and was often cited in later works.

In 1047, this lively intellectual activity encouraged Constantine IX (1042–55) to establish two official schools in the capital, one devoted to Law, the other to Philosophy. The new law school was intended to train two types of jurist: the notaries (*notarioi*) and lawyers (*synegoroi*), both organized in professional colleges. The *nomophylax*, guardian of the laws, chosen to head it was John Xiphilinos, who wrote many legal commentaries before becoming a monk on Mount Olympos, and later patriarch (1064–75). The emperor appointed Michael Psellos to direct the school of philosophy. A polymath of great brilliance, Psellos is now best known for his *Chronicle* devoted to the reigns of fourteen emperors (976–1078), but he was also the author of numerous writings on philosophical matters and mathematics and of a large collection of letters (see chapter 21). Towards the end of the eleventh century, a text called *Tipoukeitos* ('what is to be found where') provided an index to the *Basilika*, adding references to eleventh-century legislation and the legal interpretations of Eustathios Romaios. The *Tipoukeitos*, possibly the work of a judge named Patzes, facilitated use of legal sources by quoting the opening words of particular laws.

Meanwhile in the ecclesiastical sphere, individuals and bishops brought their cases to Constantinople, where the patriarch presided over a court of appeal. As the advance into and occupation of Asia Minor by the Seljuk Turks in the eleventh century forced many bishops to take refuge in the capital, they joined the permanent synod (*synodos endemousa*) attached to the patriarch and participated in his court. The court issued rulings designed to maintain the status of bishops in exile, or to provide guidance for those living under Muslim rule, who complained that 'the sixty books of the laws which are called *Basilika* are not widely known in our lands ... Is it safe for the orthodox Syrians and Armenians ... to say the office liturgy in their own language?' In writing the legal response in 1194, Balsamon emphasized that vernacular liturgies should always be translations of authorized Greek models, and pressed for greater harmonization with Constantinople. Balsamon developed the tradition of sophisticated commentaries on canon-law work and included many examples of illicit and improper Christian behaviour recorded in the late twelfth century.

Despite the immense disruption of the Latin occupation of Constantinople from 1204 to 1261, these high standards were maintained by the patriarch in exile in Nicaea and by church courts elsewhere. Records of applied law are preserved in thirteenth-century judgments given by Archbishops Demetrios Chomatenos of Ohrid and John Apokaukos of Naupaktos. Even now we can admire their judgments, for instance in the granting of a divorce on grounds of intense hatred, which prevented the consummation of the marriage even after the couple had been shut up together for a week; or where a slave convicted of theft was spared the loss of her one surviving hand, as demanded by her owner, on the grounds that to lose both hands would make it impossible for an individual to survive.

In the fourteenth century, distinguished legal experts included Matthew Blastares, who attempted to reconcile canon and civil law in his *Syntagma kata stoicheion*, an alphabetical treatise divided into sections for different topics, in which the ecclesiastical law precedes the civil ruling on the same subject, and Constantine Harmenopoulos, who issued his *Procheiron Nomon* (Handbook of the Laws) in 1354. His study in six books, thus called *Hexabiblos*, became one of the most outstanding contributions to medieval law and was rapidly translated into Serbian, as was Blastares' *Syntagma*. Harmenopoulos also compiled a selection of canons, *Epitome kanonon*, with commentaries on problems in ecclesiastical law, and Blastares composed short synopses of canon law, hymns and theological works, as well as a list of Latin legal terms. A district court in Thessalonike similarly preserves evidence of judges who cited the *Codex Justinianus* correctly and used its provisions in conjunction with laws of their own times.

In the same city of Thessalonike, where Thomas Magister composed his oration *On the Duty of a King* (cited at the head of this chapter), he praised respect for the law within a wider context of the ruler's duty to encourage broader, deeper knowledge, for as he says,

laws were originally enacted and are still in the main upheld by knowledge ... and knowledge is the most peculiar, the most profitable and the most valuable of all things to men – simply because in addition to its other benefits, it lifts men above the stature of men.

He then insists that the state and the ruler must promote education, must cultivate it and make it available to all. While Byzantine law continued to adapt to the circumstances of an empire now much reduced in size and strength, lawyers, judges and legally trained clerics took pride in their legal system.

As in all societies, Byzantium witnessed instances when the law might be abused, for example in the case of marriages dissolved on grounds of consanguinity, or in the lawless dismemberment of Emperor Andronikos I in 1185. Many judgments involved a high level of violence, for instance in the punishment of rebels, but the Byzantine legal system was based on principles distinct from the arbitrary justice common among non-Roman peoples. Its superiority was borne out by the adoption of civil and canon law far beyond the empire in both time and space, particularly through translations of the *Hexabiblos* of Harmenopoulos. Indeed, following the Greek War of Independence in 1821, the new state adapted the six books and updated them as the basis of the legal code, which remained in force into the twentieth century.

The Byzantine devotion to law may also have influenced another significant feature of its civilization: the notion of a just war. This idea developed during the medieval centuries to sanction wars of reconquest of imperial territory lost, and defensive wars to protect the empire and prevent further losses. Byzantium employed skilled diplomacy to try to avoid military action through discussion and negotiation. Emperors and generals who devoted their attention to military tactics always stressed the need to prevent warfare if possible. And when it proved unavoidable, they sought legal means to justify fighting. By the twelfth century, western crusaders condemned this reliance on diplomacy as a sign of Byzantine cowardice. But the empire continued to avoid bloodshed where possible. This policy may be related to Byzantium's preference for physical mutilation rather than the death penalty. It also reflects the separate status of ordained priests and monks within the empire, which forbade them from taking part in military activity. They might bless the troops and pray for their victory, but religious leaders and monks did not take up arms. Although emperor and patriarch were united in promoting Christian policies, they maintained their separate legal systems. By insisting on a distinct sphere for the Church, governed by its own law, Byzantium sowed the seeds of a secular state administered by civil law. Together they reflected the profound respect for written law in Byzantium, which came to have such a marked influence in neighbouring states.

II

The Transition from Ancient to Medieval

8

The Bulwark Against Islam

Sulayman, king of the Arabs said, 'I shall not cease from the struggle with Constantinople until I force my way into it or I bring about the destruction of the entire dominions of the Arabs.'

Chronicle of Dionysios of Tel-Mahre, ninth century

During the seventh century, Byzantium was almost destroyed by desert tribes who emerged from the Arabian peninsula to overrun the eastern Mediterranean. This unexpected challenge came on top of nearly a decade of warfare with Persia in the 620s and persistent Slav raiding into the Balkan provinces. Its consequences were so severe that in the 660s Emperor Constans II left Constantinople for the safety of Sicily. Some senators, however, refused to leave the Byzantine capital and their confidence in the power of the empire to resist was confirmed by a major triumph over the Arabs in 678. Nonetheless, this turbulent period transformed the ancient Roman world, and the establishment at Damascus of an Islamic caliphate created a permanent rival to Christian Byzantium.

In order to understand this devastating change (or triumph, depending on your point of view), we must consider developments of the late sixth and early seventh centuries. Under Emperor Maurice (582–602), simultaneous threats from Slavs in the Balkans and Persians in the East stretched Byzantine defences to breaking point. In the 580s, Slavonic and Avar tribes crossed the Danube frontier and captured major fortified cities like Singidunum (Belgrade), allowing them to move south with their families and flocks in search of better pasture.

By the early seventh century they besieged Thessalonike, whose patron saint Demetrios was allegedly crucial in preventing its capture. Large regions of the Balkans, Greece and the western Peloponnese were gradually overrun and temporarily passed out of imperial control. The immediate result of this pressure was that Roman troops refused to campaign north of the Danube in the winter of 602, marched on Constantinople and overthrew the emperor.

Shortly after this coup d'état, the Persians overran the eastern frontier and devastated major cities in Asia Minor. In conditions of grave disarray, the Senate of Constantinople appealed to the exarch of Carthage, who sent his son Herakleios and nephew Niketas with troops to restore order in Byzantium. But nothing could deter Persian attacks: Antioch succumbed and Jerusalem was savagely sacked in 614. After a massacre of the local population, the patriarch and remaining Christians carrying the relic of the True Cross were marched off into Persian captivity, which they compared to the Babylonian captivity of the Israelites. In 619, the Persians occupied Alexandria and prevented the grain fleet from sailing to Constantinople.

With the help of the Patriarch Sergios (610–38), who crowned him emperor in 610, Herakleios concentrated all his attention on defeating Persia. For over ten years he improved Byzantine fighting forces and planned new strategies, which were used in the prolonged campaign of 622–8, when he spent whole years away from the capital, making alliances with Caucasian tribes, and planning attacks deep inside Persian territory. During his absence, however, the Persians made common cause with the Avars, who now dominated their Slavonic allies, and advanced to the shores of the Bosphoros. The siege of 626 was a challenging moment in the history of the empire, as we have seen in chapter 2. The Byzantines believed that the Mother of God had defended the city in person and it had passed under her special protection.

Less than two years later, Herakleios advanced into Persia from the north and captured the major city of Nineveh, forcing Chosroes II to flee from Ctesiphon to Dastergard. In 628 the Shah of Shahs was overthrown, his palace was sacked, the True Cross recovered, and vast amounts of booty had to be burned because the army could not carry it all off. The official announcement of victory was sent to

Constantinople and read to the assembled population in Hagia Sophia by the patriarch: 'Let all Christians give thanks to the one God ... For fallen is the arrogant Chosroes, opponent of God.' It went on to describe the army's return from Persia and concluded: 'We have confidence in our Lord Jesus Christ, the good and almighty God, and in our Lady the Mother of God, that they will direct all our affairs in accordance with their goodness.' Herakleios probably restored the True Cross to Jerusalem in the spring of 630 before he finally returned to the capital, where a great triumph was celebrated. Patriarch Sergios, the young prince Herakleios-Constantine and the entire population went out to greet him and accompanied him into the city 'dancing with joy', as Theophanes records in his *Chronicle*.

At this high point of Herakleios' achievement, the Prophet Muhammad died in Arabia (632). The final defeat of Byzantium's most serious enemy coincided with the birth of another: Zoroastrian Persians were replaced by Muslim Arabs. In their post-victory confidence, imperial officials refused the tribute traditionally paid to tribes who guarded the edges of the desert and had previously provided an early-warning system. Byzantium was therefore quite unprepared for invasion from the south. In the regained provinces of Syria, Palestine and Egypt the military authorities set up by Herakleios after 630 were taken by surprise. They were also dismayed by the coherent military challenge of the Arabian tribesmen, whom Muhammad had united after much inter-tribal warfare.

The death of the Prophet only confirmed the Arabs' determination to spread Islamic domination throughout the known world. They adopted the year of Muhammad's flight (Hijra) from Mecca to Medina (AD 622) as the first in their own lunar calendar, and began dating the conquests that followed from that year (AH). Using camels accustomed to the desert, they developed successful military tactics of rapid raiding and effective siege technology. The great cities of the Near East fell in quick succession: Damascus in 634, Gaza and Antioch in 637 and Jerusalem in 638. At the battle on the River Yarmuk in northern Syria in 636, Herakleios witnessed a terrible defeat. He retreated to Antioch but was forced to abandon it to the Arabs. Although no one in Constantinople imagined that these huge losses would be permanent, it proved impossible to reverse them. In 661, the Muslims established their capital at Damascus and began to launch annual campaigns against Byzantium.

In a single decade (632/42) the Arabs had occupied Syria, Palestine and the richest province of Egypt, including the Christian Holy Places of Jerusalem and Bethlehem. This was a major turning point in Byzantine history. The Arabs had conquered about two-thirds of imperial territory and clearly intended to take the rest, as they pressed on with their expansion across Asia Minor and the coast of North Africa. In the process they nearly put an end to Byzantium. The capture of Jerusalem inflicted a deep humiliation on Christian prestige, while the conquest of Egypt put an end to the economic system constructed by Rome and inherited by New Rome. Using their mastery of practical astronomy to travel through the desert, the Arabs adapted to the sea without difficulty and began to attack the islands and coastlines of the empire.

From commercial contacts with the inhabitants of the Near East, Arab leaders knew that the Roman Empire had had a great history. They wanted to re-create its ancient unity around the Mediterranean under their own control. To western historians it may appear as 'the swamping of Christian civilization', but the Arabs saw it differently. Islam had replaced Christianity in the same way that Christianity had replaced Judaism and outlawed the pagan cults, and all were urged to convert to this final revelation from God. But the Arabs had to capture New Rome before they could move on Old Rome, and Byzantium proved to be the stumbling block which frustrated their initial attempt at the conquest of the known world.

The Arabs' ambitions were confirmed by their destruction of the Persian Empire: Ctesiphon, Takrit, Nineveh, Isfahan and Persepolis were all conquered by 648, and new garrison settlements constructed at Kufa, Basra and Mosul provided bases for later conquests. The Arabs combined an eastern thrust towards Kabul in Afghanistan (664) with a western advance across North Africa to Kairouan (670), near Carthage. By 711, they crossed both the River Oxus to capture Bukhara and Samarkand and the Straits of Gibraltar to invade Spain. The blue-tiled mosques of Samarkand and Tashkent, together with the Great Mosques of Kairouan and Cordoba, symbolize the extent of this expansion. From its base in Arabia, the new religion of Islam not only replaced Christianity in the lands of its birth, but also controlled the widest extent of the known world.

Ever since the 1930s, when the great Belgian historian Henri Pirenne pointed out the significance of the Arab expansion with the memorable phrase 'Without Muhammed, Charlemagne is inconceivable', Islam has been connected with the emergence of Europe. He argued that the Muslim disruption of ancient trade patterns, which had united all shores of the Mediterranean, forced northern Europe to develop its own economic base, independently of the south. Contacts across the North Sea with Britain and Scandinavia led eventually to the development of the Hanseatic League that linked Germany with the Baltic regions. Pirenne failed, however, to acknowledge the role played by Byzantium in preventing continued Muslim expansion across Asia Minor, the Dardanelles and into Europe. Instead of analysing how the empire fought for its existence, he took for granted its role in shielding the West. But if Constantinople had fallen to the Arabs in the mid-seventh century, they would have used its great wealth and imperial power to advance directly into Europe. The broad swathe of early Muslim conquests would have been replicated throughout the Balkans and farther west, where the Slavonic and Germanic peoples would not have been able to resist. And without its Christian hinterland, Rome too would surely have converted. Without Byzantium, Europe as we know it is inconceivable.

Byzantium survived. But it had to come to terms with a new enemy that had unleashed a permanent change in the world of Late Antiquity, one which it could neither defeat nor incorporate. In place of Roman rule around the Mediterranean, a threefold division produced an Islamic South, a Byzantine Christian East and a Latin Christian West. No doubt, the long wars between Byzantium and Persia had weakened both the old imperial structures, creating a partial vacuum into which the Arabs moved, maximizing their energy for additional campaigns. But the Arab conquest, initially driven by economic pressures in Arabia, owes most to the new religion of Islam, which means submission (to the will of Allah). The revelations of Muhammad, who identified himself as the 'last Prophet of God', bound the desert warriors together under a vigorous but narrow banner. His sayings were the first texts to be written down in Arabic, in contrast to the rich oral poetry of those who had previously worshipped numerous idols. The Qur'an in classical Arabic is not only the first but also a beautiful example of the previously spoken language. The Arab tribes thus became a chosen people, who had received God's final message and had recorded it in their own tongue. Insistence on monotheism and spiritual worship in easily mastered rituals inspired believers, disciplined converts, however reluctant, and gave all adherents a new sense of purpose.

Although holy war, jihad, was not one of the five pillars of Islam (the confession of faith, daily prayer, pilgrimage, fasting in the month of Ramadan and giving alms), it rapidly became a distinctive aspect of the new faith. The Arabian tribesmen who participated in the first great wave of conquest needed followers and additional forces to sustain their campaigns east and west. Initially the warriors, who were paid and encouraged by booty, lived in garrison centres separated from the conquered population. Jews and Christians, the peoples of the Book (i.e. the Old Testament), were allowed to keep their religions as long as they paid extra taxes under the rule of Islam, but many converted. As Patricia Crone and Michael Cook have shown, the history of this amazing process must be reconstructed from external contemporary accounts, since nearly all the Arabic records date from centuries later and preserve mythic aspects.

Eventually the Arab campaigns extended beyond anyone's grasp of geography in the seventh century. It is hard for us to realize how quickly the religion of Islam was carried from Arabia to the ends of the known world. In 712, the Arabs captured the Visigothic capital of Toledo and created a Muslim state in Spain. Forty years later, they defeated Chinese forces at Talas in Sogdiana, thus securing the extension of Islam through Central Asia. This new world was linked by camel trains following desert routes overland from Ceuta, opposite Gibraltar, to the Far East. But the desert zeal of holy war collided with the urban seductions of occupation: the fighters started to settle in cities, married local girls and began to lose their tribal identity. Almost inevitably, the process generated division and civil wars.

Much earlier in their campaigns, however, when the Arabs attempted to conquer Byzantium, they were checked by the fortified Taurus Mountains which separate Asia Minor from the continent of

Asia proper. Byzantium became a frontier zone, the barrier between Christianity and Islam, Europe and the Near East. During the high point of Arab power, from 660 to 740, the empire had to contend with annual raiding across the Taurus, and three major campaigns were directed against Constantinople by land and sea. As Caliph Sulayman (715–17) declared, Constantinople was a great prize, and in 717 he was determined to take it. The defeat after a twelve-month siege was all the more important for Byzantium's survival. The Arabs were rebuffed and their ambitions to make Constantinople the base of expansion farther west were thwarted.

The Arabs established in Spain found that the Pyrenees marked the limit of their westward expansion. In 733, when they campaigned farther north, combined Frankish forces under Charles Martel ('the Hammer') defeated them near Poitiers and forced them back. They remained behind this natural frontier for the next seven hundred years, generating a highly sophisticated society in Spain, especially in what is now Andalusia. Two mountain ranges thus marked the extent of Muslim conquest of the Roman world and these boundaries remained fixed for centuries. By AD 800, a new Christian society emerged in the West and identified its territory as 'Europa', while Byzantium sustained the faith in the East. Both flourished outside the newly established limits of Islamic expansion, which they gradually pushed back.

At the eastern end of the Mediterranean world, Jerusalem had passed into Muslim hands – the patriarch Sophronios surrendered the city to Umar, the second caliph (successor to the Prophet) of the Arabs (634–44), rather than permit a repeat of the Persian desecration and massacre of 614. In the Qur'an, Jerusalem was recorded as the place from which Muhammad was taken on a tour of heaven after a miraculous nocturnal visit from Arabia. The rock on the Temple Mount on which he had stood was enclosed in a building. In 691/2, Caliph 'Abd al-Malik replaced it by a most beautiful shrine, the Dome of the Rock. The interior is decorated with mosaics in the Byzantine style, executed by Byzantine craftsmen, but they carry a purely Islamic message. Verses from the Qur'an in Arabic, proclaimed on a band above entirely non-figural images of idyllic gardens, trees, flowers and ornamental urns, are directed against the Byzantines:

The messiah, Jesus, son of Mary, was only a messenger of God and His word which He committed to Mary, and a spirit from Him. So believe in God and His messengers and do not say 'three' [a reference to the Christian Trinity]: refrain, it is better for you.

This monument symbolizes the decisive shift of power and religious observance in the Near East.

Only indirect records of the contemporary Byzantine reaction are preserved, in apocalyptic stories of the end of the world which imply that the Arab tribes are the precursors of the Antichrist. Based on ancient predictions, such as the Book of Revelation, these accounts reinterpret the story of the last Roman emperor who will go to Jerusalem and hang up his crown to signify the end of time. In one version, the column of Constantine in his Forum in Constantinople will be the last monument to survive the floodwaters, which will destroy the earth. Borrowing the name of Methodios, Bishop of Patara, who was supposed to have written an Apocalypse in Syriac, these pseudo-Methodian texts reflect the anxiety of seventh-century Christians about the Arab conquest of their capital.

This was indeed the Muslim aim, but it did not happen. Byzantine resistance drew on military, dynastic, cultural and religious strengths. Constantinople's giant walls, moats and seaboard defences generated profound self-belief among the inhabitants of the city, whose faith in the support of the Mother of God inspired confidence. They also provided the vital human investment in maintaining the walls which ensured the city's impregnability. The empire's inner strength was nourished by its Christian devotion, its belief that Byzantine military victories were granted by God, and that by sincere prayer He would continue to protect them.

Behind the natural barrier of the Taurus Mountains, the few remaining troops from the Near Eastern provinces were regrouped and settled in areas of Asia Minor. In place of traditional Roman military methods of recruitment and pay, a new system, which we now characterize as 'medieval', gradually evolved: the fighting forces were allotted lands in a military region, *thema* (Greek, plural *themata*), on which their families lived and from which they equipped themselves for annual summer campaigning. The first three of these *themata*, identified as

Anatolikon (Eastern), Armeniakon (Armenian) and Opsikion (from the Latin *obsequium*, a term used for military followers), seem to have developed in the period *c.* 630–80. Shortly after, Thrakia (Thrace, the area west of Constantinople), Thrakesion in western Asia Minor and a naval *thema* on the southern coast of Asia Minor, named Kibyrraioton (based on the port city of Antalya), were created. A separate naval force (*Karabisianoi*) continued to patrol in Aegean waters but never seems to have formed a *thema*.

In these new units of military government, the general (*strategos*) combined all powers. Civilian officials were subordinate to his authority and their chief function was related to the recruitment of soldiers, whose names were recorded on military lists (*katalogoi*). Beyond this essential aspect, their task was to measure land, and calculate, record and collect taxes on all the territory under imperial control. This formed the basis of Byzantine administration to the end of the empire, eight hundred years later. But the establishment of the new provincial administration took several generations and did not prevent regular raiding by Muslim forces from Damascus. Byzantium had had to change its method of financing and organizing military defence, adapting its system of government to a smaller scale. It had to come to terms with the loss of Egypt, which had supplied wheat to feed the metropolis for centuries, as well as the prosperous regions and cities of Syria and Palestine. This decisive change moulded all subsequent history and helped to define medieval Byzantium. Despite these losses Byzantium continued to issue a reliable gold coinage and to live by its legal system. Roman law was translated into Greek as the emperor abandoned his Latin designation, *imperator*, for the Greek, *basileus*. Herakleios also issued new laws and reformed the copper currency.

In the mid-seventh century the Arabs sailed to Cyprus, Cos and Rhodes, which all fell to Muslim control. From these bases the Arabs harried shipping in the Aegean, raiding the islands and coastal sites, sometimes to cut wood for shipbuilding. In 655, they defeated the young emperor Constans II (641–68), grandson of Herakleios, off the south coast of Asia Minor. He then decided to move his court in 662 to the safer environment of Syracuse in Sicily. The Roman *Book of the Pontiffs* describes how Constans visited Rome, was ceremoniously received by Pope Vitalian and made gifts to the churches, including a gold pallium (cloth), which he laid on the altar of St Peter's:

He stayed in Rome twelve days; he dismantled all the city's bronze decorations; he removed the bronze tiles from the roof of the church of St Mary *ad martyres* . . . Entering Sicily he lived in Syracuse. He imposed such afflictions on the people . . . for years on end . . . as had never been seen before. On 15 July in the 12th indiction, the said emperor was murdered in his bath.

When a pretender claimed the throne, the Senate in Constantinople immediately had Constans' eldest son crowned emperor as Constantine IV (668–85), and Syracuse reverted to its provincial status. Sicily and southern Italy remained under imperial rule, though in the course of the ninth century the island slowly succumbed to Arab conquest. But long after the military defeat of Byzantium there, some courts still recorded their judgments in Greek, individuals founded orthodox monasteries and artistic workshops copied Greek manuscripts in a Byzantine style.

From the beginning of Constantine IV's reign, Constantinople was assaulted by persistent Arab attacks; in a five-year campaign, the besiegers wintered at Kyzikos and engaged the Byzantine navy every summer. In these battles 'Greek fire' was first used effectively to destroy enemy ships. Finally, in 678, Constantine IV turned the tide of Muslim conquest, not only by demonstrating how strongly defended his capital was, but also by persuading the Mardaites, independent mountain tribesmen of Lebanon, to attack the Arabs. He imposed a thirty-year peace treaty on Caliph Mu'awiya, who agreed to pay a yearly tribute of 3,000 gold pieces, fifty captives and fifty thoroughbred horses. In this way, the emperor ended what had seemed like an unstoppable campaign against the empire, although Caliph 'Abd al-Malik (685–705) would later resume attacks. Constantine IV negotiated favourable arrangements with the Lombards in Italy, and the Avars in central Europe, and restored good relations with Rome. By removing his brothers from authority, he insisted that his son Justinian II should succeed him.

This turning point in Arab–Byzantine relations allowed Constantine IV to shift attention from the Muslim threat to the very different one posed by the Slavs in the western provinces. Although they too were capable of besieging major cities, they tended to settle on productive agricultural land in groups identified by Theophanes as *Sklaviniai*. Their gradual infiltration throughout the Balkans had forced many indigenous communities to flee to fortified cities, mountain tops and islands. In 584, Monemvasia, the city 'with one entrance', was established on a rocky outcrop linked to the Peloponnese by a causeway. The population of Argos fled to Orove, an island in the Saronic Gulf, and the inhabitants of Patras sailed across the sea to Sicily. Both the degree of Slavonic settlement, which can be traced through place-names and archaeological evidence, and its time-scale remain disputed. But eventually nearly all the Slavs became Byzantines, whether by military force or through commercial and social interaction.

In this process of incorporation and conversion, the new system of administration and the Church played significant roles. By 695, Hellas in central Greece formed a *thema*, with its own general and staff who supported local clergy, for instance the bishops of Athens and Corinth, in maintaining orthodox traditions through parishes and monasteries. Initially through trading contacts, the Slavs learnt to speak Greek and gradually became absorbed into the empire, serving in the army, adopting Christianity and paying their taxes to Constantinople, like other imperial subjects. Their cultural conversion strengthened Byzantium and deepened the empire's Christian identity.

Slavonic names or origin are noted in the sources in a neutral fashion: Niketas, Patriarch of Constantinople (766–80), was a Slav eunuch; Thomas the Slav was a military general who aspired to be emperor. Epithets such as these fall into the category of labels derived from a person's geographical origin, personal features or trade, which were often considered humorous in Byzantium. Those called Paphlagonitis (from Paphlagonia) were often caricatured as dirty pork-eaters, while Simokattes ('snub-nose'), Sarandapechys ('forty cubits', i.e. tall) or Podopagouros ('crab-foot') could all be ridiculed. The development of family names, however, marked a social process that gave individuals stronger identity, even if it might be humble. In the eleventh century, Patriarch Michael Keroularios ('candle-maker') held senatorial rank but must have had candle-makers among his ancestors. In the long overview of medieval history, this early and widespread use of family names set Byzantium apart from other states, as a society with a developed awareness of the importance of genealogy and personal relations.

In the process of transforming the Slavs into Byzantines, the Church also played a critical role by expanding bishoprics and constructing churches. It was a long irregular process marked by setbacks such as the siege of Patras in 806, when Arab pirates linked up with rebellious Slavs to threaten the city. Thanks to the miraculous intervention of the local saint, Andreas, as well as a general based at Corinth, the besiegers were defeated. The original Greek inhabitants of Patras, who had fled to Sicily, were invited to return with their bishop to reoccupy the city. We learn from the writings of a ninth-century scholar, Arethas, that his parents were among those who returned.

In addition to converting the Slavonic tribes to Christianity, patriarchs of Constantinople also tried to impose a more uniform orthodox belief. During the Persian invasions of 611–19, many Monophysite Christians in the eastern provinces, who refused to accept the Council of Chalcedon (451), had not supported imperial forces, arguing that a Zoroastrian regime would be more tolerant than the Byzantine. Religious controversies were reflected in political problems. Using definitions designed to win over these Monophysite communities, Patriarch Sergios I and his successor, Paul II, issued theological declarations in 634, 638 and 648, which extended the debate over Christ's natures to the issue of His energy and will. But the doctrine of Monotheletism (the belief that Christ had only one will) provoked great opposition both in Byzantium and in the West, and failed to win over the Monophysites.

The search for clearer theological definitions may have been given added impetus by the expansion of Islam, which undermined the Byzantines' confidence. While they condemned the new revelation of Islam as a heresy, the Christian authorities in Constantinople anxiously questioned why God permitted the infidels to win so many battles. But the effort to bring the Monophysite churches back into communion with Constantinople was weakened by Muslim conquest, which effectively took over the areas that supported the hierarchy of rival churches and bishops. Many converted to Islam. Other Christian communities who remained loyal to Constantinople are sometimes identified as Melkite, from the Syriac term for imperial. Under Islam, all these Christians were protected people (*dhimmi*) and were tolerated. Gradually they adopted Arabic as their liturgical language and many survive to this day, for example, in Palestine and Lebanon.

The official campaign to enforce Monotheletism led to the persecution of orthodox opponents. Maximos Confessor, a Byzantine monk, and Pope Martin I were both brought to Constantinople, put on trial and then banished. The pope died in exile in Cherson on the Black Sea, while Maximos was mutilated and then moved from one castle prison to another, suffering great privations. Their writings preserve a record of this theological debacle, which implicated Pope Honorius as well as several patriarchs of Constantinople.

Monotheletism was finally condemned at the Sixth Oecumenical Council, summoned by Constantine IV in 680. The emperor himself presided over many of the sessions, when texts cited in support of the theology of One Will were analysed and found to be incorrect. He ordered that all copies of these writings should be burned, except for one example to be kept under lock and key in the patriarchal library of heresies. This procedure confirmed the vital role of the Church in supporting the imperial structure of government. In turn, orthodox emperors used church councils to consolidate their own dynastic rule.

In 692, Justinian II summoned another council, normally called *in Trullo* because it met under the dome (*troullos*) of the Great Palace, to review ecclesiastical law. This gathering of 211 bishops, including representatives of the five great patriarchates, issued 102 canons intended to enforce more coherent definitions of belief and to update regulations for more uniform behaviour. These include the condemnation of many pre-Christian activities, such as the celebration of Kalends (New Year), and the 1 March festival, with public dancing by women, cross-dressing and the use of theatrical masks; the invocation of Dionysos while pressing the grapes; foretelling the future by bears or other animals, or by cloud-chasers, sorcerers, purveyors of amulets and diviners, who pretend to predict fortune, fate or genealogy. Apparently, it was proving difficult to eradicate older traditions.

The Council also legislated for the first time on religious art: canon 100 decrees that no art which might arouse lascivious feelings should be displayed, and canon 82 prescribes the portrayal of the Saviour in His human form, as Incarnate man, rather than the early Christian symbol of the Lamb of God. The first may apply to the icons of pagan gods and goddesses, as well as to portraits of prostitutes and concubines, which decorated many cities, together with verses describing their skills. The second immediately influenced the production of religious icons, which were often painted by monks. It was reinforced by Justinian's revolutionary new gold coinage, which displayed the face of Christ on the front and put the emperor's portrait on the back (plates 11a and 11b). Two types were issued: the first used a bearded image of Christ, the second a younger model with short curly hair, both familiar from mosaic portraits. Icon painters had already developed the first style, which is preserved on a magnificent panel at Mount Sinai. The fact that the Council *in Trullo* felt obliged to address these artistic issues suggests that they were taking on greater significance as a result of increased contact with Islam. In light of the continuing military successes of the Arabs, the charge of idolatry levelled against icon worship had a certain resonance, for the Muslims observed the Old Testament commandment against graven images.

Although Justinian II represented the fourth generation of Herakleios' family, in 695 he was overthrown in a military coup and exiled to Cherson. Despite the mutilation of his nose and tongue – intended to prevent him from ever ruling again – he survived and returned to power, wearing a golden nose patch and using an interpreter to speak for him. He tried to ensure the succession of his son, Tiberios, but his second reign from 705 to 711 was marked by such cruelty and revenge against his enemies that the entire family was murdered in another coup d'état.

Nonetheless, during the initial period of Islamic threat, Byzantium derived a sense of continuity and strength from the dynasty founded by Herakleios. Although there were several crises, one imperial family held power from 610 to 695 and provided a more orderly succession of inheritance from father to son, which helped to secure the empire in its transformation from a late antique into a medieval state. Within Constantinople, the Senate displayed its importance by taking responsibility in moments of crisis. It sent the appeal to Carthage which saved Byzantium from chaotic administration; it sat as the court of highest judgment when Pope Martin and others accused of heresy were tried; it prevented Constans II from taking his family to the West, and it provided the experienced patricians who negotiated diplomatic treaties. But the Senate was unable to counter the ambitions generated by rival military leaders who took over as king-makers between 695 and 705 and again from 711 to 717. This novel power base, built up in the *themata*, destroyed the civilian authority of the Senate and empowered soldiers who competed to impose their own candidates as emperor.

Under the onslaught of Islam, the empire was reduced to a much smaller medieval state, identified by its commitment to Roman imperial traditions, orthodox Christianity and its Greek inheritance. It also adopted dynastic rule to strengthen its new government. By resisting the Arabs, the Byzantines sustained Christianity in the eastern Mediterranean and checked the expansion of Islam into Asia Minor. From this very limited base, they began the conversion of the Slavonic tribes, which was to have momentous consequences. But the primary achievement of the new medieval Byzantium was to prevent Muslim efforts to capture Constantinople, which would have opened the way to a rapid conquest of the Balkans, central Europe and probably Rome itself.

9

Icons, a New Christian Art Form

When the husband [who had commissioned a gilded wooden icon of St Michael the Archangel] felt he was about to die, he took his wife's hand and put it upon the hand of the archangel saying: 'O Archangel Michael . . . behold, in thy hands I place my wife Euphemia as a deposit, so that thou mayst watch over her.' And after his death, Euphemia continued offering the icon incense, keeping a lamp lit before it at all times, and venerating it three times a day, she begged the saint to help her and protect her from the Devil.

Sermon of Eustathios of Thrace, probably seventh century

In this simple story, we learn how an elderly couple expressed their faith, thanks to an icon of St Michael the Archangel. The painted image they had commissioned was kept by the widow Euphemia in her bedroom, where she performed acts of veneration before it. Not only did it defend her from the Devil's attempts to destroy her faith, which are described in vivid detail, but also, after her death, it was placed over her face as a protective cover. The local bishop then witnessed the appearance of the archangel himself, accompanied by many other angels all clad in golden robes, who came to take Euphemia's soul to heaven. The icon disappeared temporarily, but later it was found suspended in the air in the episcopal church, where it performed many miracles.

Burning incense and lighting a lamp in front of an image was of course an ancient way of showing respect. All imperial images had to be honoured in this way, and in the third and early fourth centuries the Christians' failure to do so had unleashed official persecution against them. Public statues of gods and emperors, sometimes colossal, dominated the urban landscape and received marks of respect in special rites. At pagan festivals, statues of the gods were washed, dressed and paraded through cities; they were set up on altars, decorated with flower garlands and worshipped. In temples of Asclepius, patients slept close to the god's statue and offered prayers requesting medical cures. Inside private homes, the family *lares* (household gods) were also venerated; women in particular attended to these in domestic shrines and made offerings to the gods. This strong tradition of seeking protection within the home provided a context in which Christian icons gradually replaced ancient ones. Although there is no record of this process, it seems likely that when Christians adopted their new monotheistic faith, they would have removed the old *lares* and set up new protecting images. As Christianity became established, pictures of Christ, the Virgin and saints took over the role of securing the well-being of the family. While this domestic form of veneration is rarely stressed, it may have been the means by which Christian icons came to be regarded by the faithful as indispensable.

Recently, Thomas Mathews has shown that in Late Antiquity icons of the pagan gods were also displayed inside houses. They could be framed and hung on a wall; sometimes they had hinged side panels which could cover the painted area or lids which fitted over them. They are painted in encaustic, using heated wax which could be coloured and applied to thin pieces of wood to create life-like portraits. These images of gods and local deities have intense large eyes that address the viewer directly. Incense and lamps were burned in their honour. Often they were associated with funerary practices. Mummified bodies from the Fayyum area of Egypt, for instance, preserve portraits placed over the face of the deceased. Not only rich women, wearing their golden jewellery, but also old men, young children, athletes and pagan gods were all commemorated in this way. Their compelling personal characters make us feel that we know them as they were when alive. Thanks to the dry conditions in Fayyum, many survived, while elsewhere, though ubiquitous in the Roman world, they decomposed.

Mathews suggests that these pagan portraits are the forerunners of

Christian icons painted using the same technique, and that images of Isis provided a model for the Mother of God, those of Zeus and Sarapis for the first images of Christ. These ancient icons are found in a private, domestic setting as well as in cult temples. Evidence that icons derived from pagan models may be supported by the stories of miraculous punishments suffered by painters when they tried to depict Christ as Zeus (one or both hands were temporarily withered). Even as late as the 580s, pagans were discovered commissioning icons so that they could appear to venerate Christ when, in fact, they were devotees of Apollo. This deception provoked trials in which the pagan worshippers of Apollo were condemned to death; it also implies that distinguishing encaustic panels of the pagan gods from icons of Christ might be difficult. Artists also worried whether Christ was to be shown with long hair and bearded, or with short curly hair. While some Christian authors praised the long-haired image modelled on what they called 'Nazarene', others claimed that the short frizzy hairstyle was more authentic.

The Greek term *eikon* can refer to any image, but by the fourth century it seems to relate particularly to the early encaustic portraits of Christ, the Virgin, the saints, local martyrs and bishops and monks (plates 21 and 27). In contrast to the domestic use of icons within the home, religious images were common in tombs. Christians buried in marble coffins (sarcophagi) chose symbols and images to reflect their religious convictions, and these elaborately carved monuments were often placed inside churches. Imperial patronage in association with holy relics frequently provided a stimulus to Christian art, for instance when Leo I (457–74) and his wife Verina brought the girdle and veil of the Mother of God to Constantinople and constructed special shrines within her church at Blachernai to house them. These chapels were decorated with large icons of the Virgin with the imperial couple and the two senators responsible for identifying the relics. On her feast days the icons were processed through the city. In less official celebrations, images of holy men, bishops, martyrs and saints were also commemorated in mosaic, painted in fresco and displayed in public places. Painted panels were rapidly copied in metal, mosaic, enamel and less precious materials; they were framed and covered with silver covers embellished with gems; silk veils were hung in front of them to protect the painted surface. Icons created a new art form, which remains particularly associated with Byzantium. They not only attained paramount importance within the empire, but also exercised immense influence outside it.

How did icons gain such a dominant place in Byzantium? Despite some theological reservations, related to the Old Testament prohibition of graven images, religious images are mentioned in early Christian texts. While there is no evidence for their existence during the life of Christ, a story that St Luke had painted the Virgin and Child, and that all later copies were endowed with that authentic power, associated such icons with the holy qualities of their subjects. Other images miraculously created, such as the Mandylion, the towel on which it was believed Christ had impressed his features, were called *acheiropoietai* (not made by hand), and were particularly cherished. At Edessa (in Syria) and Kamouliana (in central Asia Minor) icons modelled on this holy cloth performed the role of city protectors, and were paraded around the walls whenever enemies appeared. Similarly, after the First Oecumenical Council, images of the 318 Fathers were held responsible for protecting Nicaea, while the most important icon of the Mother of God played a highly significant part in the defence of the capital. As we have seen, this gave rise to Constantinople's additional name: Theotokoupolis, the city guarded by the Theotokos, she who bore God.

Belief in the power of icons was related to the theory that the icon in some way captured the essence of the holy person depicted, and that through the icon communication with that person could be established. St Basil of Caesarea (c. 329–79) enshrined this notion in a famous comment on imperial images: the honour made to the image passes to the prototype. Icons, therefore, could serve as intercessors: prayers directed to them passed on to the holy persons depicted on them. This understanding was reinforced by the manner in which icons addressed the viewer. The figures represented a dignified authority in a direct frontal manner, with large eyes which gazed out from the panel as if inviting communication. Through this immediate contact, the icons demanded attention. In response, Christians gave the images their total devotion. Visions and conversations were alleged to take place in front of Christian icons. When a childless couple visited the shrine of St Glykeria at Herakleia, for instance, the husband reported that the saint appeared and spoke to him, reassuring him that they would have a child, and in due course St Elizabeth was born. Icons thus facilitated a method of spiritual communication that did not depend on the consecrated power of a priest or bishop. They functioned in a domestic setting as well as in church and gave particular solace to individuals who made their devotions privately, as stories record. In this respect, they performed the same function as the pre-Christian household gods.

Icons were also created in other media: craftsmen continued the ancient skill of carving precious metals and expensive materials – ivory, gemstones, enamel and rock crystal. Secular ivory diptychs commissioned by Roman consuls died out with that institution in the sixth century, though emperors continued to commission ivory panels to commemorate a coronation or a marriage. Most surviving medieval ivory plaques carry Christian themes, such as St Michael the Archangel, or scenes from the life of Christ. Frequently these religious objects preserve the form of consular diptychs, joined by hinges at the centre, or triptychs (in three sections), which means that the central part can be covered; on some triptychs all external and interior surfaces are carved. Individual panels were combined to decorate large pieces of church furniture, for example ivory thrones such as the sixth-century one belonging to Bishop Maximian of Ravenna. When elephant tusk became too expensive, walrus and other bone was used for combs, needles and small round boxes. In the West, Byzantine ivories with Christian subjects were often reused as medieval book covers. Mounted on metal frames decorated with jewels and ancient cameos, they create glowing golden guards at either end of parchment manuscripts.

A set of silver plates decorated with scenes from the life of David reflects Old Testament inspiration for Byzantine art: the use of silver stamps to guarantee quality means that many of these pieces can be securely dated to specific years of the reign of Herakleios (610–41). Other silver objects are identified by dedicatory inscriptions commissioned by Syrian villagers for local rural churches, which can in turn be dated from inscriptions set into the mosaic floors. Crosses, patens, chalices, spoons, altar and book coverings intended for liturgical use suggest that at all levels of society these offerings were widespread.

Just as the cults of the ancient gods had been spread through art (sculpture and paintings), so icons became an effective way of disseminating the stories of particular saints. When pilgrims went in search of miraculous cures, achieved by contact with a saint's relics, they found churches often decorated with images – of Demetrios in Thessalonike, Artemios in Constantinople, Menas accompanied by his camels near Alexandria, and Symeon on his column near Antioch. Sometimes the icons exuded a healing liquid that proved a powerful cure; oil that burned in lamps in front of them also had healing powers. In the late sixth century, Patriarch Sophronios of Jerusalem had personal experience of this in Alexandria where he witnessed the crowds of pilgrims; individuals who believed themselves cured then purchased clay or silver flasks decorated with the healer's image (plate 9). Portable icons were made with lids which protected the painted surface and tiny icons were worn on necklaces for personal protection. Together with pilgrim flasks and small metal icons in cheaper material, they did as much to spread the fame of the healing saints as the written *Lives* and collections of their miracle stories.

Despite this concentration on religious images, Byzantine craftsmen never lost their ability to portray characters from pagan stories, and their patrons continued to order whatever they wished. Recent discoveries in the late antique provinces of Syria, Palestine and Transjordan confirm a fascination with the ancient myths – the doomed love of Phaedra and Hippolytus, Prometheus creating the first humans or the drinking contest between Dionysus and Heracles – depicted on mosaics laid in the eighth century, under Muslim rule. Images of the rape of Europa and loves of Zeus were depicted with great realism on ivory boxes. Similarly, gold- and silversmiths, traditionally restricted to guilds, which limited their numbers and ensured quality, continued to decorate their products with images from ancient mythology, for example representations of Bacchus and Silenus with scantily dressed maenads. The use of encaustic for secular portraits also continued into the sixth century and many are commemorated in verse:

I was a harlot in Byzantine Rome, granting my venal favours to all. I am Callirrhoe the versatile, whom Thomas, goaded by love, set in this picture, showing what great desire he has in his soul, for even as his wax melts so melts his heart.

The range of art decorated with what the Church considered thoroughly unsuitable subjects reminds us of the Byzantine delight in pre-Christian imagery, which extended into the twelfth century and beyond.

Apart from symbols such as the Cross, Christian images were not introduced on the coinage until 692–5, when Justinian II minted gold types with portraits of Christ, using both the long- and short-haired representations (plates 11a and 11b). Thereafter, the Virgin or saints were more commonly shown on coins to invoke their special protection and support; Emperor Alexander (912–13), for instance, introduced the image of John the Baptist, crowning him as emperor on the reverse of his coins. In the 860s, Patriarch Photios' seal displayed an image of the Virgin holding the Christ Child in a medallion, known as the Blachernitissa type after a famous icon kept in her church at Blachernai, and shortly afterwards Emperor Leo VI put an image of the Virgin on his gold coins. The fact that Photios copied the image of an icon for his own seal reflects the importance of icons in Byzantium. By the ninth century they formed the quintessential element in Byzantine art and inspired devotion in orthodox worshippers, then as now.

Nearly all the components of Byzantine art were ancient and drew on older techniques. In the case of icons, encaustic had been used to great effect to commemorate pagan gods and Roman individuals from all walks of society. In Christian Byzantium, however, the devotional icon created a new art form which became its most characteristic feature. Together with other luxury objects, made of gold, silver and ivory or coloured silks, icons were appreciated by Christians as evidence of the superior culture of Byzantium. The same artistic traditions also sustained imperial ideology, in images which portrayed the rulers as donors, on coins which associated holy figures with them, as well as in secular works of art depicting victorious emperors, patrons of manuscripts, crowns and other imperial symbols. In this way, art sustained the empire in its transition to a medieval state and artistic products remained symbolic of Byzantium even after 1453. And because of the personal devotion they engendered, Christian icons were at the centre of a great debate which shook the empire from 730 to 843.

IO

Iconoclasm and Icon Veneration

> The falsely called 'icon' neither has its existence in the tradition
> of Christ or the Apostles or the Fathers, nor is there any prayer
> of consecration to transpose it from the state of being common
> to the state of being sacred. Instead, it remains common and
> worthless, as the painter made it.
>
> *Definition* of the Iconoclast Council of 754

> The making and worship of icons is no new invention, but the
> ancient tradition of the church ... It is impossible for us to
> think without using physical images ... by bodily sight we
> reach spiritual contemplation. For this reason Christ assumed
> both soul and body, since man is fashioned from both.
>
> St John of Damascus, eighth century

Iconoclasm, literally 'the breaking of icons', is one of the few Byzantine words still in English and European use. This itself is testimony to the lasting power of the conflict which it names: the fight over the dangers and powers of religious images. In Byzantium, iconoclasm was inspired by the Second Commandment of the Law of Moses, which states: 'Thou shalt make no graven images nor shalt thou worship them.' The recapitulation of this law in the Book of Deuteronomy is even more severe:

Thou shalt not make thee any graven image, or any likeness of any thing that is in heaven above, or that is in the earth beneath, or that is in the waters beneath the earth: Thou shalt not bow down thyself unto them, nor serve them: for I the LORD thy God am a jealous God ...

But it was neither the Judaic nor the Christian tradition that brought Byzantine iconoclasm to the fore. It was the Islamic observation of this commandment against idolatry which laid down the challenge to the role of images within imperial Christendom.

In Byzantium, people had become deeply attached to icons of holy persons, as we have seen, and images of Christ circulated throughout the empire on imperial coinage. In 692, when the Council *in Trullo* insisted that Christ be portrayed in his human form, it argued that the Incarnation justified a personal Christian art which was more instructive than symbolic representations of the Lamb of God. Scribes of early Christian manuscripts regularly illustrated biblical scenes, indicating their belief in the power of images to teach scripture. In this they followed the advice given by Pope Gregory I to western bishops: pictures could teach those who could not read. This notion that paintings were 'Bibles of the illiterate' encouraged a narrative art which followed the Gospel stories rather than the portrait-style devotional icon. Both were highly developed in Byzantium by the early eighth century.

Since the Byzantines cherished their religious art and icons, why did they turn against them? The phenomenon of iconoclasm, when people destroyed the images they had previously honoured, demands explanation. Theories abound, from the claim that it was all due to Leo III (717–41) to a recent interpretation that few people were actually involved – most were indifferent to the issue. Yet iconoclasm was one of the great ideological disputes in recorded history. For over a century, battle was joined; two distinct periods of icon destruction in Byzantium are documented, from 730 to 787 and again from 815 to 843, and several deaths and martyrdoms are recorded. As for the appeal of icons to popular sentiment, perhaps this was best understood by local Soviet commanders in the 1930s: when they were ordered to campaign against the influence of the Church, they were known to line up icons, sentence them to death and then shoot them.

In order to understand the introduction of iconoclasm, it is essential to recapitulate the military problems of early eighth-century Byzantium. Leo III was the last of a string of mainly unqualified emperors imposed by troops attached to the provincial government of the themes (*themata*) who marched on the capital and disposed of rulers with impunity. In the twenty-two years between 695 and 717, there had been six changes of ruler. The resulting instability prevented any serious attention to the dangerous expansion of Arabs into Asia Minor and Bulgars in the Balkans. By the time of Anastasios II (713–15), the Arabs were clearly preparing a major assault on the capital, and the emperor could only react by repairing the walls and getting in supplies. Another revolt by troops of the Opsikion theme, with naval support, set up a provincial tax collector as an unwilling emperor (Theodosios III, 715–17). This provoked the Anatolikon and Armeniakon theme armies to try to end the constant upheavals by establishing a competent military ruler.

In March 717, Leo, general of the Anatolikon forces, negotiated with Theodosios III and Patriarch Germanos to take control, and was crowned emperor on the condition that he would not disturb the Church and that his predecessor should be allowed to retire from public life as a monk. Once recognized as ruler, Leo III immediately prepared the city to withstand the expected siege. Knowing that for decades the Arabs had intended to make the Byzantine capital their own, he reinforced the measures already taken, storing extra food supplies, preparing the navy and strengthening the city's fortifications. During the twelve-month siege of 717/18, Leo's vigorous defence, achieved with skilful use of 'Greek fire', Bulgarian aid and the intercession of the Virgin, constituted a great victory over the Arabs. It reflected both his military experience as well as popular belief in the city's divine protection, and was commemorated annually thereafter.

To prevent further Arab attacks by sea, Leo III paid special attention to naval forces, strengthening the theme of Thrakesion along the west coast of Asia Minor, promoting the Kibyrraioton to theme status, and establishing new naval commands in the Aegean Sea and on Crete (see map 3). He also suppressed a revolt in Sicily and reinforced imperial control in southern Italy. He displayed his orthodoxy by attempting to force conversion on Jews and heretical Christians, called Montanists (followers of the second-century AD prophet Montanus from Phrygia). And, by crowning his one-year-old son Constantine as co-emperor, he revealed his intention to establish a new imperial dynasty that would rule for generations. New coins were struck to spread this message. But the provinces of Asia Minor continued to suffer repeated raids, which theme forces were unable to check despite Leo's efforts. Since the Byzantines knew that God granted victory in battle, and had in the past assisted them in defeating the historic empire of Persia, they had to question why He now gave triumphs to the Arabs. Being a God-fearing people, they sought an explanation for divine disapproval in their own human failings.

Then in 726, from the depths of the Aegean, a great volcanic eruption forced boiling lava and pumice stones 'as big as hills' into the air, which darkened the sky for days and then floated up on the shores of Asia Minor, Greece and the islands. A new island emerged between Thera (Santorini) and Therasia. When Leo wondered what this divine sign meant, his advisers interpreted it as a warning against idolatry, and advised him to ban icons from churches and public places. It is not clear if he knew that Bishop Constantine of Nakoleia in Asia Minor had already noticed the failure of icons to protect cities besieged by the Arabs, or that some wonder-working icons had ceased to perform their expected miracles, but Constantine is later identified as an adviser to Leo. When the emperor learnt that divine favour was being withheld because of the excessive veneration of icons, which was tantamount to idolatry, he 'began to speak against the holy icons', as the chronicler Theophanes states. Theophanes also cites the instance of Caliph Yezid ordering the destruction of Christian art in 722/3, and claims that Leo was inspired by the same idea and was 'Saracen-minded'. For Leo, however, it was necessary to secure God's support in battle against the Arabs, and if this meant imposing iconoclasm, then iconoclasm must be imposed. It was instituted as a way of regaining divine support at a critical time for the survival of Byzantium. Leo's motives may have been spelled out in theological terms, but they expressed his understanding of the Muslims' methods of ensuring discipline and effectiveness.

The first phase of iconoclasm began in 730 when Leo III ordered church leaders to remove icons. When Patriarch Germanos refused to agree, he was dismissed by a judicial tribunal of senators and civilian officials. Anastasios, previously his assistant, was appointed to direct the new iconoclast Church. In Rome, however, Pope Gregory II (715–31) and his successor Gregory III (731–41) reacted with hostility to the official letter about the dangers of icons. Their antagonism was also fuelled by disputes over taxation in Italy, which had increased as a result of a new imperial census of the population. Apart from the removal of a prominent icon displayed on the imperial palace, very little specific destruction is recorded, as if the change in religious practice needed a fuller and firmer theological basis. Leo's son, Constantine V, later provided this in his own writings and the associated campaign to impose iconoclasm.

After a long reign of twenty-four years, Leo III died peacefully in 741. His notable achievements included a decisive defeat of the Arabs the previous year at Akroinon; a new law code, the *Ekloga*, which insisted that provincial judges receive a salary in order to avoid corruption, among other reforms designed to strengthen the legal system; and the transfer of the ecclesiastical diocese of East Illyricum from Roman control to Constantinople. This brought the Greek-speaking regions of southern Italy, Sicily, the Balkans and Greece, and their revenues, back into the orbit of the Byzantine capital and was naturally opposed by the Roman bishops. In 731, Pope Gregory III also held a local council to condemn iconoclasm, which opened a religious schism between Rome and Constantinople. His successors continued to lay claim to the territories of Illyricum. Nonetheless, the reign of Leo brought stability to the empire, consolidated imperial defences and checked Muslim expansion. Iconoclasm appeared to have succeeded in its primary aim of regaining divine favour in battle, without as yet a wholesale destruction of icons.

The century between 743 and 843 was dominated by the battle over religious images. Following a short but violent civil war, Constantine V (741–75) assumed control over the capital and began to develop his own theory of iconoclasm, arguing for a spiritual form of worship which avoided any idolatrous veneration of painted wood. This theology of Christian belief without icons was elaborated in his *Peuseis* (*Enquiries*), which stressed that the Eucharist was the true image of Christ and the Cross the most powerful symbol of the Christian. In preparation for holding an oecumenical council to consolidate iconoclast belief and practice, Constantine V organized a series of debates to counter iconophile opposition and to make sure that all bishops supported the correct theology. When they eventually met at Hiereia in 754, the iconoclast bishops denounced icon veneration as idolatry, citing scriptural texts, and emphasized that Christians should worship without base material objects such as wooden, painted images:

Because the catholic church of us Christians stands in the middle between Judaism and paganism, she walks the new path of piety and worship ... without acknowledging the bloody sacrifices ... of Judaism; despising also the entire practice of making and worshipping idols, of which abominable art paganism is the leader and inventor.

Rome did not participate in the Council and rejected its decisions. Although the records of the proceedings were later destroyed, apart from the *Definition*, which was preserved and denounced in 787, it is clear that Constantine took a leading role. The persecution and death of persistent icon venerators followed, mainly monks who both painted religious images and encouraged their cult. St Stephen the Younger was one of the most prominent.

After a recurrence of bubonic plague in the 740s, Constantine attracted workers to the capital to repair its major aqueduct, as well as to restore monuments damaged in a serious earthquake. The church of St Irene, a foundation of Justinian, was rebuilt in iconoclast style, with a mosaic cross in its apse, and can still be admired as an impress-ive example of the symbolic art then in favour. Of course, the Cross was also revered by iconophiles as the most potent symbol of Christ's power; it was used in blessing, protecting, curing and exorcizing demons by iconoclasts and iconophiles alike. In 751, however, the iconoclast emperor was unable to save Ravenna from the Lombards; no military aid was sent to the West (as noted in chapter 6). This was partly due to Constantine V's almost constant campaigns against the Arabs, Slavs and Bulgars, which were highly successful. As a result of his military triumphs, the idea of imperial victory became elided with the religious policy of iconoclasm, and those who fought in the wars often became its fervent supporters. At his death in 775 Constantine V bequeathed a much stronger empire to his son, Leo IV (775–80), whom he had married to Irene, a girl from Athens.

Despite forty-five years of iconoclast policy, when Empress Irene was widowed in 780 on the death of her husband Leo IV, she decided to reverse it, a daring and surprising shift which was supported by exiled iconophiles, especially monks. In the name of her sixteen-year-old son Constantine VI, she summoned another oecumenical meeting to Constantinople. Pope Hadrian I and the three eastern patriarchs were all invited and sent their representatives to the Council, which was presided over by a newly appointed patriarch. Irene had promoted Tarasios, leader of her civilian government, to the post. After a disastrous first meeting in 786, which was disrupted by bishops loyal to iconoclasm, the Council reconvened in Nicaea in 787 and denounced iconoclasm as an innovation in Church tradition. Icon veneration, justified by citing miracles recorded mainly in the lives of saints, was restored and twenty-one canons were issued to ensure that no new churches were built without relics and icons of the saints. The iconophiles' chief argument was that the Incarnation of the Son of God permitted a depiction of Christ as He had been seen on earth. That image could be venerated with relative honour (*proskynesis*), even if actual worship (*latreia*) was reserved for God alone:

The holy Church of God which confesses rightly that there is one hypostasis of Christ in two natures, has been instructed by God to represent Him in icons, in order for her to remember His redemptive dispensation. (Sixth session of the Council of 787)

They ordered all iconoclast texts to be destroyed.

Empress Irene undoubtedly exploited the divisions generated by half a century of iconoclasm and seized the opportunity to lead Byzantium back to the veneration of icons because it afforded her greater control. Her urge to restore the graven images was hardly pious. For when Constantine VI broke free of her influence and tried to rule alone, she had him blinded in the same purple chamber where she had given birth to him twenty-six years earlier. From 797 to 802, she replaced him and ruled as emperor, issuing laws and negotiating with Caliph Harun al-Rashid and Charlemagne. Her portrait is found on both sides of the gold coinage issued in her name, a unique style, with crosses on her crown, orb and sceptre (plate 11c). When her finance minister overthrew her in a palace coup d'état, she had ruled longer than her husband, Leo IV.

In 815, Emperor Leo V initiated the second phase of iconoclasm, a resumption intimately connected with the promise of military success.

This was now firmly associated with Constantine V. In a staged event, soldiers loyal to his memory broke into the imperial tombs at the mausoleum attached to the Holy Apostles and called on their hero to lead them to victory. Under Leo V (813–20) and Michael II (820–29), iconoclast forces engaged the Bulgars with some success, and Patriarch John, called the Grammarian (*grammatikos*) because of his profound learning, developed new justifications for the destruction of icons. During the reign of Emperor Theophilos (829–42), these were accompanied by a more vigorous persecution of those who persisted in painting or venerating icons.

On the death of Theophilos, however, his widow Theodora assumed imperial power for her young son, Michael III. Despite the challenges posed by several military officials and her own male relatives, she succeeded in making a firm alliance with the court hierarchy, led by the chief eunuch Theoktistos, and previously exiled iconophile monks, and again an empress reversed iconoclasm. Theodora chose Methodios, who had been tortured and imprisoned, as patriarch and commissioned him to write a new liturgy (the *Synodikon of Orthodoxy*) to mark the return to correct belief. Reaffirming the Council of 787, the veneration of icons was restored on 10 March 843. The destruction of all iconoclast texts was again ordered. Theodora also insisted that the Church should grant her husband Theophilos a posthumous pardon for his iconoclasm, so that young Prince Michael would not suffer from any association with heresy. The *Synodikon* was chanted with the names of iconoclasts Leo III and Constantine V, but not Theophilos, among a long list of condemned heretics; it is still performed in Orthodox churches on the first Sunday in Lent.

The 'Triumph of Orthodoxy', as the event became known, was commemorated in icons, although none survive from the ninth century. A fourteenth-century copy, now in the British Museum, portrays the empress with Michael III and Patriarch Methodios venerating an icon of the Virgin and Child above a row of iconophile martyrs, several monks and one (fictitious) nun, Theodosia (plate 27). Illuminated psalters also reflect the resumption of figural art with numerous pictures in the margins, which often illustrate the iconoclast controversy (e.g. Patriarch John the Grammarian trampled underfoot by iconophiles; plate 15). Three manuscripts of this type, including the famous Khludov Psalter, date from the period immediately after 843 and served as models for later ones. In monuments, on the other hand, symbolic iconoclast art remained in place for several years: no iconophile could possibly object to the cross. Only in 866 was the apse decoration of St Sophia in Constantinople renewed with a mosaic of the enthroned Virgin and Child. Patriarch Photios inaugurated it on Easter Sunday with a sermon describing its significance, and it remains in place to be revered. Elsewhere, figural paintings and mosaics which had been whitewashed over or covered up were restored. In miraculous fashion, lightning revealed the original Vision of Ezekiel mosaic in the church of Hosios David in Thessalonike. Although the patriarch feared the return of iconoclasm, the Triumph of Orthodoxy had secured the veneration of icons. Their honoured position was never again challenged.

From this overview of iconoclasm, it must be clear that all modern reconstructions of its impact are based on inadequate documentation. This is because the victorious icon-lovers insisted on the destruction of their opponents' arguments. As we have seen, in 787 and again in 843, they demanded the total obliteration of iconoclast theology by burning all the texts. This systematic destruction removed most of the evidence for what the icon-breakers were trying to achieve. The full text of the *Peuseis*, written by Constantine V, the acts of the Iconoclast Councils of 754 and 815, and the theological writings of John Grammatikos are all lost. We know the basic *Definition of Belief* issued by iconoclast theologians in 754 only because it was read out in 787, when it was denounced sentence by sentence. Several apse mosaics featuring monumental crosses put up by iconoclasts were eventually replaced by images of the Virgin and Child, leaving a shadowy outline. And much secular art of the iconoclast period, for example scenes of chariot and horse racing, was removed as irreverent.

Iconoclasm by its very nature involves destruction. But how many icons or paintings, frescoes or illuminated manuscripts were actually consigned to flames, overpainted or effaced is unknown. Modern estimates vary. To document the losses and to reconstruct what art might have been in existence is of course impossible. But iconoclast destruction is recorded: in the Patriarchate of Constantinople, holy figures previously decorating rooms were replaced by crosses, though not till the 760s. Surviving manuscripts from the periods of iconoclasm now lack images which had been cut out, and psalters produced immediately after 843 have representations of iconoclasts painting over icons.

The only way that we can understand this century of iconoclast debate is by setting it in its broadest context. The Byzantines turned against their holy images between 730 and 843 in a major upheaval sparked by the challenge posed by Islamic conquest, the loss of empire and expectations of the end of the world. As Byzantium came to terms with its new shape and gained confidence in its capacity to survive, it returned to the icons – first in 787 and again in 843, when Empresses Irene and Theodora took the lead. When it felt threatened, as in the early ninth century, Byzantium adopted the policy that was intimately associated with military victory, with soldiers taking the lead. The second phase of iconoclasm from 815 to 843 is only explicable as a reflection of Byzantium's reaction to a further devastating military challenge to its existence.

If we look more closely at the arguments that were used by both sides, we can see how directly these related to the threat of Islam. The iconoclasts claimed that religious images were dangerous and led people into idolatry, a sin for which they would be punished. They also pointed to the fact that the icons were no longer effective and had lost their power to defend and cure true Christian believers. Both arguments were used in 730, when Leo III introduced iconoclasm as the official policy. Against this, iconophiles developed sophisticated arguments based on the Incarnation, which permitted artists to depict the human Christ. St John of Damascus and others believed that Christians could be led up to a higher awareness of the divine through the veneration of icons.

In the course of the debate over icons, Byzantium set up its holy images as intercessors to define its art against the influence of the iconoclast Arabs. The Byzantines knew about Islam's claims to superiority over God's previous revelations to the Jews and the Christians, which were emblazoned on Muslim coins and monuments like the Dome of the Rock. Suras from the Qur'an repeated the message that

Jesus was just another prophet, not the Son of God. Christian artists countered this by depicting the Crucifixion, to emphasize their belief in the Resurrection. In the monastery on Mount Sinai, completely surrounded by Muslims who denied that Christ had risen from the dead, icons dating from the period of iconoclasm display the dead Christ on the Cross. They make the point that Jesus died, was buried and returned to life before his ascension into heaven. Debate over which divine revelation was true extended to all regions and is reflected in all aspects of political propaganda, as well as buildings and icons.

Iconoclasm also affected many levels of society, especially the icon painters themselves, chiefly monks, who were prosecuted for continuing to produce icons, and monastic communities which resisted iconoclasm – for instance Stoudios and Chora, both in the capital. Iconophile monks were exiled to various locations; others who embraced the change to iconoclasm were installed at these and other previously iconophile centres. Similarly, all those who continued to venerate icons at home, notably women, ran the risk of prison or worse. When St Stephen and his companions were incarcerated on Constantine V's orders, the wife of the prison officer is said to have brought her own icons to them in secret, so that they could maintain their venerations. Clerics on both sides, who stood by their theology and refused to compromise, were affected: iconophile Patriarchs Germanos and Nikephoros were forced to retire; Paul abdicated (something very unusual in Byzantium); the iconoclast bishops who disrupted the Council of 786 were punished, and Patriarch John the Grammarian, who refused to resign in 843, was sent into exile.

But probably the most significant sector affected was the military, such as the soldiers who became convinced iconoclasts under Constantine V, when he led them to major victories over both Arabs and Bulgars in the mid-eighth century. In their eyes, correct iconoclast theology brought military triumphs over the external enemies of Byzantium. Outside the empire, reactions recorded in other Christian centres indicate how seriously icon veneration was taken. In his monastery near Jerusalem, St John of Damascus (c. 675–753/4) elaborated a defence of the holy icons. In Rome, iconoclast theology was seen as another eastern heresy, like Monotheletism, and was firmly opposed. Farther north, however, Frankish theologians were shocked at the idolatrous aspects of iconophile justifications, when they learnt about them in a faulty translation of the acts of the 787 Council. Even beyond the imperial frontiers, the arguments and consequences of iconoclasm were considered significant.

Perhaps the most telling sign that iconoclasm had profound repercussions lies in the efforts made by iconophiles to efface all knowledge of it. For several decades after 843, Patriarch Photios feared a revival and wrote about the dangers of iconoclasm, suggesting that the policy retained power and force even when condemned. He was proved wrong. But the destruction of iconoclast theology was not completely successful, for during the European Reformation those Protestants critical of religious imagery cited precisely the same texts and concepts derived from the Byzantine experience. Comparison with the later experience of iconoclasm also confirms the underlying causes of Christian anxiety about religious images: icons had a similar function to representations of the old pagan gods. All the ancient practices were reproduced in the veneration of icons: they were kissed and adored; candles and lamps with incense were burned in front of them; and prayers were addressed to the holy persons represented. The iconoclasts condemned such behaviour as a new form of pagan idolatry, which generated a superstitious belief that the painted wood could respond. Muslims had also noticed the similarity and claimed that it made Christianity 'like the religion of the people of the idols'. Hence the iconophiles' determination to distinguish Christian from pagan icons, and veneration from true worship, which is reserved for God alone. This is still a sensitive issue in some orthodox circles today.

To claim that iconoclasm had a fundamental importance does not reduce the significance of other achievements of the period. Most inhabitants of the greatly reduced empire experienced the eighth and ninth centuries as a period of heightened military threat. By defeating Arab and Bulgarian forces, Leo III and Constantine V guaranteed the empire's survival. Provincial inhabitants of both the eastern and western frontiers were not exposed to the same regular devastation. Although Constantinople would be besieged again, it withstood all later attacks until 1204. Legal reforms, the consolidation of theme military government, the restoration of dynastic rule and the re-establishment of Constantinople as a major market in the eastern

Mediterranean were more important to the life of Byzantium than iconoclasm. The intimate connection between military victory and iconoclasm forged by Constantine V and imitated by his successors must be held responsible for the systematic destruction of figural art – barely a single Christian icon made before 730 survives from Constantinople – while iconophile artists and monks were persecuted, tortured and killed.

The iconoclast battles also draw attention to a fascinating contrast between male support for iconoclasm and female opposition, embodied in Empresses Irene and Theodora, who successfully reversed it. The two women seem to have acted from political considerations rather than from personal belief. Irene in particular set a telling precedent when she assumed imperial authority in 780, summoned the Seventh Council and later dispensed with her son's rule. Of course, this was not accepted in all quarters. Some western observers refused to believe that Irene could rule as emperor. They used the argument that the imperial position was vacant to promote the superior authority of Charles, king of the Franks. On Christmas Day 800, when he went to pray at the tomb of St Peter, Pope Leo III improvised Charles's coronation and he was acclaimed as 'emperor of the Romans'. The pope knew that Irene was ruling and that the new title would not be acceptable in Byzantium. Charles himself tried to overcome the breach in relations caused by this ceremony by responding favourably to Irene's negotiations for a marriage of convenience, which would have allowed them both to use the imperial title in their respective political spheres. This was the event that provoked the revolt against her. Nonetheless, her example was followed not only by Theodora but also by later empresses. In Byzantium, widowed imperial mothers continued to act as regents for their young sons, as Irene and Theodora had done.

In developing its own cult of icons, Byzantine Christianity broke away from the established interpretation of what was a graven image. All later Byzantine art was based on principles forged at this time. The reliance on icons was celebrated in impressive displays of public art, such as the mosaics in Hagia Sophia of Constantine and Justinian flanking the Virgin, or of Christ over the main entrance, as well as in a domestic setting. Periods of iconoclasm probably strengthened this focus, encouraging women such as the wife of a prison official to preserve their own icons in spite of the official policy of the Church. It is therefore ironic that Irene and Theodora, who reversed Byzantine iconoclasm, did so as much out of their love of power as of their peity. Perhaps inadvertently, they also encouraged artistic traditions which led to the great flowering of icon painting, ivory carving, manuscript illumination, mosaics and frescoes that have become the hallmark of Byzantine art. If the iconoclast emperors saved Byzantium from the Arabs, the iconophile empresses ensured glorious representations of Christian holy people for six hundred years – and much longer outside the empire.

II

A Literate and Articulate Society

> Read military handbooks and histories and the books of the
> Church ... If you pay careful attention you will gather from
> them ... maxims of intelligence, of morality and of strategy;
> for nearly all the Old Testament is stories of strategy. A diligent
> reader will also gather ... many from the New Testament.
>
> Kekaumenos (retired general), *Advice to his Sons*,
> eleventh century

One reason for believing that arguments about the role of icons were
widely known, stubbornly held and passed on through the generations
is that Byzantium was an articulate society in which literacy was
highly appreciated. Village and episcopal schools, priests, monks and
individual teachers provided a means of learning to read. Education
was available beyond basic reading and writing, and in the capital it
extended to the highest levels, which produced well-qualified men for
the civil administration, the army and the Church. And because leading positions in all spheres were open to talent, education was seen as
a means of social mobility, a key to the rewards of high office and
social prominence. In a circular process, the education of younger
members might bring an increase in family fortunes, which benefited
all relations, who in turn invested in the educational facilities and
intellectual activities which consolidated and enhanced the status of
scholars in Byzantium. Byzantine respect and admiration for learning
is a defining feature of the empire's culture.

In contrast to the West, where higher education was restricted to
those destined for a clerical career, in Byzantium any talented male

child could pursue it. While the vernacular speech of the street with its own vocabulary and pronunciation was used for everyday communication, classical Attic Greek dominated higher education, linking the Homeric epics with the language of medieval Byzantium. Byzantine scholars used ancient Greek in their writings and may even have spoken it. In Northern Europe, their western counterparts studied Latin or Greek as foreign languages, very distant from their native Germanic, Anglo-Saxon or the Romance tongues which were slowly evolving into French, Spanish and Italian. Although they studied the classics – Cicero, Virgil and Ovid – with a passion like the Byzantine devotion to Greek, they lacked a comparable continuity. Only the Chinese sustain a longer linguistic history than the Greeks.

The Byzantine educational system was, and always remained, classical, based on the seven liberal arts of antiquity: three literary topics (grammar, rhetoric, logic), followed by four mathematical ones (arithmetic, geometry, harmonics and astronomy). Philosophical argument informed the entire syllabus, although only advanced students studied the texts of Plato and Aristotle. Children began with basic letters and practised writing the alphabet on wax tablets or slates. They then moved on from learning Aesop's Fables to exercises based on the *Art of Grammar* by Dionysios Thrax (a grammarian of the second century BC). They learned poetry by heart, notably the Homeric epics. On average they could memorize and understand thirty lines a day, so progress through the *Iliad* with more than 15,000 must have been slow. After poetry and grammar, the teenage student was ready for rhetoric, the study of orations and how to make persuasive speeches, using short model texts (*progymnasmata*) by Aphthonios of Antioch and later compilations. They read speeches by Demosthenes and Libanios and practised delivering their own for special occasions, such as imperial marriages. All this preceded study of the quadrivium of mathematical sciences and philosophy, which was concentrated in the capital.

This pagan curriculum had great strength. It was followed without much change from the fifth to the fifteenth century. It provided educated Byzantines with a secular basis of knowledge derived from ancient Greek principles, to which Christian teaching and theology were added. As Kekaumenos, a self-taught military man of the eleventh century advised his sons, the Bible is full of useful stories as well as moral precepts. Like most high-ranking officials, he combined an awareness of the importance of secular education with deep respect for Christian beliefs. This was reciprocated among ecclesiastics by attention to the benefits of a good secular education for debating theological problems. Accounts of the Sixth Oecumenical Council, held in 680/81, for example, reveal a sophisticated procedure for checking the authenticity of Christian sources against authorized copies held in the patriarchal library. High levels of literacy and intellectual achievement among the clergy enabled the Byzantine Church to defend its theology effectively.

Byzantium took for granted a developed level of record-keeping that was almost unparalleled in the early Middle Ages – for instance, legal decisions were written out in triplicate so that the imperial chancery and both parties to the judgment would have a copy. In a dispute over land heard in the patriarchal court in 1315, a woman and her sister-in-law produced six documents between them, all relating to the same plot of land, two of which turned out to be forgeries. Diplomatic negotiations were also meticulously recorded, as we learn from Emperor Nikephoros Phokas' threat to produce a copy of an agreement made in 967 if the western embassy of 968 tried to contravene it. Tax registers preserved details of previous generations of landowners as well as the person responsible for paying, and private contracts drawn up by notaries provide similar personal details. The activity of thousands of officials and trained scribes and their filing systems and many generations of educated civil servants sustained the imperial office.

In addition, Byzantium recognized unwritten agreements made by those who were poor or humble, and encouraged a profound oral learning which developed in relationship with written culture and may be characterized as articulacy. It originated in the songs, stories and reminiscences, memorized and passed from generation to generation, as in most medieval societies. Written evidence for this spoken culture is by its nature slim, but on many occasions it is clear that parents and older relations were responsible for teaching their children proverbs derived from ancient Greek drama and poetry, stories about the ancient gods and goddesses, and moral values. Technical skills of construction, farming and midwifery, to name only a few, must have been transmitted from generation to generation within the same family, as fathers trained their sons as blacksmiths and mothers taught their daughters to cook and weave. In the most important field of medicine, the local midwife was literally a wise woman whose skill could save life, while those who looked after epileptics and lepers generally relied on experience maintained in oral forms. So alongside the manuscript tradition of medical knowledge, based on Galen and earlier experts, Byzantine doctors had access to unwritten instruction in the form of articulate methods of caring for the sick.

In parallel with the classical educational system, monasteries from the earliest times provided illiterate men and women who committed themselves to the Christian life with a much simpler form of oral learning: memorizing the Psalms and Gospel stories. Some, however, insisted that their recruits learnt to read, so that they could participate in the liturgy in an informed manner. This elementary Christian education is mentioned in the lives of Byzantine saints, who were often marked out for holiness by the speed and ease with which they committed long passages of scripture to memory. Children in general acquired some Christian education within their families. Many more learned to read than to write, which required years of practice. Saints' *Lives* were written in a simpler Greek, also used for collections of miracles and stories 'beneficial to the soul'. Some girls also acquired sufficient literacy to write wills, donate property and participate in the monastic life, though few attained the brilliance of Kassia, a ninth-century nun who composed hymns, epigrams and poems. Studies of literacy based on later documents suggest that the ability to read, if not to write, was more widespread among women in Byzantium than in medieval Europe.

Inevitably there was tension between the basically pagan content of education and the Christian culture of the empire. A text from the eighth century sheds fascinating light on the problems faced by a group of self-proclaimed local philosophers, who set out to record inscriptions on statue bases in Constantinople and to comment on ancient monuments. Their *Brief Historical Notes* include descriptions of classical statue groups and their powers, references to portraits of emperors, and identifications of buildings, pagan and Christian. The authors' research is directed towards an understanding of the pagan environment of the 'Queen City'. They warn against the malevolent powers of ancient statues, which might fall and kill the investigator, as happened to Himerios during the reign of Philippikos (711–13) in the Kynegion, an ancient arena for wild-beast shows on the acropolis of Byzantion. They provide often ridiculous etymologies for some of the names they can identify and cite unknown authorities in support of their interpretations. Reading ancient Greek inscriptions was nearly as difficult for them as it is for us today. Nonetheless, they provide clear evidence of an interest in the classical past, which is also documented in the intimately linked fields of astronomy and astrology.

Under Constantine V, hence before 775, a copy was made of Ptolemy's *Handy Tables*, the essential tool for calculation of the movement of the sun, moon, planets, and therefore of eclipses. At the end of the century, the Byzantine court employed an astrologist who used the *Tables* to cast horoscopes and to predict events. The same scientific tradition was also highly appreciated in Baghdad, where a Christian monk, Theophilos, served as chief astrologer to al-Mahdi (775–85), and translated many ancient Greek works into Syriac and Arabic. His writings were also well known in Byzantium and probably stimulated greater interest in works of astrology generally considered unsuitable by the Church. The reworking of scientific texts in Byzantium is more striking than the literary culture evident in the *Lives* of several eighth- and ninth-century patriarchs and saints, such as Tarasios (784–806) and Nikephoros (806–15) and St Theodore, abbot of the monastery of Stoudios (died 826), who received instruction in classical poetic metres and writing epigrams in the correct style.

These skills had also been kept alive in Palestinian monasteries under Muslim rule. In the first half of the eighth century, St John of Damascus and his adopted brother Cosmas were exceptionally well trained in the classical curriculum, including the mathematical sciences. Mar Saba, the monastery of St Sabas near Jerusalem, had a rich library to which many scholars and scribes contributed right up to the period of the crusades. In the 790s, however, as Muslim rule became less lenient, many Palestinian monks moved to Constantinople, bringing their learning with them. One of these was George, known as the Synkellos because he had served as *synkellos* (literally, cell-mate, assistant) to the Jerusalem Patriarch, who arrived in the capital with his lengthy *History* covering the first six millennia, from the creation of the world to the reign of Diocletian. The tradition of recording all human existence, using the system of dating from the first year of the world, *anno mundi*, had been preserved beyond the frontiers of the empire and brought a fresh impetus to historical writing within Byzantium. Its influence is clear in the *Chronicle* attributed to Theophanes Confessor, which continued the work of George the Synkellos from *anno mundi* 5777 (AD 284/5) to 6305 (AD 812/13), probably using material collected by him. Patriarch Nikephoros also wrote a shorter narrative *History*, not based on events year by year, which provides interesting comparison with Theophanes' for the period AD 602–769.

The letters written by St Theodore of Stoudios indicate a parallel concern to invigorate a distinct rhetorical form which was to have a great future in Byzantium. While he was careful to protect the anonymity of iconophile supporters, Theodore's letters from exile have a distinct purpose – to sustain opponents of iconoclasm. Through them we can trace the creation of a virtual community of icon-venerators, scattered but linked by their leader's encouragement. Similarly, the letters of a tenth-century schoolmaster contain detailed complaints: at students who failed to attend their classes and whose parents failed to pay. This teacher, who remains anonymous, records his pleasure in buying a copy of Sophocles, and writes to friends asking to borrow an ancient text that he wished to copy. Numerous scholars or their disciples organized the collection of their own letters, perhaps more for their style than content. Features of Byzantine life, such as diet, climate, friendship (particularly marked in the case of writers distant from the capital city), systems of patronage, expressions of sympathy at illness and death, and congratulations on marriage and the birth of children, predominate. Writing a letter usually remained a rhetorical exercise, in which naming names and speaking plainly were avoided. Sometimes correspondents found it hard to understand the point of the communication; often the bearer of the letter was instructed to deliver the real message orally. Yet the survival of so many letter collections in Byzantium reflects a common practice among its intellectuals, both clerical and secular, who excelled at this literary method of communication.

During the ninth century, a technical advance prompted greater literary endeavour: the development of joined-up writing (minuscule), which may have originated in the imperial chancellery. A similar improvement in writing Latin occurred at about the same time, suggesting that scribes in both cultures found writing in capitals both slow and cumbersome. In Byzantium, the change was associated with the transfer of material from papyrus scrolls onto parchment, a more durable medium. In the process, copyists not only used the new, quicker style of writing, but also made editorial changes, establishing chapter headings, inserting punctuation and including marginal notes. A significant proportion of ancient Greek learning was thus saved for posterity, such as Archimedes' *On Floating Bodies*, recently discovered on parchment that had been scraped clean in order to copy a prayer book in the thirteenth century.

The teaching of mathematics and scientific subjects developed as texts of Euclid and Ptolemy were copied from papyrus onto parchment. Two key figures in this process were John the Grammarian, later iconoclast patriarch, and Leo, nicknamed the Mathematician and the Philosopher, who also composed epigrams in the classical style. Under Emperor Theophilos (829–42), John was twice sent on embassies to the Arabs and returned with news of the scientific work undertaken by them. Leo's fame allegedly spread to the Abbasid Caliphate of Baghdad, where one of his students was taken prisoner. On learning from this student that a Byzantine expert could prove the theorems of Euclid, the caliph is said to have requested his services. But Theophilos refused to let Leo go and employed him as a teacher in the capital, where he commissioned copies of many ancient Greek scientific and literary texts. In 863 when Theophilos' brother-in-law Bardas set up new schools of higher education, Leo was appointed 'chief of the philosophers' and with a team of four assistants taught all aspects of the mathematical quadrivium.

Although the story of Leo's student seems mythical, it reflects an intense intellectual development both in Baghdad and in Byzantium. Under the ninth-century Abbasid caliphs, al-Ma'mun, al-Mu'tasim and al-Mutawakkil, court scholars were attached to a 'House of Wisdom' and in the observatories constructed by al-Ma'mum Arabic astronomers improved on the accuracy of Ptolemy's observations.

In this stimulating environment, al-Khwarizmi (*c.* 790–*c.* 850) developed a new field of mathematics – algebra – the first systematic solution of linear and quadratic equations; he also used Indian/Arabic numerals, the concept of zero and the decimal point, and wrote on geography, astronomy and astrology. These advances were stimulated by the translation of ancient scientific works from Greek and Syriac into Arabic. Of the thirteen books of theorems by Diophantos (an Alexandrian mathematician of the third century AD), ten survive in Arabic, six in Greek and three are lost, suggesting that in the early ninth century Muslim scholars translated the most complete version then known. Cultural exchange between Constantinople and Baghdad went in both directions but scientific learning advanced faster and farther in the Islamic world. In later centuries, Arabic texts were translated into Greek, bringing the enhanced inheritance of the ancient world full circle.

In both Muslim and Christian centres, imperial and private patronage was vital to the development of learning. Part of the palace in Constantinople, the Magnaura (so-called from the Latin *magna aula*, great hall), was used for classes where imperial children received instruction. Up to the fifteenth century, emperors and patriarchs continued to promote higher education in Constantinople. Their libraries ensured the copying of manuscripts and storing of orthodox texts, which could be consulted by scholars. In most provincial cities, bishops ran schools to teach boys destined for careers in the state administration, the army or the Church. Hermits and monks provided instruction and monasteries, such as the monastery of St John in the southwest of Constantinople, known as the Stoudios, developed important scriptoria, where monks learned to copy and illuminate manuscripts. The communities on Mount Athos acquired rich repositories of secular as well as Christian texts, often through the legacies of wealthy men who retired from the world taking their books with them. In 1354, when Emperor John VI Kantakouzenos abdicated, he retired to a monastery in Constantinople as the monk Joasaph and wrote his memoirs. The regular recruitment of educated older men naturally boosted the intellectual level of the community.

One high point of intellectual endeavour in early medieval Byzantium is marked by the career of Photios, whose achievements are a symbol of centuries of book culture and scholarly effort. Although he was an exceptional figure, his engagement with ancient culture was subject to the characteristic Byzantine combination of restraint and inspiration. He recorded his own thoughts – on theological, philosophical, literary and art historical topics – in most elegant Greek.

Photios came from an iconophile family persecuted during the second phase of iconoclasm (815–43). Like his uncle Tarasios before him, he had risen through the ranks of the administration to become head of the civil service. And then, also following the pattern of Tarasios' career, in 858 he was appointed to head the Byzantine Church in place of Ignatios, who was deposed. As patriarch, Photios wrote many sermons, letters and a treatise on the procession of the Holy Spirit, which remained fundamental to all later analysis of the subject. His rapid promotion from lay status to the head of the Church, however, caused problems in Byzantium, where his predecessor Ignatios had many supporters. When they appealed to Pope Nicholas I, the quarrel broadened to include the western Church (see chapter 12). Photios' appointment as patriarch (858–67) was ended by the accession of Emperor Basil I, who reinstated Ignatios. On the latter's death, Photios returned to serve a second period (877–86), and was then removed from office by Leo VI, nicknamed the Wise (886–912). During his first period of exile, however, Photios was employed as a tutor for the imperial princes – a sign of his own reputation as a teacher and the importance of the imperial palace as a centre of learning. In this capacity he may have inspired the young Leo, one of Basil's sons, who proved himself a competent writer of sermons as well as a serious promoter of legal reform, economic organization and military tactics. If so, Leo was an ungrateful pupil; one of his first decisions from the throne was to dismiss Photios, who died in unknown circumstances.

Photios' dramatic ecclesiastical career was not unusual. It was balanced by an exceptional and unwavering dedication to intellectual achievement. It is now generally agreed that he wrote the introduction to the *Epanagoge*, a revised law code issued by Basil I, which sets out the ideal relationship between Church and State. It argues that the emperor must remain subject to the laws, even as he makes them, because he is only the representative of God on earth. Photios' letter to the Khan of Bulgaria, which is heavily dependent on the rhetoric of Isocrates on the correct practice of a good ruler, describes the duties of a Christian monarch in a similar fashion. The patriarch urges his spiritual son to become a 'new Constantine', leading the Bulgarian people into the Christian *oikoumene*. In answers to questions raised by his friend Amphilochios of Kyzikos, Photios demonstrates his broad learning on a wide range of issues. But it is above all his *Bibliotheke* (*Library*) that illustrates his brilliance and has identified him as 'the inventor of the book review'. In this he lists the 279 books which he recommends to his brother, Tarasios, accompanied by detailed analysis of their contents and idiosyncratic comments. It contains a mixture of secular and Christian writings, heretical and orthodox, good and bad stylists, which permits Photios to show off his taste in literary culture. While a large number of books discussed in Photios' *Library* are theological, he preserves notes on plays of Aeschylus that are now lost and comments on a more complete encyclopaedia by John of Stobi (Stobaeus) than has survived.

His notes on individual works still make very good reading:

I read Antonius Diogenes, *Wonders beyond Thule*, in twenty-four sections. It is a novel . . . Its contents offer very great pleasure; though the narrative verges on the mythical and incredible it arranges the material in a structure of very plausible fiction.

He then gives an account of the story which has little to do with Thule (the far North) but involves exciting travel among unknown peoples with most unusual customs, marvels and adventures. He concludes:

This book appears to be the source and origin of Lucian's *True Story* . . . In this novel, as in other fictional tales of that type, there are essentially two very useful features: one, that he shows the unjust man always paying the penalty, even if he seems to escape on numerous occasions; secondly, that he portrays many innocent people exposed to great danger and often saved contrary to all expectation.

This can be compared with a later entry:

I read a substantial, indeed enormous, work in fifteen sections and five volumes. It is a collection of testimonies and quotations of whole books, not just Greek but Persian, Thracian, Egyptian, Babylonian, Chaldaean and Roman, by authors highly regarded in each nation. The compiler tries to show that they are in agreement with the pure, supernatural and divine religion of Christians; that they announce and proclaim the supernatural Trinity of one substance . . . The author was not averse to similar exploitation of the writings on alchemy by Zosimos (he was a Theban from Panopolis). Here he expounds the meaning of Hebrew words and discusses where each of the apostles proclaimed the doctrine of salvation and ceased his mortal labours. At the end of the work he offers a personal exhortation, blended from and strengthened by pagan maxims and scriptural quotations. Here in particular one can recognize the man's devotion to virtue and irreproachable piety . . . So far I have not been able to discover the name of the compiler of these volumes . . . But he lived in Constantinople with his wife and children and was active after the reign of Herakleios.

This work is now lost. Photios' account allows us to reflect on how little we know of the seventh century, and how much literature has been destroyed.

In the *Library*, Photios comments on his own reading at his brother's request and promises more notes to come. His efforts to summarize the contents of rare books were followed by later scholars, who compiled compendia of useful information, notably Emperor Constantine VII (see chapter 16). Similarly, the group which gathered around Photios to discuss some of the lesser-known writings available in the ninth century established a pattern. He did not discuss all the texts in regular circulation, which probably explains why the obvious works of Plato and Aristotle do not feature in his *Library*. Meetings where authors read their latest compositions became a common feature of Byzantine intellectual life and continued to stimulate literary debate and commentaries to the end of the empire. The literary salons run by well-educated women like Anna Komnene in the twelfth century, and foreign princesses who wanted to learn about Byzantine culture, such as Mar'ta (Maria) of Alania in the eleventh, involved philosophers, rhetoricians, poets and historians on precisely this model.

While Photios was clearly unusually brilliant, he was also representative of his society and wrote for a readership with similar tastes and capacities. In his letters to Amphilochios, we sense the shared training in classical Greek texts, which had been copied again and again, excerpted and re-ordered in compendia (*florilegia*) of ancient wisdom. The same attention was given to the Bible, studied both by ecclesiastics and lay people as a fount of knowledge. While it is true that Byzantine scholars followed a rather rigid curriculum of study, they included everything they could read in Greek, with discipline and curiosity, and copied ancient texts with care. They preserved for posterity a much larger corpus of classical Greek authors than would otherwise have survived. Photios, however, in his devotion to all aspects of the Greek inheritance, pagan and Christian, classical and medieval, scientific, legal and literary, embodied the aspirations of Byzantium. He moved beyond the boundaries of established culture to compose sermons, treatises and letters of great interest. He encouraged a clearer understanding of the importance of the ancient Greek past for medieval Byzantium, which sustained it through many centuries of political uncertainty.

12

Saints Cyril and Methodios, 'Apostles to the Slavs'

How is it that you now teach and have created letters for the Slavs, which none else have found before? ... We know of only three tongues worthy of praising God in the Scriptures, Hebrew, Greek and Latin.

Life of Constantine, probably by Methodios, ninth century

In the ninth century, two brothers, Methodios and Constantine, who lived in Thessalonike, where their father Leo was a military officer, learned to speak Slavonic. Many Slavs came to the city to trade and bilingualism was a feature of life on the imperial frontiers. But these two young men were exceptionally good at languages. When Patriarch Photios realized this, he encouraged the brothers to invent a way of writing down Slavonic. They devised an alphabet to represent the sounds of the spoken tongue and began to translate the key texts of orthodoxy. Their first attempt produced an alphabet called Glagolitic, which later developed into Church Slavonic; their second is still in use in Russia today. This alphabet is called Cyrillic after Constantine's adoption of the monastic name Cyril before he died in 869. The brothers became known as Saints Cyril and Methodios, 'Apostles to the Slavs'.

The elder brother, Methodios, initially followed a secular career and held an official position in a Slavonic principality of Macedonia, where he must have lived among Slavs. Then he became a monk on Mount Olympos. After the death of Emperor Theophilos in 842, the younger brother, Constantine, was sent to complete his education in Constantinople. His first patron, the eunuch Theoktistos, promoted him as an ordained priest and official of the church of Hagia Sophia. But in addition, he studied Syriac, Hebrew (he translated a Hebrew grammar into Greek) and philosophy. His second patron was Patriarch Photios himself, with whom he shared intellectual interests and a concern with education. Like Photios, he was sent on diplomatic missions to the Muslim court at Samarra and the Khazar centre, north of the Black Sea, where he is supposed to have discovered the relics of St Clement, a shadowy Bishop of Rome in the first century, banished to the Crimea.

According to the *Life* of Constantine, probably written by Methodios, familiarity with the language spoken by the Slavs was common enough in the region of Thessalonike. Numerous tribes had settled there after they crossed the Danube frontier at the end of the sixth century. While some groups captured major fortified cities and on several occasions besieged Thessalonike, without success, others moved south with their families and herds and occupied agricultural land. Their presence throughout the Balkans and as far south as the Peloponnese was hostile enough to cause the flight of much of the indigenous population to mountain castles and islands, according to later reports. From the late eighth century on, imperial campaigns began to reassert control from Constantinople, and in 786 Empress Irene and her son Constantine VI made a royal tour as far as Berroia (Stara Zagora in Bulgaria). Accompanied by dancers and musicians, they marked the pacification of the Slavs and dedicated the church of Hagia Sophia in Thessalonike. Twenty years later, Nikephoros I is reported to have thwarted a combined Slav–Arab uprising in Patras and invited the original population to return to their city. As Arethas, a ninth-century scholar records, his own relatives were among those who came back from Sicily to Patras, where they found the defeated Slavs under the bishop's authority.

Despite the loss of control over large areas of the Balkans and western Greece for many generations, Constantinople eventually restored imperial administration through the new system of 'theme' government. By the tenth century, there were themes in the Peloponnese, Hellas (central Greece), the islands of Kephalonia, Zakynthos, Kerkyra (Corfu), Dyrrachion (modern Durrës in Albania), Thessaly, Thessalonike and Macedonia. After many years of contact with

Byzantium, the Slavs who had originally settled in *Sklaviniai* were now aware of Christianity and the Greek language. Only on Mount Taygetos above Sparta two tribes remained hostile to the civilizing mission of Byzantium, and they were eventually incorporated. Just as Rome latinized and Christianized barbarian invaders in the West, even though it lost control over them, so the strengths of East Rome, its Greek culture, commerce, laws and wealth absorbed numerous intruders.

In 862, however, Emperor Michael III received a request from Moravia (part of ancient Pannonia, modern Slovakia and the Czech Republic) for Byzantine priests. King Rastislav was anxious to counter-balance the influence of Frankish missionaries from Bavaria and to create an independent Moravian Church. Although Patriarch Photios considered the Greek language superior, he encouraged Methodios and Constantine to use the new alphabet to translate the Gospels and the Psalms, as well as the liturgy attributed to St John Chrysostomos, into Slavonic. In 863 he sent the brothers to Moravia where they spent four years setting up a church using both the new vernacular and Greek. This was opposed by the western missionaries, who celebrated the liturgy in Latin. Perhaps at the request of Rastislav, the brothers planned to have some of their disciples ordained as priests to strengthen their church in Moravia, and in 867 they set off for Rome.

When they reached Venice, a famous debate took place over their use of the Slavonic liturgy. On one side were the westerners (bishops, priests and monks from Venice and possibly Francia), who insisted that there were only three sacred languages, Hebrew, Greek and Latin, because they were the languages used on the Cross to record the death of Jesus. On the other side, Constantine defended the newly created vernacular, pointing out that,

we know of numerous peoples who possess writing, and render glory unto God, each in his own tongue. Surely these are obvious: Armenians, Persians, Abkhasians, Iberians, Sogdians, Goths, Avars, Turks, Khazars, Arabs, Egyptians and many others . . . Falls not God's rain upon all equally? And shines not the sun also upon all?

While they attacked him 'like ravens against a falcon', according to the *Life* of the saint, Constantine retorted that they should be ashamed to command all other nations to be blind and deaf, and produced numerous scriptural justifications for allowing all nations to praise the Lord.

An invitation from Pope Nicholas I caught up with them there and they left Venice for Rome, only to find that Nicholas had just died. His successor, Hadrian II, however, welcomed the missionaries. Constantine presented the pope with the relics of St Clement, which he had brought from the Black Sea. The disciples from Moravia were duly ordained and 'they at once sang the liturgy in the Slavonic tongue in the church of the Apostle Peter'. The Slavonic Scriptures were placed in the church of St Maria ad Praesepe, and the liturgy was celebrated several times there and in other churches of Rome. In February 869, when he felt his death approaching, Constantine became a monk with the monastic name Cyril. He was buried in the shrine of San Clemente, where later frescoes commemorate his adventurous life.

Pope Hadrian not only approved of the missionaries' use of the vernacular, he also appointed Methodios as papal legate to the princes of Moravia and Pannonia, instructing him to read the lessons first in Latin and only then in Slavonic. Shortly after his brother's death, he left Rome to take up this position and for over fifteen years he continued their work of translation and conversion, despite increasing Frankish opposition. After the overthrow of Rastislav in 870 by his nephew Svjatopluk, Methodios was imprisoned in Swabia (south Germany) for several years; eventually he and his supporters were driven out of Moravia. Despite the brothers' efforts, the Church in Moravia passed increasingly under Frankish control and remains largely Roman Catholic today.

Elsewhere, however, the Slavonic liturgy had greater success. Before his death in 885, Methodios and his disciples completed translations of the Bible, liturgical services and collections of canon law. The aim of making the Slavs one 'among the great peoples who praise God in their own languages', as recorded in the *Life* of Constantine, was ultimately achieved. Not only the Bulgarians but later the Russians and the Serbs were thus allowed to celebrate using their own tongue. Given the Byzantine insistence on the centrality of Greek in the transmission of all culture, how should we view this triumph of the vernacular? It is a tribute to Patriarch Photios, who had nurtured the outstanding linguistic talent of the two missionary brothers from

Thessalonike. But it can also be seen as a radical break with tradition, another example of Byzantine innovation and creativity, which contrasts with the insistent use of Latin demanded by the western Church.

Photios was a brilliant scholar and diplomat, but when he initiated the process of converting the Bulgars to Byzantine Christianity he provoked Pope Nicholas I into a tremendous battle. Rome was already critical of Photios' rapid promotion through the clerical ranks, and in 861 condemned his appointment to the patriarchate as 'an invasion of the see held by Ignatios'. An exchange of hostile letters began, which led to a debate over Constantinople's claim to powers equivalent to those of Rome in the West, its preservation of correct Christian doctrine, and its authority to convert non-Christians to orthodox traditions, most specifically the Bulgarians.

The importance of Bulgaria lay in its position between the spheres of eastern (Byzantine) and western (Frankish) influence. In 862, when Khan Boris made an alliance with Louis the German, a descendant of Charlemagne whose territory abutted Bulgaria in the West, Michael III sent a military expedition to counter it, and Boris was forced to accept Byzantine terms and Christian baptism. Photios performed the ceremony and the Khan was given the Christian name Michael by the emperor, his godfather. Boris-Michael, however, had failed to win over his own pagan supporters, who opposed the Greek clergy and rose in revolt. Rapidly, the Khan put down the revolt and made an abrupt turn to the West, writing to Louis the German in 866 and to Pope Nicholas. He was trying to work out which of the two leading centres of Christianity would accord his Bulgarian Church the greater degree of independence.

As Boris-Michael played one side off against the other, both New and Old Rome responded to his questions about the true faith. Photios' letter on correct theology as defined by oecumenical councils, and on the duties of a Christian prince, implied the Khan's subordination to Constantinople. In contrast, the pope emphasized Roman control and use of the Latin liturgy in the nascent Bulgarian Church in his *Responsa* (*Answers*). While Nicholas cited the absolute superiority of the Bishop of Rome, based on descent from St Peter, Photios drew on the theory of the pentarchy, the five great patriarchs meeting in council, as the highest authority in Christendom. The pope mentioned papal claims to the diocese of East Illyricum, which had been transferred to Constantinople in the eighth century, and ridiculed some of the customs attributed to Byzantine priests working in Bulgaria. Both parties were trying to ensure that Boris's state adopted Christianity in a particular form, sending rival bands of missionaries to convert his subjects.

This conflict led to the mutual excommunication of Photios and Nicholas in the summer of 867. In September, however, Michael III was murdered by his favourite, Basil, who assumed full power as sole emperor (see below). One of his first actions was to dismiss Photios and restore Ignatios, as noted in chapter 11. A few months later, Nicholas I died in Rome. The removal of these two leading players in the conflict permitted the emperor to summon an oecumenical council (the eighth) to resolve the schism. It was held in the Byzantine capital from October 869 to March 870. Just four days after the closing session, Boris-Michael's envoys arrived to consult the council about the Church of Bulgaria: to which patriarchate should it belong? The question was sprung on the Roman delegates, who protested in vain that the council could not decide. But Basil I had given the Bulgarians an opportunity to settle the matter by a conciliar decision and then insisted in favour of Constantinople.

The efforts of Cyril and Methodios, and Photios, were thus brought to a successful conclusion, although the first was dead and the other two took no part in it. Through a political manoeuvre designed to reduce Roman influence over Bulgaria, Basil I made sure that the empire would secure an orthodox ally on its western border. Despite Pope Hadrian II's refusal to accept the Council's decision on Bulgaria, ten years later the Council of 879/80 confirmed the decision. This council, summoned by Photios after he regained his post as patriarch, claimed to be the eighth. Although it is not recognized in the West, its decree concerning the orientation of the Bulgarian Church could not be undone. Khan Boris-Michael kept his country within the Byzantine 'family of kings' and encouraged the use of the vernacular in secular as well as ecclesiastical education. Although, unusually, no contemporary record of Photios' *Life* survives, he is also recognized as a saint in the Orthodox Church for his efforts to convert the Bulgars.

*

Re-examining Photios' efforts today, we can appreciate that his leading role and pedagogic skills set new standards of excellence and expanded the intellectual range of interests in Byzantium. He emphasized Boris-Michael's need to adopt the Christian attributes of a just ruler, as one of a Byzantine family of kings under the fatherly figure of the *basileus* (emperor) in Constantinople, and strengthened the courtly practice of integrating foreign princes through the award of titles, insignia and official costumes. The spread of orthodoxy to Bulgaria was accompanied by the adaptation of many Byzantine art forms, church architecture, icons and painted tiles, and Khan Boris-Michael built himself grand palaces modelled on that of Constantinople. Adoption of Christianity did not check Bulgarian rivalry with Byzantium, but it did extend the orthodox faith to large areas of the Balkans.

More significantly, it created a model which could be reused in the conversion of other northern peoples. In 860, Russian warriors sailed down the River Dnieper, across the Black Sea and attacked its southern coastline near Sinope. They penetrated into the Bosphoros and threatened the walls of Constantinople. According to Patriarch Photios, who witnessed the attack, their sudden appearance caused great consternation: their red hair, wild clothing and fierce, incomprehensible shouts terrified the Byzantines, who had never seen the 'Rus'. Seven years later, Photios sent off a bishop with the missionary task of finding the ruler (*khagan*) of these Russians based at Gorodishche (later Novgorod, in northern Russia) and converting him to Christianity. Thus, even before the Bulgars had been won to the faith, Photios was looking farther afield and planning an even larger campaign. A few Byzantine coins excavated at Gorodishche confirm some commercial contact with this northern settlement, though nothing more came of the missionary effort. In contrast, when the Christian authorities in Constantinople identified heretical forces, such as the Paulicians, a dualist sect active on the eastern frontier, they tried to defeat them militarily. Basil I campaigned successfully against the Paulicians and transferred some to the Balkans, where they later re-emerged as Bogomils (see chapter 22).

By 911, however, Russian merchants probably from the much nearer centre of Kiev on the Dnieper, had made a trade treaty with

Constantinople and were regular visitors. In 941, a hostile attack on the Queen City had to be beaten off by boats loaded with 'Greek fire'. Eventually, in 944 a new treaty regulated the number of precious silks the Russians could acquire in exchange for their slaves, wax and honey. Through these more intense trading agreements, the Russians became more familiar with Byzantine culture and the Byzantines with the Rus. In the mid-tenth century, Olga, widow of the Rus leader Igor, made a visit to Constantinople with numerous merchants, two interpreters and a Christian priest. She was baptized and took the Christian name Helena, from the empress, Constantine VII's wife, who received her in special ceremonies inside the women's quarter of the palace. This was the start of a momentous development that led up to the conversion of the Rus at the end of the tenth century. I will return to it in chapter 17.

In this long process of winning non-Christian peoples to the Byzantine definitions of the Christian faith, Photios remains a commanding figure. By encouraging Saints Cyril and Methodios to develop written forms of Slavonic, he contributed to a novel solution of using the vernacular to win non-Greek speakers to the faith. In contrast, Pope Nicholas I and the Frankish missionaries insisted on the centrality of Latin in Christian worship, just as all Muslims were (and are still) expected to learn the Qur'an in the original classical Arabic, even if it is not their mother tongue. The West only caught up with Byzantium during the sixteenth-century Reformation, when the Protestants claimed the right to translate the Bible into their own languages; it is often said that Islam has never experienced a similar reformation. Photios understood that the needs of Slavonic peoples could be better met by having Christian teachings in their own tongue. Although he himself used a polished Attic Greek and considered it vastly superior to any other linguistic medium, he inspired the 'Apostles to the Slavs' to pursue their invention of a written alphabet for Slavonic, and then their translation of the Bible, Christian liturgy and law books. They gave the Bulgars, Serbs and Russians ways of worshipping in their own languages, which created their own orthodox traditions. In turn, for centuries after 1453, their religion formed a central component of the Russian claim on the imperial traditions of Byzantium.

III

Byzantium Becomes a Medieval State

13

Greek Fire

The Greeks began to fling their fire all around; and the Rusii seeing the flames threw themselves in haste from their ships, preferring to be drowned in the water rather than burned alive in the fire.

Liutprand of Cremona, *Antapodosis* (*Tit for Tat*), on the Russian attack on Constantinople in 941

Greek fire remains a mystery. It was probably made from crude oil acquired from naphtha wells in the Crimea, mixed with resin, but the precise proportions and the hydraulic mechanism for projecting it are still rather unclear. Some combination of substances nonetheless created the most important weapon in the Byzantine military arsenal, which could be forced onto enemy ships, causing terror and destruction. I have already mentioned its effects during sieges of Constantinople. In the famous illustrated *Chronicle* by John Skylitzes, which continues a historical narrative from 813, when Theophanes ends, down to 1077, the mechanics of Greek fire are vividly depicted. A small sailboat guided by rowers advances towards an enemy ship; the heated liquid is forced through a long tube; it burns on the water between the two vessels and engulfs the enemy ship (plate 25). Although scholars do not agree about the origin of the drawings, the place where the manuscript was copied or the groups of artists involved, the 524 illustrations are fascinating and apparently realistic. Known as the Madrid Skylitzes, from the library where it is now kept, it preserves a unique breadth of mainly secular images: emperors receiving or sending embassies, making triumphal entries into

Constantinople, battle scenes and sieges of cities, as well as portraits of individuals.

Greek fire was allegedly invented by a certain Kallinikos, who arrived in Constantinople just before the long Arab siege of the capital (674–8) and displayed his secret to great effect. It became one of the enhanced technical weapons used in both naval engagements and land attacks on cities, when liquid flame was thrown onto the battlements. Even unmanned fireboats could be launched, using the prevailing wind, as happened in 1204 during the siege of the capital. In 2006, John Haldon published an account of his attempt to re-create both the substance and its projection. Graphic photographs show the heated liquid emerging from a narrow tube and burning 'with a loud roaring noise and a thick cloud of black smoke'. Using a reconstructed siphon and oil from the Crimea, the flame was projected 10–15 metres and was so intense that in a few seconds it completely burned a target boat. Thanks to his modern experiment, we can begin to appreciate the horror and confusion of Greek fire in medieval warfare.

Because of its capacity to strike fear into the enemy, in the tenth century Constantine VII listed it as a Byzantine state secret that was never to be revealed to outsiders. This conceit was somewhat misplaced, since the Arabs quickly developed their own version of it. Nonetheless, in advice to his son Romanos II, he reports that foreigners often ask Constantinople for three things: Greek fire, imperial regalia and imperial brides 'born in the purple'. On no account were these to be granted, except in the case of marrying an imperial princess to a Frank. In fact, on numerous occasions imperial regalia were bestowed on foreigners in order to secure advantageous alliances, and marriages were arranged as part of foreign policy, but the secret of Greek fire was not shared.

The three requests, however, reflect Byzantium's unique position during the Middle Ages: the empire had prestigious status symbols, traditions and military secrets that were coveted by many. The widespread imitation of Byzantine regalia, titles, imperial costume, jewelled crowns, orb and sceptre, in western and central Europe, confirms their defining standing. When kings and princes tried to elevate their status to a truly imperial one, they wanted to be acclaimed in the Byzantine style, to sit on a Byzantine throne, crowned and holding

Byzantine symbols of power. In these respects, imitation is indeed the highest form of flattery. It could be indirect as well. In Norman Sicily, during the eleventh and twelfth centuries, King Roger II, who may have commissioned the Madrid Skylitzes, constructed the exquisite mosaics of the Palace Chapel in Palermo in the Byzantine manner. These were in turn copied by Ludwig of Bavaria for his fairy-tale castle at Neuschwannstein in the 1880s.

As the empire re-established control over its frontier regions during the ninth and tenth centuries, long coastlines had to be defended from naval attack, particularly after the Arab capture of Crete (*c.* 820). Boat builders, sea captains and sailors with maritime skills were recruited from all sea-faring communities to form special naval units. Islands such as Euboia, attached to the theme of Hellas, had to provide sailors, ships and naval equipment (such as ropes, sails and anchors) for maritime warfare. The imperial fleet protected Constantinople and led the major naval campaigns of reconquest. New contingents of professional, full-time troops (*tagmata*) were recruited to protect Constantinople; they were garrisoned in or near the capital and provided a bodyguard for the imperial family in the Great Palace. In contrast to the theme troops, who were called up in the spring and campaigned under their generals (*strategoi*) until the autumn, these units received a salary for permanent service and formed the army's core. Using this reorganized and energized military administration, Byzantine generals initiated campaigns that aimed not only to reconquer previous imperial territory but also to annex more distant regions.

Byzantium gradually became a stable and efficient medieval state, assisted by the upward mobility of relatively unknown men, through military or other careers. The success of Basil I (867–86) was based on his skills as a horse tamer and boxer, learnt in Macedonia where his Armenian family had been settled as peasant farmers to guard the northwestern frontier. Finding no great opportunities there, Basil made his way to the capital, where his ability to tame horses attracted the attention of wealthy patrons. From private employment he gained promotion to the imperial stables, where Michael III selected him as guardian of the imperial bedroom (*parakoimomenos*), a post normally reserved to eunuchs. Basil did everything to please Michael and ruthlessly removed anyone opposed to him. His ambition culminated in a ceremony described by Patriarch Photios: in 866 a double throne was set up in the gallery of Hagia Sophia and Michael crowned Basil as his colleague and co-emperor. Their joint rule was short. Just over a year later, Michael III was murdered, by Basil himself according to one account, and the Armenian peasant became sole ruler over Byzantium.

Despite his lack of education, Basil proved an able military commander and continued the empire's campaigns against the Arabs both in southern Italy and in the east. A generation after his death in 886, Romanos Lekapenos (920–44) used his position as commander of the navy in his successful bid for power. From a relatively humble Armenian background, he had risen through the naval ranks to lead a coup d'état in 921. He married his daughter Helena to the boy emperor Constantine VII, and as emperor organized the defence of the capital against the Russian attack of 941, instructing his navy to set up 'devices which shoot out fire ... in the prow and also in the stern and on both sides of each ship'. Taken by surprise, the Russians called Greek fire 'lightning from heaven'.

In addition to the promotion of talented men even from poor backgrounds, the Byzantine military developed its medieval power in the tenth century. After numerous attempts to regain Crete, Nikephoros Phokas finally drove the Arabs off the island in 961, and four years later Cyprus was brought back under imperial control. Byzantine expansion into Armenia created a province of Taron in 966/7, and encouraged numerous Armenian families to migrate into the empire. John I Tzimiskes continued this eastern reconquest, with the recovery of Antioch in 969, which remained under Byzantine rule until 1084, and he exercised brief control over Damascus and Beirut in 975. His aim of regaining Jerusalem was never achieved, though it reflects a constant Byzantine desire to restore Christian rule over the Holy Places.

As the Byzantines developed more effective ways of defending the empire, military handbooks of strategy began to change, although they continued to quote from earlier sources. The *Taktika*, attributed to Leo VI (886–912), emphasized how to combat the fighting tactics of the Arabs, who had developed a particular form of punitive raiding: against this activity the emperor recommended avoiding direct contact with the enemy, but shadowing and harassing the departing troops, who might be laden with booty or plunder of cattle and prisoners. In his later handbook, Nikephoros Phokas, another brilliant general who rose to become emperor (963–9), expanded this type of guerrilla warfare, which proved highly effective. Often it was followed by the exchange of prisoners that took place at frontier rivers and involved no hostilities. In this way peaceful formalities were also introduced into Arab–Byzantine relations across the eastern border regions.

As a result of the expansion of Byzantine authority in the east, a novel way of life developed among both Christians and Muslims living in frontier zones. Where previously these borderlands had been largely emptied of populations, who sought refuge in the castles that guarded the mountain passes, they now became settled. On both sides of the nominal frontier, Byzantines and Arabs extended cultivation in the fertile areas and built themselves villas. In the verse epic of Digenes Akrites, the mixed-race frontiersman, marriage alliances were added to raiding parties; the hero's father was an emir from the Arab side who carried off a Byzantine bride and later converted to Christianity. His story forms the first part of this long romance, which survives in several versions, all written down later, but seems to reflect conditions of the ninth–tenth centuries. The second part is devoted to the hero, Digenes Akrites, half-Arab, half-Byzantine, whose baptismal name was Basil. He in turn persuaded the daughter of a distinguished general to ride off with him and marry him. Although she was kept locked up in a tower, after he had serenaded her from below the young lady took the initiative, sending her nurse to give him her ring as a token of her affection. Their wedding follows and then the hero's exploits, with stories that owe much to folk tradition, such as Basil killing lions with his bare hands. The background of Christian–Muslim inter-marriage, of grand palaces and gardens on the banks of the upper Euphrates, where Byzantine control facilitated a sumptuous lifestyle, is brilliantly captured: 'In this marvellous and delightful pleasure garden, the noble Frontiersman [Basil] built a delightful house, of good size, four-square, of hewn stones', which he decorated with precious marbles, mosaic ceilings and onyx pavements. He depicted the military triumphs of Samson, David and Goliath, and Achilles, as well as the stories of Penelope and Odysseus, Bellerophon, Alexander, Moses and the Exodus of the Jews. In the church dedicated to

Theodore, the military saint, Basil buried his father and mother and constructed his own tomb.

Such activity is confirmed from Arabic sources which record knowledge of Arabic among Byzantine Christians in frontier regions and considerable movement across them. Verses inscribed on a tomb in a place near Melitene (Malatya in Turkey) were explained by the deep friendship between a local man, possibly a doctor, and an Iraqi who settled in the region. After the death of this foreigner, his Christian friend buried him oriented in the Islamic prayer direction (towards Mecca) and carved on his grave the Arabic verses he had written:

> I went on long journeys,
> travelling hither and thither in search of wealth,
> and the misfortunes of time overtook me,
> as you can see.
> I wish I knew whether my friends cried
> when they lost me
> or whether they even knew.

In around 1100, the Duke of Melitene commissioned a translation of the Persian tale of Syntipas the Philosopher, which reflected the same close contacts. The Greek version was made from a Syriac reworking of the popular story of the adventures of Sindbad, a young prince unjustly accused of sexual misdemeanours. Through this slow process of acculturation of bordering peoples – Arab, Armenian, Georgian in the east, Bulgarian, Slav and Serbian in the west – Byzantium consolidated its multi-ethnic and polyglot population.

In addition to the secret weapon of Greek fire, another feature that assisted in the recovery of Byzantium after its losses to the Arabs was the concept of an imperial dynasty. Despite his obscure origins, Basil I's family sustained control over Byzantium for nearly two centuries, from 867 to 1056. In the tenth-century, Constantine VII commissioned a biography of Basil (his grandfather), which invented a noble Armenian origin for the family and traced the portents which led to Basil 'saving' the empire from a drunken and dissolute ruler, Michael III, rather than gaining power in treacherous circumstances. By blackening the character of Basil's patron and colleague, Constantine made sure that his grandfather was given a highly original and invented role, as more legitimate and worthy of the imperial title than Michael. By such means the Macedonian dynasty, as it became known, contributed to a deeper sense of order, *taxis*, and strengthened the imperial office through a proper and controlled line of succession from father to son. Of course, rivals emerged whenever the empire seemed to lack strong leadership (for instance, during the early years of Basil II's personal rule, 976–1025), but the dynasty maintained power. It reaffirmed the principle that the empire should be ruled by one family, whose members were legitimated by precedent and blood. In some cases this gave women of the imperial dynasty a major role, as happened in the eleventh century when the sisters Zoe and Theodora represented its last generation (see chapter 17).

This resurgence was underpinned by an economic recovery, which I look at in the next chapter. But the military victories of the centuries after the Triumph of Orthodoxy in 843 constitute a major achievement, and within the sphere of warfare the secret Byzantine weapon of Greek fire played a vital role. Its technical problems are emphasized by an account of how some Bulgarians captured a supply of the substance and the tubes used to project it. Even with both, they could not work out how to use it. Although Haldon's modern experiment to re-create Greek fire has resolved many of its mysteries, back in the Middle Ages its secret remained intact and the Byzantine version of it died with the empire.

14

The Byzantine Economy

> On 8 May 795 he [Constantine VI] engaged an Arab raiding
> party ... he defeated them and then went to Ephesos, and
> after praying in the church of the Evangelist, remitted the cus-
> toms dues of the fair (which amounted to 100lbs of gold) in
> order to win the favour of the holy apostle, the Evangelist John.
>
> *Chronicle of Theophanes Confessor*, early ninth century

In this short notice, the chronicler Theophanes recorded Constantine
VI's victory over the Arabs and his thanksgiving at Ephesos. There, the
massive basilica of the Evangelist, founded by Justinian and Theodora,
surmounted the hill that had overlooked the ancient temple of
Artemis. This famous wonder of the ancient world was largely demolished so that its stones could be deployed to fortify the hill and
construct the church. As the feast of St John was celebrated on 8 May,
the emperor's detour to Ephesos was clearly related to the celebration.
In medieval times it was common for the anniversary of a saint's death
to be celebrated by a holiday fair which attracted merchants, often
from long distances. Despite the apparent incongruity between commercial activity and religious festival, fairs had become closely linked
to churches, especially those with important relics that attracted pilgrims. It is clear from the sizeable sum donated to the Evangelist that
St John's at Ephesos was a major commercial event in western Asia
Minor.

Byzantium inherited from Rome a contempt for trade as an activity
not worthy of free men, and commercial exchange rarely attracts
the attention of Byzantine chroniclers. So the mention of this fair is

exceptional and offers a glimpse into the volume and importance of the *kommerkion*, a tax of 10% of the value of goods sold, which could generate 100lbs of gold in customs dues. If the turnover of the fair indeed amounted to 1,000lbs of gold, it can be compared to the pay chest of 1,100lbs of gold for an army on campaign in Strymon (northern Greece), or 1,300lbs for the annual pay of the Armeniakon theme (*thema*) in the early ninth century. Commerical agents known as *kommerkiarioi* collected the customs paid on all commercial trans-actions throughout the empire. Through the seals of these imperial officials we can trace the state's determination to tax economic ex-change, both at fairs and at key points on the frontiers of the empire where import and export of goods took place. Such seals, which survive in thousands, name the individual *kommerkiarios*, who was appointed to a particular area for a particular year in the reign of a particular emperor (plate 8). His duty was to levy the 10% tax on all goods which passed through his customs post, and he would attach his lead seal to the sacks to indicate that duty had been paid.

This type of taxation seems to have originated in attempts to control the export of valuable goods such as silks. It also enables us to trace commercial agents active in frontier posts and later throughout the empire. At the approaches to Constantinople, the *kommerkiarioi* ran the main customs stations at Abydos and Hieron, which controlled the southern and northern ends of the Straits (between the Dardanelles and the Black Sea). In this way, they also policed shipping up and down the Bosphoros and the provisioning of the capital. After the conquest of Egypt by the Persians in 619, which put an end to the grain imports established by Constantine I, alternative supplies were sought in Thrace and parts of western Asia Minor. Local merchants must have taken on these roles and together with the *kommerkiarioi* played a critical role in ensuring food supplies for the capital. Officials probably competed to gain the position of customs officer, because it carried the possibility of trading in a personal capacity beyond the official job of collecting the 10% duty. There were opportunities for making profits in all fields of commerce in Byzantium.

Constantinople dominated the naval and land trade routes between north and south, west and east, and maintained control over lucrative markets frequented by many foreign merchants. In the seventh century, the wealth of the city attracted merchants from all parts of the eastern Mediterranean and even from Gaul. A collection of regulations governing naval contracts, known as the Rhodian Sea Law, was put together in the seventh or eighth century and ensured that local merchants received fixed compensation for damage or loss from shipowners who agreed to transport their goods by sea. In 809/10, the leading shipowners of Constantinople were so wealthy that Emperor Nikephoros I could force them each to take a loan of 12lbs of gold at the exceptionally high interest rate of 16.67%. The normal rate for usury was later fixed at between 4.17 and 6%. So despite few references to commercial activity, Byzantine merchants, shippers and tradesmen generated profits and wealth in the capital city. Much of it related to the management of supplies to feed its inhabitants.

Yet revenue from trade formed only a small proportion of the overall budget of the Byzantine state, which derived a much larger income from the taxes on land and persons. This was partly due to the reliability of land tax, which formed a steady source of revenue, and partly due to the traditional investment in land by the social elite. The senatorial classes did not involve themselves in trade. They believed, with a traditional snobbery, that higher social rank, marked by the ownership of landed estates and court position, set them apart. Those who engaged in commerce, even international trade, were despised as common and dirtied by the activity. In the ninth century, Emperor Theophilos (829–42) is reported to have had an entire ship's cargo burned when he discovered that his wife, Theodora, had some association with the vessel. Yet wealthy citizens in Thessalonike took a major role in the grain supply of the second city of the empire, and rich individuals, who supported the iconophiles exiled to islands in the Sea of Marmara, could charter and load a ship to take provisions to them. So some, usually unnamed individuals, used established patterns of commercial exchange when necessary. Nonetheless, in general the traditional attitude of the upper echelons of Byzantine society created a paradox: they scorned the very activity on which the city depended.

The Byzantine approach to trade remained very traditional: no products essential to the state were to be exported. Greek fire, supplies of gold, salt, and iron for making weapons or wood for shipbuilding

– in short, anything that might aid the enemy – should never leave the empire. The list of prohibited goods included all silks dyed with real purple (made from murex), which were reserved to members of the imperial family, though on occasion these silks might be sent abroad as diplomatic gifts. From the *Book of the Eparch*, attributed to Emperor Leo VI (886–912), which regulated the guilds of craftsmen and merchants in Constantinople, we can sense a determination to control all production, not only of valuable silks or objects made of precious metals, but of candles, soap, fish and even notarial records. Although similar guilds with regulations do not seem to have developed in other major centres, there can be no doubt that Byzantium wished to set profit margins and interest rates throughout the empire.

Nonetheless, fairs such as the one held annually at Ephesos reflect trade which sustained cities, villages and fortified castles, even during periods when coins did not circulate widely outside the capital. Through all the centuries of Byzantium, emperors issued coinage in gold, silver and copper, with their own images identified in writing. From the first gold solidus minted by Constantine I in 312 to the final issues of Basil II in the 1020s, a gold standard was maintained unchanged – an extraordinary achievement (plate 22). Gold coinage circulated through the empire via the pay of state officials and soldiers inscribed on the military catalogues (see chapter 8). In addition to its propaganda value, one of the main functions of the coinage was to facilitate the collection of taxes. The most significant form of taxation was that levied on persons and land; the central government insisted that it had to be paid in gold coins. In this way, the gold paid out to administrators and soldiers returned to the centre in the form of taxes.

The administration of detailed fiscal mechanisms reflects a traditional Byzantine assumption about the economy: that taxing the land and its population was the most efficient way of financing government expenditure on military needs, maintaining the imperial court, provisioning the capital and other urban centres, and producing the highly sought-after luxury goods, such as silk, metalwork, enamels and icons. Land was also used to support military families, who provided a fully equipped member of the theme army (or the equivalent cash payment) in return for reduced tax on their property. Although modern attempts to calculate the imperial budget seem bound to fail, because only fragmentary figures survive, the system does appear to have worked well enough. Under rulers like Justinian, expenditure on churches, fortifications and other constructions may have outstripped the proceeds from direct taxes on land and persons and indirect taxation on commerce. But this was offset by the booty from successful military campaigns and added taxation from the reconquered areas brought back into the tax orbit of the central government. Emperors were always committed to expanding the empire, regaining lost provinces and bringing new regions under their control, in order to realize the possibility of increasing these forms of income. To some extent the calculation was borne out by the tenth-century conquests and eleventh-century pacification of Bulgaria (see chapter 20). Conversely, any reduction in territory under imperial control meant an immediate drop in tax revenues. This explains in part the steady impoverishment of the empire after 1261.

During the turbulent period of seventh-century Muslim conquests, loss of territory and hostile invasions generated many refugees. As people fled to more secure regions, they broke the old Roman link between the farmer and the land he cultivated. In these circumstances, the central administration lost track of its tax base beyond the core area that remained imperial, and it took many years to reassert the capacity to extract direct taxation. From the late seventh century onwards, as imperial administration was extended to inland areas of the Balkans and eastern Asia Minor in new themes (*themata*), officials from Constantinople were sent to compile new records in order to extract these taxes. To the census of population (poll and hearth tax), they added an evaluation of the productivity of the land (if it was rocky and could support little agriculture it was taxed at a lower level than arable or pasture), and a record of what draught animals and farmyard animals such as pigs and goats the peasant household possessed. Olive groves, vineyards and mulberry plantations (to support the silk industry) represented essential products for taxation. Exemptions were offered to certain products, such as the murex shellfish used in making purple dye. The complexity of this recording process is evident from various financial treatises, which record how to assess land and property, and from later monastic documents with long lists of exemptions from taxes.

Emperors never failed to mint coins. This helps us to estimate the reality of Byzantine trade. Yet very few coins minted between 668 and 820 have been found at excavated sites in the provinces, such as Corinth, Ephesos, Sardis, Aphrodisias or Pergamon. Cécile Morrisson has recently summarized this evidence in a series of graphs, which all show the same tremendous drop in finds of coins struck during that 150-year period. It can hardly be coincidental that this is the epoch of the iconoclast disputes. At Athens, for example, after many decades of archaeological digging, hardly any gold coins of this period had been unearthed, so the discovery of a *nomisma* of Justinian II (685–95, 705–11) is particularly notable. This unique find, unearthed during excavations for the new Athens metro, may be linked to the creation of the theme of Hellas by the same emperor.

Some modern historians have interpreted the gap in coin finds to mean that Byzantium was reduced to a barter economy and taxes were paid in kind. If so, this cannot have lasted to the end of the eighth century, when officials from the central administration could tax the fair at Ephesos to produce a large sum in gold coin. A fully monetized economy seems to be clear from the measures taken by Emperor Nikephoros I (802–11), who counted on raising a substantial sum in gold from the taxes of Thrace. He was condemned for increasing taxes, sometimes by 50%, for imposing the hearth tax on previously exempted charitable foundations, and charging a new tax of two gold coins on every household slave imported from the Dodecanese, among other financial 'vexations'.

Nonetheless, very few coins minted by emperors from Constantine IV to Michael II (668–829) appear to have been in use outside the capital and the western provinces of Sicily, southern Italy and North Africa, which had their own mints. This is a problem that continues to puzzle historians. Possibly the gap is noticeable at the sites chosen for excavation by classical archaeologists, more interested in ancient than medieval finds. These cities suffered a particular decline in the period of invasions and the divisions caused by iconoclasm. They were transformed into fortified settlements (such as the Acropolis of Athens or Acrocorinth, the castle above Corinth) or temporarily abandoned. Perhaps when archaeologists start digging at castles and fortified sites on the eastern borders of the empire, more coins will be excavated. Or perhaps fewer coins were minted and they circulated only in the immediate area of the capital. The gap seems to mark the low point in Byzantine economic power, corresponding to the turbulence of the seventh-century invasions and demographic decline (see chapters 8 and 2), after which recovery can be observed in all fields.

Throughout the history of Byzantium, as in Rome, the imperial office was sustained by produce from its own extensive properties and estates in different parts of the empire. As by far the largest landowner, it controlled substantial resources, including major stud farms for the breeding of animals, as well as forests, mulberry plantations, vineyards and olive groves, administered directly by agents. Emperors often rewarded successful generals, administrators and churchmen with grants of land, which may have formed the core of large estates later controlled by wealthy and powerful families. Rulers also donated land to monasteries and granted them tax exemptions, despite the economic wealth which they accumulated. Gifts to individuals, however, could as easily be taken back. All rulers regularly confiscated the wealth and landed property of political opponents, who were exiled. Nikephoros I, for example, was responsible for transferring into imperial possession estates previously belonging to charitable foundations. He thus brought greater wealth to the imperial office, while impoverishing 'pious houses'.

From the earliest surviving financial documents, it appears that all villages were expected to pay a lump sum to the tax collectors when they arrived on their annual visit after the autumn harvest. While each household and landowner was taxed individually, the entire community provided the total sum due in gold and fractions of gold coins (half and third *nomisma*). In this process, the village elders had responsibility for making sure that any deficit would be made up. If a woman lost her husband and sons, for instance, and was unable to cultivate the family plots of land, her neighbours would be encouraged to do the work, share the harvest and make it possible for her to pay her taxes. Tax officials might also grant her some tax reduction or even exemption. Eventually, the neighbours might take over possession of the land. In contrast, there are many widows who appear in tax records as heads of household; indeed, in the register of Thebes, one male taxpayer is identified only as the son-in-law of a certain woman called Sophronia. She seems to have had responsibility for a multi-generational family with considerable land holdings.

While these records provide some evidence of family size over several generations, estimating the rural population and its growth is extremely difficult. Indirect indices, such as church building and the expansion in bishoprics, suggest that from the mid-ninth century onwards demographic expansion and an increase in surplus funds resulted in investment in fine stone buildings. The impressive church at Skripou, for instance, records the contribution made by a local general for the building, erected in 873/4. Almost at the same time, a church dedicated to St John in Athens bears the name of its founder, Constantine, his wife Anastaso and son John, otherwise unknown. Similarly, in Cappadocia, residences and churches were dug out of the volcanic tufa (plate 12). Not much is known of the people who lived in these cave dwellings and excavated the churches, yet the wall paintings reflect a wealthy and discriminating local society, who commemorated John I Tzimiskes (969–76) in fresco. After many centuries of Arab raiding and warfare, central Asia Minor was experiencing economic growth and an increase in wealth.

Within Byzantine rural communities of the ninth and tenth centuries, sales of land were regulated to maintain the fiscal unity of the village. Inequalities within the village meant that wealthier members gradually became dominant and acquired property outside the community. Outsiders were not permitted to buy village land but the existence of private landed estates, granted to individuals by imperial largesse, formed a novel force in the rural environment. The establishment of these big landowners threatened to destroy the social structure of the countryside through the buying up property in village communities. By acquiring plots of village land, the powerful (*dynatoi*) increased their own resources and made inroads into the peasant community. The impoverished peasants who had previously owned the plots generally passed into the control of the new landlord and thus became tied to the land in the manner of medieval serfs.

From the reign of Romanos I Lekapenos onwards (920–44), emperors tried to restrict the powers of these individuals by protecting the rights of villagers and forbidding the foundation of new monasteries while older ones fell into ruin. This double effort to sustain traditional arrangements probably had an economic origin: it was designed to preserve the tax base of the empire. It aimed to protect free villagers, who paid their taxes, rather than permit their land to pass into the hands of powerful landowners, who could often resist tax officials or claim exemption from tax. Tenth-century emperors issued a series of laws designed to support the collective village identity and hold their powerful neighbours in check. But the fact that Basil II felt obliged to repeat the law in 996, in order to close a loophole by which the poor had been legally deprived of their land after forty years, suggests that the powerful could not be restrained. Nonetheless, the growth of larger landed estates also encouraged the cultivation of previously fallow land, and investment in improved technology, such as water-mills, and in crops such as olives that take years to mature. Confidence in long-term agriculture is usually a sign of economic expansion. It also coincided with the aims of the Byzantine elite to expand their ownership of land, farms and manpower.

But the laws failed to prevent individuals devoting their wealth to building new churches and their own monasteries, even when others were falling into ruin. When Basil I became emperor in 867 he found a large number of ecclesiastical foundations in the capital in serious need of repair. Yet shortly afterwards a retired admiral, Constantine Lips, founded his own monastery in Constantinople, and the church which survives displays elegant tile and sculpted decoration. Some officials built themselves such tall, grand villas in Constantinople that the city eparch published regulations to prevent them from taking all the light from smaller buildings.

Rather than invest in economic activity, the Byzantine elite preferred to buy land and invested in administrative positions, from which they made extra money on the side. They also purchased honorific court titles, which carried a state pension. Nicolas Oikonomides calculated that the return on this type of investment, around 2.5–3% per annum, was much lower than the 6% official rate of interest, although it could rise to 8.3% on the highest titles such as *protospatharios* (literally, first sword-bearer). But since these titles were not inheritable and the original sum invested in the purchase was never repaid, honour and status appear to have been the motivation. Use of a grand title and the appropriate costume to be worn at court appearances was more significant than any economic benefit. A bearded *protospatharios*, for example, wore a gold collar with precious stones and a red cloak edged in gold; a non-bearded (eunuch) *protospatharios* wore white garments and a white cloak with gold decoration. Despite the traditional disdain for people who made money from trade, emperors would admit them to the elite circle of titleholders – at a price.

This mechanism also served to draw all high-ranking officials, civilian and military, as well as foreigners, into the court at the heart of the capital. The process integrated them more closely into the imperial system of government and had the additional benefit of strengthening the hierarchy of the court and the central bureaucracy. In 950, Liutprand of Cremona, an Italian envoy to the court of Constantinople, witnessed the annual payment of court officials, and his description confirms the importance of state employment in Byzantium. The event began on Palm Sunday and lasted three days:

A table was brought in ... which had parcels of money tied up in bags, according to each man's due, the amount being written on the outside of the bag ... the first to be summoned was the marshal of the palace, who carried off his money, not in his hands but on his shoulders, together with four cloaks of honour. After him came the commander in chief of the army and the lord high admiral of the fleet ...

After they had laboriously removed their bags of gold, the distribution continued down the order of patricians and the minor dignitaries. When Constantine VII (945–59) enquired whether he enjoyed the ceremony, Liutprand cleverly compared himself to Dives in hell, tormented by the sight of Lazarus at rest (a reference to the parable of the rich and poor man), and the emperor sent him a pound of gold and a large cloak.

The Queen of Cities – the ruling city of Constantine – attracted numerous foreigners who came to buy and sell in its markets, which stimulated the empire's medieval commercial revival. Its golden and silken products attracted more merchants, its schools attracted more students, its churches, relics and icons attracted more pilgrims, its imperial administration generated more jobs, and its mixed society created more opportunities than any other in the Mediterranean. In the Islamic world there were larger cities, like Baghdad, and bigger markets. But Constantinople had no Christian rivals. For the Syrian, Russian and Venetian merchants who often stayed for months in Constantinople, it remained the secure hub around which economic growth revolved. Each group was quartered in a particular district, where they worshipped in their own monuments: Arab traders in their mosques, Jewish traders in their own synagogues and western merchants in their own churches. They were all subject to the supervision of the city eparch, who also maintained law and order.

In 992, Basil II granted the Venetians a reduction in the basic tax on ships entering the Dardanelles, from 30 to 17 gold solidi each, thus giving them more favourable terms than local traders or other foreigners. The reason for this advantage was that Venice would also assist the empire militarily against its enemies by transporting Byzantine troops across the Adriatic to campaign in southern Italy. While this privileged access to the capital has often been interpreted as a blow to local merchants, who were still obliged to pay the full tax, it may have been considered a method of ensuring that western merchants continued to use Constantinople as their major market. What emperors granted could also be rescinded, and in the twelfth-century Venetian privileges were withdrawn on political grounds. Although Byzantine merchants were less able to compete in the international transport of goods, they appear to have fallen back on a less profitable carrying trade from port to port around the Aegean. And some became wealthy enough to purchase offices and titles, which strengthened the centralized focus on the court and the established sense of order and hierarchy.

Venice developed a different attitude towards commerce as a source of power and prosperity. For the small city-state, trade was a necessity imposed by the circumstances of its foundation as a refugee colony. Its citizens were obliged to trade by sea in order to survive, and made the construction of boats for fishing and commercial exchange a central feature of their lives. The Senate of Venice protected its mercantile navy with armed vessels so that trade in slaves, salt and wood to all parts of the Muslim world as well as Byzantium could flourish. In contrast, imperial insistence on service and investment in land as the sure way to make a fortune distracted the Byzantines from commercial activity. Merchants were hampered by restrictions and controls, which limited their initiatives. The empire neglected local fishing fleets and forced them to provide captains, sailors and equipment for military expeditions. In the late twelfth century, even the monks of Mount Athos were restricted in the capacity of boats used to transport grain from their estates to Constantinople.

Imperial attitudes to trade prevented the development of more flexible economic institutions and failed to respond to initiatives developed by Italian and Muslim merchants. Yet for centuries, Byzantium managed to retain its economic position in the medieval world through the issue of reliable gold currency and the presence at its heart of dynamic markets. Even after the devaluation of the eleventh century, a stable gold coinage was re-established and Byzantium maintained its traditional luxury industries, generating great wealth which deeply impressed western crusading knights. Few foreign coins minted before 1204 have been excavated in Constantinople, reflecting the high prestige and sufficiency of the Byzantine gold solidus – the symbol of an imperial, rather than a commercial, economy.

15

Eunuchs

His face was that of a rose, the skin of his body white as snow,
he was well-shaped, fair-haired, possessing an unusual softness
and smelling of musk from afar.

Life of St Andrew the Fool, probably tenth century

The use of eunuchs to guard and serve grand rulers goes back to ancient Egypt and China. In common with the great medieval empire of Japan and the Muslim Caliphate, Byzantium also employed eunuchs, whose high-pitched, unbroken voices, childishly soft skin, hairless bodies and elongated limbs added to the exotic elements of court life. These castrated men – a third sex, neither male nor female – who could not produce their own families, were trusted to attend to the Byzantine emperor and empress, to protect the women of the ruling dynasty and to run court ceremonial. In Muslim countries, they frequently guarded the sacred shrines of Islam. And in imperial China, right up to the twentieth century, poor men continued to offer themselves for castration in order to obtain a court position. The phenomenon of court eunuchs has a global history and Byzantine practice was not unusual among hierarchical, imperial governments.

Byzantine eunuchs were, however, exceptionally well integrated into society at large. In addition to exercising control over the activities of the imperial court, they attained prominent positions in the Church, the administration, the army and in the houses of great families throughout the empire. Western crusaders arriving in Byzantium were amazed, and sometimes horrified, at the ubiquity of eunuchs. During

King Louis VII's visit to Constantinople in 1147, Manuel I sent a choir to celebrate the feast of St Denis with the Franks:

These clergy made a favourable impression because of their sweet chanting; for the mingling of the voices, the heavier with the light, the eunuch's, namely, with the manly voice . . . softened the hearts of the Franks. Also, they gave the onlookers pleasure by their graceful bearing and gentle clapping of hands and genuflexions.

Since the writer, Odo of Deuil, is generally hostile to Byzantium, his appreciation of the sound of eunuch castrati performing with male singers is surprising.

Eunuchs had specific roles in ancient Persia and Rome, which were reinforced when Diocletian adopted Persian attributes, such as a crown, globe, throne and golden robes, to symbolize imperial domination. In Byzantium, the restriction of intimate duties connected with the imperial family to castrated men was based on an assumption of their loyalty to the ruling dynasty, although this was not always borne out by the ambitious schemes of leading eunuch courtiers. Those who had been castrated before puberty were known as 'beardless men'; those castrated as grown men of course retained the physical signs of masculinity. Byzantine eunuchs often accumulated considerable wealth, became generous patrons of the arts and enhanced the imperial court. All too often they also shared the whims and cruelties of uncastrated men and women.

Despite the assumption of their softness, eunuchs were appointed to lead armies. The general Narses (an Armenian), who completed the conquest of Italy in the reign of Justinian, finds a parallel in the Chinese admiral Zheng, who is said to have discovered America ninety years before Christopher Columbus, or the medieval Japanese naval commander who certainly sailed as far as the East Indies. References to eunuch military commanders occur throughout Byzantine history, though with less frequency in the fourteenth and fifteenth centuries. Some clearly were slaves who had been castrated before they entered Byzantine service, for instance Peter Phokas, who took his master's surname and excelled in personal combat with the Russians. He headed the imperial guard under Nikephoros II (963–9) and was appointed commander on the eastern front in the 960s. In the late tenth century, Basil II appointed a patrician eunuch named Nikolaos to lead the successful attack on Aleppo in 995.

Following the definitions of eunuchs given by St Matthew (19:12):

there are some eunuchs, which were so born from their mother's womb: and there are some eunuchs, which were made eunuchs of men: and there be eunuchs, which have made themselves eunuchs for the kingdom of heaven's sake,

some Christians tried to curb their sexual urges by self-castration. But the First Oecumenical Council of Nicaea in 325 issued a firm canon against self-castration: Christians who wished to adopt a religious career were ordered to resist the temptations of the flesh and control their lust by ascetic discipline. The Byzantine Church, however, accepted castrated men into the ranks of the clergy and as monks. Eunuchs became patriarchs of Constantinople and saints, indicating that castrated males were not denied the highest post in the ecclesiastical hierarchy or the possibility of attaining great holiness. Eunuch priests and monks often found an important role in female religious communities, where they performed the consecration of the Eucharist on Sundays. Indeed, some foundation charters stipulated that all clergy who had any role within nunneries must be eunuchs. Conversely, some male monasteries denied eunuchs access because they posed a sexual temptation to monks (see below).

Castration had always been considered a humiliating procedure, repugnant to free Roman citizens. So eunuchs were created among non-Roman peoples, usually those captured and enslaved in warfare. This was reinforced in the sixth century when the Code of Justinian made the operation illegal within the empire. Foreign prisoners of war were often castrated at the borders and then brought to Byzantium to supply the demand for 'safe' servants. Procopius notes that the region of Abasgia (Abkhasia, in the Caucasus) was a source of eunuchs, such as the courtier Euphratas who served as a diplomat; later, 'Scythian', Arab and Balkan prisoners were castrated and sold in the slave market to wealthy Byzantines. Eunuch servants were found in most large households, where they served the mistress, educated the children and acted as intermediaries. Saints Irene of Chrysobalanton and Euphrosyne the Younger also used their eunuch servants to communicate with their relatives and the imperial court.

The expansion of Islam, however, greatly increased the demand for slaves and eunuchs to work in the caliphate and new sources had to be found to meet it. Stray references to slave markets in Rome and Venice indicate a thriving trade in the West, while a growing number of eunuchs from Paphlagonia on the Black Sea coast of central Asia Minor reflect a novel development within Byzantium that flouted the law. Niketas the Paphlagonian, who served at the court of Empress Irene in the eighth century, was one of the first in a long line of young men from the area who were castrated by their own families. Unlike previous non-Roman eunuchs, these locally produced eunuchs were free and Greek-speaking; their families sought employment for them in the Great Palace or in the Byzantine Church.

In the tenth century, Liutprand, Bishop of Cremona, explained how the western trade worked. The operation to create 'eunuchs who have had both their testicles and their penis removed . . . is performed by traders at Verdun, who take the boys into Spain and make a huge profit'. Despite physical difficulties, those that survived often lived to an old age and were recognized by their longer than usual limbs. The market at Verdun in northern France had developed to provide slave labour in Islamic countries, such as the Umayyad Caliphate of Spain, where eunuchs were greatly appreciated. Despite repeated papal decrees against the trade, Christian merchants refused to give up the lucrative business of enslaving, castrating and selling young men, who were often Christian. Women were also in demand in the harems of Islamic courts. The exciting adventures of individuals captured by pirates and sold into captivity is a familiar theme of medieval epic and romance, both eastern and western.

In 949 when Berengar, king of North Italy, sent Liutprand on his first diplomatic mission to Constantinople, he failed to provide suitable gifts. So Liutprand, whose father and stepfather had previously served as ambassadors to Byzantium, remembered their advice and purchased some eunuchs. When the new ambassador was admitted to the imperial presence,

I therefore presented him [Constantine VII] with nine excellent cuirasses . . . two silver gilt cauldrons . . . and what was more precious to the emperor than anything else, four carzimasia; that being the Greek name for young eunuchs.

Liutprand's positive reception and the pleasures of his stay in Constantinople may or may not have been related to the gift of eunuchs, but clearly he thought he had made a good choice.

An additional reason for the employment of eunuchs is related to their sexual activity, which may have been limited but was obviously valued. The *Life of St Andrew the Fool* not only describes the beautiful appearance of a eunuch slave, but also documents how he was obliged to 'perform the sick practice of the sodomites' in his master's bedchamber, for which the saint threatened him with hell fire. When a friend pointed out that the chamberlain had to oblige his master or he would be beaten and severely punished, Andrew responded that if slaves resisted this abominable passion 'they would be blessed and thrice blessed, for thanks to the torments you mention they will be reckoned with the martyrs'. Eunuchs clearly had a sexual drive although they were regularly accused of taking the passive (i.e. female) role in homosexual activity and thus encouraging sodomy. The story of 'Bagoas', a young boy at the Imperial Orphanage of Constantinople in the eleventh century, appears to confirm this accusation: in the manner of Dorian Gray, he chose self-castration in order to preserve his good looks and retain the devotion of his older friends.

In their musical capacity, eunuchs held an unrivalled role: they formed the choirs of castrati. Together with young boys, they performed in the major churches of Constantinople and at the imperial court. It seems likely that the Orphanage may have become another source of eunuchs, who thus preserved their ability to sing in the castrato style, which was so highly appreciated. These choirs may have served as the model for the castrati who performed for bishops of Rome at the Vatican. The introduction of the new style of singing is connected with Pope Vitalian (657–72), who also installed Byzantine-style *diakoniai*, devoted to philanthropic activities, such as the care and accommodation of pilgrims. Both institutions were modelled on Byzantine practice. In the case of eunuch singers, Rome established an enduring tradition which was only abandoned, reluctantly, in the early twentieth century.

One further method of creating eunuchs must be mentioned: when castration was imposed as a punishment, for instance to prevent males from ever fathering heirs. This was often the case with young sons of a disgraced emperor (Maurice 582–602, Michael I Rangabe 811–13,

Leo V 813–20), or of rebels (Germanos, son of a rebel against Constantine IV). The mutilation effectively excluded such a man from the imperial office, as emperors were expected to produce heirs. It was the most extreme form of bodily mutilation introduced into the legal system by Leo III in his *Ekloga* (740), which punished theft by the loss of a hand and lying by the cutting of the tongue. Blinding similarly became a common method of disqualifying a rival who tried to seize the throne, or an emperor who failed to govern adequately (Philippikos in 713, Constantine VI 797, Romanos IV 1072, Isaac II 1195 or John IV Laskaris 1261). Although such physical mutilations now seem barbarous, the Byzantines reasonably enough saw castration or blinding as a lesser penalty than death.

The prominence of eunuchs in Byzantium, however, was guaranteed by the development within the imperial court of a series of key positions reserved to them. Many of these offices involved contact with the emperor and empress within their private quarters; others were devoted to the maintenance of court etiquette and ceremonial. For such sensitive positions, eunuchs were considered not merely desirable but essential. And once this tradition became ingrained, the roster of posts reserved to 'beardless men' required a regular supply of eunuchs to be trained for them. The families of Paphlagonia who castrated a son knew of this need and tried to take advantage of the potential benefits of a palace career.

In the *Treatise* drawn up by Philotheos at the end of the ninth century, which records the seating order for official dinners, eight official positions reserved for eunuchs are appointed by law, and nine additional ones are bestowed by the emperor by word of mouth. Each post has its own costume, with particular shoes and attributes of office. The first group includes the rank of *praipositos*, led by the most brilliant, *klarissimos*, who acts as the emperor's chamberlain and mouthpiece, directing the court ceremonies as major-domo. Whenever an important ceremonial event was to be held, the *praipositos* summoned all the officials who would participate and gave them instructions about their costumes, attributes and positions the night before. Then during what might be a day-long event, he set each stage in motion by instructing the next part of the ceremony to begin, ordering participants to move to new places with the words: 'If you please . . .'

This post was always held by one of the chief eunuchs who would have participated in such ceremonies many times over the years, and who trained the younger ones to remember what they had to do, and how the whole event should proceed. Before the ceremonies were written down in the record commissioned by Constantine VII Porphyrogennetos (see chapter 16), this information was transmitted by oral traditions – an instance of Byzantine articulacy.

The second group of eunuchs was led by the *parakoimomenos*, who slept across the door of the emperor's bedchamber, the *protovestiarios*, who looked after his wardrobe, and those in charge of the emperor and the empress's dining rooms, and their wine cellars. They include four officials responsible for order in the Great Palace and in two distinct parts of it known as the palaces of Magnaura and Daphne. Among their chief responsibilities was escorting the emperor whenever he left his quarters, and protecting him from the sight of bearded men (and everyone else) when he changed his costume, his shoes or put on his crown. Since imperial ceremonies often involved many changes of clothing in places outside the Great Palace, for instance when the emperor processed to the shrine of the Virgin at Pege beyond the walls, the eunuchs would form a circle, protecting and hiding him as he was crowned and robed. Their presence close to the imperial couple and responsibility for personal effects gave them positions of trust, which those outside the court were always anxious to exploit. Like doctors who attended the emperor, the chief eunuchs had direct access to his private quarters and could come and go without question. Their ability to prevent others from talking to the emperor, or even seeing the emperor at a distance, gave them great power.

The history of Byzantium is dotted with examples of what some historians condemn as over-powerful eunuch courtiers, who attempted to dominate their rulers. From Chrysaphios in the fifth century, Euphratas under Justinian and Theodora, to Staurakios and Aetios, rivals for Empress Irene's affections, Samonas in the ninth, Basil Lekapenos in the tenth, and John the *orphanotrophos* (in charge of the large Imperial Orphanage in Constantinople) in the eleventh, the list is extensive. Basil Lekapenos, an illegitimate son of Romanos I, known as 'Nothos' ('the Bastard'), made a particularly successful career. After being castrated as a child to destroy any imperial ambitions he might have developed, he was appointed *parakoimomenos* by Constantine VII. He held on to great power through the rule of Nikephoros II and John I, and practically governed the empire during the first decade of Basil II's reign (976–85). With his great wealth, he commissioned magnificent art objects such as the Limburg reliquary. He also wrote a treatise on naval battles and had it copied in a splendid manuscript of military *Taktika*.

In this respect, Basil Lekapenos was typical of several high-ranking eunuchs who became art patrons, diplomats, generals, administrators, teachers, writers, theologians and churchmen (plate 10). In many cases these officials were detached from their court duties to undertake particular missions, diplomatic or military, such as Andreas, who negotiated with the Arabs in the seventh century, or Theoktistos, who commanded the navy in the ninth century. In Byzantium, as in the caliphate, eunuchs regularly found employment as military generals and diplomats. Their high status is confirmed in the *Book on the Interpretation of Dreams*, written by a Christian Greek author, Achmet, who drew on Byzantine and Arabic sources as well as on his own dreams. In common with many authors, he equates beautiful eunuchs with angels. Both of course were considered sexless beings, since angels have no sex and eunuchs were supposed to have lost theirs. Even if this was not correct – as we have seen and as numerous accusations of eunuchs having sexual relations make clear – it reflects the important roles filled by eunuchs in Christian and Muslim societies, especially those of messenger, private secretary and intermediary.

As well as these high-ranking eunuch officials, others made careers far away from the Great Palace and imperial patronage. They appear incidentally in hagiographical sources, and sometimes feature on a list of wedding gifts, as in the story of Digenes Akrites, the frontier hero. When Basil finally married the girl (she is never named), her eldest uncle presented them with ten boys:

> eunuchs, all good-looking and with beautiful hair,
> dressed in Persian garments of silk
> and with golden torques around their necks.

This was an expensive wedding present, which could be set beside the thoroughbred horses equipped with beautiful saddles and bridles, the hunting dogs and gilded icons which are also mentioned. When the wealthy widow Danelis made the journey from the Peloponnese to Constantinople, she was carried on a litter by her eunuch servants, and among the many rich gifts she presented to Emperor Basil I were, it is claimed, one hundred eunuchs.

Two new laws (*Novels*) of Leo VI, published at about the turn of the tenth century, addressed the situation of eunuchs within the empire. The first prohibited the marriage of eunuchs with women, on the grounds that the purpose of marriage was procreation, and the second allowed eunuchs to adopt children, who could become their heirs. In this way, court eunuchs who rose to the highest positions and accumulated wealth could transmit it to their adopted sons. Leo VI reflected a more humane view of eunuchs, which coincided with the gradual relaxation of the laws against castration on imperial territory. In the case of St Metrios, whose castrated son Constantine made a successful career at the imperial court, his operation was justified by an angelic vision which foretold his future.

Eunuchs often became monks. One Kosmas, a eunuch monk from Paphlagonia (again), was on a journey to Italy when he stopped to rest near the tomb of Holy Luke in Steiris (plate 31). There he had a vision directing him to stay at the tomb, to protect it and make it more beautiful. Yet some monasteries were unwilling to accept eunuchs or young boys into their communities, presumably because they feared sexual disruption. On Mount Athos, they were gradually excluded as a danger to the other monks. The *Tragos* (*Rule*), signed by John I Tzimiskes, states:

I order you not to receive young and beardless men and eunuchs who come to the Mountain to be tonsured ... And if any abbot or *kelliotes* [hermit] disregards my injunctions and introduces into his domain or his cell a eunuch or a boy ... we believe it is best to expel him from the Mountain.

The deeply embedded presence of eunuchs at the Byzantine court, their acceptance in society at large and their established legal status gave them a more prominent role than in other medieval societies. In contrast, eunuchs provoked horror in the medieval West, where only 'whole' men could serve as bishops. Some underlying prejudice persisted, nonetheless, even in Byzantium, as Theophylaktos of Ohrid's

Defence of Eunuchs makes clear. This eleventh-century dialogue between a monk and a eunuch, written by a learned bishop, presents a general hostility to eunuchs in terms of their moral weakness, greed, licentiousness, ambition, effeminacy and wickedness in performing indecent songs, behaving theatrically like actors and drinking too much. In response, the eunuch defends his social group, distinguishing Byzantine eunuchs, who often serve as bishops and monks, from foreign ones. He praises the castration of young boys as a way of preserving their chastity, and points out how many eunuchs remain chaste and inspire others by their behaviour. Obviously some lead less moral lives, but the same is true of whole men. He urges his opponent to judge the eunuch by his spiritual achievement rather than his appearance.

Theophylaktos' treatise was dedicated to his brother, Demetrios, a eunuch, and not intended for widespread circulation. But in his preface, composed in iambic verse, he declared that he hoped to answer the charges generally made against eunuchs. The treatise is transmitted with his other orations and letters in the main manuscript collections and must have been widely read. According to Kathryn Ringrose, Byzantine authors faced a 'rhetorical dilemma' in discussing eunuchs: castrated men ought not to be powerful, were not expected to lead armies successfully, yet had to perform every service demanded of them by their rulers. Any brilliance they displayed on the battlefield had to be explained as an anomaly, due to the exceptional tactical skill of the individual, because eunuchs were considered incapable of military prowess. This contradictory situation reflects the way that Byzantine society constructed the gender of eunuchs as a third category, different from both male and female.

Although the court roles for eunuchs declined in the late Byzantine period, perhaps as the empire's military concerns became more pressing, they continued to play important roles and represent another line of continuity, which extended well beyond the fall of Constantinople in 1453. With the advent of the sultan's harem within the expanded Topkapi Palace, they were employed on a larger scale to guard the numerous wives and slaves of the Muslim ruler. With this new responsibility, they became very powerful once again as the Black (African) and White (European) eunuchs of many Ottoman scandals.

16

The Imperial Court

In the morning the king comes in [to the imperial box over-looking the Hippodrome] with his intimates and servants, all of them dressed in red. He sits on an eminence overlooking the place and there appears his wife called *dizbuna* [Greek *despoina*, mistress] with her servants and intimates, all of them dressed in green and she sits in a place opposite the king. Then arrive the entertainers and players of string instruments and begin their performance.

al-Marwazi, *Properties of Animals, c.* 1120

While the sacred liturgy and choir of castrati made a strong impression on visitors to Hagia Sophia, the ceremonies, receptions and dinners of the imperial court provided a colourful secular counterpart. Al-Marwazi followed a fuller account by Harun ibn Yahya, who was captured and taken to Constantinople in the late ninth or early tenth century. Both describe the chariot racing in the Hippodrome, with two men dressed in gold each driving a quadriga of four horses, how they enter and race three times round the place 'with idols and statues' (a reference to the monuments on the central division, Spina, of the Hippodrome). But the most impressive ceremonies took place within the Great Palace where the Byzantine court was the hub of empire; all activity revolved around it. The palace itself occupied a large area on the elevated eastern point of the city and contained classical monuments associated with the baths, churches built to display Christian relics, and reception halls designed to enhance imperial authority. Within its walls the emperor and empress had their private quarters, special areas were devoted to ceremonial activities, and barracks were reserved for the palace guards. While the rulers could meet informally with advisers, all official ceremonies took place in the court, which constituted a fixed point in the world of Byzantine politics.

Unlike the rulers of western Europe, who took centuries to settle in capital cities where they could establish permanent courts, Constantine I had transferred both the centre of Roman government and the imperial court to Byzantium. The complex known as the Great Palace of the emperors never moved from 330 to 1453, although from the twelfth-century emperors used the palace at Blachernai, an area within the northwest corner of the city walls. The Great Palace became the largest Christian court, rivalled only by ancient Persia and later by the caliphate. Court rituals impressed foreigners and subjects alike. Even before they got to the ceremonies, visitors to the Great Palace all comment on other spectacular aspects: the ancient statues which lined reception halls, some allegedly capable of predicting the future; the gold mosaic and precious metals which adorned the buildings, each one grander and more extravagant than the next; and the palace troops of different ethnic groups who carried their particular weapons.

At receptions held in the Chrysotriklinos, a golden hall built within the palace by Justinian II in the late seventh century, the emperor appeared on an elevated throne directly under a mosaic of Christ Pantokrator which decorated the apse. Elsewhere, hydraulic power was used to create amazing effects. Ancient organs operated by water pressure had survived in Byzantium and were used at imperial receptions and in the baths, where fountains and singing birds entertained the emperors. In the Magnaura Palace, the emperor sat on a great golden throne, flanked by golden lions that roared and golden birds that twittered in golden bejewelled trees. And while an ambassador made *proskynesis* (putting his forehead to the floor in the required act of reverence), this throne suddenly rose from the floor level up to the ceiling. On his first embassy to Constantinople in 949, Liutprand of Cremona pretended that this extraordinary sight did not surprise him. His father and stepfather had warned him about the ceremony. But he concedes: 'I know not how it was done.'

In addition to this aim of inducing awe and wonder in the visitor, the court served a vital function within the empire: to bind all subjects into a closer relationship with the emperor, with a more devoted loyalty – both a sense of belonging and a fatalistic subordination to authority. This was achieved in part by the promotion of talented young men and women to positions of responsibility and power, which commanded respect and admiration. Although the actual number of ordinary people so promoted remained small, the possibility of being one of their number remained open, and this motivated many a family to try to place a son or daughter within the orbit of power. The court exercised a hegemonic power which integrated all sectors of society and reinforced imperial authority; it was recognized as a centre of superior culture and unrivalled brilliance. Ambitious provincial inhabitants usually identified with it and aspired to a place in it. In the eleventh century Kekaumenos, a retired general, condemned the court as the centre of intrigue, which it must have been. But his successful career reflects the ability of the court to attract and retain the loyal services of a talented officer of Armenian origin.

Besides the eunuchs, who managed the imperial court, well-educated men found employment in the vast civil service, which often led to their promotion to high-ranking government positions. As we have seen, others competed – and paid – for the honour of holding particularly ceremonial titles, which carried a state pension (*roga*). All were expected to attend the court when invited, dressed in their costumes and carrying their staffs of office, together with leading ecclesiastics, members of the Senate of Constantinople, the circus factions in their green and blue uniforms (see chapter 3) and a variety of military units wearing their regimental colours. In a hierarchical order, they entered the ceremonial area, greeted the emperor and empress and took their places for the festivities, creating impressive ranks of different colours and identities.

Young girls were also recruited to serve at court, not only as ladies-in-waiting to the empress, but sometimes to fill the most important role open to any woman in Byzantium. In theory, one method of selecting wives for future emperors was the imperial bride show, in which the prince chose the most attractive contestant for his wife. Stories describe how the empress-mother selected a number of suitable and beautiful young girls and presented them to the future emperor in a sort of beauty contest. It seems unlikely that such events actually took place as recorded. But the idea that a provincial family with an attractive daughter of the right age might be so honoured was not without foundation. Imperial brides of the eighth and ninth centuries often came from relatively undistinguished provincial families: Irene from Athens, Maria of Amnia and Theodora from Paphlagonia. Maria and Theodora were allegedly chosen through an open contest. Even if 'beauty' was not the deciding factor, the idea points to the vitality and openness of the court. For the possibility of recruiting a new family from anywhere in the empire into the court generated an identification with its good fortune, and provincial families were drawn into the cycle of imperial ceremonial and were kept aware of court life. The prize benefited all involved. Sisters of successful imperial brides could also make advantageous marriages to courtiers, for example. Indeed, to gain a position as lady-in-waiting to the empress was a highly desirable objective, and many men sought to promote their daughters in this way. In more than one case it resulted in marriage to the emperor (Theodote in the late eighth century, Zoe Zaoutze in the ninth). So while young boys were castrated by their families and sent to make careers among the eunuch staff, young girls were groomed to attract the attention of a future emperor or a high-ranking official. The imperial court became a centre of social and thus financial promotion.

The supposed bride show itself only played a small part in the selection of empresses. Since marriage alliances were often critical to the success of diplomatic negotiations, foreign brides arrived in the Byzantine capital to seal important treaties, for instance Čiček the Khazar, renamed Irene, in 732, or Mar'ta/Maria of Alania in 1072. Byzantine brides were also sent abroad for the same purpose, and eventually even a princess 'born in the purple' had to honour a military alliance (see chapter 17). During the period of the crusades, the number of western princesses who became Byzantine empresses increased greatly. John II and Isaac II had Hungarian wives; Manuel I was married first to a German and second to a Latin princess from Antioch, and he chose a French wife for his son, Alexios II. The emperors' female relatives were also married to western rulers more often, indicating a wider use of marriage alliances in foreign relations. But the Komnenos and Angelos families took care to draw many prominent Byzantine families into strategic alliances. For all their members, male and female, marriage was a matter of politics not of personal choice.

Ever since the fourth century, when Eusebius of Caesarea formulated the theory that the ruler obtained imperial power only by God's will and served as His representative on earth, Christian and Roman ideology had been welded together to sustain Byzantine cultural supremacy. According to this theory, the imperial court was a mirror of the heavenly one, and the emperor's enhanced power was designed to implement divine rule. Foreign policy, administered by trained diplomats, court ceremonial directed by eunuchs, and the central administration all used this theory to ensure that a deep and penetrating sense of imperial authority pervaded the empire.

An original and effective system of government was run from the Great Palace. It controlled most aspects of Byzantine life, from financial matters, such as the minting of coins and commercial regulations, to the promulgation of new laws. The emperor also appointed the patriarch and could exercise considerable influence over the Church. A hierarchy of bureaucratic officials sustained this highly centralized system, which created an endless demand for scribes and copyists and had to ensure that decisions taken in the court were put into practice effectively. Government records were stored and administrators housed in the substructures of the Hippodrome, where some eleventh-century judges complained of their cramped office space. But over the centuries these vast archives have all been destroyed. The few original documents that survive are now generally found in monasteries (especially those of Mount Athos), the Vatican and other foreign collections.

It has been said that Byzantine government could survive even frequent changes of leadership because its administration was so solid. Emperors might come and go, but the routines of the bureaucracy continued. Some aspects of this system can only be reconstructed through the study of lead seals once attached to now-lost parchment documents. When the emperor appointed an official to a new post, or promoted a military officer, that man recorded his new rank and title on lead seals which he attached to his orders as a guarantee of their authenticity. These seals were made like coins from a matrix cut in mirror writing but they were of lead, a much cheaper metal (plate 8). Although very few original Byzantine parchment documents survive, the lead seals that were once attached to them are not so easily destroyed. When the University of Istanbul was constructed in the 1920s in the area of the Forum of Theodosios, the rubble excavated must have come from an archive of documents, for it contained many thousands of seals. Although this was not noticed when the rubble was tipped off the sea walls, the seals were eventually washed up on the shore and collected. Similarly, on archaeological sites like Corinth, lead seals are very common finds. From the multitude that survive, specialists can reconstruct the career paths of many individual administrators and soldiers. But centuries of medieval records themselves, authenticated by seals, are almost completely lost.

For those who became the elite of Byzantine society by contributing to the administration of the empire, court ceremonies of bestowing titles, costumes and insignia of office confirmed not only their own role but also that of their wives. When military and civilian officials received an honorary title, their wives were endowed with a feminine form of that title. Thus the wife of an imperial *kandidatos* gained the title *kandidatissa*, which was formally bestowed when her husband was promoted. A few seals with these feminine titles indicate that women authenticated their acts in the same way. All wives had to present themselves at court, correctly dressed and appropriately rehearsed to perform the ceremony. When they wore a special hat called *propoloma*, they did not make the low *proskynesis*, presumably because it might fall off.

Two major written sources permit a reconstruction of the Byzantine hierarchy of offices: the *taktika* of imperial administrators (lists which record the seating plans for major banquets) and court rituals described in the *Book of Ceremonies* (see below). The emperor headed the court hierarchy, followed by the patriarch. By the reign of John I Tzimiskes (969–76), a *taktikon* records the five highest honours held by members of the imperial family (including the title of *zoste patrikia*, patrician of the girdle or belt, *zoste*, usually reserved for the emperor's mother-in-law). They are followed by the military and naval chiefs commanding the themes; then by the rector (who held responsibility for the imperial household), *synkellos* (assistant to the patriarch), and judges, including the city eparch, and leaders (*demarchs*) of the Blues and the Greens. Next came the officers responsible for running the large divisions of the civil service and their staff, ahead of those representing the industries and trades of Constantinople, the grain stores and local monasteries. Military leaders always took precedence over civilians.

How both groups worked together to organize the resources of the empire can be illustrated by the complex preparations for a military operation planned in 949 to liberate Crete from Arab domination. Among the personnel and their equipment were 20 *dromones* (ships) with two crews each of 300 men, 230 oarsmen and soldiers, 70 cavalrymen supplied with 70 chain-mail shirts, and 12 light mail shirts for the steersmen and Greek fire siphon operators; that is 600 altogether. On the 20 *dromones* of the Vestiarion (a separate department of government), each ship had 3 siphons, i.e. 60 siphon operators altogether, 120 oars, i.e. 2,400 altogether, and 120 anchors and cables. This is a tiny fraction of a much longer list. The navy had to provide both transports and manpower, protective clothing for the steersmen and those operating the siphons for the use of Greek fire, as well as for 70 cavalrymen with their horses. With the necessity of providing water and food for the animals as well as the oarsmen and combatants, the central administration called on services from many departments of government to get the armada under way. And yet this expedition failed.

In the conduct of foreign policy and diplomacy, for which Byzantium was famous, a corps of interpreters dealt with foreign embassies and translated the diplomatic letters they brought to Byzantium. Occasionally, instructions to reply in a simpler form of Greek rather than the classical language indicate that spoken demotic Greek was well known among both Arabs and Italians. Arab sources describe an official letter from Romanos I Lekapenos sent to the Caliph of Baghdad, al-Radi, which was written in Greek in golden letters with an Arabic translation in silver. It accompanied gifts of golden glass encrusted with precious stones, with a lion in crystal, goblets, plates of gold and bowls all encrusted with jewels, clothing, spices including musk, amber, numerous perfumes and rare objects 'sans pareil'. Later in the tenth century, during the rebellion of Bardas Skleros, an Arab ambassador recorded his unsuccessful negotiations with Basil II over the status of key border fortresses, citing the triple copies of previous agreements (which turned out to be not identical). Byzantine diplomats were usually selected from among the most educated, including bishops and monks, as well as military and civilian officials, and the letters of Leo, Bishop of Synada, Leo Choirosphaktes and Constantine Manasses document their work. By the twelfth century, Manuel I Komnenos employed several Italian merchants as translators and interpreters in his negotiations with the crusaders.

The most important source for imperial administration, however, is the *Book of Ceremonies*, a compilation of detailed receptions, court rituals and activities outside the palace, to be observed on certain days, put together by Constantine VII (945–59). It includes much earlier material compiled by Peter, a senator, reflecting court activities during the reign of Justinian, which draw on documents such as the Calendar of 354, a Roman record of traditional pagan rites for the well-being of the capital city and its rulers. In Constantinople, the most important public holiday occurred on 11 May, the foundation of the city. The *Book of Ceremonies* records what should happen at particular feasts, including both Christian services and commemorations of military anniversaries, such as the defeat of the Arabs in 718, of particularly severe earthquakes, or of the annual grape harvest, which involved an expedition made by barge up the Bosphoros. Of course, all the anniversaries of saints and church festivals required imperial participation, which could take an entire day when the court processed to a shrine, attended the liturgical service and the emperor dined with the patriarch. Organized according to the liturgical calendar, which begins at Easter, the book also gives instructions for celebrating acclamations, coronations, imperial marriages and the birth of a son to the empress. In most of these events, the eunuch courtiers direct each stage and signal the participation of different groups.

Among the numerous foreigners who recorded their impressions of the Byzantine court and its workings, Liutprand of Cremona provides two vivid, detailed and contrasting accounts. As the envoy of Berengar of Italy in 949–50, the first reflects his positive reception by Constantine VII, cited in chapter 14. Eighteen years later, the second was dominated by Nikephoros II Phokas' hostility to his master, the German Emperor Otto I, who was a much more powerful ruler. On Liutprand's first trip he records how Christmas was celebrated in the Hall of the Nineteen Couches in the Great Palace, when the emperor and his guests reclined, eating from golden plates in ancient Roman style. At one point the ceiling opened and heavy gold dishes of fruit were lowered onto a table. Between the numerous courses, dancers and singers with organs and other instruments provided musical entertainment. Liutprand was particularly impressed by an acrobatic display, performed by a strong man who balanced a tall pole on his forehead, and two young men who climbed up and down performing tricks at the top of it. A similar scene is depicted on frescoes in the cathedral of Kiev and on a magnificent enamel bowl of Islamic make, reminding us of the common features of medieval court culture. Throughout the Near East, rulers collected unusual animals, exchanged luxury goods, such as enamel saddles and silks decorated with gold thread and jewels, and built themselves spectacular palaces with gardens, fishponds and fountains. Byzantium's network of contacts with the Muslim caliphs and emirs, Slavonic princes and other rulers, was sustained by such gifts, which led in the mid-tenth century to Byzantine craftsmen creating the mosaic and tile decoration of the mihrab in the expanded Great Mosque of Cordoba.

During his second, unwelcome, mission to negotiate an imperial marriage for Otto I's son, Liutprand was housed in a draughty palace and closely watched. His party was not allowed to ride to the palace when summoned to meet the emperor's brother. Sometimes they were not even allowed out to purchase water. Since relations between Byzantium and the West had changed, Liutprand found Nikephoros Phokas hostile to the proposed alliance. The emperor told him that it was impossible for a princess born in the purple to marry a western ruler. He railed against diplomatic letters from Rome which employed incorrect titles: instead of Emperor of the Romans, Nikephoros was addressed as Emperor of the Greeks. In turn he addressed Otto as king rather than emperor. After these squabbles over titles, over Latin – the original language of the Romans – and over Otto's conquests in southern Italy, Liutprand insulted the Byzantines by asserting that the name 'Roman' comprehended 'every form of lowness, timidity, avarice, luxury, falsehood and vice'. In contrast to the banquet he had enjoyed with Constantine VII, the imperial dinners, dominated by leeks, garlic and fish sauce, disgusted him. He was outraged that a barbarian embassy from Bulgaria was seated closer to the emperor and with a proper tablecloth. The final indignation occurred as Liutprand left imperial territory, when customs' officials confiscated the silks which he thought he had purchased legitimately.

Liutprand's descriptions of court ceremonies permit us to experience rituals which are prescribed in the *Book of Ceremonies*. While many document what should happen, for instance at the betrothal of the emperor's son to his future wife, the actual practice might be adjusted to take account of unusual circumstances. The Byzantines were frequently flexible and shrewd at such adaptation. In the second year of her sole rule, Irene transformed the ceremony for Easter Monday (1 April 799): instead of riding on a white horse to the church of St Mokios, distributing coin to the crowds as an emperor would, she arranged to be carried in a carriage drawn by four white horses, whose bridles were held by high-ranking military officers. In this way, the empress could maintain the act of imperial largesse, giving out money, which the crowds surely expected. Similarly, when Olga, the widowed Princess of Kiev, visited Constantinople in the mid-tenth century, the reception for a male head of state had to be revised to take account of her gender. Olga and her delegation took part in the regular ceremony of greeting, but in addition she was received by Empress Helena, the wife of Constantine VII, in her private quarters, and participated in an all-female dinner, while the men of her embassy (mainly fur and amber traders) were entertained by the emperor.

Separate events for men and women were the norm and gave the empress a particularly important role as hostess. During her visit, Olga was invested with the grand title of *zoste patrikia*, marked by a special belt of office. Thus decorated, she took part in a mixed reception of both men and women, at which she was seated beside the ruling couple and the young prince Romanos II. Since seating arrangements were of the utmost significance in the court, and proximity to the top table was greatly valued, this special privilege indicated that Olga had been granted the highest status among foreigners. Despite apparently fixed arrangements at imperial banquets, quarrels over who sat where were predictable. We have seen how Liutprand felt that his master Otto I had been insulted when the Bulgarians were seated in a higher position than himself. He also recorded a story about a banquet planned in 945 in order to assassinate Constantine VII Porphyrogennetos. The official who warned Constantine of the threat also advised him how to avoid it: at the moment when 'the dispute for pride of place begins', the prince was to strike on a shield, thus giving the signal for his loyal Macedonian troops to burst in and arrest the traitors.

Arab diplomats and prisoners of war record similarly graphic details of the life of the imperial court. Harun ibn Yahya provides a fascinating account of the palace, where Muslim captives were invited to dine on special occasions and were assured by a herald that 'there is no pork in these dishes'. He described the guards – Black Christians, Khazars and Turks – with their own weapons, four different prisons, numerous talismans (including a horse and rider with ruby eyes), an organ, the emperor's church and courtyards with marble, mosaic and fresco decoration and tables of wood, ivory and gold. Close to the church of Hagia Sophia, he noted the clock with twenty-four small doors, which opened and closed automatically to mark the hours. He was interested in a cistern from which wine and honey could be made to flow out of the statues on top of columns on feast days, and statues such as the one on the top of the column of Justinian.

In the Hippodrome, Harun thought the Serpent Column, made of four copper snakes, was intended to ward off real ones, and described other hollow statues of yellow copper representing people, horses and wild beasts. He observed with surprise that the empress sat beside the emperor to watch the chariot and horse races. This scene is portrayed in frescoes decorating the tower of the cathedral at Kiev, where the imperial couple are shown overlooking Hippodrome sports from the imperial box. In the early fifteenth century Clavijo, the Spanish ambassador, records the same tradition: the empress sits with the emperor in the Hippodrome, while other ladies watch the jousts from a gallery above the entrance. Although tumblers, jugglers, gymnasts, wrestlers, singers, jesters (often dwarves) and dancers, both male and female, were common court entertainers throughout the medieval world, Byzantium clearly had its own unusual distractions: acrobats performed on camels and on ropes strung between high columns in the Hippodrome. Inside the court, choirs of eunuchs with their permanently childish voices, and golden and silver organs played by the Greens and the Blues, as well as castanets and lyres, all provided musical diversion.

The most detailed records of Byzantine court activity, diplomacy and administration are the compilations of Constantine VII Porphyrogennetos: the *Book of Ceremonies*; a treatise *On Governing the Empire*, dedicated to his son; and another *On the Themes*. These reflect a practical need to prepare Romanos II for his imperial role, and draw on a long tradition of books of guidance. The two treatises deal respectively with territories and rulers beyond the empire, and the regions under imperial control, the themes. Both include much geographical information about the different terrains, mountains, rivers and the characteristics of their inhabitants. *On Governing the Empire* opens with a discussion of the Pechenegs, who are considered extremely dangerous enemies as well as 'ravenous and keenly covetous of articles rare among them . . . shameless in their demands for generous gifts'. Constantine advises,

when an imperial agent goes over to Cherson on this service, he must at once send to Patzinacia (the land of the Pechenegs) and demand hostages and an escort, and on their arrival he must leave the hostages under guard in the city of Cherson and himself go off with the escort to Patzinacia and carry out his instructions.

This practical information is illustrated by particular experiences.

Once when the cleric Gabriel was dispatched by imperial mandate to the Turks and said to them, The emperor declares that you are to go and expel the Pechenegs from their place . . . all the chief men of the Turks cried aloud with one voice, We are not putting ourselves on the track of the Pechenegs; for we cannot fight them because their country is great and their people numerous and they are the devil's brats.

In this section on Byzantium's northern neighbours, Constantine gives a detailed account of the way the people from Novgorod, Smolensk and other cities in Russia gather in Kiev and sail down the River Dnieper to the Crimea, and thence across the Black Sea to

Constantinople. He describes the seven rapids or cataracts on the lower Dnieper and how they may be negotiated. At the first, which is called Essoupi, which means 'Do not sleep!', the water crashes against rocks in the middle 'with a mighty and terrific din'. To provide a sense of scale, he reports that this cataract is as narrow as the polo ground in Constantinople. Here the Russians disembark the men and guide the boats around the rocks in the middle of the river on foot, also punting them with poles:

At the fourth barrage, the big one called in Russian Aeifor and in Slavonic Neasit, because the pelicans nest in the stones of the barrage . . . all put into land. They conduct the slaves in their chains by land, six miles, until they are through the barrage. Then partly dragging their boats, partly carrying them on their shoulders, they convey them to the far side of the barrage.

They continue to the seventh barrage and on to Krarion, where there is a ford as wide as the Hippodrome and as high as an arrow can reach if shot from the bottom to the top. This is 'where the Pechenegs come down and attack the Russians'.

Constantine collected this mixture of practical and political advice from older sources covering the history of Byzantium's relations with all its neighbours. Even though some of the information is not up to date, the genealogies he provides of the Prophet Muhammad, the ruling Bagratid dynasty in Georgia and Armenia, and the Franks in the West explain and elaborate on important historical developments. He shows, for instance, why the Croatians remain independent from the Bulgarians:

The prince of Croatia has from the beginning, that is ever since the reign of Heraclius, the emperor, been in servitude and submission to the emperor of the Romans, and was never made subject to the prince of Bulgaria.

In addition to these works for his son, Constantine described another of his personal efforts in the following words:

Research into history has become clouded and uncertain, either because of the scarcity of useful books or because the quantity of written material has aroused fear and dismay. This is why Constantine, born in the *porphyra*, the most orthodox and most Christian of all the emperors who ever reigned . . .

considered that the best thing ... was first of all to have an active search made and to gather together from all corners of the *oikoumene* books of every kind, full of diverse and varied knowledge.

(I discuss the *porphyra* in the next chapter.) The result was an enormous encyclopaedia in 53 books 'enshrining all the great lessons of history', and divided by topics such as military strategy, hunting and marriage. Only three of these books survive: number 1 on the election of emperors, 22 on embassies, largely culled from the work of a certain John of Antioch, and 50 on vice and virtue. Other projects in the same style are fortunately preserved intact: a complete Lexikon of Greek names and terms called the *Souda*, and a revised edition of the late antique anthology of Greek epigrams, which gives pride of place to the Christian inscriptions at the beginning but also preserves even the most indecent homoerotic verses.

These great encyclopaedias brought together the historical experience of the past in a movement which modern historians have characterized as a 'renaissance'. It could also distort the past, as Constantine showed in the *Life of Basil*, an account which he commissioned of his grandfather's rise to power. As we have seen, Basil I became emperor by murdering his predecessor Michael III. Constantine insisted on interpreting this act as one that saved Byzantium from a drunkard and emphasized all the irreverent and crazy aspects of Michael's rule. Basil I could thus be portrayed in a favourable light as the founder of the Macedonian dynasty, now in its third generation under the proud leadership of Constantine. 'Macedonian' has also become the term attached to his 'renaissance' of ancient wisdom.

The court ceremonies documented by Constantine VII continued in use for centuries and were transferred to the Blachernai Palace, when Alexios I Komnenos (1081–1118) decided to live there. After 1204, during the Latin occupation of Constantinople, all the centres which claimed to represent Byzantium adapted the ceremonies to their own courts, and in 1261, when Michael VIII Palaiologos re-entered the capital on foot, he observed the ceremony appropriate to a victorious emperor returning in triumph. In some ways the most curious text about court ceremonies is the late Byzantine *Treatise on the Dignities and Offices* by an anonymous author known as Pseudo-Kodinos. It reflects the persistence of titles, costumes and regalia well into the fourteenth century, when both the empire and the imperial court had only a shadow of their former strength. In his mosaic portrait at the Chora monastery, Theodore Metochites, the first minister of the empire, is depicted wearing a kaftan and turban, which reflect the influence of Turkish styles on court costume in this period (plate 26). So even in the last years of the empire, not only do the same responsibilities appear, together with the *roga*, the annual pension, which had once made certain offices so desirable, but also the honorific terms are grossly inflated and individuals competed to gain them as never before. During the short reign of the last ruler of Byzantium, Constantine XI (1449–53), the Grand Duke, Loukas Notaras, tried to obtain two high offices for his sons in convoluted obsequiousness:

Your Majesty made Kantakouzenos' son *stratopedarch* at your brother the despot's request, because of his relationship by marriage and because his father was *protostrator*. If you give Phrantzes such an important office which is above that of *grand stratopedarch*, what will happen? But if Your Majesty pleases, reward him with the office of *grand primikerios* which is next in rank.

At this stage, whether an official was *protostrator* or *grand stratopedarch* cannot have been of great importance in financial terms, but courtiers still fought to gain the most prestigious posts which ranked highest in the hierarchy. The emperor was embarrassed because he wanted to reward other officials who were more deserving than Notaras' sons. Meanwhile the Turks encircled the city and brought up their new giant cannon which was to bring down the walls.

17

Imperial Children, 'Born in the Purple'

In 1044, the Byzantines protested against Constantine IX's mistress, Maria Skleraina, and demanded to see the real empresses. 'We don't want the Skleraina as empress. We don't want her to cause the death of our mothers, the *porphyrogennetoi* Zoe and Theodora.'

John Skylitzes, *Chronicle*, eleventh century

The adjective 'born in the purple' (Greek, *porphyrogennetos*) derives from the *porphyra*, a special room lined with porphyry, purple stone, or hung with purple silk, which was constructed within the Great Palace before 750. In that year Irene, the Khazar princess who became Constantine V's first wife, gave birth to a male child, named Leo after his grandfather. He was later identified both as 'the Khazar' and *porphyrogennetos*; he was the first imperial child born in the Purple Chamber. This special complex was an initiative of the iconoclast emperor, who also built the church of the Virgin of the Pharos (Lighthouse) within the palace complex. It became the room in which empresses delivered their children, who all bore the epithet 'born in the purple'. This was a creative device, which introduced a new title as a way of ensuring dynastic imperial authority.

In Roman times, birth 'in purple' was a term commonly used of imperial children, who might even be wrapped in purple-edged swaddling clothes. The expensive dye, derived from tiny murex shellfish, was employed to enhance imperial dignity. As we have seen, Byzantine emperors and their families monopolized the wearing of purple silks and they sent diplomatic gifts of purple cloth, which were particularly appreciated abroad. A sarcophagus made of porphyry, the purple stone mined only from a source in Egypt, was also reserved for rulers.

Whether or not the *porphyra* was intended to guarantee the legitimacy of the *porphyrogennetoi*, Constantine V understood the important role it could play in consolidating dynastic rule in Byzantium. His wife Irene, a child bride brought to Constantinople to strengthen a political alliance, does not appear to have had any children until the birth of Leo. The happy event was celebrated and Leo was crowned co-emperor one year later. In these two measures, the construction of the *porphyra* and the coronation of his first-born son, we can sense Constantine's determination to secure the continuity of his dynasty. Although he later had many other sons by his third wife and raised them to high-ranking positions, he always regarded Leo as his heir.

By emphasizing a truly imperial birth marked by a new qualification 'born in the purple', Constantine wished to make the office of emperor hereditary. The Roman principle of election by Senate, army and people, had long been opposed by the principle of dynastic inheritance from father to son. The Purple Chamber, which contributed to Constantine's new medieval method of designating the heir apparent, also sidelined the senatorial aristocracy and the generals. Other rulers such as Herakleios had already insisted on maintaining their own families in power, and for those with no sons, ways of adopting a successor were well known. In the long transition from Antiquity to the Middle Ages, however, this is a critical moment. The special birthing chamber within the palace complex helped Constantine V find a solution to those who challenged his family's rule. From now on, he intended that only a *porphyrogennetos* would be qualified to rule over Byzantium.

Naturally, this development did not deter rivals and usurpers, who continued to try to seize power. The *porphyra* was also used for other purposes, for instance when Empress Irene ordered the blinding of her son Constantine VI in the chamber in which he had been born. Later, empresses used it for the distribution of gifts to aristocratic women at the pagan feast of the Brumalia. In an acutely difficult situation that arose in the early tenth century, we can observe the ruling emperor using it quite consciously to further his dynastic intentions.

The emperor is Leo VI, nicknamed the Philosopher and the Wise (886–912), who married three times and had the misfortune to lose all three of his wives. The first, Theophano, was a saintly recluse rather than an active empress. After her death, the emperor celebrated her life in frescoes painted in the Great Palace and then married his mistress, Zoe Zaoutze, who died without producing any legitimate heirs. To marry a third time, the emperor had to do a severe penance, because the Church had clear rules about the institution of Christian marriage. Even a second was only possible if no children had resulted from the first; and a third was considered inappropriate. After the penance, however, Leo duly enshrined Eudokia Baiane as his third empress. Then she and her baby died in childbirth in 901. This put the emperor in a very difficult situation as he desperately needed a son and heir to follow him on the throne. But Patriarch Nicholas I Mystikos reminded him of the ecclesiastical regulations: 'to enter a fourth marriage is a bestial act only worthy of lower animals'.

The emperor therefore lived with his mistress, Zoe Karbounopsina (black-eyed Zoe), until she was ready to give birth, when Leo had her moved into the *porphyra*. There, the much longed-for son was born in May 905. Although tradition demanded that the child should be named Basil after his paternal grandfather (Basil I), Leo decided to name the *porphyrogennetos* Constantine after all previous rulers of that name going back to Constantine I, the founder of the Christian empire and its capital city. But since Patriarch Nicholas remained completely opposed to Zoe Karbounopsina, the child was only baptized after Leo agreed to abandon his mistress and send her into a nunnery. Constantine was thus recognized as Leo's son. The emperor then installed Zoe in the palace and bribed a priest to marry them. Patriarch Nicholas was furious and punished this flagrant violation of Church law by excluding Leo from the church for nearly a year.

Eventually a compromise was reached and in the *Tomus of Union* Nicholas stipulated that no further fourth marriages would ever be permitted. Constantine was recognized as his father's heir and became the most famous of the purple-born children, always identified by his soubriquet *porphyrogennetos* to emphasize his legitimacy. Even this did not ensure a peaceful transition of power after Leo's death in 912. Following his brother Alexander's brief reign of only thirteen months, the eight-year-old Constantine was left as ruler. In 913, the Council of Regency included his mother and the patriarch, Nicholas, who remained, not surprisingly, unsympathetic. Six years later, under the pretext of protecting Constantine's inheritance, Romanos Lekapenos, the grand admiral of the fleet, usurped imperial authority and ruled from 920 to 944, promoting his own sons to the highest posts. Although nominally emperor from 913, Constantine only succeeded in ousting the Lekapenos family in 945. His purple aura sustained him through twenty-six years. He then reigned until 959. He became a scholar and painter, who patronized goldsmiths, manuscript illuminators and other craftsmen, and encouraged the rebirth of art often displaying themes from ancient mythology.

By this time, the term *porphyrogennetos* was recognized in the West as a special designation, which provoked regular pressure for marriage alliances involving an authentically imperial bride. As we have seen, Constantine VII Porphyrogennetos forcefully forbade these requests, treating Byzantine princesses as comparable to imperial insignia or Greek fire. During his own struggle to assert his right to the imperial inheritance, Constantine developed an exalted notion of what it meant to be born in the purple. He condemned Leo III for choosing a Khazar princess for his son, which brought 'great shame to the empire of the Romans', and Romanos I for permitting his granddaughter Maria Lekapene to marry Peter of Bulgaria. In connection with this inappropriate marriage, Constantine characterized Romanos as follows: he was

a common, illiterate fellow . . . nor was he of imperial and noble stock, and for this reason in most of his actions he was too arrogant and despotic . . . and because he did this thing [the marriage] contrary to the canon and to ecclesiastical tradition and the ordinance and commandment of the great and holy emperor Constantine [I], [he] was much abused and was slandered and hated by the senatorial council and all the common people and the church herself.

Despite this contemptuous dismissal of Romanos I, Constantine's eldest son was duly named Romanos after his grandfather and then married to a western princess, Bertha. In his book of advice, *On Governing the Empire*, Constantine takes pains to stress Bertha's distinguished heritage: her father, King Hugh, was by descent of the family of the great Charles, a man much celebrated in song and story and author of heroic deeds in war. This Charles was sole ruler over all the kingdoms and reigned as emperor in great Francia ... Bertha, who came up to Constantinople and was joined in marriage to Romanos, the son born in the purple of Constantine the Christ-loving sovereign, was named after her grandmother, I mean the great Bertha, and she the young Bertha changed her name to Eudokia after that of the grandmother and sister of Constantine, the Christ-loving sovereign.

Eudokia, however, died soon after, and Romanos II (959–63) then chose a wife who was said to be the daughter of an innkeeper.

In spite of the title, many *porphyrogennetoi* were fated to suffer in the same way as Constantine VII. His grandson, Basil II, also inherited power as a young boy in 963 and gained imperial authority in 976. During the first decades of his reign, the Phokas and Skleros families challenged it, while Basil Lekapenos, the *parakoimomenos* – his chief eunuch and chamberlain – exercised a manipulative influence. In 987, when Basil was struggling to defeat a revolt, he secured military aid from Vladimir of Kiev, but it came at a price. The young emperor was forced to pledge that his own sister Anna would marry Vladimir. In return, the Russian ruler promised to accept baptism and make his subjects Christian. The sequence of events is much disputed but the result is clear: Anna the *porphyrogennetos* became the wife of Vladimir and presided with him over his court in Kiev, which imported Byzantine habits. The numerous Byzantine clerics who accompanied her from Constantinople also imposed orthodox practices, encouraged monasticism and promoted Byzantine culture. Despite Constantine VII's warnings against allowing *porphyrogennetoi* princesses to be married to foreigners, they could be, and were, used in diplomatic alliances, while numerous princes were married to western brides.

The most striking examples of *porphyrogennetoi* overcoming difficulties to make good their claims to imperial authority, however, must be Zoe and Theodora, two nieces of Basil II. As Basil himself never married, these sisters became the last remaining heirs of the Macedonian dynasty founded by Basil I. It seems extraordinary that neither Basil II nor his brother Constantine VIII, their father, managed to ensure the family's continuity by getting them married. Zoe, who was said to be a great beauty, had been betrothed to the young half-Byzantine prince Otto III, but she arrived in Italy to learn of his death in 1002. In 1028, when her father Constantine VIII realized that he was dying, he arranged for Zoe to marry an elderly general Romanos III Argyros (1028–34), but they had no children. After the death of her first husband, Zoe raised three other men of her choice to the throne: Michael IV (1034–41), Michael V (the nephew of a powerful eunuch courtier, whom she adopted as her son and who ruled briefly, 1041–2), and Constantine IX Monomachos (1042–55) (plate 17). Michael IV retired into a monastery; Michael V tried to usurp imperial power by exiling Zoe to a nunnery, which provoked the people of Constantinople to riot. He was then blinded and the two *porphyrogennetoi* sisters were reinstated. This incident reflects the understanding within the capital that Zoe and Theodora were the only legitimate heirs of the Macedonian dynasty.

With Zoe's agreement, Constantine IX installed his mistress Maria Skleraina in the Great Palace, in a room on the other side of the imperial bedroom. He raised her to an honorary position but was prevented by popular opposition from calling her empress. Despite her three marriages, none of Zoe's husbands gave her the much-desired child and she died in 1050 leaving Constantine IX in power. He promoted another mistress to a position of great honour and privately addressed her as empress. In public, however, Theodora *porphyrogennetos* remained the only woman permitted to use the title. When she learned that Constantine IX was dying, Theodora returned to the city to claim the throne and won over the imperial guard. The eleventh-century historian Psellos writes that

there were certain factors that made her influence with them all-powerful: the fact that she had been 'born in the purple'; her gentle character; the sad circumstances of her former life.

Despite her long period of enforced seclusion, she 'assumed the responsibilities of a man', and ruled alone as if she had finally realized her imperial vocation.

Although the *porphyrogennetoi* sisters successfully asserted their right to rule, the Macedonian dynasty came to an end with the death of Theodora in 1056. The Doukas family tried to use the *porphyra* to establish its dynasty, but was only successful in coalition with the Komnenos clan, which seized power in 1081. Alexios I Komnenos and his wife Irene Doukaina produced nine children, all born in the *porphyra*, and their eldest, Anna Komnene, derived an elevated conception of her own authority from this fact. Although she thought that being the first-born she had a claim on the imperial inheritance, her younger brother John II became emperor at their father's death; in turn his son Manuel inherited the position. But the last of the Komnenos dynasty of *porphyrogennetoi* to be acclaimed as ruler, Alexios II (1180–82), was ousted by his uncle Andronikos I (1182–5) and murdered. So although the *porphyra* had helped to establish the Komnenos family dynasty, it could not ensure the succession of a young prince.

As we have seen, whenever the *porphyrogennetos* was not old enough to rule alone, others might usurp the power attached to the name. Empress-mothers, such as Theodora in 843 and Zoe Karbounopsina in 913, acted as regents for their sons, following the example of Irene. In contested circumstances, ambitious eunuchs like Basil Lekapenos or John the Orphanotrophos, uncle of Michael V, pronounced themselves protectors of the *porphyrogennetos*. But the people of Constantinople and probably further afield sustained great loyalty to those who carried the epithet 'born in the purple', and intervened on several occasions to support them against rivals. The lasting prestige of the term is shown by the fact that, after 1204, members of the Laskaris family who ruled in Nicaea claimed it, although they could not have been born in the *porphyra*. *Porphyrogennetos* thus became yet another title distinguishing the emperor and was used by the Palaiologos dynasty until 1453. The simple innovation of a purple birthing chamber to guarantee legitimate imperial authority persisted for seven hundred years and benefited four distinct ruling dynasties of Byzantium. No other empire devised such a neat and compelling device.

18

Mount Athos

> I have found by experience that it is right and beneficial ...
> for all the brothers to live in common. All together they are to
> look to the same goal of salvation ... They form one heart in
> their common life, one will, one desire, and one body, as the
> apostle prescribes.
>
> the *typikon* of St Athanasios, 973–5

The promontory of Athos is the eastern branch of the Chalkidike peninsula, joined to mainland Greece by a narrow isthmus. It projects 45km into the northern Aegean, rising sharply from the sea, wooded and relatively inaccessible, culminating in the mountain cone over 2,000m high (plate 1). Long before the first monasteries were set up, this narrow strip of land was chosen by individual holy men seeking a remote, uninhabited refuge from the world. Like other inhospitable mountain areas, such as Bithynia in western Asia Minor, it was considered an equivalent to the barren deserts to which the earliest monks retired. Nourished by the writings and brief sayings (*apophthegmata*) of the original Desert Fathers, the hermits of Mount Athos adapted fourth- and fifth-century instructions to a new environment. In this process, the iconophile monks' experience of exile may have created opportunities: after the resumption of iconoclasm in 815, when St Theodore of the Stoudios monastery in Constantinople was banished, he and several disciples spent some time in Thessalonike, near the Athonite peninsula.

Mount Athos became a famous holy mountain, inhabited by monks who refuse to admit anything female to their secluded existence. Their renown is based on inherited traditions of spiritual life dating back to the earliest days of Christianity. From the first monastic centres in Egypt, Palestine and Syria, which generated writings about monastic life, guides to spiritual development, records of ascetic achievement, prayers and hymns, Byzantine monks gained a wealth of inspiration. Every generation added commentaries on this material and developed new texts on monastic discipline and new ways of organizing monasteries. Several types of monastic arrangement were represented by isolated holy men, hermits living in loose associations (*lavra*), as well as those groups who had chosen the life in common (*koinos bios*, whence *koinobion*, one of the names for monastery). This was the arrangement that became dominant on Mount Athos in the Middle Ages.

The communities of Mount Athos were inspired by the early Christian traditions of the Near East, but they gradually came to form a different type of holy mountain, with its own constitution. From its earliest beginnings, possibly during the iconoclast controversy, it sustained self-sufficient communities living according to rules laid down by their founders. Byzantine emperors patronized Mount Athos; some became monks there. Even after the fall of Byzantium in 1453, it continued to nourish monastic life under Ottoman occupation, assisted by orthodox states, including the Russian Empire. In 1924, the Holy Mountain's independence within the modern state of Greece was recognized by the Mount Athos Charter.

While the earliest records of Christian monastic life contained many regulations, ranging from the rule attributed to Pachom, instructions in the *Life of Antony*, to the answers provided by St Basil to questions put to him (in the so-called Long and Short Rules), no single document dominated the monasteries of the eastern Mediterranean. In contrast to the Rule of St Benedict, which inspired a particular order of monks in the West, each eastern monastery established its own regulations, and individual holy men continued to pursue the eremitic life in their own way. The striking traditions of the fifth- and sixth-century stylites (column saints) inspired followers until the eleventh century at Mount Galesion in Asia Minor and in central Greece (though not on Mount Athos). Scattered groups of hermits might meet on Sundays to participate in the liturgy and then return to their isolated cells, extending the model of the Syrian and Palestinian *lavra*. Although the Islamic conquests of the seventh century forced many monks to flee from their original homes, they found more supportive environments in Byzantium, Italy (particularly Rome) and Asia Minor (the mountains of Cappadocia and Bithynia). Studying the same texts, which taught bodily self-discipline through spiritual exercises, they attracted new recruits by their example.

For those monks and nuns who cherished icons, the iconoclast persecution was not just another disruption: it encouraged the private veneration of icons which had to be hidden. For those who agreed with the spiritual reform of worship, support for iconoclasm brought rewards, including the use of buildings from which iconophiles had been removed. The period of active persecution thereby generated considerable mobility, which reinforced an ancient principle of wandering, when monks who had adopted a life of total poverty travelled from one centre to another, relying on Christian charity. This remained another feature of Byzantine monasticism and permitted monks to make pilgrimages to particularly holy monasteries and visit spiritual leaders. The western principle of remaining in one place was more often applied to nuns than monks in Byzantium.

Although monks from Athos are credited with playing a major role in the Triumph of Orthodoxy in 843, it is not clear who they were. Members of the Stoudios community, and other groups, took a more prominent part in Theodora's reversal of iconoclasm. Monastic life on Athos developed slowly, from individual hermits dispersed over particular areas to settled communities living in specially built quarters. The coenobitic principle of life in common emerged only gradually and was promoted by founders such as Euthymios the Younger, who first visited Athos in about 859. Eleven years later the same saint transformed a ruined church at Peristerai near Thessalonike into a monastery dedicated to St Andrew. By 883, another community had been established at Kolobou, near the episcopal see of Hierissos, rather than on the peninsula itself. Although many legendary figures dot the early history of monasticism on the Holy Mountain, the monk Eustathios, named in a document dating from 894, certainly existed. He acted as the spiritual father of a widowed lady, Gregoria, who decided to sell her property to his monastic community. With her children's approval, she retained only the land promised to her slave who was to be freed on her death. As a condition of this arrangement, the monks were to say prayers for her soul. The record of this sale thus reveals one of the most common ways in which monasteries on the Holy Mountain began to flourish.

To create a monastery, hermits had to start by building a church where they could perform the liturgy. Normally, the founder took a major role in this activity. Later he added cells for the monks, a refectory where they could eat together, outhouses for kitchen, laundry, medical supplies (largely produced from the herb garden) and storerooms. The founder regulated his new monastery by a charter (*typikon*), often based on existing documents, such as that written for the Stoudios monastery in Constantinople by St Theodore at the end of the eighth century, which was widely copied. It might also quote from early Christian texts, particularly the Long and Short Rules of St Basil, collections of ecclesiastical canons and the advice of holy men. These charters represent a systematization of the Christian theology of monasticism. Each one specifies the routine to be followed: at what hours the monks are to perform the liturgy, when they work in the grounds, when they are allowed to borrow books from the library, as well as what they eat and what they wear. Since the charters have many similar features, monastic routine is fairly common. Mention of an infirmary where sick and older monks could be looked after, a sort of prison where those guilty of serious sins might be detained on a bread and water diet, and outlying cells inhabited by those monks who wished to perform solitary devotions, reflect an individual founder's emphasis. There could also be a charnel house for the relics of past monks, which were transferred from cemeteries with due reverence. This was introduced at St Catherine's monastery on Mount Sinai, where visitors today are shown the skulls and bones of hundreds of past members of the community (plate 2). Whatever the variations between monasteries, all monks took the same fundamental vows of perpetual chastity, poverty and obedience to their abbot. The formal ceremony of admission included a symbolic cutting of hair, but subsequently orthodox monks normally let their hair grow and did not cut it. Although they can always be identified by their black garments, there is no circular tonsure as in the West.

Because the peninsula of Athos is mountainous and not suitable for cereal cultivation, the monks there needed gifts of nearby land and property which could supply them with foodstuffs. Hence the close relationship with local lay people, who received spiritual guidance and assistance and in turn supported the monasteries with donations. The dynamics of recruitment developed from this local integration, which in turn spread the fame of new monasteries and attracted men from farther away. As the monasteries grew in resources, they created a way for large, wealthy families to invest in the spiritual life: one son would be dedicated to the monastic life, another to the military, the youngest might be made a eunuch and together with a daughter could be sent to the imperial court.

Secular patrons also wished to be commemorated by prayers for the salvation of their souls. From the earliest history of Mount Athos, emperors sought an association with the monks, for the same reason. In 883, Basil I issued an imperial decree protecting them from local shepherds who tried to pasture their flocks on the peninsula. Romanos I Lekapenos allotted the Athonite monks an annual pension and fixed the boundary at Hierissos in 941/2. About fourteen years later, the first named monastery, Xeropotamou (literally, dry river), was in existence. Its foundation is attributed to Paul Xeropotamites, to whom a layman named John made a donation in 956. As soon as he became emperor in 963, Nikephoros Phokas made major donations to the Lavra monastery; an annual grant of 244 gold coins and supplies of wheat ensured its rapid growth.

The history of this monastery, which became known as the Great Lavra, is recorded in two versions of the *Life* of St Athanasios. He was born in Trebizond on the Black Sea in about 925 and became a teacher in Constantinople before embracing monasticism. Like all novices, he sought advice from an experienced ascetic, Michael Maleinos, who directed a group of hermits on Mount Kyminas in Bithynia. One of his companions in this spiritual training was Nikephoros Phokas, later to become emperor. From Bithynia, Athanasios went to Athos seeking a retreat from the world. Long-distance travel on this scale, from Trebizond to Athos, is not uncommon in the stories of medieval monks, who often undertook pilgrimages to Jerusalem, Rome and Sinai. Despite Athanasios' efforts to remain unknown, his fame attracted followers and imperial support made possible the foundation of the monastery in 963/4. As abbot, Athanasios wrote its charter and several other documents to guide the monks under his care. Over the next thirty years, the numbers increased so fast that substantial new buildings were necessary. A large-scale walled monastery came into existence. Athanasios died in about 1001 when he fell from a ladder which he had climbed to inspect the construction of a new church.

Monastic expansion was not limited to Athos: in all parts of the empire, including cities, dedicated Christians and lay patrons supported new foundations. In Cappadocia, startling discoveries in the tufa valleys of Göreme and Peristremon have revealed rock-cut structures, both civilian and ecclesiastical, some decorated with high-quality frescoes (plate 13). But no texts survive to document the builders, who may have been monks, of these tenth- and eleventh-century cave churches. At Steiris in central Greece, however, the *Life* of Holy Luke, composed by his disciples, describes how he made his garden into 'a beautiful paradise' but hid his cell 'in a thicket so that it would not easily be noticed by most people. His purpose was always to prune back the impulses of vainglory ... and to be more like a dead person than a living one' (plate 31). Similarly, the monk John Xenos wrote an account of his efforts to build churches, plant trees and crops, set up beehives and train and install monks at numerous mountain sites in Crete, some of which are identified. For over thirty years, he moved from one to another, recruiting local people to help in the excavation and construction of buildings, and in 1082 he travelled to the capital to obtain patriarchal protection for them.

To some Byzantines, urban monasticism was a contradiction in terms, since it brought those who were committed to a lifetime of prayer, contemplation and silence into the bustling noise of the city. But as we have seen, monks had been allowed to settle in Constantinople in the fifth century, and numerous communities flourished there behind high walls. Some like the Stoudios, Chora, Evergetis and Dalmatou monasteries became famous and sustained an unbroken existence for centuries. Dalmatou, the first to be set up, just outside the walls of Constantinople in 382, continued in use until the twelfth century when it was converted for use as a nunnery. Many others, such as the Myrokeraton, Xylinites or Koukoubiou, are known from a single mention and remain unidentified. This is also a common feature of female houses, which are much less well documented than male.

From earliest times, women had shared the determination to dedicate their lives to Christ. Some Desert Fathers established sister houses for them. Female communities were set up in an urban environment, also under the protection of a bishop. In Constantinople, Patriarch John Chrysostomos (390–404) supported the nunnery founded by Olympias, a wealthy heiress, who also made generous donations to the Church from her inheritance. In his correspondence with her, John praised her dedication and appreciated her material support for monasticism. Her foundation remained in existence for over two centuries, perhaps longer. In the early seventh century, the abbess Sergia wrote an account of the miraculous recovery of its holy relics. But this is exceptional. From the *Lives* of female saints it is clear that their commitment to monastic life paralleled that of men, but their nunneries – whether in cities or the countryside – might not survive for more than a couple of generations after the founder. During iconoclast persecution, when the veneration of icons was privatized, women sustained their devotion in their own homes rather than in nunneries. This may have encouraged a later model of domestic sanctity, which permitted married laywomen, like St Maria the Younger in the tenth century, to attain sainthood.

While monasteries expanded throughout Byzantium, Athos developed its own system of government. Initially, all those registered as monks or hermits on the Holy Mountain elected a Protos (literally, first) to represent them in their relations with the outside world. Later, a council of monasteries emerged as the ruling institution, although Lavra, Vatopedi and Iviron, a community of Georgian monks, remained independent and their abbots took precedence over the Protos. Karyes became the administrative centre of the Holy Mountain, where biannual meetings of all the monks were held. While both emperors and patriarchs attempted to influence and regulate relations among the groups in the monastic federation of Athos, the leading abbots negotiated privileges for their communities. They successfully extended exemption from all imperial taxation and an increase in the number and size of boats in which they transported their produce to markets.

In 1045, Constantine IX Monomachos issued a new charter for the Holy Mountain, which noted and corrected several bad developments. Some monks complained about the admission of eunuchs and young boys, the size of monastic boats and their use for commercial purposes, the use of cattle, the cutting of firewood and export of lumber for building: all these were to be corrected. Clearly the emperor had been made aware of factional plotting as well as uncanonical acts, such as the ordination of under-age boys as deacons and priests. He urged 'all the most devout elders' to attend the general assembly and to 'partici-pate in the decision with the fear of God and with truth, free from all favoritism and bribe-taking, from party feeling, from partiality and from any other passion: from envy, strife and vengefulness'.

Some of these problems had arisen from the rapid expansion in numbers, which meant that there was not enough to eat. The Holy Mountain attracted recruits from all corners of the Christian universe, first as visitors or pilgrims, later as brothers committed to the monastic life. While Iviron was intended to serve as a community for Georgians, Benedictine monks from Amalfi in southern Italy established three houses on Mount Athos, and numerous Armenians, Slavs and Bulgars settled on the mountain. During the twelfth century, monks from Russia, Bulgaria and Serbia came to play a much larger role on Mount Athos in their houses at Panteleemon, Zographou and Hilandar, to which the Serbian ruler Stefan Nemanja and his son Sava retired. Mount Athos welcomed Orthodox from far and wide and maintained contacts with Sinai and other distant houses. Some monks who visited the Holy Mountain and gained spiritual training there went on to found their own monasteries elsewhere, and others were appointed to bishoprics and even to the patriarchate.

While the expansion of monasticism on Mount Athos was sup-ported by imperial patronage, abbots tried to keep their large estates free from imperial taxation. Emperors were not always willing to grant charters of exemption, nor did they approve the foundation of new monasteries at the expense of older houses which often fell into disrepair. In a series of laws issued during the tenth century (see chapter 14), they aimed to concentrate religious devotion on already existing monasteries. Although he had supported Athanasios in his monastery of the Lavra, in 964 Nikephoros Phokas reinforced these laws, without success. Lay patrons often wanted to establish their own communities which would bear their name and commemorate their deaths, and the prestige of Athos continued to attract donations.

In the late Byzantine period, the monks of Athos were drawn into a vigorous theological debate over hesychasm (*hesychia*, literally, silence, quiet), which demonstrated the importance of the Holy Mountain in the religious life of the empire. In the early thirteenth century, Gregory Sinaites, who had been trained at Sinai, introduced hesychast practices to Athos. These were based on repetition of the simple prayer, 'Lord Jesus Christ, Son of God, have mercy on me', combined with breathing exercises designed to focus concentration and raise the monk's spiritual awareness to a higher level. Hesychast theory naturally appealed to those Athonite hermits who lived in isolation and followed their own routine of prayer (called idiorhythmic). It was given much greater prominence and force by Gregory Palamas (1296–1359), then abbot of Esphigmenou, one of the oldest communities on the Holy Mountain. In his writings, Palamas developed hesychast principles, inspired by the moment when the disciples witnessed the uncreated light of the transfigured Christ on Mount Tabor (Matt. 17:1–6). He believed that monks with a heightened awareness could experience the divine energy and uncreated light, and become like God:

Those who have pleased God and attained that for which they came into being, namely divinization (*theosis*), these then are in God since they are divinized by Him and He is in them since it is He who divinizes them. Therefore, these too participate in the divine energy.

This claim was hotly disputed by Barlaam of Calabria, an orthodox monk from southern Italy, and many others who ridiculed the hesychasts as 'navel-gazers'. In 1339 Barlaam, abbot of the Akataleptos monastery in Constantinople, was sent by Andronikos III on various diplomatic missions to the West connected with the proposed reunion of the eastern and western Churches. With his bilingual culture, he was aware of the theology of St Thomas Aquinas (not yet translated into Greek), which strengthened his doubts about the spiritual mysti-

16. The sea view of Hagia Sophia, the Great Church of Constantinople dedicated by Justinian in 537, showing the eastern apse and the central dome.

17. Mosaic of Christ flanked by Emperor Constantine IX and Empress Zoe, from the gallery of Hagia Sophia. Originally, Zoe's previous husbands had been depicted. In June 1042, when she married Constantine, her third husband, the inscription identifying him was changed and all three faces were reset. Constantine presents a bag of gold to Christ, and Zoe holds a scroll with her husband's name: Konstantinos, Emperor of the Romans, faithful in Christ.

18. Interior of Hagia Sophia showing the east end and the dome, with Muslim invocations on the shields hung at the level of the galleries, where the imperial mosaics are just visible. Above these the pendentives, decorated with sixth-century mosaics of seraphim (winged creatures with faces), support the dome from the four corners of the base.

19. Mosaic panel from the church of San Vitale, Ravenna, dedicated in 547, showing Theodora and her ladies-in-waiting. While the empress wears her formal crown, jewelled collar and purple cloak, the silk dresses, jewellery and red shoes of her companions reflect elegant court style.

20. Mosaic panel from the church of San Vitale, Ravenna, showing Justinian and Bishop Maximian, who completed the building in 547, with priests and soldiers.

21. Icon of Christ from the Holy Monastery of St Catherine's, Mount Sinai, painted in encaustic on wood (85cm × 45cm), sixth or seventh century. Christ as Pantokrator, the 'Ruler of All', is shown in an architectural setting, holding a thick Gospel book with jewelled covers and raising his hand in blessing. The asymmetrical treatment may reflect theological definitions of his two natures, human and divine: one eye appears to judge while the other is more forgiving.

22a. Gold coin of Constantine I (306–37) with a Victory on the back (*right*) minted at Nikomedeia (diameter 21mm, weight 4.5 gr).

22b. Gold coin of Basil II (976–1025) with a portrait of Christ on the front (*left*) and Basil and Constantine holding a cross (*right*) minted in Constantinople (diameter 21.5mm, weight 4.38 gr). Byzantium preserved a gold coinage of reliable fineness over 700 years.

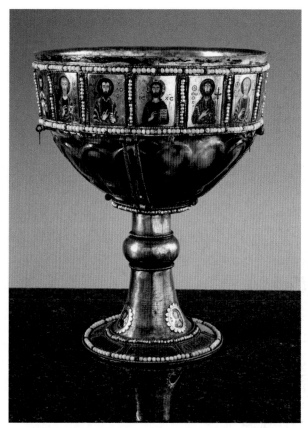

23. Chalice of Romanos II, sardonyx, gold, cloisonné enamel plaques, with representations of Christ and saints, and pearl decoration, *c.* 960. This is the type of Byzantine luxury gift sent to foreign powers. It might have formed part of the loot taken to Venice after the sack of Constantinople in 1204.

24. A sixth- or seventh-century earring made of gold decorated with semi-precious stones on nine loops that hang from a circular frame of notched gold wire enclosing two peacocks flanking a monogram with the letters N A E T O (probably a family name, not deciphered). The suspension loop is missing.

25. 'Greek fire' from the manuscript of John Skylitzes' *Chronicle*, probably made in Sicily in the twelfth or thirteenth century. The caption for the image reads, 'The fleet of the Romans setting on fire the fleet of the enemies', and shows the Byzantine mechanism of the siphon and its projection of burning liquid.

26. Mosaic of Theodore Metochites from the Chora monastery in Constantinople, restored by him between 1316–21. He is identified by the inscription on the left as the founder and chief minister, *logothetes tou genikou*. Wearing his court costume and turban, he presents the church to Christ. The central inscription identifies the church as 'the dwelling place of the living'.

27. The 'Triumph of Orthodoxy', an icon painted in Constantinople, c. 1400 (39cm × 31cm). It is a copy of an earlier icon that commemorated the restoration of icon veneration in 843. On the upper level, Empress Theodora and her young son Michael III (*left*) and Patriarch Methodios and priests (*right*) flank an image of the Virgin and Child. Below, a group of iconophile martyrs and holy figures, including the fictitious nun Theodosia (*bottom left*) carrying a cross and an icon.

28. Frontispiece of the Psalter of Basil II (976–1025), probably painted in *c.* 1000 in Constantinople. The emperor is shown blessed by God, crowned and armed by the archangels and surrounded by military saints. Below him, courtiers or defeated enemies fall prostrate at his feet.

cism embodied in hesychasm. In writings directed against Gregory Palamas, he expressed strong criticism of hesychast practices, which led to his condemnation at a local church council in 1341. One year later he converted to the Roman Catholic faith and was appointed bishop of Gerace in southern Italy. Although his opponents destroyed most of his writings, he seems to have drawn on the logical Aristotelianism of Aquinas, which he opposed to the Platonic and Neoplatonic theology of the hesychasts. In this respect, Byzantium developed a distinctive mystical spirituality which never had any parallel in the West, indeed it seems closer to many eastern religions. It set orthodox tradition apart from the intellectual theology of the West, where monks contributed directly to philosophical argument and logical reasoning.

During the civil war of 1341–7 (see chapter 26), Emperor John VI Kantakouzenos appointed Palamas as Archbishop of Thessalonike and supported his elaboration of hesychast theology. The monks of Athos thus became involved in the dispute between Palamas and Barlaam and participated in the councils of 1341, 1347 and 1351, which endorsed the former and condemned the latter (plate 39). The mystical elements of early Christian prayer, elaborated first by Gregory Sinaites and further developed by Gregory Palamas, were promoted to become a defining feature of orthodoxy. In this way, Byzantium embraced a spiritual practice that owed much to Neoplatonism, and rejected Aquinas' Aristotelian application of logic to theology developed in the West. The opposition surfaced during the Council of Ferrara-Florence (1438/9), when western scholars defeated the eastern theologians with arguments based on Aristotelian techniques. Yet at the same gathering, the exposition of ancient Platonic texts by the Byzantine scholar George Gemistos Plethon entranced western philosophers who were unfamiliar with them.

Although western crusaders had respected the independence of Athos, its prosperity attracted hostile attention from the Catalan Company of mercenaries in the early fourteenth century and later from the Turks, who reduced its properties on the mainland and forced some monks to flee. Some settled at Meteora (literally, in mid-air) in central Greece where they could withstand military attack from the top of their rocks. But new communities continued to be founded on Athos in the thirteenth and fourteenth centuries; less-organized forms of monastic life also flourished. The advance of the Ottomans into the Balkans signalled a change, marked by periods of temporary occupation and, ultimately, control of the Holy Mountain in 1430. While the monasteries were permitted to continue as independent institutions in return for an annual tribute, their spiritual and material conditions declined.

The fate of Athos during the period of Turkish rule is a sad tale of selling manuscripts and increasing reliance on Russian benefactors. As the leader of the Greek Orthodox community (*millet*), the Patriarch of Constantinople gained greater control over the monasteries; this was recognized at the end of the First World War and confirmed at Lausanne in 1923. But recent developments have favoured Mount Athos. In particular, the breakup of the USSR and the lifting of restrictions on religious observance have led to an influx of orthodox recruits to the monasteries. Many now come from the diaspora Greek communities of America and Australia, as well as the orthodox in the Asian landmass and the Balkans. Against all the odds, the history of the Holy Mountain is being rewritten, with mobile phones, computers and speedboats. Buildings are being restored, new icons painted, medieval frescoes and manuscripts preserved. A venerable Byzantine institution is finding new feet in the twenty-first century.

19

Venice and the Fork

> She did not touch her food with her hands but when her
> eunuchs had cut it up into small pieces she daintily lifted them
> to her mouth with a small two-pronged gold fork.
>
> Peter Damian, *Institutio monialis*, *c.* eleventh century

From that moment in 1004/5 when the Byzantine aristocrat Maria Argyropoulaina used her little golden fork in Venice, western dining habits would never be the same. Although initially condemned as pretentious, forks became luxury objects, often made of precious metal with ebony or ivory handles, collected by monarchs and bequeathed to churches. The Romans had used forks in their ancient style of dining on couches. But both couches and forks were forgotten in the early Middle Ages. Primitive instruments resembling a knife, with a single point, were used for piercing meat and people ate with their hands. Our familiar fork, to which Norbert Elias attributed a 'civilizing' role, returned to Europe thanks to Byzantium. Maria's golden one serves as a symbol of many aspects of Byzantine cultural influence in the West.

This influence was particularly evident in the settlement at the head of the Adriatic, founded by refugees from mainland Italy during the Lombard invasions of the sixth century, which became the city of Venice (see chapter 6). Fleeing with their wealth to the sandbanks that formed islands in the lagoon, the inhabitants became expert sailors and shipbuilders, exploiting the local supplies of fish and salt. They were governed by the exarch of Ravenna and maintained strong links with Constantinople. In the early seventh century, Emperor

Herakleios provided funds for the church of the Mother of God at Torcello (Santa Maria Assunta, which was later rebuilt with the famous mosaics and Last Judgment); and the local inhabitants created a new city named Heracleana (Civitas Nova Heracleana) in the emperor's honour. The combination of local wealth, military support from Ravenna, a bishopric established at Malamocco and cultural investment from Byzantium created the nucleus of Venice, a name which embraced scattered communities on a number of islands.

The Lombard invasions of northern Italy also put pressure on the Byzantine exarchate of Ravenna, which rarely had enough funds or troops to defend the territory reconquered by Justinian's wars. In 751, King Desiderius finally realized the Lombards' ambitions and captured Ravenna. Byzantium transferred its attention to the new settlement of Venice. But the inhabitants of Venice carefully balanced their alliance with Byzantium with their need for allies in the West. From the eighth century onwards, they cultivated close relations with the Franks in order to preserve their independence from hostile powers, notably Lombards and later Hungarians. The old Roman title Duke of Venice gradually lost its Byzantine connections; 'dux' became 'doge', and an autonomous system of city government slowly emerged under his authority. Contacts with the East were strengthened by Byzantine control of certain Dalmatian ports on the eastern shore of the Adriatic, and Venetian boats provided a regular service for ambassadors travelling between East and West. Merchants of Venice are known to have traded in wood for shipbuilding, wheat, salt and slaves, while archaeological evidence suggests the circulation of Byzantine glass and pottery, such as amphoras for transporting wine, grain and oil. At the end of the ninth century, Doge Orso II presented a set of twelve bells to the emperor, who responded with gifts of silks.

A lucrative slave trade also linked Venice with the Muslim world, although Roman popes regularly condemned commerce with non-Christians and Byzantine emperors prohibited it whenever they were at war with Islam. The Venetians continued to sell slaves (both Christian captives and non-Christian prisoners of war) in eastern Mediterranean centres where they bought spices, jewels and incense. In 829, they took advantage of local Christian anxiety in Alexandria about a possible Muslim persecution to smuggle the relics of St Mark out of

Egypt. San Marco became their patron saint and his lion still adorns the flag of the city. When a suitably grand new church was built to house these precious bones, a Byzantine style of architecture was adopted. In 976, this church of San Marco was destroyed in a fire, repaired and later replaced by the great basilica which dominates the Piazza of San Marco today (plate 29). Architects from Constantinople, inspired by the church of the Holy Apostles in the Byzantine capital, began the construction under Doge Domenico Contarini in the mid-eleventh century and created the building characterized by Byzantine-style domes and mosaic decoration, as well as western architectural elements. Bronze doors made in Constantinople were installed at the west entrance and the Pala d'Oro, a magnificent Byzantine gold and enamel altar façade, commissioned by Doge Ordelafo Falier in 1105, was displayed behind the high altar. These tributes to imperial culture were increased after 1204 by materials looted from Byzantium, such as the four bronze horses from the Hippodrome (plate 30), carved pillars from the church of St Polyeuktos and a porphyry sculpture of the tetrarchs now immured in the external wall. The Basilica of San Marco symbolizes Venice's great admiration for Byzantine culture.

Venetian magistrates also sought and obtained titles and honorific ranks from Byzantium. They regularly sent their sons to be educated in the capital and married them to Byzantine ladies. Maria Argyropoulaina embodied these strong ties. Her marriage to Giovanni, son of Pietro II (doge from 991 to 1008), was a mark of Byzantine gratitude to Venice for its recent naval assistance which had thwarted an Arab siege of Bari in southern Italy. It united the senatorial family of Argyros and Argyropoulos (son of Argyros) with the Orseolo, a leading Venetian family. Romanos Argyros, a close relative of Maria, later ruled as emperor from 1028 to 1034. The wedding was celebrated in Constantinople in the summer of 1004, in great style. The patriarch blessed the couple and Emperors Basil II and Constantine VIII placed the golden wedding crowns on their heads. When Maria and Giovanni arrived back in Venice, the whole city met them at a lavish reception, and the birth of their son, named Basil after the Byzantine ruler, was greeted with joy. Two years later, however, all three died during an epidemic. Nonetheless, their union strengthened an important relationship between the Republic and the Empire.

Constantinople cultivated these connections not only for cultural but also strategic reasons: the Venetian navy was designed to serve military as well as commercial purposes and proved an essential ally in Byzantine efforts to protect its territories in southern Italy. These relations were enshrined in a document of March 992, issued by Basil II (976–1025), which gave Venice most favoured trading status, under the direct control of the foreign minister. Guaranteed by a golden seal (*chryso-boullos*) and thus known as a chrysobull, it listed the privileges enjoyed by Venetian merchants in return for military and naval aid. The most important were reduced entry and exit fees payable to the port of Constantinople, which were restricted to Venetian merchants and could not be extended to merchants or goods from other cities. Amalfitan, Lombard or Jewish merchants were expressly excluded, as were the local Byzantines. Citing ancient customs, the imperial document recalled that the Venetians had always acted as loyal servants of the emperor, particularly when asked to assist imperial forces in Italian waters, and counted on this continuing.

While Doge Pietro Orseolo had initiated the discussion leading to the new chrysobull, its formal style suggests that it was not negotiated as a bilateral agreement. Although the province of Venice was treated as an independent foreign power, not a subordinate part of the empire, Byzantium dictated the terms which the Doge accepted. Basil II combined an insistence on naval assistance with trading privileges, and when Alexios I Komnenos (1081–1118) needed more of the former, he extended the latter. In the twelfth century, Venice established an entire quarter along the Golden Horn in Constantinople and built warehouses in numerous Aegean ports. Local Byzantine merchants still had to pay the 10% *kommerkion* tax, which generated considerable anti-Venetian feeling and contributed to a disastrous deterioration in relations. Eventually, as we shall see, Venice turned against Byzantium, and after 1204 consolidated its scattered bases into a colonial empire created on the ruins of Byzantine imperial territory.

While Venice developed its very special ties with Constantinople, the regions of southern Italy and Sicily remained under direct imperial control and became themes in the course of the early Middle Ages. Sicily was strategically important as a staging post on the naval route between Old and New Rome, while the crossing from Dyrrachion

(Durazzo in Albania) to Bari linked the two halves of the land route (the Via Egnatia). Emperor Leo III (717–41) transferred the diocese of East Illyricum, which included these areas, to the control of the patriarch, thus strengthening their Greek identity. The empire also kept allies among the seafaring population of coastal cities, including Naples, Amalfi, Salerno and Ravenna. Although northern Italy passed under Lombard control in the eighth century and the Arabs gradually overran Sicily in the ninth, the two south Italian regions of Calabria and Apulia remained part of the empire until the mid-eleventh. Byzantium then lost them to an adventurous band from Normandy, who formed part of the exodus of young knights, originally of Viking descent, seeking fame and fortune abroad.

While the Italian trading cities were drawn into a closer alliance with Byzantium by commerce, other western powers pursued a different relationship with the empire based on marriage alliances. From the eighth century onwards, numerous diplomatic agreements were negotiated on the promise of a Byzantine imperial bride, what western sources call a *porphyrogennita*, born in the Purple Chamber to the ruling imperial couple, as we have seen. In 767, Constantine V sent an organ to the Frankish king Pippin with a marriage proposal, and later Empress Irene's court eunuch remained in the West to instruct Charlemagne's daughter Rotrud in Greek customs, but neither of the projected unions was successfully concluded. Only in 901 did Leo VI send his illegitimate daughter Anna to marry Louis III of Provence (887–928). Constantine VII Porphyrogennetos not only justified the event, but also chose a western bride for his own son (see chapter 17).

Imperial brides from Constantinople were prestigious and alluring and medieval western rulers continued to seek and eventually obtained them. Theophano, niece of Emperor John I Tzimiskes, was one of the most notable. In 972, John sent her to marry Otto, the son of the German ruler Otto I (936–73). Although Nikephoros II Phokas had earlier refused Liutprand's request for such a marriage, John needed to make peace in southern Italy so that he could concentrate on the eastern frontier and reopened negotiations with the western emperor. Theophano was not an imperial princess born in the purple, but she had been well prepared by the Byzantine court for her diplomatic role in the West, and brought with her an impressive dowry. Silks, jewellery, icons and manuscripts accompanied her entourage. The marriage contract was written in gold ink on a long roll of parchment painted to resemble a Byzantine silk, and the ceremony in Rome was commemorated in an ivory plaque, which displays Christ crowning the couple in imperial style (plate 14). The marriage confirmed a central tenet of Byzantine foreign policy: the use of the emperor's female relations to strengthen diplomatic negotiations. It was as essential in the tenth century, when Theophano married Otto II, and Anna, sister of Basil II, was sent to Kiev to marry Vladimir, as in the fourteenth, when Theodora Kantakouzene, daughter of John VI, married the Ottoman ruler Orhan.

By the marriage alliance between Otto II and Theophano in 972, Byzantine influence was extended from Italy into northern Europe. Her father-in-law gave her estates near Nijmegen and Cologne, where she lived and in due course gave birth to four children, three daughters and a son, the future Otto III. As the wife of the western emperor, she participated in numerous donations to northern monasteries and after his death in 983 continued to build churches in Rome, Frankfurt, Magdeburg and Aachen, some dedicated to eastern saints such as Nikolaos, Dionysios, Alexios and Demetrios. She strengthened the cult of the Virgin and St Pantaleon at Cologne and placed her daughters in the key nunneries of Quedlinburg and Maastricht, where Byzantine silks are preserved. During her son's minority, she issued acts for him, once using the term *imperator*, rather than the normal feminine version, *imperatrix*. She made sure that he received a good education in Greek and inspired him to promote the study of classical culture. Later, he was taught mathematics by Gerbert of Aurillac, a scholar who had mastered Arabic scientific innovations through Latin translations made in Catalonia. In 999, Otto promoted him to the papacy as Sylvester II. Long before he was old enough to marry, Theophano had sent an embassy to Byzantium to find him a bride and negotiations eventually resulted in the engagement of Zoe, niece of Basil II. The proposed marriage never took place, however, as the Emperor of the West died in 1002, in his twenty-second year.

This extension of Byzantine influence north of the Alps was quite new. In Italy, the existence of orthodox churches and monasteries observing the regulations of St Basil meant that Byzantium was well known. Merchants from the cities of Naples, Amalfi and Salerno, as well as Pisa and Genoa further north and Bari on the eastern coast, traded regularly in Constantinople, and monks from the region of Amalfi established themselves on Mount Athos. Knowledge of Greek was widespread in the south and Sicily, where a Greek dialect was spoken into modern times. In the eleventh century, just as Byzantine political influence was waning, the empire set a new fashion for church doors cast in bronze, which swept Italy. Byzantine doors were imported to Amalfi, Monte Gargano, Montecassino and Venice. When Abbot Desiderius (1058–87) rebuilt the main church at St Benedict's own foundation of Montecassino, he asked Constantinople for mosaicists to create a new pavement and commissioned liturgical furniture including parts of a bronze and silver screen. The monastic scriptorium produced illuminated manuscripts inspired by Byzantine models, and craftsmen were trained in metalwork, ivory, stone, wood- and alabaster-carving and glass-making. Under the Ottonian and Hohenstaufen emperors, who ruled over both Italy and Germany, Benedictine monks from Montecassino regularly travelled across the Alps and reinforced knowledge of Byzantium in the imperial court.

While the marriages of Theophano and Maria Argyropoulaina indicate how deeply Byzantine culture was appreciated in certain parts of Europe, in other quarters there was less enthusiasm. Both women were the objects of scurrilous attacks written by western clerics, who condemned their bad influence and predicted that they would suffer torments in hell for introducing luxurious customs to the West. In a list of people who came to a bad end, the clerical reformer Peter Damian (1007–72) records Maria as an example to be avoided. In addition to criticizing her fork (see above), he considered that she lived in a very soft, delicate and artificial fashion, because she refused to wash herself in the communal waters of Venice and got her servants to collect rainwater. Maria perfumed her chamber with thyme and other aromatics, 'a bad and shameful stink', that provoked the dreadful punishments visited upon her during the epidemic of 1006.

In the case of Theophano, a vision recorded in about 1050 by Otloh of St Emmeram in Regensburg describes her bemoaning her sins and begging for forgiveness. A nun had experienced this vision, which Otloh wrote down. In the process, he accused Theophano of introducing previously unknown clothing and superfluous decorations to women at the western imperial court, which caused them to sin. These depraved customs had corrupted western women, leading them to adopt luxurious silk clothes and wicked habits. No wonder the empress was now appearing to nuns in night visions, begging them to pray for her soul.

Why should educated clerics like Otloh and Peter Damian make violent attacks on Byzantine women who had married western husbands at least two generations earlier? Apart from their obvious dislike of cultivated women, who preferred to bathe in clean water, live in scented rooms, wear silk dresses and not eat with their fingers, the reason is related to a growing awareness of Byzantium's different theological beliefs and ecclesiastical customs. Western theologians transposed their hostility to orthodox definitions and practices onto the women who had introduced Byzantine customs to the West. In attacking the personal habits of Theophano and Maria long after their deaths, the clerics found a new way of repudiating all Byzantine influence in the West.

This hostility increased during the mid-eleventh century, when contacts between Old Rome and New Rome deepened awareness of differences between eastern and western church practice, particularly the wording of the creed. At the same time, the conquest of parts of southern Italy by Norman adventurers, under their leader Robert Guiscard, prompted Emperor Constantine IX (1042–55) and Pope Leo IX (1049–54) to seek a way of limiting it. In 1054, at the emperor's invitation, a papal embassy embarked from Rome, led by Cardinal Humbert of Silva Candida, to discuss relations. But instead of creating a firm alliance, relations between the cardinal and Patriarch Michael Keroularios rapidly deteriorated, to the emperor's embarrassment. On 16 July 1054 they exchanged bulls of excommunication and hope of unity against the Normans was forgotten. This moment of mutual condemnation was quickly lifted but not forgotten (see chapter 4).

Although it can hardly justify the name 'the Great Schism', this split drew attention to differences in belief, use of unleavened bread (azymes), clerical celibacy and the underlying issue of Roman primacy. If Byzantium refused to recognize the supreme position of the Bishop of Rome, heir of St Peter, this reflected on its incorrect theology.

Western hostility to the East could overflow from ecclesiastical issues, such as the procession of the Holy Spirit, to more mundane concerns. In addition to expressing extreme antagonism to Byzantine silks, eunuchs and forks, Peter Damian accused Theophano of immoral behaviour with John Philagathos, the Greek monk from Calabria (a typical way of trying to undermine an adversary). From the issue of women wearing diaphanous silk dresses, it was a short step to condemning the long robes of Byzantine court clothing for men, viewed as less manly than western trousers. From the fork to other strange eating habits, such as using garlic, onions and leeks cooked in oil; from strange food to the even stranger custom of entrusting eunuchs with court ceremonial; and from the prevalence of eunuchs to the assumption that all Byzantine men were effeminate and preferred not to fight: these deep prejudices fed on ill-informed, anti-Byzantine stereotypes. The ninth-century collection of papal letters, especially later ones drafted by Anastasius Bibliothecarius, and Notker's *Life* of Charlemagne, identified the Greeks as most abominable (*nefandissimi*). Most of these stereotypes originated in Rome and were extended by the Franks, in contrast to the warmer relations that Venice and other Italian maritime cities maintained with the empire. But they have had a nefarious and disproportionate influence on modern historians, one reflected in repetition of Damian's condemnations (later strengthened by St Bonaventura, 1221–74). Even today, some scholars reproduce the old stereotypes without questioning their bias. They use them as a way of implying that all Byzantine influence – the introduction of the fork, the organ or Greek scholarship – was regrettable. Yet behind any western anxiety over Byzantine customs lies a deflection of the theological row of 1054 onto individual Byzantine women. Let us hope it will not take another thousand years after exposing these notions to put an end to them.

20

Basil II, 'The Bulgar-Slayer'

> We have observed with our own eyes (when we traversed the
> themes of our empire and set out on campaigns) the avarice and
> injustice every day perpetrated against the poor . . . The powerful
> who desire to aggrandize [their lands] and to enjoy in full owner-
> ship what they had wrongly expropriated at the expense of the
> poor . . . will be stripped of the property belonging to others.
>
> Law of Basil II, 996

Basil II, who ruled four generations after the first Basil (the Macedonian), is commemorated on many streets in Greek cities as 'Voulgaroktonos' (Bulgar-slayer). Yet the defeat of the Bulgars is not his
greatest claim to fame. During his extremely long reign, from 976 to
1025, he presided over a major expansion of the empire beyond the
Taurus Mountains in the east, the conversion of the Russians, the
forging of numerous important foreign alliances, the patronage of art
and learning, and the protection of the poor. In all this, he was a
worthy grandson of the famous Constantine VII Porphyrogennetos.
Yet he almost fatally weakened Byzantium by not ensuring the continuity of the Macedonian dynasty.

His portrait, the frontispiece to a magnificent manuscript of the
Psalms, has become a defining symbol of Byzantine power (plate 28).
From heaven, Christ lowers the crown which the archangel Gabriel
puts on his head, while Michael hands him his lance. On a pure gold
background, flanked by six military saints all dressed in battle attire
and holding spears, Basil imposes his rule on subjects or defeated
enemies kneeling before him. Gone are the orb and sceptre of Roman

imperial authority. This is an image of a medieval Christian military ruler which typifies Byzantine appreciation of the soldier-emperor celebrating his victories. It is a fitting tribute to Basil, who devoted himself to military action throughout his life. Other generals such as Belisarius, Constantine V and Nikephoros Phokas are just as famous for their military triumphs, which were also celebrated in Constantinople. Yet Basil is particularly associated with the defeat of the Bulgarians, which has attained a mythic quality.

When Romanos II died prematurely in 963, the five-year-old Basil and his younger brother and sister, Constantine and Anna (born two days before their father's death), were orphaned. In Byzantium, not having a father made you an orphan even if your mother remained alive. In the case of the three young *porphyrogennetoi*, their mother Theophano immediately remarried and raised Nikephoros Phokas, who had recently reconquered Crete, to the imperial throne. Basil grew up rather like his grandfather Constantine VII, in the shadow of other rulers: Nikephoros II (963–9), John I Tzimiskes (969–76) and then Basil, the leading eunuch, who dominated the decade from 976 to 985. This Basil was his great-uncle, an illegitimate son of Romanos I Lekapenos, who is said to have acted like a father to the princes. He put down an attempted coup d'état, which followed the death of John I in 976. But eventually the young emperor had to fight to establish himself both against his great-uncle and against representatives of the Skleros and Phokas military families.

Although in 976 Basil and Constantine succeeded jointly as emperors, the elder had no intention of sharing power. Once he had banished his great-uncle in 985, Basil II proceeded to exclude his younger brother so effectively that Constantine VIII was restricted to hunting, banquets and luxurious living in his palace in Nicaea. Basil's effort to rule alone, however, was challenged again in 987 by two opponents. In the face of this dangerous double attack, Basil negotiated an alliance with Vladimir of Kiev, the leader of the 'Rus', based in present-day Ukraine: 6,000 Russian mercenaries would assist the emperor in return for the promise of an imperial bride, Anna the *porphyrogennetos*, Basil's sister. As the emperor must have known, this was one of the Byzantine exports specifically forbidden by Constantine VII, but in the desperate military situation he was forced to agree to it. With the help of the Rus, both rebels were later defeated, and Basil had to send his sister off to Kiev.

As we have seen in chapter 16, Vladimir's grandmother Olga, who visited Constantinople under Constantine VII, had consolidated good relations between the Rus and Byzantium, but her son and grandson reverted to traditional pagan beliefs. The Rus were divided in their perception of Byzantium and Vladimir decided to align his forces with the Christian empire, rather than maintaining the traditional pagan hostility. He was also able to insist on his marriage to a princess 'born in the purple', a symbol of the allure of Byzantium, which added legitimacy and prestige to his own rule. Only when Vladimir managed to secure this concession were all his boyars baptized in a mass immersion in the River Dnieper. After considerable delay by Basil and pressure from Vladimir, the wedding finally took place. Anna was known as the *tsaritsa*, meaning sister of the Greek *tsar* (caesar), and lived in the palace complex, which Vladimir had built of stone, with rich mosaic and fresco decoration to provide a suitably grand residence for her. The alliance is recorded in the *Russian Primary Chronicle*, compiled in the early twelfth century from older materials, all written in the Cyrillic alphabet devised by Constantine-Cyril and Methodios.

In this momentous shift, the Rus from Kiev adopted Orthodox Christianity. Vladimir ordered the public humiliation of their idols, which were banished, and under the influence of a metropolitan, bishops, priests and monks, who had accompanied Anna from Constantinople, churches and monasteries were built on Byzantine models. Priests from Cherson also assisted in the process of conversion, and Vladimir put one of them, Anastasii, in charge of the church he dedicated to the Mother of God. This became known as the Tithe church because Vladimir dedicated regular funds for its support; built in brick and stone, with a dome, three aisles and three apses, it was a far larger building than anything previously constructed in Kiev. In the early eleventh century Antonii, who had been tonsured on the Holy Mountain, founded one of the first monastic communities at the Caves, and in 1037 Iaroslav built the Kievan cathedral of St Sophia, with Byzantine-style mosaics of a Christ Pantokrator in the dome and a standing Virgin in the apse. The conversion of Russia and the mere spread of eastern Christianity across a vast area was assured.

Meanwhile, in Byzantium, Basil II eventually managed to undo his great-uncle's web of alliances and secured control over the empire's ambitious military aristocracy. He brought effective government, peace and a huge accumulation of treasure to the empire. During his almost continuous military campaigns, he observed the dangerous results of powerful landowners extending their property at the expense of poorer villagers and attempted to legislate against this. As well as his capacity for fighting, Basil was an ascetic figure who insisted that his spiritual father, Photios of Thessalonike, should accompany him on campaigns. He supported intellectuals such as Symeon called *Metaphrastes* (the translator), whose *Menologion* (a monthly catalogue of saints' lives) established which saints were to be commemorated throughout the liturgical year, and an unnamed group of scholars who produced the first popular Byzantine lexicon, known as the *Souda*. The *Menologion* created a standard edition of 150 lives in ten volumes, to be read on specific days of each month. It concluded research left unfinished by Leo VI and Constantine VII with full and detailed lives; very few saints were added later. In contrast, the so-called *Menologion of Basil*, with a dedicatory poem to the emperor, has uniformly brief lives of the saints but a wide range of different illustrations on every page. The *Souda* is not an original dictionary, but it was much used down to the sixteenth century and copied for its explanations of rare words, proverbs, grammatical forms and names of ancient persons, places and concepts.

Basil II never married, a most unusual feature for a Byzantine emperor, and relied on his brother and heir Constantine VIII to sustain the Macedonian dynasty. In 1002, he agreed to send his niece Zoe to marry Otto III, but she arrived to find that he had died. And despite later marriages, Zoe never had a child. When Basil was well over sixty years old, those who despaired at the prospect of Constantine becoming emperor attempted a rebellion. Basil suppressed it. The successes of his long rule perhaps gave him confidence that the system of Byzantine imperial government would survive. The administration he had established did indeed last well beyond Constantine VIII's brief reign (1025–8), but Basil's failure to arrange marriages for his nieces and secure another generation of the Macedonian dynasty left the empire weaker.

Basil II's expansion of the empire began in 989 and gradually brought large areas of the Caucasus, the Balkans and southern Italy under Byzantine control. Antioch, which had been recaptured from the Arabs in 969, became the base for an eastward expansion. By a combination of tireless military campaigning and skilful diplomacy, parts of the Caucasus previously under Georgian, Armenian and Abkhasian rule were incorporated within the empire. Basil used local elites to govern these territories for Byzantium. Similarly, in the far west the emperor strengthened imperial rule in southern Italy, which had been put under the authority of a single official in the reign of John Tzimiskes or even earlier. To combat the major enemy in the region, the Muslims of Sicily, Basil secured maritime assistance from Venice through the chrysobull of 992.

In its southern Italian provinces Byzantium sustained its own Greek administrators, lawcourts, Orthodox churches and monasteries, side by side with the Lombards, who had their Catholic faith, Lombard law and Latin language. This coexistence and mutual respect helped to ensure the region's prosperity, which was encouraged by the building of irrigation canals and mills, and the planting of vines, olives and mulberries critical to the nascent silk industry of the region. Further north, as well, Byzantium sustained good relations with the Benedictine monastery of Montecassino, and the city of Amalfi. Following the alliance made in 992, stronger contacts developed between Constantinople and Venice and several doges sent their sons to be educated in Constantinople.

Basil II, however, is most intimately associated with the area which established his later sobriquet: Bulgaria. In the late tenth and early eleventh centuries, Bulgaria was Byzantium's most challenging and dangerous neighbour. Tsar Samuel ruled over a large area of the Balkans (see map 4), and in 986 he revived Bulgarian independence. After defeating the young emperor, he proceeded south into Hellas and the Peloponnese, ravaging cities and destroying fortifications. He captured the city of Larissa in central Greece and later crowned himself 'Emperor of the Bulgars'. His feats are recalled in many Bulgarian cities where streets are named after him. To combat Samuel's ambitions, Basil reorganized the administration of the area under a *doux* (duke) based in Thessalonike, and led annual campaigns from

991 to 995. In 997, his general Nikephoros Ouranos defeated Samuel at the River Sperchios, but Basil had to return to the region in 1000–1002 and again in 1005 to impose peace on the Bulgars. In 1014, a Byzantine victory at the pass of Kleidion, north of Thessalonike, was balanced by a total defeat suffered by the regional *doux*, showing that the military forces were evenly matched. Four years later, after the death of Samuel's successor, John Vladislav at Dyrrachion, and the capture and blinding of prisoners, the Bulgars realized that to continue their hostility was useless.

When he learnt of this decisive turn, Basil set out from Constantinople to secure the Bulgars' submission. As he proceeded west from Adrianople, their leaders acknowledged his authority. At Strumica he received a letter from Maria, John Vladislav's widow, who promised the submission of three of her sons and her six daughters, as well as numerous younger members of the royal family. Basil went on to Ohrid where Samuel's palace was thoroughly ransacked and quantities of silver, jewelled crowns and gold embroidered clothes were found, together with a supply of coined money, which was distributed to the troops. There he welcomed Maria and her large family. Later, she was given the title of *zoste patrikia*, an exceptional honour. From Ohrid, Basil returned to Lake Presba and Kastoria. Everywhere Bulgar leaders came to make their submission, received imperial titles and honours and were sent to Constantinople. Then the emperor marched his army via Larissa to the River Sperchios, where he was amazed to see the bones of the Bulgars killed nearly twenty years earlier, past Thermopylai where he admired the fortifications, and on to Athens. In the church of the Mother of God, within the Parthenon temple, he gave thanks for his victory and presented splendid and rich offerings. After this visit, he returned to the capital and celebrated a triumph, in which the booty from Samuel's palace at Ohrid, as well as the Bulgarian royal family, were paraded in front of the people. Finally, he entered the Great Church and thanked God for the victory.

The prolonged period of warfare must have resulted in many deaths on both sides. To ensure better relations in future, Basil insisted on marrying Bulgar nobles to Byzantine women and finding Byzantine husbands for their female relatives. He also allowed the Bulgars to continue paying their taxes in kind rather than currency and to preserve other local customs. So, in addition to slaying the Bulgars, Basil instituted methods of ensuring future control; during his extended march to Athens and back, symbols of domination were craftily associated with honours. At Basil's death in 1025, Michael Psellos reckoned that the empire was stronger and richer than ever, but he does not identify Basil as the Bulgar-slayer. So the epithet was not coined during his lifetime. In the 1090s, John Skylitzes gave prominence to the great victories of Basil II over the Bulgars for a particular reason: at that time, Alexios I Komnenos urgently needed to mobilize aristocratic families to participate in *his* campaigns against the Pechenegs in the same region. But again, the term is not yet used. The nickname Voulgaroktonos emerges only under Isaac II Angelos (1185–95), who was again challenged by Bulgaria. Then the late twelfth-century historian, Niketas Choniates, identifies Basil II as the slayer of Bulgars, to recall that emperor's long campaigns and victories.

Among the most striking aspects of this evolution is a mythical claim that after the battle at Kleidion in 1014, Basil ordered that all the 15,000 Bulgar prisoners of war should be blinded, apart from one in every hundred who would retain one eye in order to lead them back to their ruler. On seeing the pitiful spectacle, Tsar Samuel is reported to have had a heart attack and died. There are many reasons to doubt the story. Much larger conflicts had already occurred, for instance at the River Sperchios in 997. The garrison at Kleidion is unlikely to have been attacked by thousands, and many defenders as well as Bulgars were killed before the Byzantines won the battle. Although the large numbers quoted by Byzantine historians are notoriously exaggerated, blinding was commonly imposed on prisoners of war. It was also a traditional method of punishing the leaders of Byzantine revolts and political opponents, much less unpleasant than impaling on a stake. Basil imposed the loss of the right hand on Bedouin prisoners in 995, and blinded Georgian captives in 1021/2, but he was not exceptionally brutal; he was exceptionally successful. He was determined to defeat and punish rival forces, whether Christian or Muslim.

Tsar Samuel's death in 1014, however, provided a peg on which to hang the story of blinding on a massive scale. In fact, the conflict continued for four more years until his successor, John Vladislav, died. This finally brought the Bulgar wars to an end in 1018. The emperor's nickname has obscured Basil's other exceptional military achievements, the conversion of the Rus, and his patronage of Byzantine encyclopaedic culture in the style of his grandfather. His ascetic lifestyle and the founding of the church of St John at the Hebdomon, an imperial palace attached to the military parade ground outside the walls of Constantinople, where he chose to be buried, signal his piety. Verses inscribed on his tomb stress his military campaigns in the first person:

For from the day that the King of Heaven called upon me to become the emperor, the great overlord of the world, no one saw my spear lie idle. I stayed alert throughout my life and protected the children of the New Rome, valiantly campaigning both in the West and at the outposts of the East . . . O man, seeing now my tomb here, reward me for my campaigns with your prayers.

Similarly, Basil chose to display himself in the Psalter wearing his chain mail and armour. In these ways he invokes a timeless representation of military power, and the figures prostrate at his feet are as likely to be Byzantine courtiers as Bulgars.

21

Eleventh-Century Crisis

> But what it is necessary to say, I will say: it is from the time of this emperor [Constantine IX], because of his prodigality and his ostentatious magnificence, that the affairs of the Romans began to be endangered, and since then down to our own days little by little they have deteriorated to arrive at an extreme weakness.
>
> John Skylitzes, *Chronicle*, eleventh century, on the failures of
> Constantine IX (1042–55)

States that last as long as the Byzantine or the Chinese inevitably experience periods of crisis which appear to threaten their survival. For Byzantium, the challenge of Islam in the seventh century launched one of those moments and resulted in novel imperial structures over a smaller territory. The crisis of the eleventh century was perceived by those who lived through it as another turning point in Byzantine development.

The most striking sign of this crisis occurred in the summer of 1071, when Byzantium suffered two military defeats by new opponents. In the far east, north of Lake Van, Seljuk Turks defeated and captured Emperor Romanos IV Diogenes at the battle of Mantzikert. At the same time in the West, the Normans captured the city of Bari in southern Italy. The Turks were a steppe people, possibly of Mongol origin from Central Asia, identified by their ancestor, Seljuk. During their march westwards, they had successfully conquered all who opposed them, and as recent converts to Islam they took their understanding of jihad, holy war, seriously. After thirty years of raiding on the borders of Asia Minor, they gained a major victory at Mantzikert, while Robert Guiscard's campaign against Byzantine Calabria and Apulia culminated in the conquest of Bari.

As a result of this coincidence, Byzantium had to face two very different enemies on remote frontiers, separated by thousands of kilometres. Handbooks of military strategy strongly advised against allowing this situation to arise. But the failure to deal with these threats earlier was itself part of a deeper crisis, to which the Seljuks added a further humiliation by their capture of Romanos IV. The defeats of 1071 have to be set in the broader context of a range of problems dating back to the second quarter of the eleventh century. The first was a chronic political instability that followed the death in 1028 of Constantine VIII. A rapid turnover of emperors was compounded by the second: internal revolts and invasions from north of the Danube, led by a non-Christian tribal people, the Pechenegs. When the regular Byzantine armed forces proved inadequate and additional mercenary troops were needed, Constantine IX (1042–55) minted new lightweight coins of less than 24-carat gold to finance their expenses and maintain their loyalty. It was the first serious debasement of the gold solidus for over seven hundred years. This constituted the third problem, which combined with military weakness and dynastic insecurity in a most damaging way.

As we have seen in chapter 17, the two *porphyrogennetoi* sisters, Zoe and Theodora, daughters of Constantine VIII, were the last representatives of the Macedonian dynasty. Their influence on Byzantine political leadership between 1034 and 1056 was not entirely beneficial. None of Zoe's four consorts devoted sufficient attention to military affairs or brought a clear direction to imperial politics. This allowed the court a dominant role, with its coterie of civilian officials and masters of rhetoric who had little experience of military matters. When she died in 1050, Zoe left her last husband, Constantine IX Monomachos, and his Georgian mistress on the throne. Her sister Theodora outlived the emperor and was restored to imperial power in 1055. One year later, on her deathbed, she was persuaded to nominate Michael, nicknamed the Aged, as her successor, which only prolonged the period of unsettled leadership. Thus, only twenty-five years after Basil II's exceptional reign, an unprecedented internal decomposition of Byzantine authority began to unravel imperial traditions.

The lack of firm government in Constantinople provoked a series of external attacks and internal revolts which came to a head early in the reign of Constantine IX (1042–55). In southern Italy Frankish mercenaries, protesting against the lack of pay, called on the Normans led by Guiscard for help; in the Caucasus, disaffected local leaders led the provinces of Iberia, Abkhasia and frontier areas around Ani in revolt; the governor of Cyprus tried to seize power, the Bulgars rebelled, the Russians attacked Constantinople and the Seljuk Turks overran the eastern frontiers of the empire. But the most severe military challenge came from the Pechenegs, who crossed the frozen Danube during the winter of 1046/7 and initiated a six-year war in the Balkans (1048–53).

Although Constantine IX had experienced commanders, like George Maniakes and Katakalon Kekaumenos, he frequently appointed his friends – court officials – to manage military campaigns. In the 1042 expedition against the Bulgars, Michael, archon of Dyrrachion, led seven *strategoi* and supposedly 40,000 men to their deaths. On several occasions, the emperor also rejected sound military advice with disastrous results. He disbanded the army of the eastern theme of Iberia and commuted some military duties into cash payments. As Skylitzes comments with obvious disapproval, throughout his reign he continued to spend large sums on his grand building projects: the monastery and palace of Mangana in the capital, and the New Monastery on Chios; numerous donations to churches and philanthropic institutions; celebrated mosaics in Hagia Sophia, at Kiev and Bethlehem. He collected a small zoo of unusual animals and paraded his giraffe and elephant in the Hippodrome for public entertainment.

In order to defeat the Pechenegs, Constantine IX had to increase the empire's money supply so that he could pay additional military forces. That is why he minted a lightweight gold coin, the *tetarteron*, which was already used to pay mercenary troops and was treated as equivalent to the *nomisma*. The emperor also continued the devaluation of the *nomisma*, the traditional gold coin, to which Constantine VIII (1025–8) and Michael IV (1034–41) had added a small quantity of silver, reducing its gold content to below 95%. The emperors thus began to undermine the gold standard established in the fourth century by Constantine I, which had been maintained down the centuries. Under Constantine IX the process accelerated and proved difficult to control: four different gold coins were issued, increasing the devaluation to 81%. The *tetarteron* was also debased at an even greater rate to 73% of its original gold content. Later emperors continued to add melted down silver coins to the gold until the 1080s when a *nomisma* contained only 10% gold. Everyone could see the difference between these coins and those of Basil II and rejected the devalued money; they demanded payment in the good old coins.

No historical text mentions the devaluation; it was discovered by numismatists (coin specialists), who analysed the ever-lighter weight of gold coins minted in the eleventh century and measured the steady increase of silver alloy used. The decision to undermine the reliability of one of the empire's greatest assets remains perplexing. How could the rulers of Byzantium not realize what devaluing the *nomisma* would do to the authority of the empire, both at home and abroad? It seems that once the process had begun, emperors could not prevent it from accelerating. And after the defeat at Mantzikert in 1071, this became more obvious as military and economic problems increased. More coinage was minted but it did not command the same respect. Troops refused payment in the strange-looking gold *tetartera* and *nomismata*, while merchants rejected Byzantine coin in favour of Arab gold *dinars* or even silver pennies struck in European cities. Byzantium's imperial status suffered.

While we can now appreciate the dangers of devaluation, it is difficult to assess how Byzantine emperors understood and controlled the overall economics of their state. They probably could not gauge the long-term effects of reducing the gold content. Constantine IX seems to have authorized successive devaluations as the only method of paying mercenaries to defend the empire against the Pechenegs. Other factors such as a reduction in tax revenues through inefficient or corrupt collection, and through grants of land made by emperors to individuals, who thus gained control of the basic land tax, contributed to his lack of monetary resources. In the short run the policy worked. The violent Pecheneg attacks were beaten off. But in the process, Constantine abandoned a feature of Byzantine civilization that had lasted for eight hundred years. By the early twelfth century, Alexios I Komnenos realized that he had to repair the damage and in 1092 he issued a *nomisma* of 20.5-carat gold which replaced the worthless coins. Although the new coin was curved rather than flat and never gained quite the same status as the old one, the empire restored a reliable gold currency and recovered even from the damaging policy of devaluation.

The eleventh-century crisis thus linked issues of dynastic stability, provincial fighting power, the economy and imperial image in a novel fashion. Its military challenge was primarily due to unfamiliar enemies, who attacked the enormously long frontiers of Byzantium at two points simultaneously: Seljuks from the east and Normans from the west, adding to the already perceived danger of Pechenegs in the Balkans. Unfortunately, in the mid-eleventh century the imperial court was dominated by civilian officials and intellectuals, who encouraged cultural and artistic investments and paid insufficient attention to military problems. Theme forces were unable to prevent the Turks from plundering Ikonion in Central Asia Minor in 1069. Through the eyes of the philosopher and historian Michael Psellos, we can observe how the courtiers became partly responsible for a more general political failure.

Psellos was born in Constantinople in 1018 and had the great fortune to be taught by a celebrated teacher, John Mauropous, later Metropolitan of Euchaita. Among his fellow students were a group of friends who went on to attain the highest positions in the civilian spheres of law, philosophy and court rhetoric. Psellos distinguished himself from them by his mastery of advanced scientific as well as humanistic subjects. He was a true polymath, a brilliant writer, whose letters, speeches and *Chronicle* of fourteen emperors (976–1078) capture the times in which he lived with amusing personal details and a developed sense of his own importance. Due to his fame as a philosopher, when Constantine IX set up two new schools, Psellos was appointed to head the one devoted to Philosophy while his friend John Xiphilinos was nominated to the one for Law. His abiding passions become clear as one reads his exhilarating *Chronicle*, which is centred on Constantinople and the court almost to the exclusion of other aspects of empire. Yet we know from the letters he wrote to support his students and friends when they were posted out to the provinces that he was well informed about different regions and tried to make their experience of 'exile' from the capital less painful.

In his account of the debacle of 1071, Psellos notes a significant, additional element: aristocratic rivalry. Factions at court were mirrored by rivalry among the high-born families, who competed for positions, salaries and honorific titles. Despite Basil II's defeat of the Skleros and Phokas clans in the late tenth century, others such as Constantine Dalassenos plotted to capture the imperial throne under Romanos III. In 1057, the Komnenos family promoted its general Isaac as emperor, but he was rapidly overthrown by a Doukas, who was then replaced by a Diogenes. And when Romanos IV was captured by the Turks, his rival Andronikos Doukas promoted another Doukas as Emperor Michael VII. Since Psellos had been Michael's tutor, his lyrical account of this reign is highly partisan and unreliable. But clearly it represented a victory for the imperial court of office holders and intellectuals, who continued to neglect military matters.

Amid the crisis of leadership, stoked by family rivalry, there is nonetheless a definite vitality, also manifested in certain eleventh-century innovations. In a break with tradition, Constantine IX, who came from the distinguished family of Monomachos, admitted some men of non-aristocratic birth to the Senate of Constantinople. Although the Senate was no longer a constitutionally powerful body, it still had a role in legal appeals and disputed successions. It is not clear why the emperor promoted this social development: because insufficient numbers of traditional senatorial families were willing to serve, or because he felt that new blood was necessary. Most Byzantine writers were terrible snobs when they discussed a person's origins. Being well-born (*eugenes*) was considered a necessary distinction, although there was no aristocracy as such. But careers in the military, the administration and even the Church had always been open to talent, and people of foreign or lowly birth like Basil I had risen through the ranks, often to influential positions. And since the merchant classes sustained life in Constantinople, some realization of their worth (literally as well as socially) may have influenced Constantine IX.

The presence of the people of the capital – local merchants, craftsmen and residents – was becoming more pronounced and is noted by contemporaries. In 1042, for instance, when Michael V exiled Zoe from the palace, a crowd of local Byzantines marched off to the Petrion monastery where Theodora lived, demanding that she be released and Zoe recalled. In highly unusual scenes, women appeared in the streets mourning the exile of their rightful empresses, and even foreign troops attached to the court expressed their indignation. As a result of this mobilization, the *porphyrogennetoi* empresses were restored. When Constantine IX died in 1055, the same popular pressure ensured that Theodora inherited her rightful position as the last representative of the Macedonian dynasty.

Psellos calls these supporters of the imperial sisters 'a citizen army', though others identified them as a mob and denounced their activities as *demokratia*, rule by the *demos* (people). By the eleventh century, horse racing in the Hippodrome had become much less frequent, and the circus factions (demes) of the Greens and the Blues had lost much of their power over the populace. Although their leaders, the demarchs, still participated in court ceremonial, identified by special costumes in their respective colours, a different sort of urban crowd introduced a new force into the political spectrum of Byzantium. For the first time, inhabitants of Constantinople who lived close enough to the centre of the empire to mobilize easily played a critical part in the imperial succession. Their power may be related to the novel confidence and growing wealth of those who were not well-born but who contributed to the well-being of the imperial capital. And it is significant that they claimed no power for themselves, merely the right to restore Zoe and Theodora to the throne.

Of course, in the hierarchical monarchy of Byzantium neither the state nor the Church authorities could ever tolerate any suggestion of *demokratia*. But the crowd had entered political life in a new way, quite distinct from urban participation in the rituals that invoked the Theotokos, she who bore God, in the city's protection against hostile forces, as in 626. And it continued to play an important part. This was clear from the way in which the Patriarch Michael Keroularios used the crowd to whip up local support against an embassy from Rome in 1054. Pope Leo X had sent the legates, led by Cardinal Humbert, to discuss ecclesiastical matters. The Byzantines' hostility played a small but significant role that summer, when Cardinal

Humbert and the patriarch excommunicated each other. Keroularios was able to draw on a noisy crowd to reinforce his own opposition to Rome, and in this way the *Byzantinoi* began to understand their new and influential role.

They also began to make their own vernacular speech better known among courtiers who used only the high-style Attic Greek. A further innovation of the eleventh century is the growth of literature written in this spoken, vernacular Greek. Its association with the *demos* is immediately apparent from the term used to describe it: demotic. The lower level of Greek used on the streets, in the ports and in trading agreements with foreigners had probably existed for centuries. Merchants from all over the Mediterranean and Black Sea who came to trade in Constantinople used this simpler form of Greek. In the eleventh and twelfth centuries, demotic began to influence literary output. Versions of the verse epic of Digenes Akrites, which had previously circulated orally, were written down in the fifteen-syllable metre known from political acclamations. This encouraged other compositions in a mixed literary medium with strong vernacular elements. Using the same metre of imperial acclamations chanted by the Greens and Blues, satirical verses, animal fables and eventually verse romances were created, such as that devoted to the sixth-century general Belisarius. Although most examples of Byzantine secular music, songs and dances are lost, it seems likely that vernacular Greek songs were first written down at this time. In certain musical manuscripts, the scribe has noted, 'to be sung to the tune of X', suggesting that a well-known melody was reused for Christian purposes. The earliest documents with neumes – musical signs in red painted above the words to indicate pitch – also date from the eleventh century.

Linguistic innovation was matched in other fields, indicating that the old empire of Byzantium could overcome the straitjacket of its inherited traditions and adapt to new forces. As we saw, some eleventh-century judges recorded minority decisions in the courts of Constantinople, thus demonstrating a much greater interpretative freedom and reliance on legal precedent to mount new arguments. The *Peira* of Eustathios Romaios contains particularly striking examples of flexible adjustments to novel circumstances, for example, when a grandmother had concluded an engagement for her grandson, who reneged on it when he came of age. Such court cases suggest that Byzantine high court judges felt confident in reforming the ancient system, based on Justinianic law, to take account of medieval realities. The change may not have been universally accepted but it continued to influence legal developments.

In the field of medicine, another major innovation of this period was the growth of dissection, previously banned. While certain surgical operations recorded in the late antique textbook of Paul of Aegina continued to be practised – the survival of surgical instruments confirms their use – the study of anatomy and internal organs depended on investigation of cadavers. Normally, the Church forbade such activity, but in the eleventh and twelfth centuries it resumed. A twelfth-century intellectual, George Tornikes, noted the importance of dissection for advancing Byzantine medical knowledge. In the West, a similar trend is observed in the medical school at Salerno, which preserved and developed ancient Greek traditions. Michael Psellos wrote on a number of medical issues and his contemporary Symeon Seth composed a treatise on diet and the advantages and disadvantages of particular foods. Although Kekaumenos condemned all doctors as more interested in fees than cures, others began to distinguish between good and bad medical practice, praising those who operated with skill and saved lives. The provision of quite advanced medical care, at least for members of the imperial family and elderly monks, is documented in the detailed description of the Pantokrator monastery, founded by John II in 1136. It had a sophisticated hospital where imperial women could be treated by a female doctor, men and monks by male doctors, and a *leprosarion* for lepers.

Constructive adaptation of legal and medical traditions was related to a heightened awareness of the importance of education and the classical past. Constantine IX was a generous patron of scholarship and funded the two specialist schools of philosophy and law. Since the study of ancient Greek philosophy had never ceased in Byzantium, by the eleventh century numerous medieval commentaries and additions had enriched this tradition. Michael Psellos had been well trained by John Mauropous, whose appreciation of Plato and Plutarch led him to compose a prayer begging God to admit them to heaven because they were good men who had lived before the Christian revelation. Using a large number of ancient texts preserved in Byzantine copies, Psellos extended his philosophical interests far beyond the study of Plato and Aristotle to the Chaldean Oracles – fragmentary records concerned with the dualistic world of good/white and bad/black forces. He claimed that he could practise theurgy, the art of summoning up ancient spirits, which was strictly forbidden by the Byzantine Church. He also wrote a treatise on alchemy, the transformation of normal metals into gold, and practised astrology. Other, unidentified scholars compared ancient texts of Ptolemy with their own astronomical knowledge, which may have derived from Arabic advances in the field. Greek versions of Arabic works of astrology were included in eleventh- and twelfth-century compendia and encouraged Manuel I Komnenos (1143–80) in his interests. As observation of the stars and prediction of fortune were intertwined, the two fields progressed together and feature prominently in the books of dream interpretation popular in Byzantium.

Profound interest in the eternity of the world, the existence of matter, or the laws of nature, manifested in commentaries on ancient writings, extended to the spherical structure of the world and natural phenomena. Symeon Seth provided an explanation for the delay in hearing thunder after seeing lightning: 'sound requires time for its transmission while sight is independent of time', though Psellos considered the hollowness of the ear as opposed to the bulging of the eye to be responsible for the difference. Attaleiates ridiculed the idea that thunder was generated by a huge dragon, but he could not explain what caused it. Rational scientific study led perhaps inevitably to conflict with the Christian authorities. Psellos' successor in the newly founded Chair of Philosophy, John Italos, was brought to trial for applying logic to the theology of the Incarnation and the miracles performed by Christ, and for denying the immortality of the soul and the resurrection of the body. In 1082, he was condemned for heresy and paganism and later some of his own students shared his fate. However, their study of ancient philosophical texts, including works of physics, astronomy, mathematics and logic, strengthened a tradition which continued until the end of the empire. Despite moments of tension, it usually managed to coexist with Christian belief, although at Mistras the scholar Plethon abandoned any loyalty to the Church and wrote complete liturgies in honour of Zeus and Apollo.

In addition to their profound knowledge of ancient philosophy, Psellos and others created new ways of writing history. His *Chronicle* may exaggerate his own contributions to political developments, but the narrative is based on direct observation and personal involvement in court events. He observed how Empress Theodora's intimate friends planned a succession that would protect their interests, 'seeing with my own eyes and hearing with my own ears how they played fast and loose with the Empire, like men playing at dice'.

His language, while based on the Attic Greek used by the ancient authors he so greatly admired, displays irony, humour and psychological insight. Here he gives a colourful description of Constantine X Doukas (1059–67):

Constantine had a hearty contempt for offices of great dignity and preferred to live in retirement. He used to dress in a rather careless fashion, going about like a country yokel. Lovely women, of course, enhance their beauty by the wearing of simple clothes: the veil with which they conceal it only serves to make more evident their radiant glory and a garment carelessly worn is just as effective when *they* wear it as the most carefully prepared make-up. So it was with Constantine. The clothes he threw round him, far from hiding his secret beauties, only rendered them more conspicuous.

Not many followed him in writing with such flair, though many copied his exciting and innovative features, such as offering first-person opinions.

The crisis of the eleventh century was eventually resolved by the usurpation of Alexios I in 1081, who united two competing families, the Komnenos and the Doukas, by marriage alliances. Together they struggled to defeat the empire's enemies – Norman, Pecheneg and Seljuk – and to overcome the negative effects of the currency devaluation. As we shall see in the next chapter, Alexios I managed to establish his own dynasty, which ruled Byzantium for a century. Yet John Skylitzes recorded an 'extreme weakness' in the late eleventh century; the crisis had left distinct traces. Some modern historians have singled out this period as a stage in the 'feudalization' of the empire; others note the decline of Byzantium from an empire with ancient claims to world domination to a smaller medieval state administered by one family, the Komnenos. All point to the increased power of Italian trading cities – Amalfi, Pisa, Genoa and Venice – and the growth of distinct identities, particularly among Balkan peoples previously ruled from Constantinople. These new republican and separatist forces within the Mediterranean world were bound to affect Byzantine claims to imperial hegemony, though they also contributed to the exploration of novel forms of expression in a variety of fields of learning. Beyond all this, the drumbeat of Turkish expansion can be heard, still distant and underestimated, but announcing what would become the final displacement of Byzantine rule.

22

Anna Komnene

> A woman wiser than men in words, more manly in acts, more
> firm in plans, more prudent in tests . . . a woman enriched by
> three eyes of perception, those of her natural perspicacity, of
> scientific penetration and of consummate experience.
>
> George Tornikes' *Funeral Oration*, for Anna Komnene,
> twelfth century

No book on Byzantium worth its salt would lack a chapter devoted to the twelfth-century princess Anna Komnene. She is one of Byzantium's best historians and most celebrated scholars and the author of the *Alexias*, a history of her father Alexios I Komnenos. She began work on it in about 1137 and was writing the final pages ten years later as she was dying.

Anna regularly reminds the readers of her book that she was born in the *porphyra* of the Great Palace in 1083, the eldest child of Alexios and his wife, Irene Doukaina. Her birth symbolized the alliance of the Komnenos and Doukas families, which brought greater stability to the turbulent eleventh century. As part of this alliance, her father adopted Constantine Doukas, son of Michael VII (1071–8) and Maria of Alania, and betrothed Anna to him. When she was a child, Anna could remember occasions when her father was acclaimed in public, and she and Constantine were also acclaimed. Whenever the emperor and his family left the palace, the factions would accompany them chanting: 'Many years to the emperor! Many years to the empress!', usually repeated three times. Anna anticipated that they would in due course inherit imperial power. This future was dashed by the birth of a son, John, to Alexios and Irene in 1087. He replaced Constantine as heir apparent and Anna lost her role as future empress. As she describes these events sixty years later, she is still full of hatred for her younger brother, although she must have known that it was normal for a Byzantine ruler to appoint his own son as his successor.

Anna had very happy memories of Constantine Doukas and his mother Maria of Alania. In the custom of arranged marriages, when she was about seven years old Anna was sent to live with them, and she recalled this period of her early life with great happiness. She cannot praise Maria and her fiancé enough. Constantine, who was about nine years older than Anna, was 'seemingly endowed with a heavenly beauty not of this world, his manifold charms captivated the beholder, in short, anyone who saw him would say, He is like the painter's Cupid'. The widowed empress Maria 'was considered Love incarnate ... a living work of art, an object of desire to lovers of beauty'. From other sources it is clear that Maria was considered very beautiful; she also succeeded in protecting her son's rights to the throne for several years. She ran a literary salon and commissioned works from distinguished authors such as Theophylaktos of Ohrid and Eustratios of Nicaea. She may have encouraged Anna to read and study.

Some time after 1094, however, Constantine died and Anna returned to her own family. At this stage in her life her intellectual studies began in earnest, developing her obvious aptitude and curiosity. She mastered the higher quadrivium of mathematical subjects as well as philosophy and medicine. When her parents tried to restrain her from pursuing more advanced knowledge of Aristotelian texts, she engaged Michael of Ephesos, a known expert, in secret. She greatly admired her paternal grandmother, Anna Dalassene, after whom she was named, who held supreme power in Constantinople while Alexios I was away on campaigns. Anna describes her in loving detail as a paragon of womanhood with a manly mind wedded to extreme piety, great strength of character and intellectual capacity. Her example may have nourished Anna's own political ambitions.

At the age of fourteen she was married to Nikephoros Bryennios, another ally of her father's, and in due course they had four children. Nikephoros came from a well-known military family and served

Alexios loyally throughout his reign. Anna always speaks with devotion of Bryennios, whom she calls 'my caesar'. Throughout her adult life, she pursued her studies of philosophy, medicine, scientific works and literature, reading widely in both ancient and contemporary writings. Like Maria of Alania, she ran a literary salon where scholars, poets and clerics read and discussed their recent work.

Despite her brother's natural determination to succeed their father, Anna never seems to have accepted her fate – to be denied the role of empress. Her mother, Irene Doukaina, encouraged her in this misguided opposition to John. Irene tried to persuade her husband to nominate Bryennios as his successor, and Alexios did not rule out the possibility. But Bryennios himself realized that a son-in-law would stand no chance against a legitimate son, and refused to participate in Anna's schemes. So when Alexios I lay dying, in 1118, it was John who took the ring from his father's finger and got himself acclaimed emperor. Even after this normal succession, Irene and Anna still continued to plot against him, and one year later he forced them to retire to the monastery of the Virgin Kecharitomene (Full of Grace). There, in 1127, her mother died and after her husband's death in about 1137 Anna set to work on her *magnum opus*.

The *Alexias* (usually identified as *Alexiad* in English) is devoted to Alexios. The title echoes Homer, implying that her father was an Odysseus. Although it is not as extended and is written in prose rather than verse, Anna's history is conceived on an ambitious scale to cover most aspects of Alexios' rise to power and his long thirty-seven-year reign. It runs to nearly five hundred pages in the Penguin Classics translation and is full of exciting stories and amusing details. The first three books are designed to absolve the Komnenos family of blame for usurping imperial power. Books IV to IX are devoted to the wars against Normans, Scyths (northern tribes who fight with 'barbaric' weapons), Turks and Cumans. In Books X to XI she gives a famous account of the First Crusade (1096–1104), which may be compared with western records. She continues with the Norman invasion of the empire led by Bohemond, Robert Guiscard's son, in 1105, and its defeat. Two final books cover additional military campaigns, the treatment of dualist Manicheans and Bogomils (heretics whom Alexios had to root out) and the founding of the Orphanage in Constantinople. Amid this concentrated account of heroic military and other activity, Anna frequently relates events out of chronological order and says little about internal developments.

Yet clearly her father restored imperial power and left a much strengthened empire to John II. Anna documents this process indirectly, showing how he developed imperial qualities:

> Once he had taken over the leadership of the Romans, being always a man of action, he at once became immersed in matters of state ... Alexios, the master of the science of government, directed all his innovations towards the good of the Empire itself.

He relied mainly on his own relations to fill key posts in the administration, including his mother, Anna Dalassene. One of his first acts as emperor was to commit the entire administration to her care:

> I therefore decree ... that in virtue of her ripe experience of worldly matters ... whatever decrees she gives in writing ... shall have the same abiding validity just as if they had been dispensed by my own serene Majesty ... And whatever solutions or whatever orders, written or unwritten, reasonable or unreasonable, she shall give, provided they bear her seal ... shall be accounted as coming from my sovereign hand.

Dalassene proceeded to establish a monastic routine in the imperial palace, which helped to impose greater order on the administration. She clearly played an important part in the transition to Komnenian rule, and was still active in 1095 when she ordered the blinding and exile of Nikephoros Diogenes, who had plotted against Alexios.

This powerful lady had raised at least eight children, whom she married most advantageously to create alliances with several other elite families. Although she had previously opposed the Doukas clan, Anna Dalassene could see that the union of her son Alexios with Irene Doukaina would consolidate the new Komnenos dynasty by an unmatched network of support. As Alexios I reorganized the administration, he created a series of new court titles, which he restricted to his family and members of this network – a major and lasting addition to the hierarchy. In her history, Anna Komnene documents the loyal service provided by men of humble birth, even foreigners who were also drawn into ruling circles. Although she does not detail his currency reforms, the new 20.5-carat gold coin which he issued is documented in a treatise on taxation, the *Logarike*. This includes reports by tax officials and Alexios' responses, which reflect how taxation was calculated in the provinces in line with the new gold currency. And of course, she praises the emperor for maintaining orthodoxy, particularly in condemning the revival of the Bogomil heresy. Its leader Basil was burned at the stake.

In the field of foreign relations, Anna draws particular attention to the stability and order which her father imposed after a decade of civil war. Even before his accession in 1081, she emphasizes his negotiations with Venice. The chrysobull of privileges he granted to the Republic favoured its merchants over the Byzantines, but it reinforced Venetian naval assistance against the Normans. When the Turks were raiding Damalis on the Bosphoros, Anna records how her father forced them to retreat:

He ordered the men hurriedly conscripted to embark on small ships . . . with bows and shields only . . . to make their way secretly at night around the headlands off-shore and then . . . to leap from their ships and raid the Turks; they were then to re-embark and return to base at once . . . He warned them to instruct their rowers to make no noise with their oars.

Gradually the Turks withdrew and immediately Alexios instructed the troops to seize the villages and buildings:

The infantrymen were commanded to ride on horseback, use a lance and make cavalry excursions against the enemy . . . in broad daylight . . . So the hidden spark of Roman prestige began gradually to burst into flame . . . and the sultan was constrained to make the most urgent pleas for an armistice.

Playing off one Turkish leader against another, Alexios won back considerable territory, but was unable to prevent the fall of Ikonion in 1084, which became the capital of the Seljuk Sultanate of Rum.

The capture of Jerusalem in 1087 by the Turks prompted Alexios to launch his appeal to Pope Urban II for Christians to unite against Muslim warriors (see chapter 24). This inaugurated a completely new policy in Byzantium, which brought western forces into the eastern Mediterranean. And in 1097, with the help of these crusaders, Alexios regained Nicaea from the Turks. Four years later, crusading forces assisted in the recapture of Ankara, and then Alexios proceeded to re-establish imperial control over the northern, western and southern coasts of Asia Minor. Although the arrival of ambitious western knights and merchants brought additional problems, Byzantium also benefited from them, and Anna can justifiably praise her father for consolidating stronger ties with western Christendom.

The *Alexiad* is full of thrilling descriptions of battles, debates and receptions, peppered with sketches of the different characters involved, including their mannerisms, clothing and philosophy. After one particularly galling defeat by the Pechenegs, for instance, she recounts how George Palaiologos survived the loss of his horse, wandering on foot for eleven days until he found shelter with a widow, whose sons had also escaped from the battle and who showed him a way back to his own supporters. During the invasion of Cyprus she claims that Rhapsomates, the usurper, was so inexperienced in military matters that he was seized with panic and vertigo whenever he mounted a horse. And she devotes considerable space to the ingenious deception by which the Norman leader, Bohemond, escaped from Antioch in 1104: spreading the story that he had died, he then lay in a coffin with a dead cock which smelled like a corpse and was transported by sea to Rome. 'I wonder how on earth he endured such a siege on his nose,' Anna muses, claiming that this was 'an unprecedented and unique ruse . . . designed to bring about the downfall of the Roman Empire'. She was not aware that the same ploy had been used before by Normans, though Anna repeatedly denounces them as a crafty and treacherous people.

In the *Alexiad*, she expresses no doubt about the significance of her father's role, and presents lengthy reasons for negotiations which failed, for defeats suffered at the hands of the Normans, Robert Guiscard and Bohemond, and excuses for imperial plans that went wrong. Other sections stress the emperor's cunning in outwitting the Turks and the Scyths, and his skill in persuading them not to fight. Any slight hint of apology is overlaid by florid declarations of her father's 'supreme virtue', 'his marvellous qualities', which he displayed equally in battles against external enemies and against heretics. She repeatedly alludes to the conflict between her desire to praise, which arises from her filial loyalty, and her duty to record history in a professional manner, in order to reassure the reader that she is a historian first and foremost.

Anna concludes that Alexios' final triumph over the Bogomil heretics ends his 'reign of surprising boldness and novelty'. She claims that 'men who were alive then and who associated with him must still be amazed at what was accomplished in those days'. Here she identifies three features of her father's reign: boldness, novelty and surprise, which contributed to his successful restoration of imperial power. She confirms that Byzantium always possessed the capacity for innovation. Of course, Alexios could not turn the clock back: the empire had been weakened by the crisis of the eleventh century. But Anna leaves us in no doubt that her father's boldness, novelty and surprise were effective in renewing Byzantium as a world power.

Readers of the *Alexiad* should not forget that it was written by a woman. Although Byzantine women wrote letters, hymns, verses and saints' lives, this is the only known full-length history. At this time, women writers in the West were very active: Hildegard of Bingen was writing medical treatises and accounts of her visions, Marie de France composed her *Lais* (Tales) and Christine de Pisan her *City of Women*. But their stories, visionary literature and troubadour songs were not on the same scale and they did not write equivalent secular histories. Indeed, the *Alexiad* is so ambitious that recently some historians have doubted that Anna actually wrote it. In particular, they have presumed that she could not have described the military action in such detail and must have used a dossier of notes compiled by her husband, Nikephoros Bryennios. He had been commissioned by Empress Irene to continue the history of Psellos from the reign of Romanos Diogenes (1068–71) to that of Alexios I Komnenos, but he only managed to complete four books, ending in 1079, leaving an unpolished account. Although Anna repeatedly refers to his *History*, she makes no direct reference to additional material collected by her husband which she might have used in writing her own work. And even when she cites Nikephoros' *History*, she rewrites the material in her own literary style, which is more developed than his. Since all historians, female or male, use the sources of others, Anna's ability to draw on reports of events she did not witness herself, and allow the readers to judge their reliability or prejudice, does nothing to diminish her stature.

She does, of course, indicate how she learned about particular events, military strategy and battles. Like other historians, she follows established traditions of history-writing in Byzantium, where the classical models of Thucydides and Herodotos were closely studied. Whenever possible, historians used accounts of eyewitnesses, or stories circulating among soldiers who had experienced the campaigns, or reports written after the event. Anna follows this practice, as do all authors when they describe campaigns in which they did not participate. She names a Latin envoy, for instance, who had been sent by the Bishop of Bari to Robert Guiscard during his campaign against Dyrrachion, as her source for the account of a frightful storm which destroyed most of the Norman fleet. Since Anna and her mother accompanied Alexios on several of his campaigns, she also listened to her father's accounts of what happened, to discussions between him and his military commanders, such as George Palaiologos, and to evidence from other participants. Her account is full of debates and conversations; she frequently quotes actual words as spoken, which she may indeed have witnessed in person.

She also drew on written sources, which included governmental records of alliances concluded and planned strategy, reports on which military tactics worked, which failed, and how the enemy responded. Individual acts of bravery or treachery and deaths in action were recorded. News from the battlefront was also announced on the Forum of Constantine in the capital, for example when Eustathios Kamytzes described his extraordinary escape from the Turkish campaign against Nicaea. While other – male – authors often had direct experience of warfare, Anna was well placed at the centre of Byzantine power to find out what happened. Naturally, she is always anxious to portray her father in a favourable light, even when his battle plans failed and he was forced to flee.

Another reason for emphasizing her father's diplomatic skills may have arisen in 1147 when Manuel I Komnenos welcomed the leaders of the Second Crusade to Constantinople. Anna probably wanted to contrast her nephew's pro-western sympathies with her father's more careful and calculated reactions to the leaders of the First Crusade.

The arrival of the massed forces of Latin knights and pilgrims in 1096 constituted a critical turning point in East–West relations, which had coloured all later negotiations between the Christians. Since Manuel was highly praised by court orators for his imperial bearing and military prowess, Anna may have felt it necessary to draw attention to Alexios' achievements, which were in danger of being overlooked. Her history forms a counterweight to the political propaganda produced by court rhetoricians of the mid-twelfth century in favour of Manuel's brilliance.

Manuel also supported strange new western habits, like jousting and the wearing of trousers, which were both introduced into Byzantium during the twelfth century. While court costume remained full-length tunics of different coloured silks, Byzantine military uniform continued the Roman style of shorter tunics worn with leg covers; neither admitted a use for trousers, which were considered a rather indecent novelty. Similarly, although the court elite had played polo since it was introduced from Persia in the fifth century, jousting was a relatively new sport. In the ninth century, there are references to displays of mounted combat between individuals in which a local Byzantine successfully unhorses a foreign challenger, but the western style of jousts was unknown. Both these inventions provoked the opposition of conservatives, so in connecting Manuel with them Anna may be expressing a personal disapproval of her nephew. She may also have considered his enthusiasm for western customs distasteful and even dangerous.

Anna was writing her history when the Turkish conquest of central Asia Minor became a more permanent reality. Ever since the Byzantine defeat at Mantzikert in 1071, various tribes had infiltrated the region, forcing the local population to flee westwards; whole villages, bishops and landowners sought new homes in the European provinces of the empire. This movement from East to West resulted in greater development of the Balkan and Greek provinces, which helped to compensate for the losses in Asia. But the empire's inability to curb Turkish settlements, despite crusading help, was much clearer in the 1130s. Although Alexios I had stabilized the gold coinage in 1092, the empire's wealth had declined. In the West, Venice, Pisa and Genoa were the main beneficiaries, while the Turks established their caravanserais across the conquered provinces of Asia Minor, linking it to their already distant homeland. Anna may have felt critical of Emperor Manuel's close relations with western monarchs, which did nothing to regain the lost imperial territory.

Anna concludes her *Alexiad* in deep sadness brought on by her own sense of failure: she had been unable to persuade her husband, Nikephoros Bryennios, to make a bid for supreme power when Alexios I was dying. This helps to explain why she ends her history with tears, as she describes the accession of her brother and laments over her fate. Nonetheless, her *Alexiad* is exciting to read. It is a history of her father's reign, a biography of her family and her own autobiography, for she often comments on her personal reaction to events, her thoughts and fears. And it is composed in the most developed Byzantine style of Attic Greek, replete with obscure words and ancient proverbs. Anna's style is very cultivated and rather difficult. Like the reign of her beloved father, Alexios I Komnenos, her history is bold, novel and surprising. No other medieval woman, East or West, had the vision, confidence and the capacity to realize an equally ambitious project.

23

A Cosmopolitan Society

One finds me Scythian among Scythians, Latin among
 Latins . . .
And also to Persians I speak in Persian . . .
To Alans I say in their tongue:
'Good day, my lord, my archontissa, where are you from?
Tapankhas mesfili khsina korthi kanda, and so on' . . .
Arabs, since they are Arabs, I address in Arabic . . .
And also I welcome the Ros according to their habits . . .
'Sdraste, brate, sestritza', and I say, 'dobra deni'.
To Jews I say in a proper manner in Hebrew:
'Your blind house devoted to magic, your mouth, a chasm
 engulfing flies,
Memakomene beth fagi beelzebul timaie . . .'

> John Tzetzes, showing off his knowledge of languages he
> used to address all the different people he met on the
> streets of Constantinople, twelfth century

In the twelfth century, when John Tzetzes wrote these verses intended
to welcome visitors to the Byzantine capital, apart from the Jews
for whom he reserved insults, he did not exaggerate the number of
foreigners. Indeed, he might also have mentioned the more famous
Varangian guard formed in 988 by Basil II, which included Russians,
Scandinavians and Anglo-Saxons, or the German contingent settled
in their own quarter from the 1140s, or Catalans from Barcelona who
also frequented the empire's markets and served as mercenaries in its
armies.

In his attitude towards the Jews, John represents one of the prevalent Byzantine views, namely that the Jews had failed to understand the universal message of Christianity and still clung to their own tribal faith. His verses continue with following line: 'You stony Jew, the Lord has come, lightning be upon your head.' Yet since God had revealed the Law to Moses, as recorded in the Old Testament, the Jews were also a chosen people and could not be dismissed as heretics or pagans. This double-edged comment reflects an uneasy relationship: the allusion to Beelzebub (from Hebrew, *beelzebul*, fly-lord) indicates a popular belief that he was Lord of the Flies, while magic was often connected with Jewish practices. Yet Jewish communities had lived and worked in the major cities of Byzantium ever since the time of Constantine I. They were not obliged to reside in distinct ghettos but probably gathered in areas close to their synagogues. Although they must have spoken Hebrew, as John recounts, from the sixth century they had used the Greek translation of the Hebrew Bible (the Septuagint) and were thoroughly Hellenized.

Occasionally they were subjected to persecution, for instance under Emperor Herakleios in the seventh century, who ordered them to convert to Christianity, and again in the eighth, when Emperor Leo III forced them to accept baptism. But they knew how to circumvent this as Theophanes reports: 'The Jews . . . were baptized against their will and then washed off their baptism and they partook of holy communion on a full stomach and so defiled the faith.' Leo VI issued a similar law at the end of the ninth century, probably with the same results. It is unlikely that permanent conversions of large numbers occurred. In tenth-century Sparta – medieval Lakedaimonia – St Nikon attacked the local Jewish community, claiming that they were responsible for an epidemic in the city. He drove them out and refused to allow them to return to their jobs as weavers and cloth finishers unless they converted. Jews were regularly held responsible for unexplained disease, death and other misfortunes of Christians. In the early eighth century, for example, the first outbreak of iconoclasm against Christian churches in Muslim Syria was attributed to a Jewish magician.

Yet the Jews in Byzantium were generally tolerated and their distinctions permitted. Throughout the empire, they worked as merchants, bankers and money-lenders and were also employed as silk weavers and finishers of cloth. Thanks to the *Itinerary* of Benjamin of Tudela, a Spanish rabbi, which records his visit to nearly thirty communities in Byzantium during the 1160s, we learn of about 9,000 Jews who followed a variety of activities. They range from one poor agricultural community of two hundred on Mount Parnassus, near Delphi, to small and larger urban groups, including the Jews resident in Constantinople, especially in Galata, the settlement north of the Golden Horn which formed the thirteenth region of the capital and which Benjamin knows by its later name as Pera. He found that Byzantine Jews there, and in Thebes and Thessalonike, were prominent in the silk-working industry, and all enjoyed quite a high standard of living. He does not appear to have visited the community at Kastoria in northern Greece, which produced new hymns for use in synagogue services at the end of the eleventh century, but everywhere he notes the names of rabbis and outstanding Talmudic scholars.

In Constantinople itself, Benjamin was amazed at the stir and bustle caused by merchants from all parts of the world, and he includes Mesopotamia, Babylon, Persia, Egypt and Palestine, as well as northern and western countries. He mentions the emperor's doctor, Rabbi Solomon (the Egyptian), who is the only Jew allowed to ride on horseback, and observes the separation of Karaites, a sect which rejected the Talmud of normative Jewry, from Rabbanites, who lived by its regulations. In Pera, the Byzantine tanners made a point of emptying their filthy water in front of Jewish houses, which engendered hatred and bad relations. But the Byzantine communities were not disturbed by anything approaching the degree of hostility witnessed in the Rhineland during the First Crusade (as we shall see). During his later travels in Persia, Benjamin records that the Jews there were wealthier than those in Byzantium. But he emphasizes that he had seen no city like Constantinople, 'it is only equalled by Baghdad'. The Jews were a permanent part of the cosmopolitan society of Byzantium.

In contrast, many other groups sought temporary employment in the empire and worked for the imperial system or the court in particular capacities. For centuries, Byzantium had attracted adventurers, pirates, false prophets and heretics, all seeking their fortunes or an audience for their views, as well as merchants and mercenaries offering their services. Armenians frequently found employment in the Byzantine armed forces. As the empire's reach expanded from the tenth century onwards, a larger orbit of countries and cultures became linked to it. One striking example occurred in 1034, when Harald Hadrada arrived in Constantinople with five hundred Vikings armed with their traditional double-headed axes. The young prince had been forced to leave Norway and travel to Byzantium via Novgorod, the Russian river routes and Christian colonies, over the rapids of the lower Dnieper and the Black Sea. In Constantinople, which the Norsemen called Miklagard (the Great City), he served for ten years with the Varangian guard and campaigned in Sicily. His success attracted other soldiers of fortune from Iceland, Scandinavia and Anglo-Saxon England, after the Norman victory at the battle of Hastings in 1066. In addition to their duties as members of a professional fighting unit, they were stationed in the Great Palace as guard troops, marked out by their distinctive appearance and weaponry.

Considerable confusion surrounds the account of Harald's departure from Constantinople: his *Saga* alleges that he quarrelled with Empress Zoe, tried to kidnap her niece Maria and was involved in the blinding of Michael V. It also describes how Harald succeeded in leaving the Golden Horn, which was sealed by iron chains:

He told some of the oarsmen to pull as hard as they could, while those who were not rowing were to run to the stern of the galleys laden with all their gear. With that, the galleys ran up on to the chains. As soon as they stuck on top of the chains, Harald told all the men to run forward into the bows. Harald's own galley tilted forward under the impact and slid down off the chains; but the other ship stuck fast and broke its back. Many of her crew were lost, but some were rescued from the sea.

Harald later set Maria ashore and sailed back to Novgorod, where King Jaroslav gave him his daughter in marriage. Finally, he reclaimed his heritage as King of Norway, where he issued a regular silver coinage which appears to imitate the Byzantine silver coin, the *miliaresion* (worth one twelfth of a gold *nomisma*); similar imitations are also found in Sweden and Finland. He probably founded a church for St Olaf in the Scandinavian colony in Constantinople, to which devotees of the northern cult sent donations.

In the twelfth century, this recruitment of soldiers from the north was complemented by Christian pilgrims, such as King Erik of Denmark and his successor King Sigurd, who both visited Constantinople en route for Jerusalem and Rome, and returned with gifts of relics, gold and silver church fittings and a Greek prayer book. Sigurd had sailed down the river systems and across the Black Sea to the Byzantine capital in his Viking ship, which he presented to Alexios I Komnenos. It is shown with its dragon head in a famous fifteenth-century image of Constantinople. The emperor placed the gilded dragon head cover in the church of St Peter. The Varangian guard continued. In July 1203, the western crusader Geoffrey Villehardouin described an impressive honour guard: 'Englishmen and Danes equipped with battle-axes', lining the route from the gates of the Palace of Blachernai right up to the main door, where Isaac II Angelos was enthroned. And these same warriors also fought against the crusaders during the siege of 1204 and died with the Byzantines defending the city.

The Varangians left their mark in Constantinople: a graffito in runes (an early Germanic script), scratched on a marble parapet in Hagia Sophia, may suggest a moment of boredom during a long liturgy, while the runic inscription on a lion from Piraeus near Athens (which is now in Venice) is written in a more formal style. After their service they went home with Byzantine coins, silks used as shrouds and altar cloths, weapons and distinctive clothing. According to the *Laxdaela Saga*, Bolli Bollason came back dressed in a magnificent, gold-embroidered costume with a purple cloak, 'clothes of silk, given him by the king of Miklagarth'. As a result of these close relations and exchange of gifts, Byzantine influence in church architecture, fresco painting, manuscript illumination and ivory carving became widespread throughout the north, even as far as Iceland. Runic stones were raised in memory of those who had travelled to Byzantium as merchants, pilgrims and mercenaries, whose exploits are commemorated in Icelandic and Scandinavian poems and histories.

Another ethnic group that made a distinct impact in Byzantium in the eleventh century was recruited from the eastern regions of Armenia and Georgia. Two families of Kekaumenos and Pakourianos, in particular, stand out as a source of successful military commanders. Of the first, the Armenian general Kekaumenos mastered the art of writing in order to record his memoirs, which include military strategies and surprising victories over the Bulgars, as well as much advice for his sons based on personal experience. Of the second family, we know most about the Georgian Gregory Pakourianos, who fought for Byzantium from 1064 until his death in battle against the Pechenegs in 1086. He and his wife Kale supported the Georgian monastery of Iviron on Mount Athos, and her will describes in detail the distribution of her possessions to her relatives and freed slaves. In addition, Gregory founded his own at Petritzos (modern Bačkovo in Bulgaria), and wrote its foundation charter with provision for fifty-one Georgian monks and one notary, who should know Greek in order to deal with the local authorities. The monks were to receive their annual pension at Easter, when the monastery held a fair at its gates. Many of his comrades in arms retired to this retreat, which Gregory endowed with extensive properties.

Gregory also built three hostels for travellers who made their way from the central Balkans, down the Marica valley towards Adrianople and Constantinople. This followed a Byzantine tradition dating back to the earliest Christian times, reflecting the ideal of philanthropy, which was practised by rulers as an imperial virtue and imitated by others like Pakourianos. In Constantinople, Empress Irene established soup-kitchens, homes for the elderly and special cemeteries where proper burial could be provided for foreigners who fell ill and died in the capital. Social services were more developed in urban centres but rural monasteries could also provide basic medical care. In 1152, for instance, Isaac Komnenos established an imperial monastery at Vera (Pherrai in Thrace), with a 36-bed hospital and a bathhouse for the local villagers as well as the monks. Pakourianos, therefore, added to an established tradition of charitable foundations, which incorporated a higher level of care for medieval travellers and enhanced the movement and mingling of peoples.

During the twelfth century, the Komnenos dynasty founded by Alexios I employed more foreigners and sometimes rewarded them by a grant known as *pronoia* (literally, care). Although the precise meaning of the term is disputed, these grants gave the recipient, often a soldier, the right to collect state taxes for a limited time from an estate or a group of peasants living on it, or from pious foundations like monasteries. The grant was considered temporary and could be revoked at any time, but its original connection with military service, whether as a reward for past action or in anticipation of future duty, gradually weakened. Under Michael VIII Palaiologos (1259–82), it became hereditary and thus deprived the state of revenues on a permanent basis; holders of a *pronoia* simply collected the taxes without providing any service. If the system was introduced in the twelfth century to reward foreign mercenaries, its later development was one of the causes of Byzantine weakness.

All this cosmopolitan mixing raises the question whether Byzantium was more open to outsiders in the eleventh and twelfth centuries than before. Obviously, the arrival of western crusaders was to make a significant change in both elite and popular attitudes to Latin Christians. But from the late tenth century onwards, Byzantium attracted and employed a wider range of foreigners, who found jobs and rewards in the developed markets of the eastern empire. Their search for wealth was balanced by the empire's capacity to absorb outsiders and its need for skilled labour. The imperial structure could accommodate much diversity, provided it was loyal, and emperors delighted in the novelty and range of skills of fighters such as the Varangians. Byzantium's confidence in its own political and social organization admitted a higher degree of tolerance than other less-established medieval societies.

For all those who settled in Byzantium and paid taxes, knowledge of Greek was one essential, and learning Greek became easier in the eleventh and twelfth centuries because the spoken vernacular of the streets was simpler than the Attic Greek used by intellectuals (see chapter 21). Demotic gradually became the common language of trade in the eastern Mediterranean, spoken by Arabs, Syrians, Venetians, Genoese and Pisan merchants. The Italians regularly worked as translators for the imperial court, but by no means exclusively. During the debate between Cardinal Humbert, who led the Roman embassy, and Patriarch Keroularios in 1054, John 'the Spaniard' had to handle their disagreements; and in 1192, a Byzantine embassy to Genoa included one interpreter named Gerard Alamanopoulos ('son of Alaman'), a German who had probably married a Greek woman. Newcomers, therefore, had access to Byzantium through a less complex language system and could pick up the rudiments of spoken Greek without learning the higher forms.

Literary scholars have long noted a similarity between western *chansons de geste*, such as the *Song of Roland* or the *Pilgrimage of Charlemagne*, and the epic of Digenes Akrites and the Byzantine revival of late antique romance, raising the question of possible western influences on Byzantium. While three of the four Byzantine romances are composed in Attic Greek, the military exploits of Digenes are written in the vernacular spoken Greek of the twelfth century. In this it shares common features with topical verses making fun of prominent officials, Christian miracle stories and tales considered 'good for the soul'. Similar vernaculars are used in western *chansons*. Spoken vernacular Greek was also encouraged by Maria of Alania, mother-in-law of Anna Komnene, in the 1090s, by Bertha of Sulzbach, the first wife of Manuel I (1143–80), and by other western princesses who commissioned authors such as John Tzetzes to produce demotic versions of the *Iliad* and *Odyssey* to assist their mastery of Greek culture.

The growth of this literature, which could be appreciated by both Latins and uneducated Byzantines, reflects a new awareness of the difficulty of mastering Attic Greek and a need for simpler literary texts. Although some historians believe that Eleanor of Aquitaine, often considered a famous patron of the troubadours, accompanied her husband King Louis VII of France on the Second Crusade in 1147, and could have met Bertha at the Byzantine court, her encouragement was not essential to this literary development. The empire was changing and adapting to new pressures, and these included an alternative form of Greek, corresponding to the spoken language.

In addition to the increasing number of foreign visitors to the imperial court, the thriving economy of Byzantium continued to attract merchants from all parts of the Mediterranean. In a satirical story, written by an anonymous twelfth-century author, the hero Timarion, who describes himself as a tourist from Cappadocia, visits Thessalonike at the time of the annual festival of St Demetrios. He wants to see its sacred places, the church with its miracle-working oil which dripped from the saint's icon, and is surprised by the scale of the fair. He climbs up the hill of the castle to look out at the immense sea of tents:

The merchants' booths facing each other [were] set up in parallel rows . . . and at various points at an angle to the rows, other booths were set up . . . I couldn't help but compare it to the centipede with a very long body showing innumerable little feet under its belly . . . There were all kinds of men's and women's clothes, everything that comes from Boeotia and the Peloponnese, from Italy and Greece, Phoenicia, Egypt, Spain and the Pillars of Hercules, where the finest altar cloths are made.

In this way he expresses his amazement at 'the most important fair held in Macedonia', on 8 October, the saint's feast-day.

Such fairs stimulated the local economy and clearly attracted merchants from far and near, reflecting a constant commercial activity, even when the provinces were bereft of imperial coinage and the names of traders are not recorded. By the twelfth century, the export of olive oil and local silk products, which depended on mulberry plantations, is documented in Italian sources. Venetian merchants frequented numerous ports in the Peloponnese and central Greece and clearly made profits on their trade, but Constantinople itself remained the outstanding venue for trade. Its prosperity was also dependent upon the presence of foreign merchants, some established permanently in their own quarters, others more transient. In the mid-twelfth century, the Arab geographer Idrisi noted: 'Constantinople is prosperous, having markets and merchants, and its people are affluent.' The imperial capital could still impress and retained the cosmopolitan character which had attracted so many earlier travellers across the centuries. Even after 1261, Abdullah, a Muslim merchant, found the city most striking:

It is a great city on the seashore, comparable to Alexandria, and it takes one morning to cross it from end to end. There is a place as large as two-thirds of Damascus, surrounded by walls with a gate, which is reserved exclusively for the occupation of the Muslims. There is equally a similar place for the Jews . . . There are one hundred thousand churches, less one . . . He [the emperor] completed the number by building the Great Church . . . it is one of the most considerable and marvellous buildings that can be seen.

From its greatest extent in the sixth century, when it covered the entire eastern Mediterranean, to its smallest, when it became a tiny cluster of city-states in the fourteenth, Byzantium was always an empire, not a nation. Its resident peoples, whether Greek, Latin, Armenian, Jewish or from another community, understood themselves to be its citizens, paying its taxes and benefiting from its protection and its laws. The language of authority and command was Greek, although this language itself evolved from its classical roots into a demotic which was easier to learn and could be shared by those with other native tongues. At the same time, Byzantium never lost its Homeric world-view of migration and hospitality to strangers, which newcomers continued to enjoy.

As with many empires, the court imported outsiders as mercenaries and functionaries, free from loyalty to any other interest in the capital or beyond. Byzantium's cosmopolitan mixture, drawn across astounding distances by commercial opportunities or just curiosity, was not limited to Constantinople, as we have seen from the fair at Ephesos (see chapter 14). However visitors travelled, sailing from port to port or following the overland routes, the entire empire was organized for trade and open to pilgrims, its hospices, taverns and guesthouses ensuring that however proud and self-regarding the empire was, it was never parochial or closed.

IV

Varieties of Byzantium

24

The Fulcrum of the Crusades

Consider, therefore, that the Almighty has provided you, perhaps for this purpose, that through you He may restore Jerusalem from such debasement . . . With God's assistance we think
this can be done through you.

Guibert of Nogent reporting Pope Urban II's preaching of
the First Crusade at Clermont in 1095

In 1087, the balance of power in the Middle East shifted decisively
when the Seljuk Turks captured Jerusalem. Following their victory at
Mantzikert (1071), the Turks had been moving steadily south towards
their goal, Muslim Egypt. Their capture of Jerusalem cut pilgrim
routes to the Holy Land and prompted Christians throughout the
known world to action. Inspired by Pope Urban II's gruesome
accounts of 'the base and bastard Turks . . . an accursed race' and the
'pollution of paganism', knights, soldiers and even poor pilgrims 'took
the cross' (painted the sign of the cross on their clothes) in the West
and set out in the spring of 1096 on their own campaign to win back
the Holy Land. The ensuing crusades against the infidels in the Near
East brought West and East into much closer and often hostile contact
during the twelfth century, with Byzantium at the centre.

After a decade of civil war between 1071 and 1081, Alexios I
Komnenos (1081–1118) found Byzantine fighting forces in disarray
and realized the impossibility of campaigning both in the East against
the Turks and in the West against the Normans. He was forced to
concentrate on driving the Normans out of Epiros (1081–5), while one
group of Seljuk Turks established themselves at Nicaea in western Asia

Minor. In 1088, Alexios requested and obtained the use of a company of five hundred knights attached to the Count of Flanders, which provided excellent mercenary service. So in 1095, when he sent an appeal for western help to Pope Urban II, he anticipated the arrival of additional military forces of the same kind to assist in his battles against the Turks in Asia Minor. He may have thought that *his* needs could be made to coincide with the aims of the Latin Christians. Together they would drive the Turks out of Asia Minor and go on to reconquer Jerusalem.

Despite the Arab conquest of Jerusalem, for centuries Christians continued to make pilgrimages to the Holy Land. Once the Hungarians had been converted to Christianity, the overland route to Jerusalem via the Balkans and Constantinople was reopened, and western travellers became more familiar with the wealth of Byzantium and its amazing collection of relics. Their visits also made the Byzantines aware of the military strengths of Latin knights. While the emperor may not have appreciated the vitality of the papacy, reformed by Gregory VII (1073–85), and the growing influence of the Benedictine monastic order in the West, he had cultivated good relations with individual bishops of Rome and wished to promote Christian unity. Similarly, even if Pope Urban II saw the crusade as an opportunity to bring the Church of Constantinople under Rome's control, in all the accounts of his speech at Clermont an appeal was made to the western knights, 'who are accustomed to wage private wars even against Believers', to redirect their strength against the Infidel. Fulcher of Chartres reports that he urged them 'to help your brothers living in the Orient, who need your aid for which they have already cried out many times', which clearly reflects the idea of a common Christian front against the resurgence of Islam. Robert of Rheims adds that Urban II encouraged them in a material fashion as well:

Enter upon the road to the Holy Sepulchre; wrest that land from the wicked race, and subject it to yourselves. That land which as the Scripture says 'floweth with milk and honey', was given by God into the possession of the Children of Israel.

But as the pope preached the need for Christians to take the cross, and offered a pardon (indulgence) for their sins if they did so, large numbers of pilgrims, often poor and unarmed, including women and children, decided to set off for the East, led by charismatic preachers like Peter the Hermit, Walter the Penniless and Gottschalk, a priest from the Rhineland. Most followed a route from northern France and Germany across central Europe to Constantinople, inspired by Urban II's instructions to 'rush as quickly as you can to the defence of the Eastern Church'. Their presence fundamentally altered the idea of a combined Christian military campaign against the forces of Islam.

Some western knights had already fought the Muslims in Spain, and many pilgrims were familiar with the routes to the relics of St James at Santiago de Compostela. But the massed pilgrimage to Jerusalem of 1096 brought together for the first time thousands of largely unarmed civilians. The idea of participating in a holy war against the infidel may have increased their consciousness of the 'other' in medieval society, which was then turned against the Jews. According to an account attributed to Solomon ben Simpson of Speyer, which forms part of a longer twelfth-century Jewish chronicle, the Christian pilgrims said to each other:

Behold we journey a long way . . . to take vengeance upon the Muslims. But here are the Jews living amongst us, whose ancestors killed him [Christ] and sacrificed him groundlessly. Let us take vengeance first upon them.

As well as seeking out and killing as many Jews as they could find in Cologne, Mainz, Speyer and Worms, those who had taken the cross also destroyed synagogues and burned the Torah. Similar violence occurred in Hungary, where pilgrims quarrelled with local Christians. Albert of Aachen, who wrote his history fifty years after the crusade, records that they behaved badly towards the Hungarians: 'Like a rough people, rude in manners, undisciplined and haughty, they committed very many other crimes.' Such disorders in the passage of the pilgrims created difficulties for those who followed. They also established a negative pattern in western attitudes to the unfamiliar inhabitants of eastern Europe, including the Byzantines.

Although Anna Komnene may exaggerate when she claims that 100,000 knights and 80,000 foot soldiers participated in the great pilgrimage, modern historians reckon upwards of 30,000 knights and many more pilgrims descended on the Byzantine capital. The movement therefore took on a very different form from that requested by the Byzantine emperor of a compact body of disciplined soldiers. Although it is now known as the First Crusade, at the time its participants identified themselves as pilgrims, travelling to Jerusalem in the company of armed and mounted contingents, who would fight to regain the Holy Places. Those led by Peter the Hermit arrived at Constantinople first, intent on completing the pilgrimage on foot but seriously in need of rest before they undertook the most dangerous part of the route across Asia Minor. Markets were set up so that they could purchase food and they were ferried across the Bosphoros. When the fighting forces eventually arrived, the emperor insisted that the leaders should swear an oath to return to his rule any previously Byzantine territory they conquered from the Seljuks, which some were loath to perform. Despite many difficulties in their cooperation, the combined Christian forces followed the pilgrims into Asia Minor and succeeded in recapturing Nicaea (June 1097). The city was returned to Byzantine control and the crusading forces then set out across the Anatolian plateau in the extreme heat of summer.

Numerous accounts of the progress of the First Crusade, by western, Byzantine and Arab authors reflect dissensions between the crusaders and Alexios I, among the crusaders and within the different Muslim authorities. These came to a head outside the walls of Antioch, which was strongly defended by local Muslims. After a siege of seven months, the crusaders finally broke in and occupied the city (June 1098). But they were immediately confronted by a powerful Turkish army, raised by emirs and smaller tribes, which came to the city's relief. Some westerners who fled the city dissuaded Alexios I from sending Byzantine forces to assist the crusaders, claiming that Antioch was bound to fall to the Turks. His decision was later denounced as treachery. The final Christian victory, attributed in part to the miraculous discovery of the Holy Lance (a relic of the Passion of Christ), established Bohemond, son of the Norman ruler Robert Guiscard, as ruler of Antioch, in clear opposition to his oath to the Byzantine emperor.

The chequered history of Antioch during the crusades illustrates the contradictory aims of the participants. In Byzantine eyes, although the city had passed under Arab control in 636/7, it remained the target of Byzantine campaigns and had been regained in 969. But just over a century later, the Seljuks occupied it on their march south to Jerusalem. This symbolic loss was to be rectified by a Christian holy war, which would return Antioch to Byzantine rule. But to Bohemond and many of the leading knights on the campaign, who were actively seeking to found their own principalities in the East, the capture of Antioch was the first occasion to combine pilgrimage with territorial occupation. The Normans had already demonstrated their ambitions in this regard with Guiscard's occupation of the Byzantine provinces of southern Italy and the conquest of England by Duke William in 1066. Bohemond himself only managed to avoid Byzantine reprisals against his claim to Antioch by declaring himself dead and leaving the region in a smelly coffin, as Anna Komnene recounted.

By 1098, when the crusaders set out from Antioch to capture Jerusalem, they learned that the city had been retaken by the Fatimids. Since the Seljuk and other Turkish tribes had adopted the Sunni definition of Islam, and thus opposed the Shi'ite dynasty ruling in Egypt, Muslim forces in the Near East were divided. Thanks in part to this disunity, the First Crusade proved amazingly successful. After a six-week siege of Jerusalem (June–July 1099), the Latins overcame the defenders and slaughtered the entire population. The western knights then elected Godfrey of Bouillon, one of their leaders, as king and thus established a Christian enclave in the Holy Land. The triumph provoked a deep sense of loss among Muslims and Jews, to whom Jerusalem was a particularly holy city. Their exclusion from the city that had been under Islamic rule since 638 was particularly resented.

Jerusalem remained the central focus of rival claims throughout the twelfth century. As Muslim forces renewed their efforts to regain the city, the Latin kingdom required additional support from western knights. The Second Crusade failed to capture Damascus, and never reached Jerusalem, but additional forces got through by sea. Despite considerable success in establishing an efficient colony, with an exuberant artistic production patronized by Queen Melisende, who ruled Jerusalem from 1131 to 1153, the Christian enclave was constantly threatened. Crusader castles such as Krak des Chevaliers were constructed to guard the kingdom, while the church of the Holy Sepulchre, dedicated in 1149, symbolized the mixture of early Christian, Arab, Romanesque and Byzantine elements in crusader architecture. Eventually, in 1187 Saladin, a Kurdish general who had made himself Sultan of Egypt, recaptured the holy city for Islam, and his merciful treatment of its non-Muslim population was widely praised. Nonetheless, the shift back to Islamic control triggered a reaction in the West, where Church leaders again called for further crusades. The Third, from 1189 to 1192, and Fourth, from 1202 to 1204, were the result.

In all these meetings of East and West, language was a basic problem: few Greeks knew Latin, and even fewer westerners knew Greek. During the twelfth century, Emperor Manuel I (1143–80) increased the number of westerners employed at the imperial court, where they served as translators and ambassadors. Growing western influence in Byzantium was also clear from the emperor's delight in the sport of jousting, wearing trousers and selecting western princesses to marry into the imperial family. While this policy was sometimes denounced, there was a grudging appreciation of the Latins' fighting capacity and bravery. Whether mounted or on foot, these 'Franks' – as all westerners were called – were admired for their strength. Anna Komnene concedes that Bohemond, her father's Norman enemy, was a tall handsome man, and Niketas Choniates, the late twelfth-century historian appreciated Conrad of Montferrat, ally and son-in-law of Manuel I. Choniates even makes an unflattering comparison between the effeminate, cowardly Byzantines and their broad-shouldered, brave and daring Latin counterparts.

In addition to linguistic difficulties, Italian merchants generated a certain amount of tension within the empire. As we have seen (chapter 19), in Constantinople the Venetians controlled an entire quarter with its own church and warehouses along the Golden Horn, while Genoese and Pisan traders also maintained a presence in ports along the Adriatic, Mediterranean and Aegean coastlands. Despite the importance of international trade for Byzantium, political relations were not always good and local merchants resented the Italians' advantageous trading terms. Tensions became inflamed in 1171 and again in 1182, when Manuel I and his successor Andronikos I (1182–5) ordered attacks on Venetian merchants, their property and ships. The losses sustained were so great that the republic made a claim for compensation: this long list of houses, ships and goods destroyed was still not settled in 1203, which probably exacerbated antagonism.

Linguistic, social and economic grounds for mutual hostility between Christians were augmented by liturgical differences. The *filioque* clause, 'and from the Son' (see chapter 4), recited in the Latin creed might have passed unnoticed by local Greeks until 1054, but thereafter it became a major divider, while differences over leavened or unleavened bread, the number of genuflections and the days and degrees of fasting were obvious and visible to all. The Byzantines were shocked that western bishops and clergy fought on horseback like knights, and the Latins thought it improper for orthodox priests and lower clergy to marry. For the Patriarch of Constantinople and his staff, the claim of papal primacy was particularly threatening as it gave Rome, the see founded by St Peter, superior power over all the churches.

Another serious misunderstanding arose from the Byzantine policy of maintaining diplomatic relations with the Muslim caliphs, other Arab leaders and Turkish emirs. The western knights did not appreciate the long tradition of exchanging embassies with the enemies of the empire, which had established a web of diplomatic contacts and intelligence. On this basis, the Byzantines were often able to avoid war, to exchange prisoners and maintain peace. This was condemned in the West as treachery. The charge resurfaced in a more pointed fashion during the 1180s, when Andronikos I was reported as being in league with Saladin and the Turks. Magnus of Reichersberg, a German monk, simply denounced the Greeks as treacherous and hostile to western forces. The accusation contains a degree of propaganda and may be a forgery. But clearly the Latins were surprised that Byzantine emperors traditionally engaged in diplomatic contacts with Muslim leaders of the Near East and did not appreciate their behaviour.

These ambiguous feelings also generated suspicions and fears which accumulated as Byzantine requests for western military help against the Turks continued through the twelfth century. During the Second Crusade, in 1147, King Louis VII of France and the German Emperor Conrad came to the capital, where Emperor Manuel laid on extravagant entertainments and made sure the rulers visited the most important monuments and relics of Constantinople. Echoes of this royal visit appear in Icelandic sagas and the epic of Charlemagne's pilgrimage to

Jerusalem. Western knights were astonished at the wealth of the empire, particularly the churches and markets of the great metropolis of Constantinople, while the Byzantines feared that the crusaders might become covetous. In Frederick Barbarossa they recognized a brilliant and ambitious leader who might well turn his forces against the Queen City.

Meanwhile, the Turks consolidated their hold on the central plateau of Asia Minor. In 1176 Manuel confronted Sultan Kilij Arslan near Myriokephalon and was soundly defeated. This confirmed a permanent Turkish presence in the Sultanate of Rum, which forced bishops to flee and pressured Christians to convert to Islam.

In the last two decades of the twelfth century, both western and Byzantine forces had reason to be wary of each other. During the Third Crusade, Emperor Isaac II Angelos (1185–95) was fiercely criticized for negotiating a truce with the Mamluks of Egypt while the crusaders restored Christian control in Acre. It was in order to secure Jerusalem that Pope Innocent III preached the Fourth Crusade in 1198. One year later Alexios III Angelos (1195–1203), who replaced his brother Isaac II as emperor in Constantinople and blinded him, sent an embassy to Rome requesting support for an attack on the Turks. The pope responded that Alexios would have to contribute to the crusade and that the Eastern Church would have to return to the authority of Rome. This threat to the independence of the Church of Constantinople coloured all later negotiations between the crusaders and Byzantium.

Knights from northern Europe, led by Geoffrey Villehardouin, adopted a novel strategy for the Fourth Crusade: it would attack the Muslims from Egypt. So they requested the help of Venice in transporting their forces across the Mediterranean to Alexandria, and this was agreed at considerable expense. But too few crusaders arrived at Venice to pay for the transport in specially designed ships. The Venetians then proposed to make a slight detour from the planned route to attack Zara, a Christian city on the Dalmatian coast. In order to set sail, the crusaders had to agree, and with the plunder they accumulated at Zara they were able to finance the crusade. But at Zara they also learned about Prince Alexios, son of Isaac II, who had escaped from prison in Byzantium and came to meet the leaders of the crusade. The young pretender, plotting against his uncle Alexios III, offered 200,000 silver marks in support if they would restore him to the imperial throne. He also accepted that the Church of Constantinople should become subject to the pope. After much discussion, it was agreed that the fleet should make another detour, to Constantinople, to install Alexios as rightful emperor, collect the sums promised and then proceed to Alexandria. Many knights, however, left the expedition at this point, disillusioned by the delays in getting to the eastern Mediterranean.

In the spring of 1203, the fleet duly set sail from Zara, anchored outside the walls of Constantinople, and within a few weeks installed Alexios IV Angelos on the throne. But then he had to fulfil the terms agreed at Zara, which proved much harder. After nearly a year when Alexios failed to pay the crusaders, a delegation went to warn him:

Our lords have frequently called on you ... to carry out the contract made between yourselves and them. If you do this, they will be extremely pleased; but if not, they will no longer regard you as their lord and their friend, but will use every means in their power to obtain their due.

Geoffrey Villehardouin continued: 'The Greeks were much amazed and deeply shocked by this openly defiant message ... The noise of angry voices filled the hall.' In his history of the crusade, written later, he reported that he was extremely glad to get out of the Blachernai Palace alive. Once the challenge had been made, hostile action became more likely, and when no payment was forthcoming it became inevitable. In April 1204, the crusaders attacked Constantinople with their most sophisticated siege weapons, which had been destined for Muslim-held Jerusalem. After four days, they forced an entry over the sea walls and subjected the Byzantine capital to a five-day sack. They then elected Count Baldwin of Flanders as emperor and the Venetian, Thomas Morosini, as patriarch, setting up a Latin Empire. The Byzantines were forced into exile.

In this development, the Doge of Venice, Enrico Dandolo, played a decisive role. He had lived in Constantinople in the 1180s and lost an eye in an attack on Venetian property. Now he suggested that the besiegers agree a division of the estimated spoils of war, a Venetian technique which had also been used at Zara. The *Partitio terrarum*

Imperii Romaniae was drawn up in 1204 to justify and consolidate anticipated gains, not only of the city's wealth but also of the territory of Romania, a western name for the empire. When the city's impressive fortifications looked secure, it was Dandalo's expert knowledge of the Golden Horn that proved critical to the success of the final attack. Venice was also the power that gained most from it, in that the conquest of Constantinople gave it rights of occupation over all the trading ports it used. The Venetian commercial empire, established as a result of the Fourth Crusade, was far more successful and permanent than the Latin Empire of Constantinople, which lasted less than sixty years.

For Byzantium, however, the experience of the sack of April 1204 left indelible wounds. Both Greek and Latin authors preserve vivid eyewitness accounts: Geoffrey Villehardouin, Robert de Clari, Gunter of Pairis (a monastery in Germany) on the western side, and Niketas Choniates, the greatest Byzantine medieval historian, on the eastern. Both sides agree about the extensive looting and devastation, which was increased by fires. Gunter writes:

so great a wealth of gold and silver, so great a magnificence of gems and clothing, so great a profusion of valuable trade goods, so great a bounty of foodstuffs, homes so exceptional and so filled with commodities of every sort . . . suddenly transformed [the crusaders] from aliens and paupers into very rich citizens.

Niketas laments:

Constantine's fine city, the common delight and boast of all nations, was laid waste by fire and blackened by soot, taken and emptied of all wealth, public and private, as well as that which was consecrated to God, by the scattered nations of the West . . . the dashing to earth of the venerable icons and the flinging of the relics of the saints . . . seizing as plunder the precious chalices and patens . . . the outcries of men, screams of women, the taking of captives . . . and raping of bodies.

After five days, Choniates and his family only escaped from the destruction thanks to a Venetian friend, a wine merchant, who pretended that these Greeks were his booty.

The Latin occupation of Constantinople had many long-lasting effects, not least the removal of many relics, antiquities and treasures to the West. In 1207, for example, Heinrich von Ülmen offered a magnificent gold and enamel reliquary of the True Cross, made in about 963, to his local bishop. Its presence today in the treasury of the cathedral of Limburg is a reminder of the looting of the greatest Christian city of the medieval world. Four ancient bronze horses that had guarded the Hippodrome and inspired competitors from the fifth century, were taken to Venice to adorn the façade of San Marco, where replicas are now visible (plate 30). The crusaders removed sixth-century carvings from the church of St Polyeuktos, sculptures, icons, silks, manuscripts and precious liturgical objects – all part of the vast booty divided between the crusaders.

In this way the leaders of the Fourth Crusade subverted the ideals of the First. The spirit of Christian pilgrimage and adventure, inspired by Pope Urban II's sermon at Clermont, was destroyed by the Latin occupation of Constantinople. Although this did not put an end to crusading, its dark shadow hung over all attempts to re-create Christian unity against Islam.

25

The Towers of Trebizond, Arta, Nicaea and Thessalonike

A colossus in height and clearing the air, it strives somehow
to reach even the sky ... the shape of the tower, namely the
shape of a delicate honey-comb; a hexagon raises its most
beautiful shape to the stars and to the beauties of the firmament. To us God gave a tower of strength ... a towered
fortification of beauty, a tower of ineffable joy.

John Geometres, poem on a tower, post 989

By 12 April 1204, the greatest city in Christendom was full of smoul-
dering ruins; its palaces and the great houses of its leading families
had been pillaged, their hangings and glorious wardrobes torched,
their roofs gutted by fire. Entire libraries and archives of documents
within, if not already burned, were exposed to rain and would become
food for insects and rodents. Many of the revealing small objects of
daily life, from tools to kitchenware, icon corners and prayer books,
accumulated over hundreds of years, were smashed and broken. Some
of the booty taken by the conquerors now survives in western
treasuries, but many fine Byzantine objects were lost in 1204. How
many, we don't know, and whether even more would have been lost
later to other enemies is beside the point – the destruction took place
there and then.

Those days in April 1204 have recently been subjected to intensive
re-examination as scholars all over the world noted the 800th anniversary of the sack of Constantinople. Pope John Paul II apologized for
the event, which provided an occasion to take stock of the attitudes
of modern historians to Byzantium. Despite the obvious presence of

Byzantium in the medieval West, there is still a widespread ignorance of the empire's contribution to European development as the force which checked the expansion of Islam into the Balkans and the protective shield behind which the fragmented western kingdoms developed the notion of Europe. This still influences some western debate about the Fourth Crusade, which relies on a stereotype of Byzantium as a grey, dead zone: a series of emperors and battles for over a thousand years and little more. Byzantinists may be to blame for writing complicated histories which fail to bring to life the inner dynamic of the empire. In turn, specialists of western medieval history cling to this dull picture. It is all too easy to fall back on the initial Enlightenment view of the empire as a moribund state, peculiar unto itself, and not worthy of closer attention.

One source of this stereotype, although this is very difficult to document, seems to be the very storming and destruction of the Byzantine capital in 1204. In part, the empire brought the attack upon itself. Emperor Alexios IV and his advisers were extraordinarily stupid and complacent to allow a fully equipped siege army to remain camped outside its gates, neither paying off the crusaders as they had been promised, nor attacking and destroying them. The doge's detailed knowledge of the sea walls contributed to the successful assault, but the Venetians had learnt the skills of diplomacy and the savage combination of trade and force from Byzantium. Venice was partly a product of the empire, as well as its competitor. After the capture of the city, when the crusaders divided up the empire, Venice claimed the largest part. Pope Innocent III sent western clerics to occupy the lands now brought under the authority of the Church of Rome, and forced orthodox bishops and monks into exile.

But now the Christian West had to explain to itself and to justify the philistine massacre and destruction of the finest city in Christendom. How could the forces dedicated to fighting the Muslim infidel have burned the icons and desecrated the churches of the greatest Christian metropolis? Only because Byzantium deserved it! The Byzantine empire had to be seen as treacherous, doomed, effeminate, somehow repugnant, and disobedient to Rome. The outcome of the Fourth Crusade also confirmed to Pope Innocent and his successors, and to western rulers and monks who had participated in the crusades, that the Greeks were essentially crafty and treacherous. They always used diplomacy to conceal their weakness, and when forced to fight they proved cowardly. The Byzantine system of imperial government was also considered unstable, because it permitted a rebel to become emperor and an unsuccessful ruler to be deposed and blinded. This appeared weak to the nascent monarchies of Europe, where rulers were trying to strengthen their authority. Condemnation of its ancient political system went hand in hand with admiration for its relics, gold and silver objects, icons and silks, which deserved better homes than Byzantium. In this way, the crusaders justified their own pillage and looting. The negative stereotype of the term 'Byzantine', as if it characterizes a culture which does not deserve to exist, stretches back to the bad faith of the sack of 1204.

The devastation was such that Byzantium might never have recovered. Where many states would have succumbed to such a blow to the heart, occupied for fully half a century, Byzantium in fact reemerged in a plurality of new forms in different centres. Thanks to the inner vitality of its civilization, the empire was to last another 250 years.

This is one of the most surprising things I discovered in writing this book. I fully expected that Constantinople itself would play a central role, as a fabulous and exceptional city with its buildings and its trade. What I had not expected was how often I would be recording the compelling inventiveness and novelty of the broader aspects of Byzantine civilization, from its government and religion to its military and intellectual skills. It had the ability to develop a secret, sea-borne explosive artillery and keep the secret for centuries. It could generate and survive a profoundly divisive argument over the role of icons, identity and religious belief. When Latin Christendom and the Muslim East insisted on keeping the Holy Book in its sacred languages of Latin and Arabic, Byzantium had the audacity to translate the Greek Bible into a written language which its own scholars had invented in order to facilitate the conversion of the Slavs. It had the discipline to mint and maintain a stable coinage for over seven hundred years. It had the ingenuity to develop royal forms of power while maintaining Roman administration. Time and again, the extraordinary combination of Roman, pagan, Christian and Greek inheritances gave it the capacity to recover from adversities rather than to disappear, leaving only a trace of its achievements. The Byzantium that gainsays the generally accepted stereotype is this lively, inventive society, passionately believing in itself.

The test of this argument, that the greatness of the metropolis was sustained by the profound resources of the civilization of which it was the head, came at the moment when Byzantium was decapitated and the hinterland had to respond to its capture and takeover by foreign forces. What happened after 1204, when westerners set up a Latin empire at its centre and occupied its palace for fifty-seven years, should reveal the essential elements of the rest of Byzantine society. And what happened is that mini-Byzantine empires sprang up and Byzantium re-emerged in a plurality of cities, accompanied by an outpouring of Byzantine artistic activity.

In Trebizond on the eastern border, two Komnenos brothers established an empire which was far more than a city-state and continued to rule itself from 1204 to 1461. In the far west, 2,000km away in western Greece, Epiros became the centre of another Byzantine power, based on the cities of Arta and Thessalonike, the most active port in the empire, and declared itself to be the true heir of Byzantium. And closer to the walls of Constantinople, across the Sea of Marmara, another empire, based on Nicaea and staffed by refugees from Constantinople, enjoyed a magnificent revival. Even areas which remained permanently under Venetian rule, as Crete did until the Turks captured it in 1669, never lost their Byzantine character, which was indelibly embedded in the Greek language and religion, and is manifested in new frescoes, icons, histories and poems. The strengths and landscapes of different responses to the loss of Constantinople all confirm the depth of the educational, administrative, cultural and military capacities of Byzantium's traditions and their ability to respond to challenges, The stereotype of a monolithic, bureaucratic, feeble, corrupt, over-complicated and ineffective empire seems completely false.

During the last two decades of the twelfth century, provincial uprisings had already occurred, reflecting a growing antagonism towards the ruling centre of Constantinople. The usurpation of Andronikos Komnenos in 1182 and the murder of his nephew, the young emperor Alexios II, appear to have been the signal for Balkan revolts – in

Serbia Stefan Nemanja extended his power, founding an independent dynasty which would rule until 1371, while in Bulgaria two brothers, Asen and Peter, broke away from Byzantium and established a new capital at Trnovo. A sense of frustration in outlying areas at paying heavy taxes to Constantinople and receiving nothing in exchange is evident in the complaints of Michael Choniates, Metropolitan of Athens (1180–1205):

What do you lack? Not the wheat-bearing plains of Macedonia, Thrace and Thessaly, which are farmed by us; nor the wine of Euboea, Ptelion, Chios and Rhodes, pressed by us; nor the fine garments woven by our Theban and Corinthian fingers, nor all our wealth, which flows, as many rivers flow into one sea, to the Queen City.

This disaffection was mirrored on Cyprus, which rebelled in 1185 and gave Richard I of England ('the Lionheart') a pretext for his conquest of the island during the Third Crusade. (Later he sold it to Guy de Lusignan, the ex-king of Jerusalem.) Similarly, within Byzantium independent leaders emerged in control of their own cities: at Philadelphia in western Asia Minor, Theodore Mankaphas minted his own coins. In Greece, Leo Sgouros made the castle of Acrocorinth his centre, and an unidentified ruler took control of Methone, on the southwest coast of the Peloponnese. These local leaders (archons) claimed quasi-imperial authority and disrupted central government from Constantinople.

The events of 1204 sealed the splintering of imperial authority: the Komnenos brothers in Trebizond, Michael Komnenos Doukas in Arta and Theodore Laskaris in Nicaea strengthened a regional partition of Byzantium. Meanwhile Alexios III Angelos continued to consider himself emperor in absentia. He allied with Leo Sgouros, campaigned against Laskaris in Asia Minor, and died in captivity at Nicaea in 1211/12. Some crusaders who had participated in the sack of April 1204 returned home with their booty, but others set out to lay claim to the territories distributed by the *Partitio terrarum Imperii Romaniae*. As western knights jostled with local archons to conquer lands for themselves, all the provinces of the empire were affected by political turmoil. From Constantinople, Boniface of Montferrat led a crusader group towards Thessalonike, which the Latin Emperor Baldwin had allotted to him; members of the de la Roche family made their way to Thebes and Athens, and Geoffrey Villehardouin, nephew of the historian, and William of Champlitte continued south to set up their own principality of Achaia in the Peloponnese. They all met resistance organized by the ex-emperor Alexios III, other dissatisfied Byzantine leaders and Bulgars. Meanwhile, the Venetians established their control over numerous ports in the Aegean, to which they added Crete, bought from Boniface, who had no naval means of conquering it. These maritime centres formed the core of their commercial empire in the eastern Mediterranean down to the seventeenth century.

The fragmentation of imperial territory could have positive results locally, as all the pretenders to Byzantine imperial power established courts, which required administrators, rhetors, teachers, artists and generals to support their claims. Thanks to the educational systems in each centre, and the ecclesiastical hierarchy of highly educated bishops, the new courts emerged well staffed. The rulers of Trebizond, Arta and Nicaea all invested in buildings, law, agriculture and trade, promoting development and patronizing art in new churches and monasteries. In their rivalry to represent Byzantium, the new centres drew on a wealth of regional skills, and competed using local propaganda brilliantly expressed by their historians and intellectuals, sermons written by their churchmen and imperial-style buildings constructed and decorated by local workmen.

The plethora of successor states also had to confront another consequence of 1204: the opportunity, eagerly seized by Pope Innocent III and his successors, to bring the Eastern Church under his control, as agreed by Alexios IV Angelos at Zara. Latin bishops were immediately appointed to all the major sees in Byzantium controlled by the crusaders; Dominican, Franciscan and Cistercian friars were sent out to occupy monasteries, which became centres for the conversion of the Greek Orthodox to Latin Christianity. Byzantium was thereby invaded a second time by a religious force, determined to show the Greeks the errors of their theology. But this attempt at spiritual conquest was largely unsuccessful. The inhabitants of the empire remained loyal to their own clergy, even when their bishops were forced into exile. Byzantium resisted and maintained its cultural heritage, even in those far-flung regions never recovered by the rulers of Constantinople.

In Cyprus, for instance, Orthodox churches with frescoes, mosaics and icons remained a dominant feature of the island, although the late medieval and early modern history of the island is marked by its foreign occupiers: crusaders, Franks, Venetians and Ottomans. Beside the soaring Gothic cathedral of Famagousta, the monastery of Bellapais and the castles of St Hilarion, Kyrenia and Saranda Kolonnes, local Byzantine traditions were adapted and developed. Similarly, in central and southern Greece arched windows adorn the Gothic churches and monasteries rebuilt by western friars at Daphni and Andravida (plate 34); western-style castles at Karytaina and Mistras, and Frankish towers dotted through central Greece, reflect western building techniques. The acropolis of Athens was transformed into a fortified castle, enclosing the palace celebrated in Shakespeare's *A Midsummer Night's Dream*, as the idyllic home of Duke Theseus. But it remained Greek, not Latin.

This mixed society of Greeks and Latins, Byzantines and crusaders, is wonderfully illustrated in the *Chronicle of the Morea*, an epic of the conquest of the Peloponnese written in the early fourteenth century. The name 'Morea' may reflect the ubiquitous cultivation of the mulberry, *morea* or *murus*, an essential ingredient in the production of silk. The *Chronicle* in verse survives in Old French, Aragonese, Italian and demotic Greek versions, reflecting the polyglot population. Intermarriage created *gasmoules*, half-Greek half-Latin, whose rights and status were regulated by the Assizes of Romania, modelled on the law book of the kingdom of Jerusalem. Although a western type of feudal rule was imposed by the conquerors, the Byzantine character of the regions is very clear in the surviving monuments, especially village churches decorated with frescoes and icons in traditional style. While new provincial centres encouraged this growth, it was fired by local loyalty to the Orthodox Church, which embodied Byzantine traditions beyond the purely religious.

Trebizond

Of these new centres, Trebizond, at the southeast corner of the Black Sea, is especially notable because it became the centre of a flourishing independent empire which lasted for over 250 years, from 1204 to

1461. During the Seljuk inroads of the eleventh century, a local notable, Theodore Gabras, fought and negotiated to make it relatively independent from Constantinople. In 1204, two grandsons of Emperor Andronikos I (1182–5) gained control of it with the help of Queen Tamar of Georgia. Drawing on its traditions of autonomy, as well as its natural resources, David and Alexios Komnenos made Trebizond a new capital city. It became an international centre of Black Sea trade, partly because it controlled the western end of one of the most important overland routes from the Far East, and thus raised income from commercial taxes. Trebizond also derived considerable wealth from silver mines in the Pontic Alps, which form a natural defence to the south.

The alliterative title of Rose Macaulay's novel *The Towers of Trebizond* is based on romantic views of the picturesque Black Sea port, with its grand citadel rising above the sea, its magnificent churches and monasteries, including one dedicated to St Eugenios, the city's patron saint. The towers were largely rebuilt in the thirteenth and fourteenth centuries by the emperors, who also constructed their palace on the citadel that offers wonderful views out over the Black Sea. They adopted the title of Grand Komnenoi to bolster their political claims as successors to the rulers of Byzantium, and followed the same philanthropic traditions of building churches as well as monasteries. In the mid-thirteenth century, Manuel I founded the monastery of St Sophia, extensively rebuilt later, which preserves outstanding frescoes and carved external decoration. In both the sphere of administration and international trade, the institutions of the empire of Trebizond were modelled closely on Constantinople's. Genoese and Venetian merchants were granted privileges and allowed quarters close to the harbour, which was also used by numerous Caucasian and Russian traders.

Trebizond was always appreciated as a spectacularly beautiful site. In the eleventh century, the local scholar John Xiphilinos (later Patriarch of Constantinople) wrote an account of the martyrdom of Eugenios and recorded his miracles, which include the curing of several Scythian soldiers (Varangians). Later the local sacristan, John Loukites, rewrote the miracles with interesting new details; he describes the saint as 'the great attraction and the glorious name of all the East and of golden Trebizond'. But the most important descriptions of Trebizond occur in two famous speeches: by John Bessarion, who was born in the city in about 1400 and later became a cardinal of the Catholic Church; and by the cleric John Eugenikos, who visited it to pay tribute to his father's birthplace in the mid-fifteenth century. These are rhetorical works of praise, which follow an established genre (*ekphrasis*) and include many set elements, but they reveal much about the life of the city. Bessarion praises it as the 'marketplace of the world', with strong fortifications and a fine palace, while Eugenikos notes particularly its beautiful setting and fertile agriculture. Together they provide a rich and contrasting picture of a justly famous city.

Due to its frontier position, Trebizond served as a conduit for ideas as well as goods from the Muslim Caliphate and lands farther east. In the 1290s, Gregory Chioniades, a Greek monk, travelled via Trebizond to Tabriz, capital of the Mongol Ilkhans (in modern Iran), to learn more about Arabic astronomy with a famous scholar called Shams Bukhari. His long period of study there resulted in the translation of key Arabic texts on astronomy and the astrolabe, one of the few instances of Byzantium accepting the superior scholarship of a foreign culture. After his return, Chioniades was appointed to teach both astronomy and medical science in Constantinople, using his substantial library of scientific and medical writings. The significance of his translations into Greek was recognized much later by Copernicus, who used them in his work on planetary models. In 1305, he was sent back to Tabriz as bishop, and served the Christian community of the Ilkhanate for about five years before retiring to a monastery in Trebizond where he died in about 1320.

By judicious diplomatic and marriage alliances with Turkish, Mongol and Georgian rulers, the Grand Komnenoi sustained Byzantine rule until 1461, when their capital finally succumbed to the Ottomans. Thanks to the extensive research of Anthony Bryer, we can see how they made an excellent case for 'small is beautiful' in imperial terms. Gradually, Trebizond became Trabzon but many of its Byzantine characteristics lived on, notably the monasteries in the Pontic Alps, such as the foundation of Soumela, which survived to the early twentieth century. Isolated communities preserved a dialect of Pontic Greek and the art of playing the one-string lyra. Today,

Trabzon remains a most impressive city perched above the Black Sea, and it secures some of its wealth through the sale of local hazelnuts to Cadbury's of Birmingham, England, to be made into fruit and nut chocolate bars.

Epiros

In 1205, another rival empire was set up by Michael Komnenos Doukas in Epiros, hugging the Adriatic coast on the western edge of Greece. He was a cousin of the Byzantine Emperors Isaac II Angelos and Alexios III, but inherited from his father John the names of Komnenos and Doukas, which allowed him to claim membership of those more distinguished clans. After serving briefly in Boniface of Montferrat's Latin forces, Michael fled to Arta in western Greece, where he organized local resistance to the crusaders. In ten years he succeeded in taking control of the coastland from the Gulf of Corinth north to the Albanian border, as well as Kerkyra (Corfu) and land as far east as Larissa in central Thessaly. This small state, based on the capital, Arta, was isolated from the rest of Greece by the Pindos Mountains. It was oriented mainly to the west and encouraged the exploitation of its rich agricultural produce by local and foreign merchants. Michael's illegitimate son Michael II Komnenos Doukas adopted the title of *despotes* (lord) in 1249, which later historians used to identify his state as the Despotate of Epiros.

In 1215, Theodore Komnenos Doukas succeeded his half-brother Michael I. He regained Ohrid and defeated and captured the Latin emperor, Peter of Courtney. By 1224 he had control of Thessalonike and went on to capture Adrianople (modern Edirne), only a couple of days' march from Constantinople. When he was crowned emperor (*basileus*) in the cathedral of Thessalonike by the senior metropolitan, Demetrios Chomatenos of Ohrid in around 1225/7, he made good his claim to inherit the mantle of Byzantium. For nearly twenty years, Theodore ruled the second city of the empire as well as the Despotate of Epiros. He was succeeded by Michael II Komnenos Doukas, who consolidated the independence of the Despotate. From their capital at Arta, despots ruled until 1318 and embellished their territory with elegant monuments.

It was difficult for these rival states to attain a dominant position: their small scale meant that they had to form alliances even with their enemies. In Greece, this involved dealing with crusader leaders and western powers hungry for a foothold. As a result, the history of western Byzantium after 1204 is one of constant rivalry, realignment of forces, pitched battles and self-destructive murders perpetuating division. Ambitious western rulers, such as Charles of Anjou – king of Naples and Sicily (1265–85) – or the Italian families of Tocco and Acciajuoli, and mercenary groups like the Catalan and Aragonese Companies, intervened in the political ferment, both as allies and opponents of the crusading kingdoms and Byzantine successor states.

Nonetheless, the despots of Epiros created a capital city at Arta with a court and administration based on Byzantine models. They used their imperial patronage to attract artists and scholars and founded monasteries and churches. With their encouragement, archbishops like John Apokaukos and Demetrios Chomatenos applied Byzantine law in their own courts and extended Constantinopolitan practices to ecclesiastical administration. As I noted in chapter 7, the records of their legal decisions make unusually interesting reading and reveal a humane concern to improve unsatisfactory arrangements. While Michael II built a major church at Arta dedicated to the Virgin (which is now known as Kato Panagia, the lower church), his wife Theodora constructed a monastery and was buried in the narthex which she had added in about 1270. She is recognized as a saint and her *Life* records her pious activities. Her son Nikephoros was also a patron of the arts. In around 1290, he founded the most outstanding Byzantine monument of the despotate: the church of the Panagia Paregoretissa (the All-Holy Virgin of Comfort, plates 35 and 36). This tall, five-domed structure rises through three storeys supported on tiers of columns to the central dome with a mosaic of Christ Pantokrator. Marble revetment faces the walls up to the gallery level. While some of the relief carving reflects a western, Romanesque style, the impact of the interior is undoubtedly Byzantine.

Nicaea

The empire established at Nicaea was different. It remained in every sense closest to Constantinople, a short boat ride and day's march away. Nicaea was a well-fortified, ancient foundation, with a famous and prestigious history as the site of two oecumenical councils, and all the urban monuments necessary to a capital city. From the beginning, it was dominated by exiles from the capital and sustained the most imperial pretensions. Theodore Laskaris had married Anna, a daughter of Alexios III Angelos, and transported whatever could be salvaged of the imperial system of government from Constantinople to Nicaea. When Patriarch John Kamateros refused to move to Nicaea, Theodore persuaded a suitably qualified cleric, Michael Autoreianos, to become Orthodox patriarch in exile. And in 1208, Autoreianos performed an imperial coronation which made Theodore the first Byzantine emperor acclaimed in the successor states.

Before he became its ruler in 1254, the first Theodore's grandson and namesake composed a eulogy of the city, which he delivered in the presence of his father, John III Vatatzes, and the citizens. He stresses that

the city of you Nicaeans now ... crowns your heads with the purple of grandeur and truth ... And in return being well endowed by you with majesty it is indeed a city among cities, since it contains inhabitants made illustrious by learning rather than by wealth and a great army ... [Nicaea] is the queen of all cities and has, on account of its learning, the truly supreme rank.

Drawing attention to the physical beauty of the site, the riches of its agricultural land and lake, vineyards and supplies of water, he claims that these can satisfy any lover of food or luxury, while the city's education pours forth over the surrounding fields, making even the country people wise.

This appreciation of the civilizing role of a city is a commonplace, but Theodore emphasizes the benefits of Nicaea's learning to raise it above ancient Babylon, the cities of India and even Athens. In 1290, the set rules of eulogy were more closely followed in a later oration composed by Theodore Metochites for the visit of Emperor Andronikos II Palaiologos. The future civil servant draws attention to the fine situation of Nicaea and its lake, and 'the plentiful enjoyment of baths, with a charm that adds luxury to utility', the common shelters for those suffering in illness joined to poverty, including those stricken by the sacred disease (epilepsy). He gives more detailed descriptions of the churches, monasteries, walls and houses, reminding Andronikos that Nicaea contains

reverend treasures of beauty, the illustrious monuments of the wisdom of our times, the fruits of it, its brilliant and superb rites, the holy places of meditation for those who have chosen to withdraw from material things and to give their time only to God.

While Constantinople was occupied by the Latins, the emperors in Nicaea created a viable imperial structure in western Asia Minor and developed the region's agricultural potential to enhance its economic capacity to survive alone. During his long reign (1224–54), Emperor John III Vatatzes was able to ban the import of foreign goods and food supplies because Nicaea could provide all basic needs. Numerous foundations contributed to this agricultural development, which is documented in the records of the monastery dedicated to the Virgin Lembiotissa near Smyrna (modern Izmir). Judicious alliances with the Genoese, who were the first Italian community to gain a foothold in the lucrative Black Sea commerce, brought an increased investment in international trade. The emperor preferred to live at Nymphaion, where the mint and treasury were sited, and moved his court there in the 1230s, but the patriarch remained at Nicaea.

In addition to campaigning vigorously against Latins, Turks and the forces of Epiros and Thessalonike, emperors of Nicaea and their patriarchs took an active part in the negotiations for church union. Numerous embassies, often led by western friars, passed through Nicaea and Constantinople for discussions, which involved Elias of Cortona and John of Parma, both general masters of the Franciscan order. In 1249/50, a papal delegation led by John debated the key issue of the *filioque* (see chapter 4 for discussion of the procession of the Holy Spirit) at the court of Nymphaion. Nikephoros Blemmydes, a thirteenth-century theologian, represented the Byzantine side. Some of these westerners had broader interests: the Flemish Dominican William of Moerbeke was particularly interested in ancient Greek philosophy. He collected manuscripts, requested help in learning Greek, visited Nicaea and Thebes in 1260, and made translations of Aristotle's *On the Parts of Animals*, works of Alexander of Aphrodisias, Proclus, Archimedes and Galen. As papal legate, in 1274 he worked for the reunion of the churches and in 1278 was appointed Latin Archbishop of Corinth. His Latin translations were based on such a strict word-by-word method (called *kata poda*, 'by foot', or 'step by step') that they can help in reconstituting the original Greek of texts now lost or only partially preserved.

To the Byzantines the friars seemed unlike other westerners. They were imbued with Christian ideals such as poverty and humility, and unlike the crusading clergy they did not take part in fighting. Byzantine disapproval of armed western clergy had stoked anti-Latin feeling after 1204 and also reinvigorated orthodox opposition. But the educated friars seemed anxious to engage with Greek theology, rather than condemn it outright, and many debates conducted at Nicaea set the stage for later attempts at church union. Popes Gregory IX and Innocent IV supported exploratory talks, though they refused to authorize another universal council. And Emperors John III and Theodore II both played major roles in directing and presiding over the negotiations. In his letter to Pope Alexander IV (1254–61), Patriarch Arsenios of Nicaea (1254–60, later Patriarch of Constantinople, 1261–65), emphasized the utterly crucial role of the emperor: no question concerning a possible reunion of the churches could be raised without his participation. The danger of this position, which was strengthened by the Nicaean experience, was that the emperor would usurp patriarchal functions and thus overturn the delicate balance between civil and ecclesiastical powers.

After the Latin occupation of 1204, Byzantium was never the same and anti-western sentiment expanded, intensifying memories of the sack. On the other side, the embattled Latin Empire of Constantinople never had sufficient manpower to create a flourishing society. Like other western enclaves in the Near East, it made constant appeals to the West for armed knights to assist in its defence. The Venetians sustained its trade, Franciscan and Dominican friars converted Byzantine churches to western use, and the dynasty established by Baldwin of Flanders made judicious marriages with other powers in attempts to increase its strength. Christian rivalry of course also reduced the possibility of a reunion of the churches. Orthodox loyalty resisted all western attempts to secure 'the submission of the church of Constantinople to the church of Rome', and this refusal then became the stumbling block to further crusading cooperation against the Turks. This complex relationship was in its infancy in the summer of 1261, when the naval commander of Nicaea had the good fortune to learn that the entire Venetian fleet had gone on campaign in the Black Sea, leaving Constantinople undefended. He immediately took possession of the capital in the name of Michael Palaiologos, protector of the boy emperor John IV Laskaris, who became the first Greek ruler to re-occupy the heart of Byzantium.

26

Rebels and Patrons

Among us [the poor], the tillers of the soil, the builders of
houses and merchant ships and the craftsmen are drawn . . .
and who comes from among you? . . . Gamblers, voluptuaries,
people bringing public calamities with their greediness, disrup-
ters of civic order, spreading poverty.

Alexios Makrembolites, *Dialogue between the Rich and the
Poor*, first half of the fourteenth century

Behind the façade of unchanging hierarchy, cultivated by the ceremonies of the imperial court, there was considerable flexibility, social
mobility and innovation in Byzantium, as we have seen. Both before
and after 1204, 'good birth' was naturally recognized as a qualification for the elite category of rulers – both civil and clerical – and
educated administrators. Similarly, those in charge assumed that
people born into families of low status, who were settled on the land
in agricultural labour or in urban trading activities, should continue in
those positions. Education and the army provided avenues of upward
mobility, and marrying into an established family was also a common
method of social advancement. Conversely, the emperor's power to
confiscate property and exile opponents created some dramatic down-
ward movement. But among underprivileged members of Byzantine
society, higher status, however urgently desired, usually remained out
of reach.

The imperial notion of *taxis* (order), however, could not imagine
any change in rule by the elite. At the first sign of popular unrest,
contemporary authors denounced the mob and its ambitions, using

terms such as *demokratia* (rule by the people) and *ochlokratia* (mob rule). In Constantinople, crowds might be organized by the Blues and Greens, but they could also take to the streets spontaneously to protest against unpopular policies. In 1203, when he fled from the city, Alexios III Angelos is reported to have said that the people were 'intent on turmoil', and 'infected with instability'. They were also the first to welcome Byzantine forces back to the city in July 1261. The Latin emperor, Baldwin II, and the Latin patriarch immediately left for the West, together with the Franciscan and Dominican monks.

Byzantine rule was restored to Constantinople. One month later, Michael VIII Palaiologos, who had usurped power, walked into the city of Constantine behind an icon of the Virgin on 15 August, the feast of her Dormition (or Assumption), which was already famous in the life of the empire, and gave thanks in the cathedral of Hagia Sophia for the liberation of Constantinople from Latin rule. He had never seen the Queen City, which had been neglected by the Latins. Michael and his wife, Theodora, were crowned for the second time in Hagia Sophia by the restored Patriarch Arsenios Autoreianos, and the emperor commissioned a new mosaic of Christ flanked by the Virgin and the Baptist for the church's gallery. Following imperial tradition, he put up his own honorary column at the church of the Holy Apostles. Churches used by Latin priests were restored to the orthodox rite and the city walls were strengthened by new fortifications. The Venetian merchants were punished for their role in 1204 by exile from the city, and the Genoese, re-established in their own quarter in Pera, took over control of international trade.

After this triumphant return, Michael had the legitimate emperor, John IV Laskaris, blinded and thus made incapable of ruling, though he lived on for forty years. The usurper, like Basil I, founded his rule in violence, but established the Palaiologan dynasty, which, like the Macedonian, lasted for nearly two hundred years. Despite civil wars in the 1320s and 1340s, a Palaiologos occupied the Byzantine throne until the Ottoman conquest of the city in 1453. Most patronized the arts and erected new churches, monasteries and castles. Many were scholars; Manuel II wrote numerous treatises, including a *Dialogue* on religion between a Greek and a Turk, and another on the benefits of marriage; and all encouraged the remarkable flowering of Byzantine art and culture which is the hallmark of the late empire.

Although Michael VIII Palaiologos re-established Byzantine rule in Constantinople in 1261, the rival empires of Epiros and Trebizond had no intention of submitting to him. He could claim authority only over the western provinces of Thrace, Macedonia, parts of the Morea (the Peloponnese), and the territory of the empire of Nicaea (western Asia Minor). His chief asset was control of the sea passage linking the Aegean with the Black Sea, which permitted Byzantium to tax merchandise moving in either direction, whence the modern name 'Empire of the Straits'. This greatly reduced empire could not withstand the new threat of the Ottoman Turks, who added yet another divisive factor to the already fragmented Byzantium. There was no chance of a full imperial recovery after 1204.

While many Turkish groups were still pastoral peoples, from about 1282 the tribe led by Osman/Othman (which became known as Ottomans) took over the campaign against Byzantium in the tradition of holy war. By overcoming underlying tribal rivalry, Osman managed to persuade the leaders of small emirates to join him in attacking the Byzantine province of Bithynia. Several major Byzantine landowners in the region who felt no loyalty to Michael VIII also went over to Osman on condition that they could continue to control their properties. Other Christian mercenaries served with Turks in units commanded by their own leaders, wearing their Byzantine uniforms and armed in the Greek style. With these additional forces, Osman was able to attack the strongly fortified ancient cities of Nicaea, Nikomedeia and Prousa. In 1302 a major victory in Bithynia opened the region to Turkish settlement, and just before Osman's death, in 1326, his son Orhan captured Prousa after a prolonged siege.

Orhan made it his capital, calling it Bursa, and continued to threaten the remaining Byzantine regions of western Asia Minor. Nicaea capitulated in March 1331 and Nikomedeia six years later. Orhan transferred his father's remains to a grand new mausoleum (*turbe*) attached to the church of St Elias, now transformed into a mosque. Many later emirs and sultans constructed mosques and funerary structures in Bursa. Turkish administration of the conquered territory usually followed Byzantine practice, often using the same Christian officials to record land ownership, property rights and taxes due. With this strategic control over the eastern approaches to Byzantium, Orhan forced the empire to rely even more on its European hinterland. But not all his relations with Byzantium were hostile. He cooperated with Andronikos III (1328–41) in the emperor's efforts to regain Phokaia (near Smyrna), which had become the centre of alum production under the Zaccaria family from Genoa. Alum is the substance which fixes colours and is vital to all dyeing processes, as well as in leatherwork and painting, and the alum mines had become highly profitable. Later, Orhan made an alliance with John VI Kantakouzenos and married his daughter Theodora. This was only one of several political marriages that united Turks and Byzantines. But during the civil war that broke out in 1341, the Turks and other neighbours of Byzantium were quick to intervene.

When Andronikos III died in June 1341, his eldest son John was only nine years old. No clear provision had been made for a regency. The widowed empress, Anna of Savoy, was determined to protect her son's rightful inheritance, and was initially supported by John Kantakouzenos, her husband's closest adviser, who assumed the role of regent. But Patriarch John Kalekas also claimed the right to direct the regency, setting up a rivalry which Serbs, Bulgarians and Turks were quick to exploit. While Kantakouzenos left the capital in July 1341 to defend the empire, Kalekas plotted against him and persuaded the empress of his treacherous intentions. The property of the Kantakouzenos family in Constantinople was attacked and Anna ordered the disbanding of the army. In his bid to control the young emperor, Kalekas was supported by the Grand Duke Alexios Apokaukos, head of the fleet and eparch of Constantinople.

In response, Kantakouzenos proclaimed himself emperor at Didymoteichon (Thrace) in October 1341, opening a civil war characterized by traditional aristocratic in-fighting. In Constantinople, Patriarch Kalekas excommunicated the 'pretender' (John VI Kantakouzenos) and crowned John V Palaiologos as emperor. The news of Kantakouzenos' challenge to the ruling Palaiologan dynasty generated increased unrest, as people took sides for or against the rival emperors. But in a relatively new development an anti-aristocratic wave of violence swept through Adrianople, led by Branos, a labourer, who encouraged people to attack the properties of the rich. Since the Kantakouzenoi were extremely wealthy, there may well have been a good deal of pent-up ill feeling against them and the poor saw an opportunity to take revenge. In an entirely calculating fashion, Grand Duke Apokaukos supported them and appointed his son Manuel as governor of Adrianople. Apokaukos himself had only risen to a position of influence through the patronage of Kantakouzenos, who encouraged his ambitions and allowed him to amass considerable wealth. (Incidentally, some of this wealth he spent on commissioning manuscripts: a famous copy of Hippocrates, now in Paris (graecus 2144), displays his portrait as the donor. Apokaukos also supported medical practice, and the distinguished doctor and court physician John Aktouarios dedicated his work *The Method of Medicine* to him.)

At this time, Thessalonike was a major port and an important centre of fourteenth-century learning and culture, represented by local scholars and painters, such as the anonymous artist who decorated the church of St Nikolaos Orphanos. The declaration by Kantakouzenos provoked an anti-aristocratic reaction within the city. Calling themselves Zealots (literally, 'enthusiasts', 'zealous' for their cause), they expelled the governor and set up a council of twelve archons to rule the city. In seizing political power they drew on a well-organized guild of seamen, who exercised influence in the port, itself a city within the city. Their rebellion appears to have won some support from those of moderate means (the *mesoi*, a recognized stratum of middle-ranking home-owners and proprietors, including Jewish merchants). For the next seven years, the Zealots effectively ruled the city and gained support in other centres. Since they officially declared for John V Palaiologos, Apokaukos again sought to win control over the city by appointing another of his sons as governor, but this seems to have had little effect on the Zealot council of twelve.

Who were these unexpectedly successful rebels? The names of several leaders are recorded: Andreas Palaiologos, leader of the seamen's guild; Alexios Metochites; Michael Palaiologos, who also served as archon until he was murdered on the orders of Apokaukos; and perhaps the most radical, George Kokalas, whose family was well represented in the area. Although Andreas and Michael share the name of the imperial family, they were not from its ruling circle; the relationship between Alexios Metochites and other members of that family is not known. Not many Zealots seem to have risen from the lowest levels of society, but they claimed to represent the poor against the depredations of the rich. Probably they succeeded because Thessalonike was a great port with a large number of sailors who protected their livelihood in some sort of guild. Certainly, they were able to form a militia led by Andreas Palaiologos to defeat the pro-Kantakouzenos faction.

While the administrative arrangements put in place by the rebels remain obscure, it is evident that they managed the defence of the city against foreign enemies as well as supporters of Kantakouzenos. In 1343, when Umur, the Ottoman Emir of Aydin, sent 6,000 additional troops to reinforce a siege of the city, they held out defiantly. Two years later, the murders of Michael Palaiologos in Thessalonike and then of Grand Duke Apokaukos in Constantinople prompted the Kantakouzenos faction to try to throw out the Zealot council. But the Zealots retaliated by murdering Apokaukos' son and all the pro-Kantakouzenos allies. Their bloodshed was condemned but no one could doubt their hold on the city. Indeed, when Gregory Palamas was appointed Metropolitan of Thessalonike in 1347, the Zealots prevented him from entering. It is not clear if they were opposed to the hesychast traditions of spiritual worship and mystical contemplation that he supported, or simply refused to accept any cleric chosen by Constantinople, but they effectively kept him out and retained control for two more years.

Since most of the sources describing the Zealots are written by their opponents, it is difficult to work out what they stood for. Among historians of the period, Nikephoros Gregoras condemns the rebel government as *ochlokratia* – mob rule was truly dreadful to traditional Byzantines. Another account is provided by Demetrios Kydones, a native of Thessalonike, who wrote a monody for those killed in the 1345 uprising. This oration bemoans the 'world turned upside down' created by the Zealots, where slaves, peasants and villagers attacked their betters. He naturally takes the part of those aristocrats who suffered most, though he mentions that even the radical Zealot Kokalas was unable to save his son-in-law from being killed by the crowd.

Similar concerns occur in letters written by Thomas Magistros, long-time resident of Thessalonike, addressed to friends in Constantinople. As a scholar and teacher of conservative views, Thomas was disturbed by the disorder of the Zealots, identified as good-for-nothing people, worth no more than three obols (pennies). He condemned their lack of respect for decent house-owners, people who invest in landed property and who maintain ancestral graves.

In contrast to these predictable complaints, Alexios Makrembolites wrote a *Dialogue between the Rich and the Poor* which presents a number of issues that may well have motivated the Zealots. In this fascinating text, the speaker for the Poor accuses the Rich of numerous inappropriate attitudes and evil actions, particularly greediness, selfish exploitation of nature's benefits, insatiable determination to seize and hoard as much as possible, and a preference for corporeal rather than spiritual values. In reply, the Rich tries to justify his superior situation and accuses the Poor of being at the origin of 'theft, drunkenness, laxity, slander, envy and murder'. The Poor comments:

The means of acquiring money are obvious to any intelligent man: some become rich through knowledge, or through trade, others through abstinence, still others through rapine, many through domination, or inheritance or similar paths. Opposite reasons lead others to poverty.

But he is even more irritated by a series of humiliating social measures, including refusal to sit at the same table or to speak to the poor in normal discourse, or to permit the rich and poor to marry, a strategy which the Poor believes would cause poverty to disappear. Through sharing the abundance of the rich, 'the mixing of opposites . . . produces, astonishingly enough, the salutary mean'. The extremes of difference are listed: elaborate food and good wines, fine clothing, elegant accommodation, good medical advice, front-row seats at assemblies, as opposed to bad bread and soured wine, one shabby cloak 'full of filth and pestering lice', and inadequate protection against the weather. 'Conspicuous consumption' at rich funerals (with splendid graves, psalms and chants, eulogies, candle-bearers, wailing relatives and mourning women) is contrasted with the humble burial 'which contributes to a more splendid resurrection'. The Poor taunts the Rich, claiming that even Jews and Muslims look after their kin better than wealthy Christians, who fail to imitate Christ and deserve to be deprived of the rewards of the future life.

Makrembolites was by no means a rebel. Like other fourteenth-century writers, he belonged to a group of literati – scholars who wrote speeches to be delivered at the imperial court and earned a living in the civil administration. But his interpretation of fourteenth-century developments, particularly the success of the Turks, made him more of a realist than others. He interpreted the collapse of the dome of Hagia Sophia in 1346 as a sign of the end of the world (although it was patched up again) and blamed the Byzantines for their sinful greed and immoral behaviour.

The *Dialogue* is a contrived text, not a straightforward account of poverty in Byzantium. But the aggrieved complaints put into the mouth of the Poor, just like the justification and contempt of the Rich, must have resonated with contemporaries. Many who joined the Zealots and other anti-aristocratic forces to oppose the extremes of wealth accumulated by families like the Kantakouzenos would have reacted like the Poor against such a vast divide between the haves and have-nots. What remains exceptional is the lasting impact of the Zealot revolt, which removed Thessalonike from imperial control for seven years when traditional control broke down.

Eventually, however, the council of twelve divided over how to deal with the apparent resolution of the civil war. In February 1347, John Kantakouzenos gained entry to Constantinople and forced Empress Anna to agree to a compromise, which included the resignation of Patriarch Kalekas and the marriage of Helena Kantakouzene (John VI's daughter) to young John V Palaiologos. The two rival families were thus united, even if some supporters of the Kantakouzenos faction were disappointed that the emperor did not establish his own dynasty. Faced with this change, the Zealots displayed their hostility by the public burning of all orders from the capital. They proposed to invite Stefan Uroš IV Dušan, who was already calling himself Emperor of the Serbs and the Greeks, to become their leader, calculating that their own independence would be less compromised by accepting Serbian overlordship than by recognizing John VI Kantakouzenos as their ruler. Stefan Dušan was only too delighted to intervene in the squabble and sent forces to take control of the city.

But this invitation provoked a split among the Zealots that pushed Alexios Metochites into action against Andreas Palaiologos. He defeated the seamen's guild, announced his support for Kantakouzenos and refused to let the Serbs into the city. At this news, John VI set sail from the capital with his young co-emperor, sending his son Matthew with an army reinforced by Turkish auxiliaries. With the help of a dissatisfied Serbian military officer and Turkish naval forces, he gained entrance to Thessalonike in 1350, forcing Andreas Palaiologos to seek refuge on Mount Athos. The remaining Zealots were arrested, exiled or sent to Constantinople to be tried. John V Palaiologos, whom the Zealots had supported, was hailed as emperor, and Gregory Palamas was duly installed as metropolitan of the city. In one of his first sermons, he condemned the rebels as wild beasts, but called for peace and harmony under the rule of the Palaiologos family.

When John VI Kantakouzenos was forced to retire from public life by another demonstration of popular disapproval of his policy of alliance with the Turks, he adopted the monastic name Joasaph and wrote his *Memoirs*. In an attempt to justify his own role in the civil war, he accused the Zealots of excessive violence and presented their rebellion as a widespread movement:

it spread like a malignant and horrible disease, producing the same forms of excess even in those who before had been moderate and sensible men . . . All the cities joined in this rebellion against the aristocracy and those that were late in doing so made up for their lost time by excelling the example set them by others. They perpetuated all manner of inhumanity and even massacres. Senseless impulse was glorified with the name of valour and lack of fellow feeling or human sympathy was called loyalty to the Emperor.

He also characterized the aristocrats as an elite picked on for their good birth by the poor seeking revenge, and claimed that those of the middling sort were compelled to support the rebels. This denunciation of the violence of the urban mob is corroborated by a Constantinopolitan official, Theodore Metochites, who lost nearly all his property when his palace in the capital was attacked in 1328, long before the events in Thessalonike. Later he would re-found and decorate the monastic church of the Saviour (Chora), in which he is shown as the patron wearing his court costume (plates 26 and 33). Clearly the

Zealots could call on popular and aggressive antagonism to men considered super-rich in Byzantium. But just as predictably, the wealthiest could also restore their fortunes.

In the subsequent history of Thessalonike, John V Palaiologos' mother Anna of Savoy reinstated rule by the elite. From 1351 to her death in about 1365, she governed the city as if it belonged to her. When she had been short of money in Constantinople during the civil war, she had pawned the crown jewels to the Venetians for a loan of 30,000 ducats, which was never repaid. Later governors of the city included the young Manuel II (emperor from 1391 to 1425), who was forced to flee in 1387, and his son Andronikos, who handed over its defence to Venice in 1422. By then, Thessalonike was under an almost continual blockade by the Turks, and Venetian officials were no more successful than Byzantines in preventing the final capitulation in 1430. The Zealot experience was not repeated, but their seven-year experiment with a more communal and popular form of government represented the trend of the future: several Italian cities had already embraced largely republican forms, and major centres in the West, as distant as Barcelona and Gdańsk, were following in their train. Thessalonike's commercial activity and the guild of seamen facilitated the overthrow of the natural order, when the rich ruled the poor, and the Zealots proved that Byzantium could also generate rebels who discarded traditional government and took account of social disadvantages.

At almost the same time as the rebels took over Thessalonike, a spectacular Frankish castle perched above ancient Sparta emerged as a new centre of Byzantine culture. From 1348 to 1460, Mistras was the capital of the Morea, ruled by sons of the emperors of Constantinople who were titled despots (*despotes*, lord or master). William II Villehardouin, the fourth Prince of Achaia, had founded this castle in 1247 atop Mount Taygetos overlooking medieval Lakedaimonia. During the next forty years it changed hands several times. Following the common practice of calling on outside forces to sustain the crusading states, William made an alliance with Charles of Anjou, ruler of Naples and Sicily, who inherited the principality after William's death in 1278. To counter the serious threat posed by this French development, Michael VIII Palaiologos arranged various European alliances, which led ultimately to the massacre of French troops in 1282 in Sicily. These intrigues, which provided Verdi with a splendid libretto for his famous opera *The Sicilian Vespers* (1855), also generated competition between the West and Byzantium for control over the Morea. But Mistras remained a Byzantine possession.

From the late thirteenth century onwards, the inhabitants of medieval Lakedaimonia moved up the hillside to settle closer to the fortifications of Mistras, creating a new town below the castle. This settlement was dominated by the governor's palace, probably built on Frankish foundations, and churches, including the cathedral dedicated to St Demetrios, to which later churchmen made additions. Constantinople maintained a governor (*strategos*, also called *kephale*, literally, 'head'), and the city gradually expanded. One of these governors was a member of the Kantakouzenos family and the father of John VI. Monasteries flourished under local patrons, some commemorated in portraits and others by inscriptions. At the complex of the Brontocheion monastery with its two churches built between 1290 and 1310, the variety of architectural designs and fresco decoration suggests a considerable range of skilled craftsmen, and painted copies of imperial chrysobulls preserve a list of its privileges.

Cut off from the capital by the Frankish duchies of Athens and Thebes, which continued to occupy central Greece, and constantly threatened by other westerners – the Catalan and Aragonese Companies (mercenary bands), the Italian families of Acciajuoli and Tocco, and the titular princes of Achaia – the Peloponnese gradually became a distinctive Byzantine region. In 1349, John VI Kantakouzenos nominated his son Manuel as *despotes* of this autonomous province. It thus became known as the Despotate of the Morea, and was usually ruled by a younger member of either the Kantakouzenos or Palaiologos dynasty. Manuel's long rule as despot from 1349 to 1380 brought greater stability and prosperity. He was probably responsible for the main part of the palace, a two-storeyed residence with spacious rooms on the upper floor above a central courtyard and looking out over the plain of Sparta. He also built the local church of Hagia Sophia, which may have functioned as the palace church. It was later incorporated into a monastery. In 1361 his father, the ex-emperor John VI Kantakouzenos, now the monk Joasaph, fled from Mount Athos when it was afflicted by an outbreak of plague and sought refuge in Mistras. On Manuel's death in 1380, John V Palaiologos appointed his son Theodore as despot, and Mistras remained an appanage of the ruling dynasty for the next eighty years.

Like every part of the Byzantine world in the fourteenth century, however, Mistras was not free from the fear of Ottoman attacks. The first invasion of the Peloponnese occurred in 1388, and further raids in the 1390s seem to have included a siege of Mistras itself. Against Turkish military threats, the despots sought alliances with western powers, drawing Latin forces into the defence of the despotate. They married noble and wealthy ladies such as Isabelle of Lusignan, Bartolomea Acciajuoli, Kleopa Malatesta, Maddalena-Theodora Tocco and Caterina Zaccaria, and then found they also had to contend with a series of ambitious fathers-in-law. Yet by 1430, the despotate had put paid to Tocco and Zaccaria claims and had incorporated the principality of Achaia and the Venetian city of Patras perched on the northwest corner of the Peloponnese. Thus extended and strengthened, Mistras was also appreciated as a peaceful refuge. Manuel II left his wife and children in the Peloponnese when he went on his long embassy to the West. When an epidemic broke out in Constantinople in 1417/18, it was also used as a safe haven, and five years later, when Andronikos Palaiologos, the last Byzantine governor of Thessalonike, was forced to give up the city to the Venetians, he retired to Mistras. The apparently impregnable fortress of the despotate seemed to guarantee safety, even amid the devastation caused by the intense rivalries of competing forces.

Although it never developed into a major urban centre, being confined by its geographical setting to a small area of the slopes of Mount Taygetos, Mistras became rich and cosmopolitan. This small walled area resembled an ancient city-state and took inspiration from its proximity to Sparta. The population lived off a prosperous agricultural territory where vines, olive groves and mulberries flourished. There was an established Jewish community engaged in weaving and carpet-making, cloth and silk production, and many foreign merchants were attracted to the area – Genoese, Venetians, Spaniards and Florentines. Via the River Evrotas and the sea, communication with the West was easier than with Constantinople, and many embassies from the capital travelled via Mistras. The city characterizes the exceptional vitality of Byzantium, even in the empire's most fragmented state.

In earlier centuries, Byzantium had reserved the term Hellene (*ellenes*) to designate pagans, but in the late twelfth and early thirteenth centuries it had been transformed into a Greek way of claiming cultural superiority over the Latins. The literati at the imperial court in Nicaea incorporated ancient Hellenic wisdom, especially philosophy, into their Byzantine identity; John III Vatatzes spoke of his 'Hellenic' descent. Of course, all scholars of Byzantium felt this affinity with the ancient world and even monks like Isidore (later Bishop of Kiev and Roman cardinal), Bessarion, Bishop of Nicaea (and also later cardinal) and George Scholarios, later patriarch, who lived for some time at Mistras, saw no difficulty in combining it with their Christian upbringing. During the late Byzantine period, schoolteachers in Constantinople, Trebizond and Thessalonike perpetuated and deepened awareness of it. But at Mistras this strand of the Greek inheritance became more striking and obvious, in such close connection with one very particular aspect of the ancient world: the civilization of Sparta. Demetrios Kydones wrote to an otherwise unknown philosopher named George: 'In your excessive love of Hellenism you imagined that the very soil of Sparta would enable you to see Lycurgus' (the lawgiver of ancient Sparta).

This was the context into which George Gemistos, also known as Plethon, stepped in about 1410 when he was exiled by Emperor Manuel II from Constantinople to Mistras for heresy. His family name was Gemistos; Plethon was his pseudonym, under which he wrote his greatest work of philosophy, *On the Differences of Aristotle from Plato*. Both names mean 'full' but the second suggested a connection to the ancient philosopher Plato, with whom Gemistos was so closely connected. While his enemies retorted that 'he called himself Plethon as if insinuating a link with the soul of Plato', his supporters regularly described him as 'a second Plato', or 'second only to Plato'. The court of the despots at Mistras had already attracted scholars and artists, who created a vibrant centre of Byzantine and Hellenic culture. Having been a teacher in the capital, Plethon brought this expertise to the Peloponnese. More than other philosophers, he cherished the notion that fifteenth-century Greek scholars embodied ancient Hellenic wisdom and that it could serve a practical purpose. At Mistras, he constantly made radical proposals for administrative and political developments, while serving as a judge. The despots rewarded him with grants of land and his advice was solicited by rulers in Mistras and Constantinople alike.

To Manuel Palaiologos, Plethon recommended drastic changes which echo the aims of the Zealots: 'all the land should be the common property of all its inhabitants . . . the produce of the labour of all . . . should be divided into three parts', which would be distributed to the labourers, the farmers and the exchequer. He thought that the military should be exempt from taxes and should be maintained by the state and the services of one tax-paying labourer, called a helot:

Each infantry soldier should have one helot assigned to him, and each mounted man should have two; and thus each soldier . . . will be in a position to serve in the army with proper equipment and to remain permanently with the standards.

He also wished to reform the currency: 'It is the height of folly to use these foreign – and bad – bronze coins which we now use: it only brings profit to others and much ridicule on ourselves.' With additional recommendations for the control of trade, to encourage self-sufficiency, Plethon hoped to see the creation of an effective citizen army and the provision of a well-organized tax base, which would ensure better government and military success. As in other regions which aimed at independence, in Mistras Plethon saw the need to make government more responsive, and to incorporate popular demands for greater equality in local administration.

In association with these suggestions for a Spartan-style society, Plethon proposed a revival of ancient Greek social values and religion. His *Book of Laws* must have contained a complete liturgy for the worship of Zeus. Only 16 of the 100 chapters in three books, and some only in parts, survive. But the chapter headings reflect the broad concerns of this work devoted to theology, ethics, politics, ceremonies and natural science, which include a prayer to the gods of learning:

Come to us, O gods of learning, whoever and however many ye be; ye who are guardians of scientific knowledge and true belief; ye who distribute them to whomsoever you wish, in accordance with the dictates of the great father of all things, Zeus the King ... Grant that this book may have all success, to be set as a possession forever before those of mankind who wish to pass their lives, both in private and in public established in the best and noblest fashion.

Zeus is understood to be the absolute good; he is ungenerated, ever-lasting, the father of himself, the father and pre-eminent creator of all other things. The Olympian gods are few and supracelestial; they have no bodies and exist outside space. The lower, lesser gods are more numerous, as are the terrestrial daemons.

While many of the chapters must have been devoted to matters of religious observance (prayers for morning, afternoon and evening), priestly functions and the names of the gods, sections are also devoted to metaphysics (abstract questions concerning the eternity of the universe), ethics (against incest and polygamy) and practical matters of government (administrative, judicial, economic). Plethon had distinct proposals for improving late Byzantine society, notably that indecent sexual behaviour could be curbed by the threat of death by burning. Women convicted of adultery were to have their heads shaved and should be forced to live as prostitutes. Rape, homosexual and bestial acts would be punished by burning in a special place, beyond the public cemetery, where distinct areas for the graves of priests, ordinary citizens and criminals were to be kept apart. In his final appendix to the *Book of Laws*, Plethon invoked the powers of the gods, and the doctrines taught by Pythagoras, Plato, Kouretes and Zoroaster, as superior to any other. He dismissed the teaching of certain sophists, who misled people by promising greater happiness through a genuine immortality (a reference to Christian teachers), pointing out that their idea of eternity was only a future one. In contrast, he believed the philosophy outlined in his *Book* offered the soul an absolute eternity, both past and future – a reference to the doctrine of continued and repeated reincarnation of souls.

When the negotiations for church union were initiated in 1438, Plethon travelled to Ferrara and on to Florence, where he made contact with Italian scholars. His interest in Christian theology may not have been profound, but he could settle an argument with a logical tour de force when necessary. With one brilliant intervention, he proved that a Latin document, supposedly issued by the Seventh Oecumenical Council of 787, which recorded the creed with the *filioque* clause, could not be authentic. For if it was, he pointed out, and everyone both Greek and Latin had accepted it then, there would be no problem. But there was no evidence that the additional *filioque* had been cited in 787. On the contrary, Popes Hadrian I and Leo III, who welcomed the ending of iconoclasm, both recited the creed without it. It was only in the course of the eleventh century that the papacy had accepted what had become standard practice in the rest of Europe, namely reciting the creed with the clause.

Plethon's lectures on Platonism given to Italian scholars in Florence made a great impression on contemporaries, who were enthusiastically trying to identify, translate and read every ancient text by Plato that they could find. Their relative ignorance stimulated his major work, *On the Differences of Aristotle from Plato*, which attacks Aristotle and exalts Plato. His scholarship gave a major boost to the study of Platonic philosophy in the West, which later bore fruit in the foundation of the Florentine Academy by Cosimo de' Medici in about 1460. Under the direction of Marsilio Ficino, who translated Plato's *Symposium* into Latin and wrote an important introduction to it, the discovery and study of Platonic texts expanded greatly. Plethon was interested in problems of geography and his discussion of Strabo's *Geographika* may also have played a significant role in the debate among Renaissance scholars during the 1430s. Paul Toscanelli was one of those who met Plethon and showed him new maps of the northernmost islands of the earth: Scandinavia, Greenland and Thule, which were then being explored. In 1474, Toscanelli would write that the quickest way to the Far East was by sailing west from Europe. Strabo was certainly considered a reliable guide for the greatest voyage of exploration: Christopher Columbus' attempt to reach the Indies by crossing the Atlantic in 1492.

Until his death in 1452, Plethon continued to defend Plato against the Aristotelianism of George Trapezountios ('of Trebizond') and George Scholarios. His devoted pupils, Michael Apostoles and John

. The west front of San Marco, Venice, completed in the twelfth century, largely in zantine style. The horses (see below) stand on plinths above the central door.

. Two of the four ancient classical bronze horses brought to Constantinople probably by eodosius and set up over the entrance to the Hippodrome, and then taken by the Venetians er 1204 and erected on the west front of San Marco.

31. The monastery of Hosios Loukas, Steiris, central Greece, eleventh century, with the domes of the two adjacent churches: the earlier foundation dedicated to St Barbara and the main church enriched with mosaic and marble decoration.

32. The poor widow appeals to Emperor Theophilos while he rides out to the Palace of Blachernai. An illustration from the *Chronicle* of John Skylitzes probably made in the twelfth or thirteenth century in Sicily. The emperor shown with a halo is identified by an inscription, as is the Palace. The widow is one of two women presenting their petitions.

33. The Chora monastery in the north-west corner of Constantinople, in a photograph taken in the early twentieth century. Founded in the sixth century, the buildings were restored, expanded and redecorated by Theodore Metochites in 1316–21.

34. The monastic church at Daphni, central Greece, dedicated to the Mother of God. Founded in the late eleventh century, it was extended with a Gothic exonarthex and cloister by Cistercian monks (1207–11) and remained under Latin control until the Ottoman conquest of 1458.

35. Exterior of the church of the Virgin Paregoritissa at Arta, constructed by the Despot Nikephoros I Komnenos Doukas in *c.* 1290.

36. Interior of the church, showing the mosaic of Christ Pantokrator in the central dome.

7. View of the castle of Mistras, founded by William II Villehardouin in 1247, with buildings of the late Byzantine city on the slopes of Mount Taygetos.

8. Illustration from a Commentary on the Book of Job, copied by Manuel Tzykandeles in 1362, probably in Mistras, depicting four people in a rural setting observed by Christ. The letters between the two couples refer to chapter 27 of Job's tribulations, when he defends his own faith in God: 'Men shall clap their hands at him and hiss him out of his place.' The hats, owl, long-sleeved tunic and the woman's dress suggest clothes worn at the time of painting.

39. John VI Kantakouzenos presiding at the Church Council of 1351 that condemned the anti-hesychast writings of Barlaam of Calabria and others. He is surrounded by four bishops (Kallistos, Patriarch of Constantinople, Philotheos Kokkinos of Herakleia, Gregory Palamas of Thessalonike and Arsenios of Kyzikos), monks, soldiers and courtiers. One of the rare pictures of Byzantine church councils.

40. Manuel II Palaiologos and his wife Helena blessed by the Mother of God, with their three children, the *porphyrogennetoi*, John, Theodore and Andronikos. They all wear their imperial costumes and hold crosses. The image occurs in the manuscript of the writings of Pseudo-Dionysus, copied for King Charles VI of France, which Manuel Chrysoloras presented in the emperor's name to the monastery of St Denis, north of Paris, in 1408.

وقموا الرصاص نغسل هكذبي بعمل الصلابه لها يدين رصاص ويصب

فيهاماء ويذكها يدها الى ان يسود الى ان وتحن ثرصفاخرقه ويعمل ذلك

ثانيه وأكثراذا اجتمج الذلك ونغسل كما ينغسل الاطلميا ويعمل ذلك

صناع الرصاص

الى ان يصير في السواد ويعمل منه اقراصا وترفع ه ع ع ع ع

صفه اخرى

من الحكمان أخذرصاصا نقيا فبرده واخذ لك لبزاده نهد هلي صلابه

حرثما ثم صفا الاول فالاول تررفق من مجلس وينزع ذلك الى الجعل

41. 'Making Lead', a page from an Arabic translation of the pharmaceutical treaty of Dioscorides, *De materia medica*, copied in 1224 by the scribe 'Abd Allah ibn al-Fadl. Many Greek copies of this famous text have annotations in Arabic, indicating that they were read in Muslim countries, such as the copy that Romanos II sent to the Caliph of Cordoba in the tenth century.

Argyropoulos, and his defenders, including Cardinal Bessarion, continued his study of Platonic texts, though they were in a minority. Aristotelian arguments had been incorporated into Christian theology as early as the sixth century and were an accepted part of Byzantine learning. In the West, the study of logic in medieval schools and St Thomas Aquinas' *Summa contra gentiles* (1259–64) had developed Aristotelianism into a precise tool of rational argument. Scholarios championed this new western scholasticism, which he tried to introduce into the traditional Byzantine curriculum; he also translated and commented on writings by Aquinas. His opposition to Plethon was based not only on Plethon's attack on Aristotle but also on the *Book of Laws*, which was sent to him after the fall of Constantinople to the Turks. Scholarios, by then a monk with the name Gennadios, had been installed as patriarch by Mehmet II the Conqueror. In this capacity, Scholarios condemned as heretical Plethon's fervent enthusiasm for Hellenic religion, and ordered all copies of his *Book* to be burned. He thus made sure that the rest of Plethon's writings would also remain almost unknown.

A few years after this forceful censorship, Sigismondo Malatesta led a campaign against the Turks, who had forced the Despot Demetrios and his wife Theodora to flee to Constantinople in 1460 when Mistras was captured. In 1464, Malatesta regained the lower town, where he found Plethon's grave. Years before, he had tried to persuade Plethon to head his court school at Rimini, to no avail. Now, however, he could ensure a more appropriate burial for his hero. He removed Plethon's bones from Mistras to inter them with due reverence in the wall of his Tempio Malatestiano, where the dedication inscription may still be read: 'The remains of Gemistos the Byzantine, Prince of Philosophers in his time . . .'

Mistras thus lost the tomb of its most famous philosopher. During the long period of Turkish domination over the Peloponnese, Mistras was largely abandoned. Many of its churches, monasteries and houses fell into ruins. But they are now being restored, their frescoes conserved and their inscriptions published. The Palace of the Despots is to be roofed over once again and may serve as a tourist attraction in the newly founded Centre for Byzantine Studies. In appreciation of the historian Steven Runciman's devotion to the site, celebrated in his book on Mistras, a street was named after him. Perhaps it is also time that in this most spectacularly beautiful Byzantine city a road or square may be named after George Gemistos Plethon.

'Better the Turkish Turban than the Papal Tiara'

proverbial saying attributed to Loukas Notaras,
grand admiral in the years 1444–53

Between the recovery of Constantinople from the Latins in 1261 and its fall to the Ottomans in 1453, Byzantine foreign policy was dominated by the question of the union of the churches. Political considerations required emperors to pursue this policy because they desperately needed military help from the West to combat the Turks, and the spiritual leaders of the West had made the reunion of the churches, with Constantinople subordinated to Rome, a precondition of any assistance. After the crusaders' actions in 1204, many in Byzantium considered this abhorrent, if not heretical, and consistently refused to support it. The Palaiologan emperors therefore found themselves in a cleft stick: if the price of an alliance with effective western military forces was reunion, then they had to find an ecclesiastical policy of compromise and agreement. But any such policy would be condemned by those concerned with correct theology, and by the great majority in Byzantium who remained devoted to their own church, icons and ideas of orthodoxy. Most Byzantines wanted support not subordination.

As the Christian *oikoumene* had expanded in the early medieval West, contracted in the East under the pressure of Islam, and then reunited during the crusading period, specific features of liturgical practice emerged as major differences. For the Byzantines, any change in the wording of the creed was always considered incomprehensible and unacceptable. The primacy of St Peter, as interpreted by his successors – the bishops of Rome – jarred with the eastern concept of the pentarchy, the rule of the five patriarchs. And in the different forms of the Eucharistic bread (leavened or unleavened), all Christians could appreciate a very obvious visual divergence. Whether all clerics were obliged to maintain celibacy, and whether all Christians fasted on the same days, was perhaps less of a problem. Similarly, geography accounted for the use of Greek or Latin in the liturgy and certain unfamiliar habits, which had given the churches distinct histories within the world of Christendom.

Nonetheless, there was a fundamental desire to sustain Christian unity, especially in the face of Muslim beliefs. Bishops of Old and New Rome traditionally accorded each other great respect and ensured that prayers for the other were included in their services. Despite a breakdown in these relations in the ninth century under Patriarch Photios and Pope Nicholas, and again in 1054, mutual excommunication did not last beyond the lifetimes of the individuals involved. When Alexios I Komnenos appealed to Pope Urban II to support the Christians of the East against the infidel Turks, he did so precisely because they shared a common faith. Whatever the divergences in their practices, the First Crusade was duly preached on this basis and Christian control over Jerusalem was restored.

The events of 1202–4, however, deepened the sense of profound difference and left both parties hostile and wary. The orthodox were particularly outraged by the crusaders' occupation of their churches and monasteries, not to mention the desecration of Hagia Sophia. From the new centres established after the Fourth Crusade, Greek prelates denounced the Latin bishops and friars appointed to 'their' sees and monasteries in the occupied capital and conquered territory. Yet in the empire of Nicaea, John III Vatatzes and Theodore II Laskaris had supported contacts between Latin and Greek representatives, finding the western friars less dogmatic than Cardinal Humbert. Serious discussions took place about rebuilding unity among the Christians. After 1261, Michael VIII Palaiologos determined to intensify these contacts.

Political developments, however, continued to impede the process. When the last Latin emperor Baldwin II fled from Constantinople, Pope Urban IV received him at Rome and promised to restore him to his throne, a policy actively supported by his successor, Clement IV (1265–8). At Viterbo in 1267, the pope gave his blessing to a formidable anti-Byzantine alliance led by Charles of Anjou and sealed by political marriages: Charles married his daughter to Baldwin's son, and his son to the daughter of William Villehardouin, prince of Achaia. Fortunately for Byzantium, Clement IV died, and after a papal interregnum of three years, Gregory X was elected in 1272. The new pope's overriding concern was to plan a new crusade against the Muslims, and to this end he announced a general council of the Church which would impose ecclesiastical reforms and reunite the western and eastern churches.

This promising declaration encouraged Michael VIII to try to win over the clerics in Byzantium who had expressed doubts and even denounced the idea of reunion: Patriarch Joseph, numerous bishops and monks who were opposed to 'submission' to Rome. Against the emperor's wish 'to spare the Greeks the terrible wars and effusion of blood threatening the empire', they considered his proposal for rebuilding Christian unity unacceptable, because it conceded the primacy of St Peter over all churches and the Latin wording of the creed. They had additional concerns, but because the declaration of faith was held to be a critical method of teaching and preaching Christianity, any disagreement over the text was bound to cause splits (see chapter 4). During twelfth-century debates between western and eastern theologians, the *filioque* regularly formed a stumbling block: both Peter Grossolano and Anselm of Havelberg wrote about this after their visits to Constantinople and Thessalonike. In response, Niketas 'of Maroneia', later Archbishop of Thessalonike, wrote six dialogues which defended the western interpretation, although perversely he refused to add the clause to the creed.

With full knowledge of this background of disagreement, Michael VIII began a campaign to win over the Byzantine opponents of union. In 1273, he imprisoned Patriarch Joseph and obliged John Bekkos, archivist of Hagia Sophia and later patriarch, to spearhead the campaign. But very few clerics were won over to the Latin position by John's treatise on the subject, even though the emperor and his son and heir declared their personal adherence to the Roman definition of the faith. It even became difficult to find high-ranking clerics to represent the Church of Constantinople at the General Council which Pope Gregory X had summoned to meet in Lyons in 1274. The Byzantine delegation was led by George Akropolites, the head of the government, the former Patriarch Germanos III (who held the authority very briefly in 1266) and Archbishop Theophanes of Nicaea. It was much stronger on the civilian than the ecclesiastical side.

After a difficult journey, in which all their gifts of icons and church treasure intended for the pope were lost at sea, they arrived at Lyons, where the Council had been opened with tremendous fanfare and ceremonial on 7 May 1274. In their two weeks at the council, the *filioque*, papal primacy and a relatively new aspect of western theology – the existence of Purgatory – were debated. Since the 1230s, theologians on both sides had been discussing what could happen to sinners who did not have time to repent before death. Pope Innocent IV (died 1254) and Thomas Aquinas in 1263 had elaborated on the purging of minor sins in the fire mentioned in the Gospels. But the Orthodox Church had no notion of an alternative post-mortem existence, as the soul would ultimately be judged and sent either to heaven or to hell, so it was unwilling to accept the new western definition. As a result, the compromise wording adopted in 1274 did not refer to Purgatory, though it stressed the power of masses, prayers and pious almsgiving to assist the souls of the departed, which both sides accepted.

At Lyons, the three Byzantine delegates signed the profession of faith previously agreed with the emperor, George Akropolites swore an oath of loyalty to the pope and the Roman version of the creed, and the Council duly accepted the 'submission' of the Emperors Michael VIII and Andronikos. The reunion of the churches was celebrated on 6 July 1274 in the cathedral of Saint Jean, and Pope Gregory welcomed the Greeks back into the fold. The Council was interpreted by Rome as the submission of the entire Orthodox Church, rather than of its rulers; in the East, Michael VIII was legitimized and could demand Christian support against the infidel, but he could not persuade the orthodox to accept the terms of union. After 1274, the emperor begged the pope that their church be permitted to recite the sacred creed as it had been before the schism and up to our time, and that we may remain in observance of the rites we had before the schism – these rites not being contrary to the faith declared above.

In their later professions of faith sent to Rome, however, both Michael VIII and his successor Andronikos II accepted the existence of Purgatory, citing 'penalties of purgatory or purification'.

The union was duly celebrated in Constantinpole by John Bekkos, who became patriarch in place of Joseph I, but George Metochites, one of the Byzantine delegation, recorded serious opposition:

Instead of a conflict of words, instead of refutative proof, instead of arguments drawn from the Scriptures, what we envoys constantly hear is, 'You have become a Frank'. Should we who are pro-unionists . . . be called supporters of a foreign nation and not Byzantine patriots?

From Constantinople, where memories of the sack of 1204 were still vivid, to Epiros, where the despot presented himself as a true representative of orthodox tradition, an anti-unionist party was created. Serbia and Bulgaria also supported this view, which conveniently combined their political antagonism to Byzantium with correct theology. Nor did the union produce the promised military results, partly because Gregory X died in 1276 and Charles of Anjou continued to campaign for the restoration of the Latin empire. Eight years after the Council, when Michael VIII died, his unpopular policy was immediately abandoned. Andronikos II (1282–1328) took vengeance on John Bekkos, who was deposed, brought to trial and imprisoned; three years later the new patriarch, Gregory II, repudiated the union.

From texts that circulated in the East, it is clear that opposition to the union was based on numerous differences between Latin and Greek Church practice. On the issue of what bread should be used in the Eucharist, raised bread or the western wafer called azymes, because it lacked yeast, *zymos*, the Byzantines believed:

Those who still partake of the azymes are under the shadow of the Law and eat of the table of the Jews, not of the reasonable and living table of God nor of the bread which is both supersubstantial and consubstantial to us men . . . For indeed the azymes plainly are lifeless, as the very nature of things even more plainly teaches.

Later on this anonymous tract asks:

Why do you priests not marry? . . . The Church does not forbid the priest to take a wife, but you do not marry. Instead you have concubines and your priest sends his servant to bring him his concubine and puts out the candle and keeps her for the whole night.

The same text criticized the Latins for not venerating icons, calling the Theotokos 'Santa Maria', i.e. simply a saint, using two fingers to cross themselves from the other side, eating 'strangled meat' and numerous other habits which seemed strange and wrong to the Greeks. These differences would all re-emerge in the 1440s as the population of Constantinople disavowed the Union of churches negotiated by John VIII.

Although the attempt to achieve the union of churches had failed in 1274, the hope that western Christian forces with papal blessing would eventually come to the aid of the Byzantines was kept alive by a growing interest in Latin theology and the first translations of Latin Fathers by Greek scholars. Knowledge of medieval Latin in Byzantium, as well as the vernacular tongues spoken by merchants, crusaders, diplomats and pilgrims, had expanded from the eleventh century onwards. When the scholar and monk Maximos Planoudes (c. 1255–c. 1305) began to translate classical Latin authors and St Augustine, he revolutionized Byzantine understanding of the West. His complete prose version of Ovid's *Metamorphoses*, *Heroides* and some amatory verses; Boethius' *Consolation of Philosophy*; Cicero's *Rhetoric*; Macrobius and sections of Augustine's *City of God*: all of these made some fundamental Latin texts available to a Byzantine audience for the first time. The brothers Demetrios and Prochoros Kydones and Manuel Kalekas extended this work, while Gregory Chioniades demonstrated the importance of Islamic astronomy through his translations from Persian into Greek.

This was a new development in Byzantine culture which reflects an awareness of the value of foreign, non-Greek learning. It marked a departure from assumptions of intellectual superiority in all fields and shows that Byzantium could adapt and learn from both sides in the arguments over church union. Most of those who translated from Latin into Greek had learnt the new language from friars in Byzantium. Like the 'Apostles to the Slavs', they used their linguistic skills to enhance Byzantine culture. Planoudes also served as ambassador on a diplomatic mission to Venice in 1296. He drew upon a very broad interest in ancient Greek culture. He made an edition of Diophantos' theorems and other mathematical works, as well as copying and adding to the *Anthologia Graeca*, the late antique collection of epigrams. In contrast, two generations later, Demetrios and Prochoros Kydones were primarily concerned with theology and were directly involved in fourteenth-century church politics. The brothers were responsible for translating St Thomas Aquinas' *Summa contra gentiles* and *Summa theologiae* into Greek, works which infused new vigour into the unionist camp. They also devoted attention to the works of Augustine, Boethius and St Anselm of Canterbury, and translated a *Refutation of the Qur'an* by Ricoldo de Monte Croce.

Despite growing interest in western philosophy, the style of Aristotelian logic adopted in the nascent medieval universities of Europe did not make a great impact in Byzantium. The educational system had its own traditions, based on the original texts of Aristotle and enriched by many later commentaries devoted to metaphysics, cosmology, ethics and logic, which had always been taught in the East. Another reason may lie in the growth of hesychasm and the teaching of enlightenment through spiritual contemplation, which owed more to Plato than Aristotle (see chapter 18). The hesychast monks of Mount Athos proved to be implacable opponents of church union on the terms negotiated at Lyons. On the other side, those Byzantine intellectuals who favoured union were more impressed by western argumentation based on Latin translations of Aristotle – a tradition of logic that ignored the eastern commentaries.

John V Palaiologos, however, sought to realize plans for western military cooperation against the Turks by making a personal conversion to Catholicism. His travels to Hungary and Italy in 1366–9 culminated in his submission to Roman authority. While this remained his own decision and did not involve the Byzantine Church, he hoped it would secure military assistance. But the fact that on his way home the Venetians arrested him for debts revealed the precarious situation in Byzantium. His son Manuel was forced to ransom him, and before John V could return the island of Tenedos had to be handed over to Venice in lieu of money owed. Although the promised military intervention took shape under Serbian leadership, the Turks defeated this Christian force at the Marica in 1371 and the emperor abandoned his pro-western policy. Several leading Byzantine intellectuals nonetheless converted to Roman Catholicism and continued to urge the reunion of the churches as the only way of defeating the ever-tightening Ottoman encirclement of Constantinople. One of them, Demetrios Kydones, wrote a treatise proposing terms for winning Latin help in 1389, but it was ignored. Divisions within the elite thus contributed to weakening Byzantium while the Turks concentrated on expanding into Europe.

In 1422, the capital survived a major siege, but eight years later Thessalonike was captured, enabling the Turks to surround Constantinople from the West as well as the East. In these parlous circumstances, John VIII Palaiologos began another attempt to reunite the churches and thus win a serious commitment to western military aid supported by the papacy. In 1438, he led a high-level delegation – including Patriarch Joseph II, the two chief spokesmen Mark Eugenikos of Ephesos and Bessarion of Nicaea, sixteen metropolitans, officials and monks, making up a party of over seven hundred – to Ferrara to meet the papal party. Patriarch Joseph was so incensed at the demand that he, like all officials, kiss the pope's foot that he refused to leave the ship until the issue was resolved. As a result, Pope Eugenius IV accorded him only a private reception rather than a grand public ceremony. The Council opened officially on 9 April after twenty days of debate over where the thrones for the leading figures should be placed. After many delays and inconclusive meetings, an outbreak of plague and shortage of money forced the parties in January 1439 to move to Florence, where the Medici family supported the Council.

While detailed records of the long debates that preceded the agreement were kept, the most interesting account of the Council was written by Sylvester Syropoulos, a patriarchal official. His memoirs record impressions of the unofficial discussions which accompanied the negotiations: how the Byzantine participants argued among themselves (for there were major disagreements between John VIII and Mark Eugenikos) and picked topics for discussion which would not reveal these rifts (such as the existence of Purgatory); how it became ever clearer that if the Greeks knew no Latin, they could not debate with the western theologians, who countered every eastern text with an argument of their own, often drawn from unfamiliar writings.

The *filioque* addition to the creed remained a major barrier, both as an extra clause in the wording of the creed as agreed at the First and Fourth Oecumenical Councils, and as a statement of orthodox theology. After many months of Latin pressure, agreement was reached on the grounds that all saints are inspired by the same Holy Spirit, whether they are western or eastern, and their faith must therefore be the same in substance even if it is expressed differently in Latin and Greek. Disagreement over papal primacy proved more fundamental, however. While the words of the creed might be accepted, the power claimed by Rome meant subjection, which the Church of Constantinople found much harder to bear. After centuries of elaboration and reinforcement through Rome's judicial position in the West, popes had asserted superior authority over all churches based on their founder St Peter. They considered that patriarchs in Byzantium should submit to Rome before the union of churches could be celebrated. This not only implied inferiority, it also denied the tradition of the five leading sees meeting in Council as the highest authority in Christendom. While New Rome/Constantinople recognized Old Rome's higher place of honour, the eastern theory of the pentarchy was hard to reconcile with Rome's claim to overall primacy.

Under pressure from John VIII, the eastern clerics were persuaded nonetheless to agree a form of words which permitted the Union to be drafted. Remaining issues, like the use of leavened or unleavened bread, the marriage of lower ranks of orthodox clergy, and fasting and genuflecting habits were identified as local customs, which could be accepted. When the Act of Union was finally read in Latin and Greek in Florence on 6 July 1439, and acclaimed by all present, the churches were formally united in one faith. John VIII was commemorated in miniatures, bronzes and a medallion by Pisanello, which show him wearing the large peaked hat then fashionable. The process of negotiating the Union took nearly three years; the imperial party only returned to Constantinople in February 1440.

As a consequence, the princes of central Europe – Hunyadi of Transylvania, Vladislav I of Hungary and George Branković of Serbia – led a crusade into the Balkans which defeated the Turks in 1443/4.

Murad II agreed to a ten-year truce, which might have been effective had not some of the western crusaders broken the terms at Varna. In November 1444, they attacked the city and were defeated. Constantinople was now abandoned to its fate; the 'crusade of Varna' was to prove the last. Although Hunyadi remained committed to the policy of assisting Byzantium, and Branković, who had not participated in the attack, remained a Christian ally, Constantinople's essential weakness was symbolized when John VIII Palaiologos was forced to congratulate the sultan on his victory.

Only Mark Eugenikos of Ephesos and one other metropolitan had refused to sign the Union, and Eugenikos became the spokesman of resistance to it. Claiming that he had signed under duress, Syropoulos later joined the majority of Greeks who felt that both their beliefs and their traditions had been abandoned. In 1452, Pope Nicholas V sent Isidore of Kiev, who had converted and become a cardinal of the Catholic Church, to preach the Union in the beleaguered Byzantine capital. He arrived with a body of two hundred archers recruited at his own expense, which initially cheered the inhabitants. The Greek historian Doukas, reported, 'Of the greater portion of the sacerdotal and monastic orders, abbots, archimandrites, nuns . . . not one among them assented to the Union. Even the emperor only pretended to do so.' Nuns, he said, were particularly hostile and they implored Gennadios Scholarios of the Pantokrator monastery in Constantinople to support them. He finally wrote his tract in opposition to the Union and nailed it to his door: 'Wretched Romans, how you have been deceived . . . Together with the city which will soon be destroyed, you have lost your piety.' As these monks and nuns spread news of the resistance, the people called on the Mother of God to protect them against the Turks as she had done in the past against Chosroes and the Avars and the Arabs. They also implored her to 'Keep far away from us the worship of the Azymites.'

On 12 December 1452, the Union was celebrated in desperation in Hagia Sophia, with the Turks encamped outside the walls of Constantinople. Although Isidore of Kiev reported to the pope that the liturgy was a triumph, Gennadios and other monks failed to participate, and the Union was not widely accepted in Byzantium. Nonetheless, Isidore himself fought on the walls in 1453, was wounded and taken prisoner.

By disguising himself, he managed to escape to Crete and constantly mourned the loss of the city. Bessarion, the other major proponent of the Union, also continued to support efforts to regain Constantinople after the fall. As cardinals who served as papal legates, they were considered traitors by the orthodox. Both, however, encouraged humanist scholarship, wrote numerous works of theology and contributed to the growth of Greek libraries in the West. Bessarion's legacy to Venice in 1468 ensured that his collection would remain intact as the core of the Marciana Library, while Isidore enriched the Vatican library with writings of his own and scholia in numerous manuscripts.

Among those opposed to the Union, Gennadios was also taken prisoner in 1453 but was discovered in the slave market, ransomed and installed as patriarch by Mehmed the Conqueror. His fierce loyalty to what was the original and true Christian theology reflects contemporary opinion voiced by Loukas Notaras, an adviser to the last three emperors: 'Better the Turkish turban than the papal tiara.' Byzantium could not accept the theory of papal primacy and the subordination of Constantinople to Rome. The Byzantines, however few, remained faithfully committed to what they understood to be orthodox. They preferred to maintain their own theology under Ottoman rule than to suffer union with the Church of Rome and western rule. This was surely an echo of the sacrilege of 1204.

28

The Siege of 1453

On the twenty-ninth of May, our Lord God decided that He
was willing for the city to fall on this day ... in order to fulfil
all the ancient prophecies ... All these three had come to pass
seeing that the Turks had passed into Greece, there was an
Emperor called Constantine, son of Helen, and the moon had
given a sign in the sky.

Nicolò Barbaro, *Diary of the Siege of Constantinople*

In 1354, a major shift in the balance of power between Byzantium
and the Ottomans occurred, when an earthquake destroyed the entire
coastline of Thrace. The fortifications of the cities on the European
side of the Hellespont collapsed, forcing the population to flee and
allowing Orhan's son Süleyman to cross the Dardanelles with many
Turkish troops and families. Meeting no resistance, he began a cam-
paign to secure the permanent occupation of the western provinces of
Byzantium from his new base at Kallipolis (literally, beautiful city;
modern Gallipoli). Turkish expansion into the Balkans against the
Serbs was matched by threats to Constantinople from Thrace. Sultan
Murad I (1362–89) captured Adrianople (Edirne), which became the
Ottomans' western capital. In 1371, at the battle of the Marica, the
Turks defeated the Serbian king Vukasin and proceeded to capture
Sofia and Thessalonike, thus incorporating Serbia, Bulgaria and Mace-
donia into the Ottoman state. Both Vukasin and John V Palaiologos
became vassals. By 1387 Theodore Palaiologos, despot of the Morea,
recognized Murad's authority, although he resisted the Turks'
attempts to capture Mistras.

In less than twenty-five years, the sultan had surrounded Constantinople and was able to exercise a pincer movement on it from both east and west, by land and sea. Yet the city held out for another eighty years, partly because Murad I had made all the Byzantine rulers his vassals and could therefore count on their support. In 1372/3, he obliged John V Palaiologos to assist with his military campaigns against the remaining Christians in Asia Minor. As the historian Chalkokondyles put it:

John entered into an alliance with Murad, who had recently crossed over to Europe ... As homage to Murad, John and his sons also had to follow him wherever he campaigned.

The same author reported that this pattern of treatment was also imposed on Dragaš, the Serbian leader, and Bogdan, who had been put in charge of territory near the River Axios. In this way, the sultan accumulated troops and vassals. Some Serbs and Bosnians, however, continued to resist and mounted a combined challenge to Murad I. In 1389, the Turks met this force at Kosovo Polje, where the sultan was assassinated. Historians are divided over which side actually won the battle, but the result was increased Turkish control over the Balkans.

The history of Byzantium in its last century was written from contrasting viewpoints by Doukas, on the Byzantine side, and Chalkokondyles on the Ottoman. Both wrote after the conquest of Constantinople. What Doukas considers humiliation of the emperor, Chalkokondyles passes over as the normal treatment of a vassal by his lord. Both, however, emphasize the almost suicidal rivalry of John V's many sons, who tried in turn to take power during his long reign (1341–91). The eldest, Andronikos IV and his son John VII, the second, Manuel II, and the third, Theodore, all participated in revolts, using Genoese, Venetian and Turkish allies. The emperor had tried to prevent this by appointing them to rule over the scattered remnants of Byzantium, which gradually became autonomous units: the Morea, with its capital at Mistras; Thessalonike, centre of its remaining Balkan territory; and Selymbria, fortified by John VI Kantakouzenos as his base in Thrace during the 1340s. These little kingdoms, or appanages in which each son could act as an independent ruler, suggest a quasi-feudal system similar to Western Europe, where numerous small kingdoms and duchies vied for territorial dominance. But whereas in the West the nominal kings of France, England, Castile and Germany were trying to extend their authority, the Palaiologoi were dividing the once-united empire of Byzantium into smaller units. In contrast to the centralizing forces that were empowering the states of western Christendom, the opposite centripetal pressure was reducing imperial resources and territory in the East.

Murad's death at Kosovo Polje in 1389 intensified Ottoman pressure on Constantinople. His successor, Bayezid I (1389–1402), constructed the fortress of Anadolu Hisar on the eastern shore of the Bosphoros to prevent the Byzantines from bringing in naval reinforcements. When Manuel II was crowned emperor in the city in 1391, he knew he would face an almost immediate siege, and by 1394 the Turks had effectively invested the city by sea and land. News of this stranglehold finally galvanized the Christians in Europe to organize military aid in the form of an international force, led by King Sigismund of Hungary and Marshal Boucicaut of France. The western crusade advanced as far as the Ottoman fortress on the Danube at Nikopolis (modern Nikopol in Bulgaria), and was considered such a serious challenge to the Turks that Sultan Bayezid left the siege to meet it. In 1396, the crusade was crushed with few prisoners taken alive. Among the survivors, Sigismund and Boucicaut were both captured and later ransomed. The French marshal refused to abandon the Christians in the east and persuaded King Charles VI of France to send a small force to relieve Constantinople. In 1399, it successfully broke the Turkish blockade of the city and Boucicaut joined Manuel II in military actions.

At this point, the marshal suggested that the emperor should leave his nephew John VII in charge of the defence and make a tour of western monarchs to raise further military support for Constantinople. John VII had been crowned by his father Andronikos IV and had plotted with the Turks to win sole power against Manuel II's claims. But after a period as Sultan Bayezid's hostage, John was now entrusted with the defence of the capital, while Manuel and the marshal slipped through the blockade in December 1399. Manuel embarked on what proved a lengthy tour of Europe, wonderfully evoked in his letters to the brothers Demetrios and Manuel Chrysoloras, to Euthymios, later Patriarch of Constantinople, and Manuel Pothos.

Since he had visited Venice before, he reserved his most elaborate reports for the other major capitals: Paris, where he was welcomed with lavish ceremonies by Charles VI in the summer of 1400, and London, where he celebrated the following Christmas with Henry IV at the palace of Eltham. From Paris, Manuel described the 'nobility of soul, the friendship and constant zeal for the faith' displayed by the king, his kinsmen and officials. He stayed in the palace of the Louvre, where he noticed a fine tapestry and composed an account of its beauty. He hoped that he would shortly be able to return to Constantinople with military aid. Charles VI also invited him to celebrate the eighth day of the feast of Saint Denis at the famous monastery north of Paris. Some criticized this, saying that the Greeks were not in communion with Rome, but the king insisted and Manuel was reminded that his attempts to obtain aid would be dependent on the union of the Latin and Greek churches.

In the winter of 1400/1401, he visited London where he appreciated the hospitality of Henry IV, who

has made himself a virtual haven for us in the midst of a twofold tempest, that of the season and that of fortune . . . His conversation is quite charming; he pleases us in every way . . . He is providing us with military assistance, with soldiers, archers, money and ships to transport the army where it is needed.

Adam of Usk, who observed the embassy, wrote of the Byzantines:

This emperor always walked with his men, dressed alike and in one colour, namely white, in long robes cut like tabards . . . No razor touched head or beard of his chaplains. These Greeks were most devout in their church services, which were joined in as well by soldiers as by priests, for they chanted them without distinction in their native tongue. I thought within myself, what a grievous thing it was that this great Christian prince from the farther east should perforce be driven by unbelievers to visit the distant lands of the west to seek aid against them.

While Manuel II was in the West trying to persuade the rulers of France and England to send troops to defend his capital, an unexpected ally emerged in Asia Minor. Timur (Tamerlane), the Mongol leader, known as 'the Sword of Islam', had devastated Georgia in 1399/1400, and ransacked and burned the great cities of Aleppo,

Damascus and Baghdad. He now turned west to attack Sultan Bayezid with his highly disciplined troops, organized in typical Mongol fashion in units of 100 and dedicated to jihad. They engaged the Turks outside Ankara on 28 July 1402. Not only were the Ottomans defeated, but the sultan and his son Musa were both taken prisoner. Bayezid later died in captivity. While Timur's success shocked and terrified them, the western rulers Henry III of Castile, Charles VI of France and Henry IV of England sent their congratulations to the victor of Ankara who had destroyed their enemy Bayezid. From Constantinople, the regent John VII Palaiologos promised tribute if Timur would continue to protect Byzantium from the Turks. For the Christians enclosed in Constantinople, the Mongols had performed a great service, but there was still anxiety about what Timur would do next. After destroying the Knights Hospitallers in Smyrna, however, he then returned to the east where he entertained the much greater ambition of conquering China. There he would realize the title that became his epitaph, 'Conqueror of the World'.

After the defeat of 1402, Manuel returned to Constantinople while the four sons of Bayezid immediately began a struggle for supreme power, which was resolved in 1413 when Mehmed I triumphed over his brothers and resumed the campaign against Byzantium. Manuel commissioned a copy of the writings of Pseudo-Dionysus, with a fine group portrait of the imperial family, which he sent to the monastery of Saint Denis as a way of thanking Charles VI (plate 40). But no military aid came to Constantinople as it faced another serious Ottoman siege in 1422. In that year, Manuel suffered a stroke and John VIII took over control of Byzantium, now reduced to the capital city without hinterland, no longer Queen of any empire. In 1453 Mehmed I's grandson would ride into Constantinople as the Conqueror.

The creation of Ottoman power took place over many centuries in continuous interaction with Byzantium. As the former expanded and grew stronger, the latter shrank and became weaker. The long period of political rivalry, coupled with close relations, led to mutual influence. The Byzantine princesses sent to marry Turkish husbands introduced a Christian presence into their courts. The Byzantine system of land grants (*pronoia*) was transformed into the Ottoman *timar*, while Muslim tax registers continued to be maintained by Christian officials in the Byzantine style. For social services, Byzantines and Ottomans adopted similar patterns of philanthropy, although the Islamic insistence on giving alms meant that a proportion of every Muslim's income would be set aside for this purpose, while in the Christian world it was left to the individual's conscience. Institutions like the Muslim *wakf* closely resembled the Christian monastery with its myriad social functions. But during the Ottoman conquest, Christian resources, population, church property and taxes were redirected to Islamic institutions: caravanserais, medressehs and mosques, often staffed by Christian converts (*gulams*). Although they provided free accommodation and food for travellers of all faiths, *wakf* foundations strengthened Islam at the expense of Christianity.

This is evident from the number of active metropolitans and bishops in Asia Minor, which declined sharply as churches were converted into mosques, church property was confiscated by the conquerors, and Christian peasants found it more profitable to renounce their faith and convert to Islam. As Kydones reported in a speech urging the emperors to seek western aid:

The entire region which used to sustain us, extending to the East from the Hellespont to the mountains of Armenia, they have stripped away. They have completely destroyed cities, despoiled churches, looted graves and filled everything with blood and corpses. They have even polluted the souls of the inhabitants, forcing them to reject the true God and to take part in their own filth.

Episcopal sees in the European provinces replaced the traditional dominance of Asia Minor in the hierarchy of ecclesiastical centres. In 1324, when the Patriarch of Constantinople appealed for financial assistance, only three major sees were named: Kyzikos, Proikonessos and Lopadion. Many clerics appointed to churches in Asia Minor were unable to reside in their sees and became refugees in the capital, dependent on patriarchal support. And by the late fifteenth century, an official *notitia* (list of churches) records that in Asia Minor 'fifty-one metropolitanates, eighteen archbishoprics and four hundred and seventy-eight bishoprics are desolate'. Only one archbishop and three bishops survived.

In artistic terms, the Seljuks had already adopted the double-headed eagle from Byzantium and, inspired by Hagia Sophia, fourteenth-century mosques had adapted domes and ceramic tiles for their own use. The Green Mosque at Bursa, built with a fine dome in 1424 by Mehmed I, served as a model for many later mosques, for example at Edirne, and achieved a new distinction in sixteenth-century buildings built by the architect Sinan, notably the Blue Mosque in Constantinople–Istanbul. Sinan, born a Christian, was enslaved by the Muslims in their regular forced recruitment of boys for palace service (*devşirme*), and attained great honour through his designs for magnificent baths and secular structures, as well as mosques.

Despite this long process of mutual influence, major differences in the realm of family law and customs continued to set Islam apart. Against the Christian insistence on monogamy and reluctance to permit remarriage, Muslim men were allowed four wives, if they could support them appropriately. Sultans indulged their sexual preferences not only with their official wives but also with numerous concubines who formed the core of their harem. These women hoped to produce a large number of sons, who *all* wanted to inherit their father's power. The result was a tremendous rivalry among the mothers, as well as fratricidal warfare among the brothers and half-brothers when a sultan died. Islam did not recognize the medieval practice of primogeniture, which ensured that the eldest son inherited his father's land. The sultan might favour a younger son born to his favourite concubine over his older half-brothers. The civil war of 1402–13, between Bayezid's sons, was a portent of many similar struggles to come.

Of course, such conflicts were also familiar in Byzantium and the West. Andronikos II had been challenged by his grandson Andronikos III in the years 1321–8, and John VI Kantakouzenos provoked a six-year struggle when he claimed the throne inherited by John V (1341–7). When John VIII (1425–48) and Constantine XI (1449–53) called on their younger brothers Theodore and Demetrios for help in defending the capital, the despots of Morea were too busy fighting each other. But in the Muslim world, the court structure and harem encouraged greater competition and instability at moments of succession. And since the Ottomans had adopted monarchy as their political form, one ruler had to establish his authority over all his rivals. Each sultan usually came to power after a series of fratricides and murders, which heightened his own determination to survive. And each wanted to be the Ottoman ruler who captured the Christian metropolis of Constantinople.

In 1422, Murad II anticipated this triumph and gave precise instructions regarding the expected booty. An eyewitness records:

> The despot of the Turks also dispatched heralds to proclaim to all the ends of the earth that the emir promised to deliver all the riches and people of the city to the Muslims. This he did to gather all the Muslims ... they came to profit, not only the profiteers in looting and war, but the adventurers and the merchants, perfumers, shoemakers, and even some Turkish monks ... Some came to buy prisoners, some women; others came to take the men and still others, the infants; others came to seize the animals, and others goods; and the Turkish monks came to get our nuns and free booty from the despot of the Turks.

On this occasion, according to John Kananos, who witnessed the siege, the Mother of God protected Constantinople; even the Turks saw her fighting on the battlements. Emperor Manuel, however, managed to secure the proclamation of a rival sultan in Bursa, which forced Murad II to abandon the siege.

Thwarted in his ambitions, the sultan turned his attention to the Morea and forced Demetrios and Thomas Palaiologos to pay tribute. While Demetrios welcomed this alliance with Murad II, Thomas led an anti-Turkish coalition in alliance with his Genoese relations, the Zaccaria family. In 1448, when Emperor John VIII died, his mother Helena insisted that Constantine, who was older than Demetrios and Thomas, should be crowned emperor. Since it was clear that Constantinople was threatened more seriously than ever before, Constantine immediately appealed to his brothers for military help. But they refused and by 1451 it was already too late.

In that year Mehmed II succeeded his father Murad as sultan. He was only nineteen but determined to complete the Ottoman conquest of Constantinople. Both he and Constantine XI knew that the survival of Byzantium was at stake. The construction of a second major Ottoman castle at Rumeli Hisar on the European shore achieved the Ottoman aim of controlling all shipping in the Bosphoros, and prevented any large-scale military aid from reaching the city. From that point on, Constantinople's fate was decided. Had Constantine XI been able to pay the Hungarian engineer who offered to cast new cannon for the defence of the city, it might have survived for a few years. But the Byzantine ruler was very short of money, and so the engineer took his invention to the Turks. It was this giant weapon, larger than any previous cannon, that ensured their victory. No late antique city walls of the fifth century, built in a straight line of triple fortifications, could withstand the power of gunpowder at this fifteenth-century strength.

The Byzantine emperor sent copious appeals to the West, to which some allies responded. In the autumn of 1452, the papal legate Cardinal Isidore (previously Bishop of Kiev) and Leonard of Chios arrived in the city with the body of archers recruited and paid by the cardinal. Ships from Ancona, Provence and Castile added to the naval forces, and a group of Greeks from Crete elected to remain in the city, though six ships later slipped away. The inhabitants were greatly cheered by the arrival in January 1453 of the Genoese *condottiere*, Giovanni Giustiniani Longo, who braved the Turkish blockade and got through with his two ships and about seven hundred men. Constantine XI put him in charge of the weakest part of the land walls, the section by the Gate of Romanos, and

he invigorated and even instructed the people so that they would not lose hope and maintain unswerving trust in God ... All people admired and obeyed him in all things.

In his diary of the siege, Nicolò Barbaro, a surgeon from Venice, records his experience of living through the last days of Byzantium. When people realized that only a miracle could save them from 'the fury of these wicked pagans', they wept and prayed and

when the tocsin was sounded, to make everyone take up their posts ... women, and children too, carried stones to the walls to put them on the battlements so that they could be hurled down upon the Turks.

His vivid account is naturally biased in favour of the Venetians, and he accuses Giustiniani of abandoning his post at the Romanos Gate.

After master-minding the defence with the emperor, the Genoese leader had been hit by an arrow and died later at Chios.

Constantine XI's appeals to General Hunyadi resulted in an embassy which arrived to negotiate with Mehmed II in April 1453. But by that stage the sultan sensed victory and dismissed the Hungarian threat to attack him. He had assembled a vast army of perhaps 60,000 soldiers and up to 140,000 extras, while Constantine could muster at most 8,000 defenders. With the boom in place across the Golden Horn, the emperor concentrated on defending the 19 kilometres of perimeter wall against overwhelming Turkish forces. The siege was dominated by the sultan's new longer-barrelled cannon, nicknamed 'the imperial', which fired cannon balls weighing between 12,000 and 13,000lbs at the walls. Despite valiant efforts to repair the defences with barrels, rubble and any other material, after twenty days of bombardment a breach was opened through which the Turks forced their entry. On 29 May 1453, they raised their flag over the city.

The heroic emperor, Constantine XI, who inspired the resistance, was lost during the attack, and his body was never found, creating a Byzantine rumour that he had been swallowed up into the walls and would return. The night before the final attack, he rode out on one last tour of the walls with his adviser, Sphrantzes, who records how they saw the vast encampment of the Ottomans, their bonfires and preparations, and knew that only divine intervention could save Byzantium. Instead, the city was subjected to a three-day plunder, in which Sphrantzes and many others were taken prisoner. When Mehmed II finally entered the city, some reports claim that he wept at the losses and at the beauty of the buildings; others note that the Turks dressed themselves and even their dogs in ecclesiastical robes, threw all the icons onto a huge bonfire over which they roasted meat, and drank unwatered wine from chalices.

The sultan ordered what remained of the population to stay in the city under Ottoman rule, and organized 5,000 extra families to move in, thus beginning the process of Islamicization. He installed the well-known scholar and monk Gennadios Scholarios as patriarch in 1454. As leader of the Greek *millet* (an ethnic grouping employed by the Ottomans to control conquered people), he tried to protect the orthodox from injustice. To this day, his successor, now Patriarch Bartholomeus of Constantinople, resides in his see, through terms negotiated with the first ruler of modern Turkey, Mustafa Kemal – better known as Atatürk – at the Treaty of Lausanne (1923). Although there are few Christians in the city, the Church of New Rome, recognized by Constantine I and elevated to the same position as Old Rome by Theodosius I, persists as a beacon of orthodox faith. But it is the young Mehmed the Conqueror whose victory is commemorated in the Mosque of the Conqueror, Fatih Camii, erected on the site of the church of the Holy Apostles. With this symbolic replacement, he made Byzantium the capital of what became the Ottoman Empire.

Conclusion:
The Greatness and Legacy of Byzantium

The most striking characteristic of Byzantium was not its Christianity, spelled out in its historic councils and conversions, and celebrated in immense churches like Hagia Sophia or in the domestic intimacy of household icons; nor its Roman organization and administration and imperial self-belief; nor its enduring ancient Greek inheritance and system of education: it was their combination. This dated back to the fourth century with the creation of the new capital, its monuments and harbours, which rooted Byzantium in a rich ecology of traditions and resources.

Yet the modern stereotype of Byzantium is tyrannical government by effeminate, cowardly men and corrupt eunuchs, obsessed with hollow rituals and endless, complex and incomprehensible bureaucracy. Montesquieu developed these caricatures during the seventeenth century as he tried to explain the reasons for the decline of the Roman Empire, and Voltaire gave them greater prominence, adding his own passionate elevation of reason above religion. While the former dismissed 'the Greek Empire', as he called it, because of the excessive power of monks, attention to theological dispute and an absence of the recommended separation of ecclesiastical from secular matters, the latter could condemn it utterly as 'a disgrace for the human mind'. Perhaps both were also provoked by Louis XIV's use of Byzantine models as a means of celebrating despotic kingly rule.

Gibbon's more familiar account in his *History of the Decline and Fall of the Roman Empire*, which extended to 1453, built on these features and identified Byzantium as a 'passive' link with Graeco-Roman antiquity. In itself, he argued, it was of no interest except that it connected the classical period to the barbarian nations of Western

Europe and 'the most splendid and important revolutions which have changed the state of the world'. Perhaps the most forthright expression of Byzantium's negative reputation belongs to the nineteenth-century Irish historian William Lecky. In a withering, misogynistic judgement, he claimed:

Of that Byzantine empire, the universal verdict of history is that it constitutes, without a single exception, the most thoroughly base and despicable form that civilization has yet assumed. There has been no other enduring civilization so absolutely destitute of all forms and elements of greatness, and none to which the epithet 'mean' may be so emphatically applied ... The history of the empire is a monotonous story of the intrigues of priests, eunuchs, and women, of poisonings, of conspiracies, of uniform ingratitude.

As I hope to have shown, far from being passive, Byzantium was active, surprising and creative, as it reworked its prized traditions and heritage. It bequeathed to the world an imperial system of government built upon a trained, civilian administration and tax system; a legal structure based on Roman law; a unique curriculum of secular education that preserved much of classical, pagan learning; orthodox theology, artistic expression and spiritual traditions enshrined in the Greek Church; and coronation and court rituals that had many imitators. In the sixth century, the merchant Cosmas Indicopleustes also noted:

There is another mark of the power of the Romans, which God has given them, I mean that every nation conducts its commerce with their *nomisma*, which is acceptable in every place from one end of the earth to the other ... In no other nation does such a thing exist.

For centuries after the fall of the Queen City to the Turks, the term 'bezant' was still used, redolent of the famed reliability of Byzantine gold. Despite the eleventh-century devaluation, the name bezant provides an echo of the gold coin's powerful contribution to trade in the early Middle Ages, when Byzantium protected the growth of Venice and other Italian city-states.

Artistically, its silks and ivories set standards for beauty and craftsmanship, while its images still continue to inspire icon painters in orthodox communities throughout the world. Theologically, its intense, century-long inner struggle with the iconoclast strictures of the Ten Commandments, precipitated by their forceful adoption by Islam, became a reference point for Puritans nearly a thousand years later. Its ability to conquer and, above all, to defend itself and its magnificent capital was to shield the northwestern world of the Mediterranean during the chaotic but creative period that followed the collapse of the Roman Empire in the West. Without Byzantium there would have been no Europe.

During this critical early-medieval period, when the Arabs stormed out of the desert to capture the Holy Places of the Jews and the Christians and the granaries of Egypt, only Constantinople stood in the way of their ambitions. Had the fortifications of the Queen City and the determination and skills of its inhabitants – emperor, court and people – not ensured the security of this defensive system, Islam would have supplanted Byzantium in the seventh century. Having accomplished the conquest of Damascus, Jerusalem, Alexandria and the Persian empire, the Muslims would surely have overrun the Mediterranean empire created by Rome, once they had incorporated Constantinople with its resources and revenues, its shipyards and commercial networks. In the same way that they progressed along the southern littoral of the Mediterranean into Spain, they would have advanced across the Balkans to dominate the northern shore as well.

Byzantium was thus partly defined in rivalry with successive Arab states, and relations between Christianity and Islam had a formative influence in the empire's development. As we have seen, its initial contact with Islam in the seventh century came as a complete surprise. Byzantium's historic defeat of Persia distracted attention from what seemed at first no more than tribal marauders, if with a chiliastic twist. Instead, the appearance of the Arabs under the banner of the Prophet turned into a long trauma. The impact of their immediate military triumphs in the decade 632/42 forced Byzantium to withdraw into Asia Minor, abandoning the most holy centres of Christianity, as well as some of the earliest monastic sites in Egypt, Palestine and Syria. Yet it was also able to beat off many Muslim sieges of its capital and to hold a border at the Taurus Mountains. The rise and frustration of Islam resulted in a formative three-way division of the ancient world into unequal parts: the Muslim east which extended from Syria and Egypt across the coast of Africa and deep into Spain; the western part which adopted the name 'Europa'; and the eastern part which remained the core of Byzantium.

During the first protracted encounter with Islam, Byzantine consternation at the Muslims' enduring military success was coupled with condemnation of their theology. It was considered a heresy, albeit rather different from other seventh-century doctrinal errors. While Byzantium later accepted that Islam was a revelation from the same one God, they were slow to develop any detailed knowledge of the Qur'an, or the claim that Islam had replaced Christianity as the true revelation. Instead, arguments long used in Christian polemics with Judaism were refashioned and turned against the new opponent; vigorous dialogues were produced to reassure the Christian side while condemning the Muslim. In the eighth and ninth centuries, these took on even more strident forms with the development of Byzantine iconoclasm – both a reaction to Islam and a means of consolidating the empire to combat the Islamic challenge.

After 750, internal strife and civil war among the Muslims led the Abbasid dynasty to move the capital from Damascus to Baghdad, on the banks of the Tigris in Iraq. The rise of the Abbasids split the Islamic world into rival caliphates, leaving the Umayyads based in Spain. This eased pressure on Byzantium. Although the new centres of Muslim power in Baghdad and Cordoba were now more distant from Constantinople than Damascus, they remained a focus of constant negotiation. Byzantium tried to maintain diplomatic relations with all the rival Islamic authorities.

From the eleventh century onwards, other Muslim peoples reshaped the Islamic world. In their long journey west from Mongolia, the main activity of the Seljuk Turks was to defeat all opposing forces and capture and sack major cities for booty. In the eleventh century, as they conquered Baghdad and made it their capital, they first came into contact with Byzantium. Their Sunni beliefs made them hostile to all Shi'ite authorities in Islam, such as the Fatimid dynasty based in Cairo. When Fatimid control over Jerusalem was broken by the Seljuks, Byzantium and the Christian West were inspired to regain the Holy Places. And the triumphant recapture of the city for Christianity in 1099 was achieved in part by the crusaders' exploitation of the divisions between many local Sunni and Shi'ite Muslims. Finally, after nearly eighty years, Christian control was reversed by the Kurdish general Saladin in 1187.

For Byzantium the differences between Arabs and Turks were clear. The Seljuk Turks were a Mongol people speaking an ancient Uighur language (which is a common tongue still in use today from Turkey to the Far East, where it is spoken by the Muslim minority in western China). The Seljuk and later Ottoman Turks were not Arabs by culture or history, and initially they demonstrated their determination to challenge established Muslim authorities rather than Christian ones. Their move into Asia Minor and towards the Queen City occurred almost as a detour, when they realized that there was no serious opposition to prevent their advance. As they gradually replaced imperial control in Asia Minor during the late eleventh and twelfth centuries, Byzantium recognized them as a new hostile force, divided into several distinct emirates, and tried to come to terms with their military victories. Eventually the Ottoman Turks united a larger force that crossed the Dardanelles in 1354 and began the conquest of the western provinces of the empire.

Soon after this dramatic event, Constantinople found itself surrounded on all sides by the Ottomans, in quite different circumstances from the Arab besiegers of the city seven hundred years before. Their long exposure to the empire had helped to transform the Ottomans from nomadic tribes to a settled people. While they built mosques for prayer and caravanserais to assist overland trade with the Far East, they had adapted Byzantine administrative traditions and imperial norms, absorbing ancient skills. At the same time, Byzantine centres surrounded by the Turks flourished for centuries in a symbiotic relationship with them, for instance in Trebizond, where the Grand Komnenoi maintained Christian rule by making alliances with their Muslim neighbours and later overlords. Considerable intermarriage among the rulers of these states engendered continuing tolerance and exchange.

In 1391 the newly installed emperor, Manuel II Palaiologos, had inherited from his father the status of an Ottoman vassal and was obliged to pay considerable taxes and to campaign by the side of Sultan Bayezid I. After military operations that summer, the emperor accompanied the sultan to a camp near Ankyra in Anatolia, where they went out hunting by day and feasted by night. This happened several years before Manuel's visit to London and Paris, discussed in the previous chapter. As the winter drew in, with the first snowfall, low temperatures and long dark nights, Manuel and his companions devised a way to pass the time. They would debate with the local Muslim *müderris* (a technical name for a religious judge or teacher, *qadi*) about the relative merits of their religions. In this philosophical way, they would fill the evenings and provide some thoughtful entertainment. Manuel II was a prolific writer of letters and rhetorical exercises in the ancient Greek style, and he later set out his version of the wintry discussions held near Ankyra in a considerable volume of 300 pages.

This aspect of Byzantium's legacy was picked up by Pope Benedict XVI in the special lecture he gave in Regensburg, his old university town, on 12 September 2006. He chose to cite a particularly harsh attack on Islam from the seventh section of Manuel II's *Dialogue with a Persian*, written some time after 1391. He quotes the emperor as saying:

Show me just what Muhammad brought that was new, and there you will find things only evil and inhuman, such as his command to spread by the sword the faith he preached.

Suddenly, the name of a hitherto obscure though scholarly ruler of late Byzantium was to be found on the front pages of serious newspapers. The emperor's words were deployed to legitimize what seemed to be a frontal assault on the nature of Islam – and for a moment Byzantium was recruited into the 'war on terror'. The pope himself in footnotes added later said that he only quoted the passage to emphasize his agreement with Manuel II about the 'the essential relationship between faith and reason . . . without endorsing his polemic'. In this, he displayed an ignorance of Byzantium, for the full version of the *Dialogue* is much more complex and curious than the tiny snippet selected, with its unequivocally hostile and reductive description of Islam. Manuel's text also demonstrates that Muslims under Ottoman rule could engage in reasoned argument and debate with their Byzantine Christian opponents.

Pope Benedict's lecture poses the broader issue of Byzantium's overall relationship to its Islamic opponents. The text also suggests that the pope's most important theological adversary was less Islam than his fellow Christians of evangelical belief. For the main thrust of his argument is on the divine nature of the fusion of the teachings of Christ with the Hellenistic traditions of the Word, which, he insists, integrated reason into revelation, thus refuting any claims that Christianity can be reduced to the preaching and presence of Christ alone. But it seems disingenuous to suggest that there was not also an anti-Muslim intent behind the lecture as well. For Pope Benedict proposes that

the inner rapprochement between biblical faith and Greek philosophical enquiry was an event of decisive importance . . . This convergence . . . remains the foundation of what can rightly be called Europe.

In contrast, he presents Muslim faith as a monolithic, implicitly anti-European, religious ideology, whose believers are, thanks to their allegiance, deprived of the capacity to combine faith with reason. Instead, they fuse violence with revelation and are thus intrinsically unable, the pope seems to imply, to accept the idea of the rule of secular law, or even the concept of the university.

In this *Dialogue*, quoted by Pope Benedict, the *müderris* is identified as the Persian. He does not respond immediately to the charge that the Prophet is evil and inhuman, but counters it by reminding the emperor that Islam is God's final revelation to man and replaces the previous ones. In the same way, he says, that Christianity replaced Judaism, now Islam has replaced Christianity and it is the duty of all who believe in the one God to convert to Islam. Of course, the text was written in Byzantine Greek to reflect the superiority of the Christian faith as practised by Manuel II. It is unlikely that he preserved Muslim arguments in their strongest form. In most of the disputes, the emperor displayed his theological and philosophical skills, arguing that the Paraclete mentioned in the Gospel of St John (normally associated with the Holy Spirit) could not possibly be the Prophet Muhammad; disputing the novelty of Islamic law, which he said was Mosaic; and criticizing the Muslim view of Paradise as deeply immoral and a deceptive promise. In the final books he even suggested that he had convinced the *müderris* of the superiority of Christianity and expected him to convert.

The debate was conducted through interpreters, as Manuel did not know Turkish and the *müderris* did not speak Greek. So the *Dialogue* must have been a slow process, lacking the repartee of direct exchange, while providing employment for those who made a living from the interrelationship of the two societies. Both sides, apparently, complained of the translators getting together and whispering among themselves, a symbol, perhaps, of the interweaving of Byzantine and Turkish interests. Yet every evening, when the session came to an end, the parties reported how interesting their discussion had been and resolved to meet again the following day. And thus they passed part of the winter in Anatolia.

By the late fourteenth century, Islam had developed a multitude of different theological schools, Sunni and Shi'ite, including an Ottoman tradition of mystical poetry. And much earlier, the Arabs of Baghdad, Cairo and Cordoba had incorporated the writings of Aristotle into their educational system, which was elevated to a higher level of logical reasoning. It was this Arabic version of Greek philosophy, expounded in a highly rational style by the twelfth-century philosopher and polymath Averroes in Muslim Spain, which made such a forceful impact in the West when it was translated back into Latin. Like Byzantine intellectuals who were accused by the Church of spreading heretical opinions, Averroes was also criticized by the religious authorities of Muslim Spain. Islam was clearly in no way a monolithic religion.

This may be why the pope's extraction of a quotation from a Christian dialogue with Islam to demonstrate that Islam is incapable of reasoned debate seems misjudged. For over seven hundred years, Byzantium was engaged in a contest with different Islamic states and societies. It also coexisted with them, distinguished between them and marked them with its own legacy, most profoundly in Turkey, but also, for example, in the mosaic decoration of Muslim shrines in Jerusalem and Cordoba. This external legacy of Byzantium reflected its internal achievement which made it so resilient.

Byzantium for its part also represented one particular strand of Christianity, the Greek Orthodox, which existed side by side with a plurality of other versions. And although the empire was profoundly shaped by Christian beliefs, it was further distinguished from the medieval West by its active incorporation of much pre-Christian culture from antiquity. Some pagan elements were relatively primitive, such as the veneration of images of the gods and burning of incense in their honour; others derived from sources external to the world of Rome, such as the court practices of Persia. At the highest levels of learning, Byzantine culture included ancient notions of philosophical debate – whether the world is eternal or created, flat or round. Mathematics, geography, medical and veterinary science, literature, ethics and morality, encompassing most human concerns, were rooted in its scholarship and transmitted with many commentaries. Literary models were adapted and developed in Byzantium so that the ancient Greek romance, various forms of metric verse, hymns and epic all flourished. Although the ancient theatre did not survive long into the Christian era, the great Greek dramatists were read, studied and committed to memory by generation after generation of Byzantine schoolchildren.

In this fundamental way, therefore, Byzantium was intrinsically classical and still partly pagan. When Constantine XI found his empire reduced to a hopeless city-state surrounded by the Ottoman Turks, who were about to breach the walls using the cannon he could neither afford to buy nor was able to manufacture, the most Christian emperor called out in Greek to his people to prove themselves to be true Romans. In so doing, he summoned a history that stretched back from 1453 to the dedication of the city in 330, one thousand, one hundred and twenty-three years earlier, and identified the Byzantines with their glorious forebears, the pagan Greeks and Romans.

This pagan inheritance is often hidden within the enveloping Christian culture. Patriarch Photios' own account of the many books he read, most of Christian origin, includes the Pyrrhonian writings of Ainesidemos (an obscure Greek sceptic), works of Galen and Oreibasios, physician to Julian the Apostate, as well as the sixty-five genuine speeches of Demosthenes, which he sets in an account of the life and times of the great orator. Observations on the Homeric epics by the twelfth-century Archbishop Eustathios of Thessalonike present a more direct and immediate engagement with ancient verse. In general,

Byzantine scholars and officials considered the compositions of ancient authors superior to their own (a modesty we might reflect upon). This did not mean that they were inhibited from criticizing their illustrious predecessors. They read, edited and commented on pre-Christian texts of all varieties and thus kept available a larger proportion of pagan writings than would otherwise have survived.

Byzantine scholarly activity was made possible by the educational system, which remained based on the ancient Greek curriculum and was sustained by a profound knowledge of the most outstanding pagan texts. While the Church added its own component of theological and spiritual writings, it could never rival the training provided by memorizing ancient material. This secular practice penetrated every part of the empire across the centuries. In favourable circumstances, it led to original and elaborate analysis, as in the verse of the nun Kassia or the monk John Geometres, the bishops John Mauropous and George Chioniades, Anna Komnene and the members of her literary circle, or the philosophers Michael Psellos and George Gemistos Plethon. As John Mauropous demonstrates in his prayer for the souls of Plato and Plutarch, there was a genuine appreciation of the moral qualities of some pre-Christian writers.

Others, who may have lacked that kind of serious education, also reflected a Byzantine curiosity about what ancient authors had written, how their cities had been constructed and who was commemorated in pre-Christian inscriptions and sculptures. These self-styled philosophers dedicated themselves to a different sort of commentary on the pagan past, such as the identification of ancient buildings, monuments and sculpted busts, which continued to decorate the cities of the Near East long into the Middle Ages. Of course, they regularly made errors and elided ancient with Christian ideas, for example when they wrote that Athena, the virgin goddess, prefigured Mary, the virgin Mother of God. But Plethon's totally pagan devotion to Zeus, which produced his liturgy in honour of the ancient gods, could not have flourished without a long tradition of observing and studying the ancient world.

In the court and the households of ruling families, this education was bestowed on daughters as well as sons, enabling women to play an active role in Byzantium. This always depended on circumstances, of course, but could ensure their participation in the highest levels of society. Some exercised their influence indirectly but openly through their relationship to male rulers, as we saw in the case of Empresses Irene and Theodora, who reversed iconoclasm, or the sisters Zoe and Theodora, who sustained the last years of the Macedonian dynasty. For nearly 1,200 years, a succession of prominent women without parallel extends from Helena, the mother of Constantine I, who went on a pilgrimage to Jerusalem to build churches and distribute money to the troops in 326, to Helena Palaiologina, who was married to John II, the Lusignan ruler of Cyprus, and became regent of the island from 1442 to 1458.

Its continual fascination with the classical past distinguishes Byzantium from Western Christendom throughout the early Middle Ages. Byzantine devotion to the ancients was a constant, ongoing traditional activity of such long-term importance that it functioned both as a restriction as well as a source of inspiration. Although there were particularly creative phases, for instance in the late thirteenth and early fourteenth centuries, they were not fundamentally novel developments. By contrast, when the Italians began to explore their pre-Christian past, they were able to generate a rebirth of interest, which gave rise to what we now call the Renaissance. Their relative deprivation from ancient Greek and Roman thought and culture encouraged a different kind of curiosity and commitment, which led to an increasingly self-confident use of science and the birth of secular history. Following in this tradition, the western Enlightenment condemned most of Byzantine culture as irrational or irrelevant, even while its leaders established the modern study of history. I hope I have provided a reasoned explanation for what they could not appreciate.

The Enlightenment thus continued a western antagonism to Byzantium which had built up over many centuries. Although the continuation of the Roman Empire in the East for over a thousand years was vital for the West and provided it with many resources, a clear line of systematic hostility can be traced from the eighth century onwards. Not only was Byzantium responsible for iconoclasm – denounced as heresy – but the Byzantine use of Greek was also seen in a negative light, associated with the pagan, pre-Christian world. Nor could such intolerance directed against Greek be assuaged by the final condemnation of iconoclasm in 843. Instead, as Chris Wickham has shown, the West's attitude to Byzantium hardened in the ninth century with Notker's dismissive evaluation of the Greeks as cowards and fools. This became such a long-running prejudice that another historian, C. M. Woodhouse, claimed: 'Even almost a century after 1439 [the Council of Ferrara-Florence], Erasmus was to find that . . . an aptitude for Greek excited suspicion in the Church.'

Hostility to Greek coincided with the growing economic vitality of Venice and Genoa, while the Byzantines struggled against the steady advance of the Seljuks. The turning point, as I have tried to show, was 1204: the degrading sack of a Christian city by crusaders supposedly on their way to confront the infidel, and the tremendous plunder shipped back to the West. The only way to justify the desecration of ancient Christian places, the murder, rape and mistreatment of fellow believers, and such ill-gained loot, was to denounce the Byzantines as schismatics, heretics and worse. The systematic calumnies against Byzantium as an empire which continue to this day originated in the crusaders' attempt to justify their greed and pillage of Christian co-religionaries.

Byzantium did not lose its denigrated status even when its own scholars, such as Manuel Chrysoloras, made notable contributions to Italian Renaissance learning. In late fourteenth-century Florence he provided lessons in ancient Greek and made available a structured knowledge of the language. His grammar helped many western intellectuals to read the texts of Plato and Aristotle in the original, and his pupils extended awareness of ancient as well as Byzantine scholarship through their translations. A few Italians such as Francesco Filelfo even sought out Greek teachers in Constantinople; in the 1420s, he studied with George Chrysokokkes, married a daughter of Chrysoloras and prepared Latin translations of Xenophon and Plutarch, among others.

Neither could the Council of Ferrara-Florence (1438/9), which formally reunited the churches, turn prejudice to sympathy. While Plethon's lectures on texts of Plato generated admiration among the Florentines he met, and his fame attracted patrons, including Cosimo de' Medici and Sigismondo Malatesta, western representatives at the Council did not appreciate their Greek counterparts. It was only

Plethon's mastery of classical Greek texts that was appreciated, whether his admirers knew that he truly believed in the ancient gods or not. Chrysoloras' student Guarino used Plethon's complete text of Strabo's *Geographika* for his translation into Latin, and later, Marsilio Ficino was to translate Plethon's edition of the Chaldean Oracles (another highly suspect ancient source of obscure prophecies). Nor did the Byzantines appreciate Plethon's great work *On the Differences of Aristotle from Plato*, which was systematically burned as an encouragement of paganism. So the stereotype of Byzantium was also strengthened by forces internal to the empire.

The fall of Constantinople to the Turks did encourage western appreciation of Byzantine scholarship. That is clear from the welcome given to refugees and their manuscripts. In particular, among the collection of Cardinal Bessarion bequeathed to Venice, which forms the core of the Marciana Library, there were numerous important witnesses to ancient Greek science as well as philosophy. A Latin translation was made from his Greek manuscript of the *Arithmetica* of Diophantos, composed in the third century AD, complete with the comments of generations of Byzantine mathematicians – from Theon, his daughter Hypatia, who taught in fifth-century Alexandria, to Psellos in the eleventh, Planoudes in late thirteenth-century Constantinople, and Chortasmenos in the early fifteenth. This translation in turn is related to the bilingual Greek/Latin version of Diophantos that Fermat read in the seventeenth century, in which he wrote his famous note: 'I have discovered the most marvellous proof of this theorem but the margin is too small to contain it.' These great prizes of scholarship and learning were accepted, however, with the same sense of superiority that can be traced back to the pillaging of the Queen City in 1204. The West's gain was not a measure of Byzantium's contribution but further evidence of its intrinsic inferiority.

After the Ottoman conquest of 1453, Byzantium was maintained in a symbolic and ecclesiastical form by the patriarch based in Constantinople. The monk Gennadios (formerly George Scholarios) was appointed to this post by Mehmed the Conqueror and was made the first leader of the Greek *millet*. Although Moscow was later to claim the mantle of orthodox leadership, the patriarch in Constantinople retained the tradition of the ecclesiastical government, based on the pentarchy of five great patriarchates, and insisted upon the hesychast tradition of spiritual prayer, which had little resonance in the West. This sustained the Orthodox world through centuries of Ottoman rule, and continues to generate devotion not only in the Middle East but in many diaspora communities around the world.

Mehmed the Conqueror also insisted that Christian craftsmen should remain in the city. Not all their churches were converted into mosques. As we have seen, Byzantium lived on in a new Ottoman guise with its cosmopolitan population, which spoke numerous languages and attracted merchants from far and wide. Constantinople became an even more glorious city under the early sultans, who added elegant new public buildings, a grand new palace at Topkapi and the magnificent domed mosques which emulate Hagia Sophia. The city, thus renewed, resumed its role at the heart of a great eastern Mediterranean empire, this time Ottoman. It made the Turks heirs to a history which also fused different traditions and enabled Greeks and other Christian minorities such as Armenians to become prominent traders, administrators and diplomats. When the Sephardic Jews were expelled from Spain in 1492, they found a new home in Constantinople, which accepted their Ladino dialect and Judaic traditions.

Later, when the Ottomans marched deep into Europe, they were to meet an invigorated Christianity. The two forces interacted for centuries, clashing repeatedly as the Turks pushed westward and were rebuffed. For centuries the Ottoman Empire was a European power. In its nineteenth-century decline, indeed, it became known as 'the sick man of Europe'. When the last sultan looked ready to die, it was the European powers who stood by, waiting to carve out protectorates on the soil of the previously great empire. In Anatolia, their ambitions were thwarted by Mustafa Kemal, now known as Atatürk, who led the revolt that created the modern Republic of Turkey. In a reaction to the 'sickness' and weakness of the Ottoman Empire, he insisted on adopting a European-style national, secular constitution, which established a parliament and lawcourts, romanized the Ottoman script and banned the fez (the traditional hat). Today, Turkey still lives under this constitution, which permits Muslims to attend Friday prayers but gives everyone the weekend of Saturday and Sunday as days off work.

As the builders in King's College London observed, Byzantium has something to do with Turkey, and Turkey certainly has something to do with Byzantium. Whether or not you believe that Turkey's rich Byzantine past entitles it to take its place among the other states of the European Union, something of the spirit and legacy of the medieval empire continues to influence the world from its ancient emplacements on the Bosphoros and across Anatolia. Even today, in the enormous sprawling conglomeration of suburbs, with two bridges linking the European with the Asian side and a subway system under construction, Istanbul retains its Byzantine character – not only in the Christian presence, but also in the grandiose form of the city, its bustling commercial activity as an international metropolis and its polyglot population.

I hope I have convinced the reader who has accompanied me this far that Byzantium must be saved from its negative stereotype. Recently, major exhibitions held in the Metropolitan Museum of New York, the Benaki Museum in Athens and the Getty Museum, Los Angeles, have revealed the 'Glory of Byzantium', its 'Faith and Power' and 'Holy Image, Hallowed Ground', which displayed Byzantine art treasures from around the world and icons and manuscripts from the monastery of St Catherine on Mount Sinai. Through these sympathetically curated, and unexpectedly popular, presentations of Byzantium the public has glimpsed part of the Byzantine world which has no modern successor state but has influenced so many. Byzantine art helps to correct the stereotype in part because of its skill and sheer beauty, but also because it has stimulated a much wider interest in the society that could produce unfamiliar objects of such high quality over such a prolonged period. Together with the International Congresses of Byzantine Studies, most recently held in London in 2006, a new phase of appreciation has begun.

So if we need a word to describe the mendacity of our present political leaders, the bizarre incompetence of our own bureaucracies, the cunning selfishness and illegal mechanisms of our great corporations, or the intricate glamour of our global corridors of fame, then we should find the appropriate, modern adjective – and it is not 'Byzantine'. That empire was not without its corruption, cruelty and barbarities, far from it, but by projecting onto it the notions which are still insinuated by the term 'Byzantine', we suggest that these failings belong to some remote and doomed society, foreign to our character and quite unconnected with our own traditions.

Have I overemphasized the ingenious, educated and resourceful perseverance of Byzantine society, from its builders to its eunuchs, its monks to its empresses, its silk-weavers to its schoolteachers, rather than centring more of the story on its great emperors and generals or the repetitions of its court ceremonial? If so, it is for two reasons.

First, because we should be aware of Byzantium's exceptionally persistent, skilled fusion of traditions and inheritance, and how it created a varied and self-confident civilization that grew as often as it lost ground and fought to the end to survive. It is astounding that Byzantium continued after 1204, when the West captured and occupied its capital for fifty-seven years, even if the mini-empires which sprang to life in its place were not truly imperial states. Something of that same combination of resources – classical, pagan, Christian, eastern and western – was in the founding DNA of Byzantium, and provided a reliably constant life force across the centuries.

Second, because I hope to have shown that the spirit of Byzantium survives not just the capture of 1453, but also the intervening centuries between then and now, and its legacy lives on beyond the world of central Europe, the Balkans, Turkey and the Middle East. I have sought to convey some aspects of what it was like to be a Byzantine. In doing so, my aim is to expand, however slightly, our knowledge and experience of others, and to glimpse how people of a cosmopolitan, city-based society, with a consciously historical belief in who they were, as well as a pious belief in the hereafter, could be so different from ourselves and yet so recognizably like us.

Sundial flanked by peacocks, Skripou, central Greece, 873–4

Further Reading

Suggested reading for additional information and sources of quotes, chapter by chapter.

Introduction: A Different History of Byzantium

The Oxford Dictionary of Byzantium (ed. Alexander P. Kazhdan), 3 vols. (Oxford 1991)

Henry Maguire, ed., *Byzantine Court Culture from 829 to 1204* (Dumbarton Oaks, Washington DC 1997).

Elizabeth Jefferys, ed., *Rhetoric in Byzantium* (Aldershot 2003).

Fernand Braudel, *The Mediterranean and the Mediterranean World in the Age of Philip II*, 2 vols. (London 1975).

Chris Wickham, *Framing the Early Middle Ages: Europe and the Mediterranean, 400–800* (Oxford 2005).

Judith Herrin, *The Formation of Christendom* (Oxford and Princeton 1987).

Judith Herrin, 'The Imperial Feminine in Byzantium', *Past and Present* 169 (2000), 3–35.

Judith Herrin, *Women in Purple: Rulers of Medieval Byzantium* (London and Princeton 2001).

Meyer Schapiro, *Late Antique, Early Christian and Medieval Art* (London 1980).

Chapter 1: The City of Constantine

Chapter quote: Zosimos, *New History*, tr. Ronald T. Ridley (Canberra 1982), pp. 37–8.

Quote on p. 11 from *The Acts of the Council of Chalcedon*, tr. with introduction and notes by Richard Price and Michael Gaddis, 3 vols. (Liverpool 2005), vol. 2, p. 240.

Eusebius, Life of Constantine, tr. Averil Cameron and Stuart G. Hall (Oxford 1999).

Leslie Brubaker, 'Memories of Helena: Patterns of Imperial Female Matronage in the Fourth and Fifth Centuries', in Liz James, ed., *Women, Men and Eunuchs: Gender in Byzantium* (London 1997), pp. 51–75.

Marina Warner, *Monuments and Maidens: The Allegory of the Female Form* (London 1985).

Chapter 2: Constantinople, the Largest City in Christendom

Chapter quote: Niketas Choniates, *O City of Constantinople, Annales of Niketas Choniates*, tr. H. Magoulias (Detroit 1984), p. 325.

Quote on p. 19 from al-Marwazi, V. Minorsky, 'Marvasi on the Byzantines', in his *Medieval Iran and its Neighbours* (London 1982), 455–69.

Quotes on p. 20 from Nadia Maria El Cheikh, *Byzantium Viewed by the Arabs* (Cambridge, Mass., 2004), p. 204.

John F. Matthews, *Laying Down the Law: A Study of the Theodosian Code* (New Haven/ London 2000).

Cyril Mango and Gilbert Dagron, eds., *Constantinople and its Hinterland* (Aldershot 1995).

Sarah Guberti Bassett, *The Urban Image of Late Antique Constantinople* (Cambridge 2004).

Cyril Mango, 'Constantinople as Theotokoupolis', in Maria Vassilaki, ed., *Mother of God: Representations of the Virgin in Byzantine Art* (Milan 2000), pp. 209–18.

Philip Mansel, *Constantinople: City of the World's Desire, 1453–1924* (London 1997).

Chapter 3: The East Roman Empire

Chapter quote: *The Fall of the Byzantine Empire: A Chronicle by George Sphrantzes 1401–1472*, tr. Marios Philippides (Amhurst, Mass., 1980), p. 122.

Procopius, *Secret History*, tr. G. A. Williamson, Penguin Classics (London 1981).

Peter J. Heather, *The Fall of the Roman Empire: A New History of Rome and the Barbarians* (Oxford 2005).

Leslie Brubaker, 'Sex, lies and textuality: the Secret History of Prokopios and the rhetoric of gender in sixth-century Byzantium', in Leslie Brubaker and Julia M. H. Smith, eds., *Gender in the Early Medieval World: East and West, 300–900* (Cambridge 2004), pp. 83–101.

Janet Nelson, 'Symbols in context: inauguration rituals in Byzantium and the West in the early Middle Ages', *Studies in Church History* 13 (1976), pp. 97–111; reprinted in her collection *Politics and Ritual in Early Medieval Europe* (London 1986).

Chapter 4: Greek Orthodoxy

Chapter quote: St Maximos Confessor, *Mystagogia*, quoted by Patriarch Germanos in his *Commentary on the Divine Liturgy*, tr. Paul Meyendorff (Crestwood, New York, 1984), p. 93.

Eusebius of Caesarea, *A History of the Church from Christ to Constantine*, tr. G. A. Williamson (rev. edn; London 1989); on Blandina, see Book 5.i.47–61, pp. 144–8.

Peter Brown, *The Rise of Western Christendom: Triumph and Diversity AD 200–1000* (2nd edn; Oxford 2003).

William Dalrymple, *From the Holy Mountain: A Journey in the Shadow of Byzantium* (London 1997).

Helen C. Evans and Bruce White, *St Catherine's Monastery, Sinai, Egypt: A Photographic Essay* (New York, 2004).

Evangelos Chrysos, '1054: Schism?', in *Cristianità d'Occidente e Cristianità d'Oriente (secoli VI–XI)*, 2 vols. (Spoleto 2004), vol. 1, pp. 547–67.

Chapter 5: The Church of Hagia Sophia

Chapter quote: Procopius, *The Buildings*, tr. H. B. Dewing and Glanville Downey (Cambridge, Mass., 1940), p. 21; also in Cyril Mango, *The Art of the Byzantine Empire 312–1453* (Englewood Cliffs, New Jersey, 1972), pp. 72–8.

Quote on p. 56 from *The Russian Primary Chronicle (Laurentian Version)*, trs. and eds. Samuel Hazzard Cross and Olgerd P. Sherbowitz-Wetzor (Cambridge, Mass., 1973), p. 111.

On the construction of Hagia Sophia, see Mango, *The Art of the Byzantine Empire* (as above), pp. 78–102.

Averil Cameron, *Procopius and the Sixth Century* (London 1985).

Anna Muthesius, 'Silken diplomacy', in Jonathan Shepard and Simon Franklin, eds., *Byzantine Diplomacy* (Aldershot 1992), pp. 237–48.

Glen Bowersock, *Mosaics as History* (Cambridge, Mass., 2006).

Eunice Dautermann Maguire and Henry Maguire, *Other Icons: Art and Power in Byzantine Secular Culture* (Princeton 2007).

Chapter 6: The Ravenna Mosaics

Chapter quote: Agnellus, *Book of the Pontiffs of the Church of Ravenna*, tr. D. M. Deliyannis (Washington DC 2004), p. 200.

Quote on p. 63 from Cassiodorus' *Variae* I.1.3, in *Theoderic in Italy*, tr. John Moorhead (Oxford 1992), p. 44.

Quotes on p. 64 from Cassiodorus, *Variae*, tr. S. J. B. Barnish (Liverpool 1992), V.6 to the illustrious senator Symmachus, pp. 75–6; II.27 to the Jews of Genoa, pp. 34–5.

Charles Barber, 'The imperial panels at San Vitale: a reconsideration', *Byzantine and Modern Greek Studies* 14 (1990), pp. 19–42.

Chapter 7: Roman Law

Chapter quote and p. 78: Thomas Magistros, *On the Duty of a King*, tr. Ernest Barker, in *Social and Political Thought in Byzantium from Justinian I to the Last Palaeologus* (Oxford 1957), p. 166.

Quote on p. 75 from Ruth Macrides, 'The Ritual of Petition', in Dimitrios Yatromanolakis and Panagiotis Roilos, eds., *Greek Ritual Poetics* (Cambridge, Mass., 2004), pp. 356–70.

Quote on p. 77 from Gilbert Dagron, *Emperor and Priest: The Imperial Office in Byzantium* (Cambridge 2003), p. 257.

Matthews, *Laying Down the Law* (as above in chapter 2).

Nikos Oikonomides, 'The Peira of Eustathios Romaios', *Fontes minores* 7 (1986), pp. 169–92.

Angeliki Laiou, 'On Just War in Byzantium', in *To Hellenikon: Studies in Honor of Spyros Vryonis Jr.*, vol. 1 (New Rochelle 1993), pp. 153–72.

Ruth Macrides, 'The law outside the lawbooks: law and literature', *Fontes Minores* 11 (2005), pp. 133–45.

Chapter 8: The Bulwark Against Islam

Chapter quote: *Chronicle of Dionysios of Tel-Mahre*, tr. Andrew Palmer, *The Seventh Century in the West-Syrian Chronicles* (Liverpool 1993), p. 212.

Quote on p. 85: *The Chronicon Paschale, 284–628 AD*, tr. Michael and Mary Whitby (Liverpool 1989), pp. 183–8.

Quote on p. 90: Chase F. Robinson, *'Abd al-Malik* (Oxford 2005), p. 7.

Quote on p. 92: Raymond Davis, tr., *The Book of Pontiffs (Liber pontificalis): The Ancient Biographies of the First Ninety Bishops of Rome to AD 715* (rev. edn; Liverpool 2000), pp. 73–4.

Judith Herrin, *The Formation of Christendom* (as above in Introduction).

Henri Pirenne, *Mohammad and Charlemagne* (London 1939).

Patricia Crone and Michael Cook, *Hagarism: The Making of the Islamic World* (Cambridge 1977).

Richard Fletcher, *The Cross and the Crescent: Christianity and Islam from Muhammad to the Reformation* (London 2003).

Vasso Pennas, 'The Island of Orovi in the Argolid: Bishopric and Administrative Center', *Studies in Byzantine Sigillography* 4, Nicolas Oikonomides, ed. (1995), pp. 163–72.

Chapter 9: Icons, a New Christian Art Form

Chapter quote: Sermon of Eustathios of Thrace, in E. A. Wallis Budge, *Saint Michael the Archangel: Three Encomiums* (London 1894), pp. *79–*80.

Quote on p. 103: *Greek Anthology* XVI 80 tr. W. R. Paton, 5 vols. (New York and London 1916), vol. 5, p. 201.

Lucy-Ann Hunt, 'For the Salvation of a Woman's Soul: an icon of St Michael described within a medieval Coptic context', in Anthony Eastmond and Liz James, eds., *Icon and Word: The Power of Images in Byzantium* (Aldershot 2003), pp. 205–32.

Hans Belting, *Likeness and Presence: A History of the Image Before the Era of Art*, tr. Edmund Jephcott (Chicago 1994).

Michele Bacci, '"With the Paintbrush of the Evangelist Luke", Mother of God', in Vassilaki, ed., *Representations of the Virgin in Byzantine Art* (as above in chapter 2), pp. 79–89.

Averil Cameron, 'The Language of Images: The Rise of Icons and Christian Representation', in D. Wood, ed., *The Church and the Arts*, Studies in Church History 28 (Oxford 1992), pp. 1–42.

Thomas F. Mathews, *Byzantium: From Antiquity to the Renaissance* (New York 1998).

Robin Cormack, *Writing in Gold: Byzantine Society and its Icons* (London 1985).

Maria Vassilaki, ed., *Images of the Mother of God: Perceptions of the Theotokos in Byzantium* (Ashgate 2005), esp. Thomas F. Mathews and Norman Muller, 'Isis and Mary in early icons', pp. 3–11.

Chapter 10: Iconoclasm and Icon Veneration

Chapter quotes: Daniel Sahas, ed. and tr., *Icon and Logos: Sources in Eighth-Century Iconoclasm* ... (Toronto 1986), pp. 96, 101; and St John of Damascus, *On the Divine Images: Three Apologies Against those who Attack the Divine Images*, tr. D. Anderson (Crestwood, New York, 1980), pp. 64, 72.

Quote on p. 105: Old Testament, Exodus 20:4; Deuteronomy 5:8–9.

Quote on pp. 110–11: from Sahas, *Icon and Logos* (as above), p. 101.

Robin Cormack, *Painting the Soul: Icons, Death Masks and Shrouds* (London 1997).

Charles Barber, *Figure and Likeness: On the Limits of Representation in Byzantine Iconoclasm* (Princeton 2002).

Judith Herrin, *Women in Purple* (as above in Introduction).

Chapter 11: A Literate and Articulate Society

Chapter quote: Kekaumenos, *Book of Advice and Anecdotes*, unpublished translation by Charlotte Roueché (very kindly made available to the author).

Quotes on pp. 128–9 from N. G. Wilson, *Photius: The Bibliotheca* (London 1994), no. 166, pp. 149–53; no. 170, pp. 154–5.

Robert Browning, 'Teachers', in Gugielmo Cavallo, ed., *The Byzantines* (Chicago 1997).

Averil Cameron and Judith Herrin, eds., *Constantinople in the Early Eighth Century: The* Parastaseis Syntomoi Chronikai (Leiden 1984).

Liliana Simeonova, *Diplomacy of the Letter and the Cross: Photios, Bulgaria and the Papacy, 860s–880s* (Amsterdam 1998).

For a helpful entry on the founder of Arab algebra, see www-history.mcs.st-andrews.ac.uk/Biographies/Al-Khwarizmi.html

Catherine Holmes and Judith Waring, eds., *Literacy, Education and Manuscript Transmission in Byzantium and Beyond* (Leiden 2002).

Chapter 12: Saints Cyril and Methodios, 'Apostles to the Slavs'

Chapter quote: *The Vita of Constantine and the Vita of Methodius*, tr. Marvin Kantor and Richard Stephen White (Ann Arbor, Mich., 1976), p. 49.

Quotes on pp. 133–4: *The Vita of Constantine* (as above), pp. 49 and 55.

V. Vavřínek, 'The Introduction of the Slavonic Liturgy and the Byzantine Missionary Policy', in *Beiträge zur byzantinischen Geschichte im 9–1. Jh.* (Prague 1978), pp. 255–84.

V. Vavřínek and B. Zástěrová, 'Byzantium's Role in the Formation of Great Moravian Culture', *Byzantinoslavica* 43 (1982), pp. 161–88.

Chapter 13: Greek Fire

Chapter quote: Liutprand of Cremona, *The Embassy to Constantinople and Other Writings*, tr. F. A. Wright (London 1930; repr. London 1993), p. 136.

Quote on p. 145: from Elizabeth Jeffreys, ed. and tr., *Digenis Akritis. The Grottaferrata and Escorial versions* (Cambridge 1998), p. 205.

Quote on p. 146: from *The Book of Strangers: Medieval Arabic Graffiti on the Theme of Nostalgia*, tr. Patricia Crone and Shmuel Moreh (Princeton 2000), p. 40.

J. F. Haldon et al., 'Greek Fire revisited', in Elizabeth M. Jeffreys, ed., *Byzantine Style, Religion and Civilization in Honour of Sir Steven Runciman* (Cambridge 2006), pp. 290–325, with photographs at p. 312.

John Haldon, *Warfare, State and Society in the Byzantine World 565–1204* (London 1999).

Chapter 14: The Byzantine Economy

Chapter quote: *The Chronicle of Theophanes Confessor*, ed. and tr. Cyril Mango and Roger Scott (Oxford 1997), Anno Mundi 6287, p. 645.

Quote on p. 157: from Liutprand of Cremona (as above in chapter 13), p. 156.

Angeliki Laiou, 'Exchange and trade, seventh–twelfth centuries', in A. Laiou et al., eds., *The Economic History of Byzantium* (Washington DC 2002), and online at *http://www.doaks.org/EconHist/EHB36.pdf/*

Cécile Morrisson, 'Byzantine money: its production and circulation', in Laiou et al. (as above), and online at http://www.doaks.org/EconHist/EHB42.pdf/

Jacques Lefort, 'The rural economy, seventh–twelfth centuries', in Laiou et al. (as above), and online at http://www.doaks.org/EconHist/EHB14.pdf/

Warren Treadgold, *The Byzantine State Finances in the Eighth and Ninth Centuries* (New York 1982).

Nicolas Oikonomides, 'Title and Income at the Byzantine Court', in Henry Maguire, ed., *Byzantine Court Culture from 829 to 1204* (Dumbarton Oaks, Washington DC 1997), pp. 199–215.

Leonora Neville, 'Taxing Sophronia's son-in-law . . .', in Lynda Garland, ed., *Byzantine Women, Varieties of Experience 800–1200* (Aldershot 2006), pp. 77–89.

Chapter 15: Eunuchs

Chapter quote: *The Life of St Andrew the Fool*, Lennart Rydén, ed., 2 vols. (Uppsala 1995), vol. 2, pp. 81–3.

Quote on p. 161: Odo of Deuil, *de Profectione Ludovici VII in Orientem* (The Journey of Louis VII to the East), ed. and tr. Virginia Gingerich Berry (New York 1948), p. 69.

Quote on p. 163: Liutprand of Cremona, *Antapodosis* (as above in chapter 14), p. 154.

Quote on p. 167: Elizabeth Jeffreys, *Digenis Akritis. The Grottaferrata and Escorial versions* (Cambridge 1998), p. 205.

Quote on p. 168: John Thomas and Angela Constantinides Hero, eds., *Byzantine Monastic Foundation Documents* (Washington DC 2000), no. 12, *Typikon* of Emperor John Tzimiskes, p. 238; also available from www.doaks.org/typikaPDF/typo19.pdf

Kathryn M. Ringrose, *The Perfect Servant: Eunuchs and the Social Construction of Gender in Byzantium* (Chicago and London 2003).

Timothy S. Miller, *The Orphans of Byzantium: Child Welfare in the Christian Empire* (Washington DC 2003).

Shaun Tougher, ed., *Eunuchs in Antiquity and Beyond* (London 2002).

Chapter 16: The Imperial Court

Chapter quote: al-Marwazi, court physician of Malik Shah, *Properties of Animals*, tr. V. Minorsky, 'Marvasi on the Byzantines', in his *Medieval Iran and its Neighbours* (London 1982), pp. 455–69.

Quotes on p. 181: Constantine Porphyrogenitus, *De Administrando Imperio*, Gy. Moravcsik, ed., and R. Jenkins, tr. (Washington DC 1967), p. 55–7.

Quotes on p. 182: Porphyrogenitus, *De Administrando Imperio* (as above), pp. 59–61, 151.

Quote on pp. 182–3: Paul Lemerle, *Byzantium Humanism: The First Phase*, tr. Helen Lindsay and Ann Moffatt (Canberra 1986), pp. 325–6.

Quote on p. 184: *The Fall of the Byzantine Empire: A Chronicle by George Sphrantzes 1401–1472*, tr. Marios Philippides (Amhurst, Mass., 1980), p. 67.

A. A. Vasiliev, 'Harun ibn Yahya and his description of Constantinople', *Seminarium Kondakovianum* 5 (1932), pp. 149–63.

Nadia Maria El Cheikh, *Byzantium Viewed by the Arabs* (Cambridge, Mass., 2004).

John Haldon, 'Chapters II, 44 and 45 of De Cerimoniis. Theory and practice in tenth-century military administration', *Travaux et Mémoires* 13 (1999).

James Trilling, 'Daedalus and the Nightingale: Art and Technology in the Myth of the Byzantine Court', in Henry Maguire, ed., *Byzantine Court Culture from 829 to 1204* (as above in chapter 14), pp. 217–30: excellent on the virtuosity of Greek fire and court technology, two related aspects of the Byzantine ability to impress foreigners and courtiers alike.

Alexander P. Kazhdan and Michael McCormick, 'The Social World of the Byzantine Court', in Maguire, *Byzantine Court Culture* (as above), pp. 167–97.

Chapter 17: Imperial Children, 'Born in the Purple'

Chapter quote: Jean Skylites, *Empereurs de Constantinople*, tr. Bernard Flusin and Jean-Claude Cheynet (Paris 2003), p. 361.

Quotes on pp. 188–9: Constantine Porphyrogenitus, *De Administrando Imperio* (as above in chapter 16), pp. 73–5, 113.

Quote on p. 190: Michael Psellos, *Fourteen Byzantine Rulers*, tr. E. R. A. Sewter (London 1966), p. 260.

Chapter 18: Mount Athos

Chapter quote: the *Typikon* of Athanasios (973–5), tr. George Dennis, para. 38, *Byzantine Monastic Foundation Documents* (as above in chapter 15), no. 13, p. 260; also at *http://www.doaks.org/typikaPDF/typo20.pdf*

Quote on p. 199: *Typikon* of Constantine IX Monomachos, tr. Timothy Miller, para. 14, *Byzantine Monastic Foundation Documents* (as above), no. 15, p. 289; also at http://www.doaks.org/typikaPDF/typo22.pdf

Quote on p. 200: Robert E. Sinkewicz, *Saint Gregory Palamas: The One Hundred and Fifty Chapters* (Toronto 1988), p. 201.

Anthony Bryer and Mary Cunningham, eds., *Mount Athos and Byzantine Monasticism* (Aldershot 1996).

Carolyn L. Connor and W. Robert Connor, trs., *The Life and Miracles of St Luke* (Brookline, Mass., 1994).

Norman Russell, *The Doctrine of Deification in the Greek Patristic Tradition* (Oxford 2006).

Alice-Mary Talbot, ed., *Holy Women of Byzantium: Ten Saints Lives in English Translation* (Washington DC 1996); includes 'The Life of St Maria the Younger', tr. Angeliki Laiou.

A. A. Karakatsanis, ed., *Treasures of Mount Athos* (2nd edn; Thessalonike 1997): an exhibition catalogue with a marvellous range of essays and photographs of the monasteries of the Holy Mountain and their art collections.

Chapter 19: Venice and the Fork

Chapter quote: Peter Damian, *Institutio monialis,* Opusculum 50, addressed to the nun Blanca, chapter 11, in J. P. Migne, ed., *Patrologia Latina*, vol. 145, col. 744.

Norbert Elias, *The Civilizing Process,* rev. edn tr. Edmund Jephcott (Oxford 2000).

Johanna Vroom, *After Antiquity: Ceramics and Society in the Aegean from the Seventh to the Twentieth Century* (Leiden 2003), p. 321.

Judith Herrin, 'Theophano: On the Education of a Byzantine Princess', in A. Davids, ed., *The Empress Theophano* (Cambridge 1995), pp. 64–85.

Donald M. Nicol, *Byzantium and Venice: A Study in Diplomatic and Cultural Relations* (Cambridge 1988).

William H. McNeill, *Venice: The Hinge of Europe 1081–1797* (Chicago 1974).

Chapter 20: Basil II, 'The Bulgar-Slayer'

Chapter quote: from Basil II's law of 996 partly translated by Geanakoplos in *Byzantium: Church, Society and Civilization* (as above in chapter 18), pp. 245–7.

Quote on p. 219: from Marc D. Lauxtermann, *Byzantine Poetry from Pisides to Geometres: Texts and Contexts* (Vienna 2003), pp. 236–7; verse tr. in Paul Stephenson, *The Legend of Basil the Bulgar-Slayer* (Cambridge 2003), p. 49.

Catherine Holmes, *Basil II and the Governance of Empire* (Oxford 2006).

Barbara Crostini, 'The Emperor Basil II's Cultural Life', *Byzantion* 66 (1996), pp. 55–81.

Chapter 21: The Eleventh-Century Crisis

Chapter quote: Jean Skylitzes, *Empereurs de Constantinople*, tr. Flusin and Cheynet (as above in chapter 17), p. 393.

Quote on p. 230: Michael Psellos, *Fourteen Byzantine Rulers*, tr. E. R. A. Sewter (London 1966), p. 327–8.

Costas Kaplanis, 'The Debasement of the "Dollar of the Middle Ages"', *Journal of Economic History* 63.3 (2003), pp. 768–801.

Nikos Oikonomides, 'The Peira of Eustathios Romaios' (as above in chapter 7).

Katerina Ierodiakonou, ed., *Byzantine Philosophy and its Ancient Sources* (Oxford 2002), with helpful articles on Psellos by the editor, John Duffy and Polymnia Athanassiadi.

Chapter 22: Anna Komnene

Chapter quote: from *Eulogy for Anna Comnène*, in Jean Darrouzès, ed., *Georges et Dèmètrios Tornikès, Lettres et Discours* (Paris 1970), pp. 220–323.

Quotes on p. 233–8: from *The Alexiad of Anna Comnena*, tr. E. R. A. Sewter, Penguin Classics (London 1969), pp. 104–5, 112, 115–20, 129–30, 366–8, 504.

Thalia Gouma-Peterson, ed., *Anna Komnene and Her Times* (New York and London 2000).

Paul Magdalino, *The Empire of Manuel I Komnenos, 1143–80* (Cambridge 1993).

Chapter 23: A Cosmopolitan Society

Chapter quote: John Tzetzes, tr. A. P. Kazhdan and Ann Wharton Epstein, in *Change in Byzantine Culture in the Eleventh and Twelfth Centuries* (Berkeley and Los Angeles 1985), pp. 259–60.

Quote on p. 245: Snorri Sturlson, *King Harald's Saga*, tr. M. Magnusson and H. Pálsson, Penguin Classics (London 2005), p. 63.

Quotes on p. 250: Barry Baldwin, tr., *Timarion* (Detroit 1984), pp. 43–5; Nadia Maria El Cheikh, *Byzantium Viewed by the Arabs* (Cambridge, Mass., 2004), p. 206.

Krijnie Ciggaar, *Western Travellers to Constantinople: The West and Byzantium, 962–1204* (Leiden 1996).

Sandra Benjamin, ed., *The World of Benjamin of Tudela: A Medieval Mediterranean Travelogue* (Madison, Calif., 1995).

S. Blöndal and B. S. Benedikz, *The Varangians of Byzantium* (Cambridge 1978).

Lynda Garland and Stephen Rapp, 'Mary "of Alania": Woman and Empress Between Two Worlds', in Garland, ed., *Byzantine Women* (as above in chapter 14), pp. 91–123.

Chapter 24: The Fulcrum of the Crusades

Chapter quote: Pope Urban II, as reported by Guibert of Nogent, tr. A. C. Krey, from *The First Crusade. The Chronicle of Fulcher of Chartres and other source materials*, Edward Peters, ed. (2nd edn; Philadelphia 1998), pp. 35–6.

Quotes on p. 256: from Fulcher of Chartres (as above), pp. 52–3; and from Robert of Rheims (as above), pp. 27–8.

Quotes on p. 257: from Solomon ben Simpson of Speyer (as above), p. 126; and from Albert of Aachen (as above), p. 139.

Quote on p. 263: from Geoffrey Villehardouin, Joinville and Villehardouin, *Chronicles of the Crusades*, tr. M. B. B. Shaw, Penguin Classics (London 1963), pp. 82–3.

Quotes on p. 264: from Gunther of Pairis, in Alfred. J. Andrea, ed. and tr., *The Capture of Constantinople. The 'Historia Constantinopolitana' of*

Gunther of Pairis (Philadelphia 1997), p. 107; and from Niketas Choniates, tr. H. Magoulias, *O City of Constantinople* (as above in chapter 2), pp. 315–16.

Paul Magdalino, *The Empire of Manuel I Komnenos, 1143–1180* (as above in chapter 22).

David Abulafia, *Frederick II: A Medieval Emperor* (2nd edn; London 2002).

Jonathan Harris, *Byzantium and the Crusades* (London and New York 2003).

Site with images of the famous Psalter made for Queen Melisende in the British Library *http://en.wikipedia.org/wiki/MelisendePsalter*

Chapter 25: The Towers of Trebizond, Arta, Nicaea and Thessalonike

Chapter quote: from John Geometres, tr. Henry Maguire, 'The beauty of castles: a tenth-century description of a tower at Constantinople', *Deltion tes Christianikes Archaiologikes Etaireias* 17 (1993–4), pp. 21–4.

Quote on p. 270: from Michael Choniates, tr. Judith Herrin, 'The collapse of the Byzantine Empire in the twelfth century: a study of a medieval economy', *University of Birmingham Historical Journal* 12 (1970), p. 198.

Quotes on p. 277: *Nicaea: A Byzantine Capital and its Praises*, tr. Clive Foss (Brookline, Mass., 1996), pp. 132, 143.

Quotes on p. 278: from Theodore Metochites, in *Nicaea*, tr. Foss (as above), pp. 177–9.

A. Laiou, ed., *Urbs Capta: The Fourth Crusade and its Consequences* (Paris 2005).

Rose Macaulay, *The Towers of Trebizond* (London 1956, and frequently reprinted).

N. Oikonomides, 'The Chancery of the Grand Komnenoi: Imperial Tradition and Political Reality', *Archeion Pontou* 35 (1979), pp. 321–32.

J. O. Rosenqvist, ed. and tr., *The Hagiographic Dossier of St Eugenios of Trebizond in Codex Athous Dionysiou 154* (Uppsala 1996).

A. A. M. Bryer, *The Empire of Trebizond and the Pontos* (London 1988).

On Byzantine influence in the Balkans, see S. Ćurčić, 'Religious Settings of the Late Byzantine Sphere', in Helen C. Evans, ed., *Byzantium: Faith and Power 1261–1557* (New Haven 2004), pp. 65–77.

Michael Angold, *A Byzantine Government in Exile: Government and Society under the Laskarids of Nicaea, 1204–61* (London 1974).

Michael Angold, *Church and Society in Byzantium under the Comneni: 1081–1261* (Cambridge 1995).

Donald M. Nicol, *The Despotate of Epiros* (Oxford 1957).

Harold E. Lurier, tr., *Crusaders as Conquerors: The Chronicle of Morea* (London 1964).

Chapter 26: Rebels and Patrons

Chapter quote: 'Alexios Makrembolites and his Dialogue between the Poor and the Rich', tr. Ihor Ševčenko, in *Zbornik Radova Vizantološgog Instituta* 6 (1960), p. 222.

Quote on p. 287: from Alexios Makrembolites (as above), p. 219.

Quote on p. 289: from John Kantakouzenos, tr. Donald M. Nicol, *The Last Centuries of Byzantium 1261–1453* (2nd edn; Cambridge 1993), pp. 193–4.

Quote on p. 294: from Plethon, tr. C. M. Woodhouse, *George Gemistos Plethon: The Last of the Hellenes* (Oxford 1986), pp. 104–5.

Quote on p. 295: Plethon's prayer to Zeus (as above), pp. 328–9.

John W. Barker, 'Late Byzantine Thessalonike: A Second City's Challenges and Response', *Dumbarton Oaks Papers* 57 (2003), *Symposium on Late Byzantine Thessalonike*, pp. 5–26.

Franz Tinnefeld, 'Intellectuals in late Byzantine Thessalonike' (as above), pp. 153–72.

Steven Runciman, *Mistra: Byzantine Capital of the Peloponnese* (London 1980).

Steven Runciman, *The Sicilian Vespers: A History of the Mediterranean World in the Later Thirteenth Century* (Cambridge 1958).

Manolis Chatzidakis, *Mystras: The Medieval City and the Castle* (Athens 1981).

Chapter 27: 'Better the Turkish Turban than the Papal Tiara'

Chapter quote: attributed to Notaras, see Doukas, *Decline and Fall of Byzantium to the Ottoman Turks*, tr. Harry J. Magoulias (Detroit 1975), p. 210.

Quotes on p. 303: from Michael VIII Palaiologos, tr. in Geanakoplos, *Byzantium: Church, Society and Civilization* (as above in chapter 18), p. 219; from George Metochites, *On the Procession of the Holy Spirit*, in Geanakoplos, *Byzantium* (as above), p. 158; and from an anonymous pamphlet, the *Libellus* of *c.* 1274, against the union of churches, tr. in Geanakoplos (as above), pp. 179–88.

Quotes on p. 304: from the *Libellus* (as above).

Quote on p. 308: from Doukas, *Decline and Fall* (as above), p. 204.

Colin Imber, *The Ottoman Empire 1300–1656: The Structure of Power* (Houndmills and New York 2002).

Donald M. Nicol, *The Last Centuries of Byzantium* (as above in chapter 26).

Deno Geanakoplos, *Interaction of Sibling Byzantine and Western Cultures in the Middle Ages and Renaissance* (New Haven 1976).

Jacques le Goff, *The Birth of Purgatory* (Chicago 1984).

Chapter 28: The Siege of 1453

Chapter quote: Nicolò Barbaro, *Diary of the Siege of Constantinople, 1453*, tr. J. R. Jones (New York 1969), p. 61.

Quote on p. 311: from Laonikos Chalkokondyles, *Demonstrations of Histories*, tr. Nicolaos Nicoulides (Athens 1996), pp. 131–3.

Quotes on p. 313: from the letters of Manuel II, tr. George Dennis, *The Letters of Manuel II Palaeologus: Text, Translation and Notes* (Washington DC 1977), pp. 100–103; and from Adam of Usk, tr. E. M. Thompson, *The Chronicle of Adam of Usk, AD 1377–1421* (2nd edn; Oxford 1904), p. 220.

Quotes on p. 315: from Demetrios Kydones, tr. Speros Vryonis Jr., *The Decline of Medieval Hellenism in Asia Minor and the Process of Islamization from the Eleventh through the Fifteenth Century* (Berkeley/Los Angeles/London 1986), p. 307; on the number of bishoprics, ibid., p. 286.

Quote on p. 317: from John Kananos, tr. in Geanakoplos, *Byzantium: Church, Society and Civilization* (as above in chapter 18), pp. 387–8.

Quotes on p. 315: from Nicolò Barbaro, *Diary of the Siege of Constantinople* (as above), p. 60.

Justin Marozzi, *Tamerlane: Sword of Islam, Conqueror of the World* (London 2004).

Roger Crowley, *Constantinople: The Last Great Siege, 1453* (London 2005).

Steven Runciman, *The Last Byzantine Renaissance* (Cambridge 1970).

Conclusion: The Greatness and Legacy of Byzantium

Quote on p. 321: Edward Gibbon, *History of the Decline and Fall of the Roman Empire*, J. B. Bury, ed. (London 1909–14), stresses the passivity of Byzantium in the ninth volume, at the beginning of chapter 48, where he lists the defects of the empire and outlines the plan of the last four volumes.

Quotes on p. 322: from William Lecky, *A History of European Morals from Augustus to Charlemagne*, 2 vols. (London 1869), vol. 2, p. 13; and from Cosmas Indicopleustes, *The Christian Topography*, tr. J. W. McKrindle (London 1897), p. 73.

Quote on p. 326: from Manuel II's Dialogue with a Persian, *Entretiens avec un Musulman, 7e controverse*, tr. Theodore Khoury (Paris 1966), quoted by Pope Benedict XVI, Lecture given in the Aula Magna of the University of Regensberg. The extract from Manuel II's Dialogue had been edited with a French translation by Professor Theodore Khoury. The full Greek text was edited with a German commentary by Karl Förstel, *Manuel II. Palaiologus, Dialoge mit einem Muslim*, 3 vols. (Würzburg-Altenberge 1993–6).

Quote on p. 327: from Pope Benedict's Lecture. For the full text, see http://www.vatican.va/holyfather/benedictxvi/speeches/2006/september/documents/hfben-xvispe20060912university-regensburgen.html

Quote on p. 332: C. M. Woodhouse, *George Gemistos Plethon* (as above in chapter 26), p. 150.

Steven W. Reinert, 'Manuel II and his Müderris', in S. Ćurčić and D. Mouriki, eds., *Twilight of Byzantium* (Princeton 1991), pp. 39–51.

Chris Wickham, 'Ninth-century Byzantium through western eyes', in *Byzantium in the Ninth Century: Dead or Alive?*, Leslie Brubaker, ed. (Aldershot 1998), pp. 245–56.

Chase F. Robinson, *'Abd al-Malik* (as above in chapter 8), p. 7.

Sidney Griffith, 'Images, Islam and Christian icons', in P. Canivet and J. P. Rey-Coquais, eds., *La Syrie de Byzance à l'Islam* (Damascus 1992), pp. 121–38.

On bezants, see *The 'Historia Constantinopolitana' of Gunther of Pairis*, Alfred. J. Andrea, ed. (as above in chapter 24), p. 100; '"modern people" call these gold coins byzants, because they were minted in Byzantion'. In *c.* 1400, Wyclif used the term 'bezant' to translate the Greek drachma of the Bible, and it occurs in the Morte d'Arthur and Chanson de Roland.

Glen Bowersock, *Mosaics as History* (as above in chapter 5).

Judith Herrin, 'Mathematical Mysteries in Byzantium: The Transmission of Fermat's Last Theorem', *Dialogos: Hellenic Studies Review* 6 (1999), 22–42.

Helen C. Evans and William D. Wixom, eds., *The Glory of Byzantium: Art and Culture of the Middle Byzantine Era AD 843–1261* (New York 1997).

Helen C. Evans, ed., *Byzantium: Faith and Power* (as above in chapter 25).

Robert S. Nelson and Kristen M. Collins, eds., *Holy Image, Hallowed Ground: Icons from Sinai* (Los Angeles 2006).

List of Emperors
Named in the Text

During the Latin occupation of Constantinople

Baldwin, count of Flanders	1204–5
Peter of Courtney	1217–19?
Baldwin II	1240–61

Rulers in Nicaea

Theodore I Laskaris	1204–1222
John III Vatatzes	1222–54
Theodore II Laskaris	1254–8
John IV Laskaris	1258–61

In Epiros

Michael I Doukas Komnenos	1205–15
Theodore I Doukas Komnenos	1215–30
Michael II Doukas Komnenos	1230–66/8
Nikephoros I Doukas Komnenos	1266/8–1296/8

In Trebizond

Alexios I Komnenos and his younger brother David Komnenos (1204–12, ruler of Paphlagonia)	1204–22
Manuel I Megas Komnenos	1238–63

After the recapture of Constantinople

Michael VIII Palaiologos	1259–82
Andronikos II Palaiologos	1282–1328
Andronikos III Palaiologos	1328–41
John V Palaiologos	1341–91
John VI Kantakouzenos, rival emperor during the civil war	1347–54
Andronikos IV Palaiologos	1376–9
John VII Palaiologos	1390
Manuel II Palaiologos	1391–1425
John VIII Palaiologos	1425–48
Constantine XI Palaiologos	1449–53

Chronology

533	Defeat of Vandals in Africa
534	*Codex Juris Civilis* issued
540	Capture of Gothic king Vitiges in Ravenna
541/2	Bubonic plague spreads throughout Mediterranean
547	Dedication of the church of San Vitale, Ravenna
608	Senate of Constantinople appeals to Herakleios, exarch of Carthage
610	Phokas overthrown by Herakleios, son of exarch
622	Flight of Muhammad from Mecca to Medina
626	Siege of Constantinople by combined Avar and Persian forces
628	Herakleios defeats Persia, Chosroes II dies
630	Herakleios returns the True Cross to Jerusalem
632	Death of Muhammad
636	Arab victory at battle of Yarmuk
638	Arabs capture Antioch and Jerusalem
642	Arabs overrun Egypt
655	Arabs defeat Constans II at naval battle of Phoinix
662	Constans II moves court to Syracuse in Sicily
674–8	Long blockade and siege of Constantinople by Arabs
680/81	Sixth Oecumenical Council at Constantinople
691/2	Caliph 'Abd al-Malik constructs Dome of the Rock
692	Council *in Trullo* (Quinisext) at Constantinople
698	Arabs overrun exarchate of Carthage
711	Arabs defeat Visigoths in Spain, cross River Oxus in Uzbekistan
717–18	Siege of Constantinople by Arabs
726	Underwater volcanic eruption at Thera (Santorini)
730	Leo III dismisses Patriarch Germanos and imposes iconoclasm
740	*Ekloga* issued by Leo III and Constantine V; Byzantine victory over the Arabs at Akroinon
750	Abbasid revolt and removal of Caliphate to Baghdad
751	Fall of Ravenna to Lombards
754	Iconoclast Council at Hiereia; Alliance between Pope Stephen II and Pippin, king of the Franks
787	Seventh Oecumenical Council at Nicaea
800	Pope Leo III crowns Charles, king of the Franks, emperor in Rome
815	Iconoclast Council in Hagia Sophia
829	Relics of St Mark taken from Alexandria to Venice
843	Theodora ends Iconoclasm with Synodikon of Orthodoxy

858–67	Patriarch Photios, first reign, conversion of the Bulgars and baptism of Khan Boris
860	Russian attack on Constantinople
863	Mission of Constantine-Cyril and Methodios to Moravia
867	Murder of Michael III by Basil I the Macedonian
869/70	Eighth Oecumenical Council in Constantinople
877–86	Patriarch Photios, second reign
905	Birth of Constantine Porphyrogennetos
907	Fourth marriage of Leo VI
911	First treaty between Byzantium and the Rus
941	Russian attack on Constantinople
944	Second trade treaty with Rus, followed by Olga's visit to Constantinople
961	Byzantine reconquest of Crete by Nikephoros Phokas
965	Byzantine reconquest of Cyprus
972	Marriage of Theophano to Otto II in Rome
969	Byzantine reconquest of Antioch by John Tzimiskes
989	Baptism of Vladimir of Kiev and marriage to Anna Porphyrogennetos
992	Basil II issues first Byzantine chrysobull for Venice
1004	Marriage of Maria Argyropoulaina and Giovanni Orseolo
1004/5	Introduction of the fork to Venice
1034	Harald Hadrada arrives in Constantinople with Varangians
1046–53	Pechenegs cross Danube frontiers and devastate Balkans
1048	onwards Constantine IX Monomarchos devalues gold coinage
1054	Schism between Constantinople and Rome
1071	Normans capture Bari in southern Italy; Seljuk Turks defeat and capture Romanos IV Diogenes at the battle of Mantzikert
1082/4	Alexios I Komnenos issues second chrysobull for Venice
1082–5	Norman invasion of Epiros
1087	Seljuk Turks capture Jerusalem
1092	Alexios I Komnenos reforms the gold coinage
1095	Alexios I Komnenos appeals for western military help against the Turks
1096–9	First Crusade
c. 1111	Basil the Bogomil burned at the stake
1146–8	Second Crusade
1171	Byzantine attack on Venetian colonies throughout the empire
1182	Further Byzantine attacks on Venetian, Pisan and Genoese property

1187	Saladin recaptures Jerusalem, expels crusaders
1189–92	Third Crusade, Richard I, 'the Lionheart' of England, invades Cyprus
1202–4	Fourth Crusade
1203	First siege of Constantinople, flight of Alexios III Angelos, Crusaders install Alexios IV with his father Isaac II Angelos
1204	Crusaders' second siege and sack of Constantinople, establishment of the Latin Empire of Constantinople
1204/5	Foundation of rival Byzantine states in Trebizond, Nicaea and Epiros
1208	Theodore I Laskaris crowned as emperor in Nicaea
1216	Theodore Komnenos Doukas captures Ohrid
1224	Theodore Komnenos Doukas captures Thessalonike
1225/7	Theodore Komnenos Doukas captures Adrianople, crowned emperor in Thessalonike
1248	Mistras founded by William II Villehardouin
1249	Michael II Komnenos Doukas adopts the title Despot of Epiros
1249/50	Theological debates between Byzantines and friars at Nymphaion
1259	Michael Palaiologos defeats forces of Epiros and Achaia, William II Villehardouin taken prisoner
1261	Latins driven out of Constantinople, Michael VIII Palaiologos returns in triumph
1274	Council of Lyons declares union of churches
1278	William II Villehardouin dies, Charles of Anjou inherits principality of Achaia
1282	'Sicilian Vespers' attack on Charles of Anjou halts his projected invasion of Byzantium
1327	Ottomans capture Prousa/Bursa
1331	Ottomans capture Nicaea/Iznik
1337	Ottomans capture Nikomedeia/Izmit
1341–7	Civil war between John V Palaiologos and John VI Kantakouzenos
1342–9	Zealots seize control of Thessalonike
1351	Council in Constantinople approves doctrine of Hesychasm
1354	Ottoman forces cross Dardanelles and capture Gallipoli
1369	Ottomans capture Adrianople/Edirne
1396	Crusade of King Sigismund defeated at Nicopolis
1397–1402	Siege of Constantinople
1399–1403	Manuel II's travels in Western Europe

1402	Timur (Tamerlane) defeats Ottomans at Ankyra, Sultan Bayezid and son Musa captured
1422	Sultan Murad II besieges Constantinople
1438/9	Council of Ferrara-Florence, another attempt at church union
1444	Murad II defeats Crusade of Christian forces at Varna
1453	29 May, Sultan Mehmed II captures Constantinople, death of Constantine XI on the walls of the city
1460	Ottomans capture Mistras
1461	Ottomans capture Trebizond/Trabzon

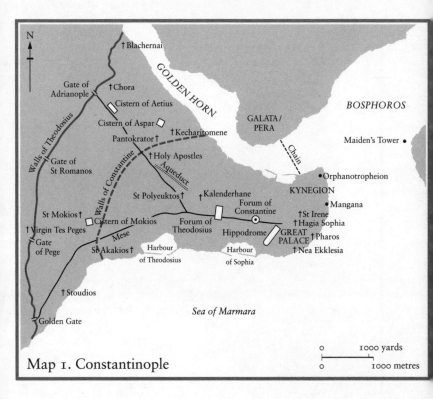

Map 1. Constantinople

Map 2. The Roman World

† monastery

0 ————————— 500 miles
0 ————————— 500 kilometres

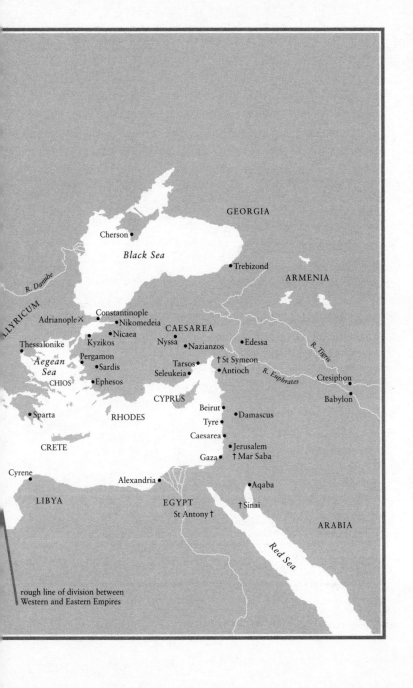

GEORGIA

Cherson •

Black Sea

• Trebizond

ARMENIA

R. *Danube*

ILLYRICUM

Constantinople
Adrianople ✕ • Nikomedeia
• Nicaea

CAESAREA

Thessalonike
Kyzikos   Nyssa • Nazianzos   • Edessa   R. *Tigris*

*Aegean
Sea*   Pergamon
• Sardis   Tarsos •   † St Symeon   R. *Euphrates*   Ctesiphon •
Seleukeia •   • Antioch
CHIOS   • Ephesos   Babylon •

CYPRUS

• Sparta   RHODES   Beirut •   • Damascus
Tyre •
Caesarea •
CRETE   • Jerusalem
Gaza •   † Mar Saba

Cyrene •   Alexandria •   • Aqaba

LIBYA   EGYPT
St Antony †   † Sinai

ARABIA

Red Sea

rough line of division between
Western and Eastern Empires

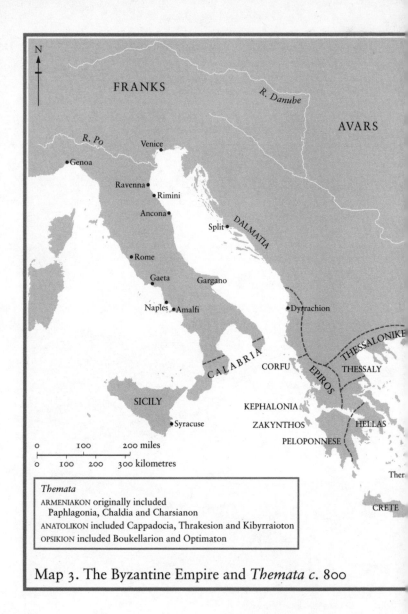

N

FRANKS

R. Danube

AVARS

R. Po

Venice

Genoa

Ravenna
Rimini

Ancona

DALMATIA
Split

Rome

Gaeta
Gargano

Naples Amalfi

Dyrrachion

CALABRIA
CORFU
EPIROS

THESSALONIKE

THESSALY

SICILY

KEPHALONIA

ZAKYNTHOS

HELLAS

Syracuse

PELOPONNESE

Ther

CRETE

0   100   200 miles
0   100   200   300 kilometres

Themata
ARMENIAKON originally included
  Paphlagonia, Chaldia and Charsianon
ANATOLIKON included Cappadocia, Thrakesion and Kibyrraioton
OPSIKION included Boukellarion and Optimaton

Map 3. The Byzantine Empire and *Themata* c. 800

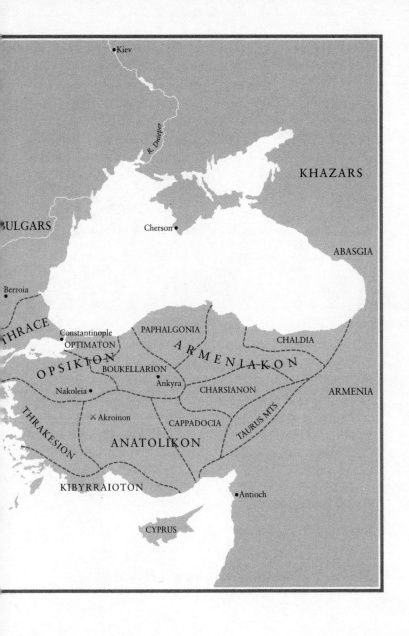

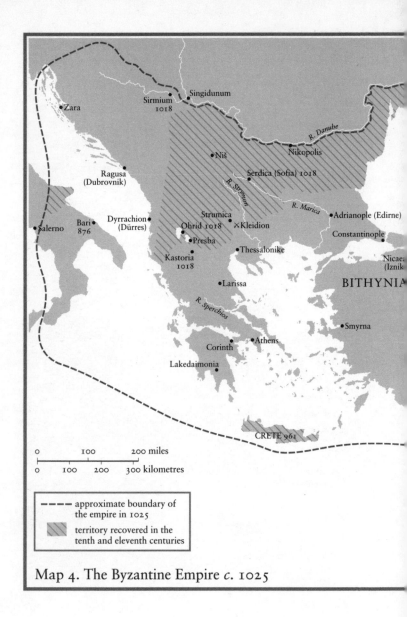

Map 4. The Byzantine Empire *c.* 1025

Map labels:

Zara

Sirmium 1018

Singidunum

R. Danube

Nikopolis

Niš

Serdica (Sofia) 1018

Ragusa (Dubrovnik)

R. Strymon

R. Marica

Adrianople (Edirne)

Strumica

Dyrrachion (Dürres)

Obrid 1018

×Kleidion

Constantinople

Salerno

Bari 876

Presba

Thessalonike

Nicaea (Iznik)

Kastoria 1018

BITHYNIA

Larissa

R. Sperchios

Smyrna

Corinth

Athens

Lakedaimonia

CRETE 961

Scale:

0   100   200 miles

0   100   200   300 kilometres

- - - - approximate boundary of the empire in 1025

territory recovered in the tenth and eleventh centuries

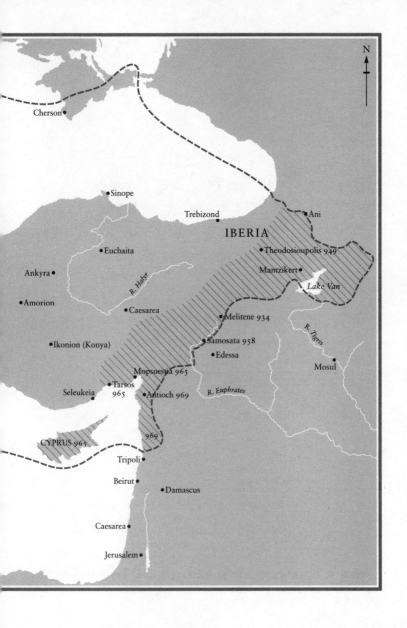

N

Cherson•

•Sinope

Trebizond•

•Ani

IBERIA

•Euchaita

•Theodosioupolis 949

Ankyra•

R. Halys

Mantzikert•

•Amorion

Lake Van

•Caesarea

•Melitene 934

R. Tigris

•Ikonion (Konya)

•Samosata 958

•Edessa

Mopsuestia 965

Mosul•

Seleukeia

•Tarsos
965

•Antioch 969

R. Euphrates

CYPRUS 965

969

Tripoli•

Beirut•

•Damascus

Caesarea•

Jerusalem•

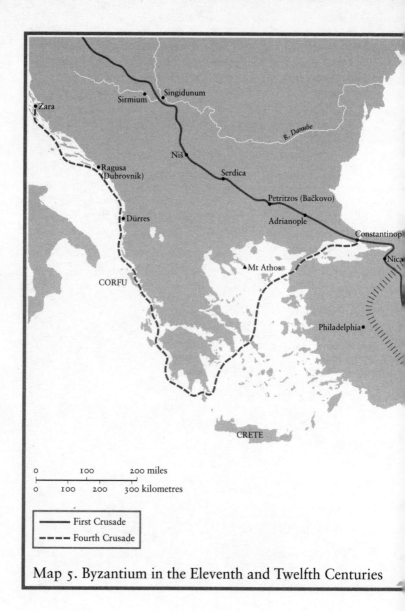

Map 5. Byzantium in the Eleventh and Twelfth Centuries

Zara

Sirmium • Singidunum

R. Danube

Ragusa (Dubrovnik)

Niš •

Serdica •

Petritzos (Bačkovo) •

Dürres •

Adrianople •

Constantinop

Nica

CORFU

▲ Mt Athos

Philadelphia •

CRETE

0   100   200 miles

0   100   200   300 kilometres

——— First Crusade
- - - Fourth Crusade

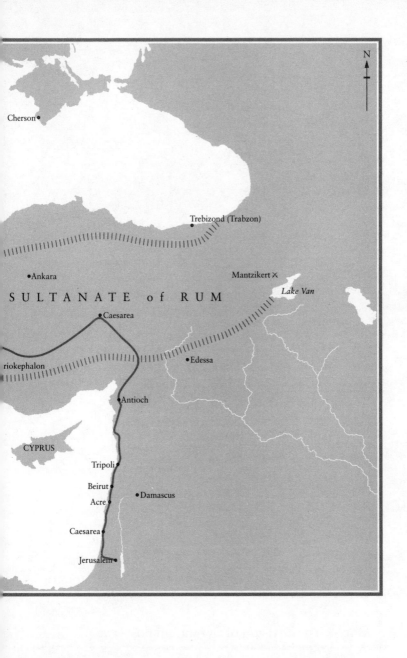

N

Cherson •

Trebizond (Trabzon) •

• Ankara

Mantzikert ✕

SULTANATE of RUM

• Caesarea

Lake Van

riokephalon

• Edessa

• Antioch

CYPRUS

Tripoli •

Beirut •

Acre •

• Damascus

Caesarea •

Jerusalem •

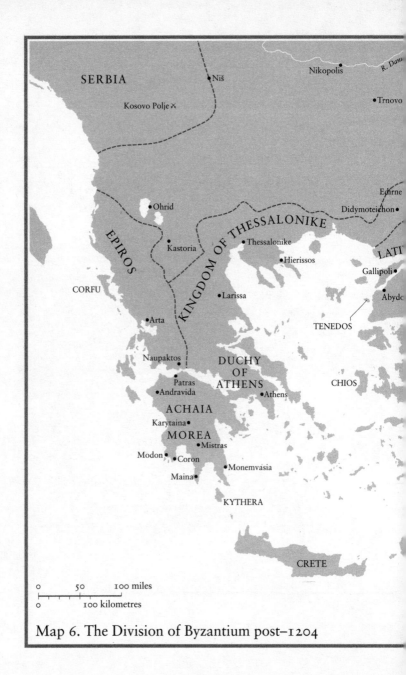

SERBIA

Niš

Nikopolis

R. Danu

Kosovo Polje ✕

Trnovo

Ohrid

Edirne

Didymoteichon

KINGDOM OF THESSALONIKE

Kastoria

Thessalonike

Hierissos

EPIROS

LATI

Gallipoli

CORFU

Larissa

Abydo

TENEDOS

Arta

Naupaktos

DUCHY
OF
ATHENS

Patras

CHIOS

Andravida

Athens

ACHAIA

Karytaina

MOREA

Mistras

Modon

Coron

Monemvasia

Maina

KYTHERA

CRETE

```
0        50      100 miles
0              100 kilometres
```

Map 6. The Division of Byzantium post–1204

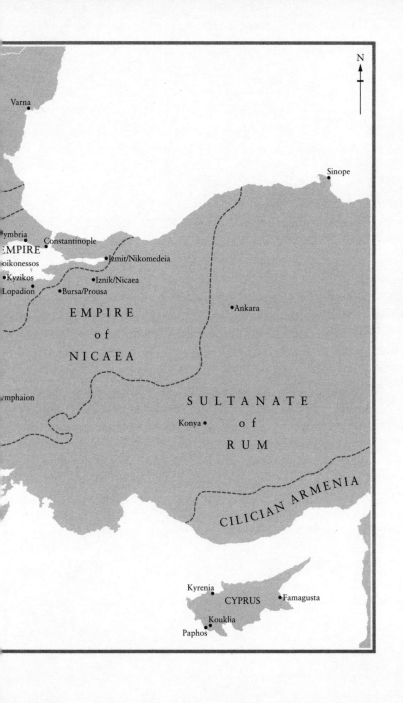

N

Varna

Sinope

ymbria   Constantinople
EMPIRE   •Izmit/Nikomedeia
oikonessos
•Kyzikos   •Iznik/Nicaea
Lopadion   •Bursa/Prousa
                                        •Ankara
        EMPIRE
            o f
        NICAEA

                    S U L T A N A T E
mphaion
                    Konya •   o f
                                R U M

                                    CILICIAN ARMENIA

                        Kyrenia •
                                    CYPRUS   •Famagusta
                            Kouklia •
                        Paphos •

Acknowledgements

In writing this book I gratefully acknowledge the financial support of the A. G. Leventis Foundation, the Michael Marks Charitable Trust, Dr Alkisti Soulogianni, Director of International Relations of the Ministry of Culture of the Hellenic Republic, and Professor Rick Trainor, Principal of King's College London. I would also like to thank my colleagues in the departments of Classics and Byzantine and Modern Greek Studies who gave me time and encouragement.

For wise advice in the final stages of writing I thank in particular Stuart Proffitt, who went through the text twice. At a critical stage in composition Dr Alexandros Papaderos, Director of the Orthodox Academy of Crete, provided most generous hospitality. My friends Dionysios Stathakopoulos, Charlotte Roueché and Carol Krinsky found time to read drafts and make numerous improvements; Murat Belge, Neil Belton and Anthony Cheetham helped with their attention to detail; and reports by Bob Ousterhout and Chris Wickham and two other readers not identified by the publishers saved me from errors and suggested new topics to include in the final version. I am most grateful to Clive Foss and Uroš Milivojević who suggested useful corrections.

I also thank Georgina Capel, for her enthusiastic support, Brigitta van Rheinberg for her belief in the end product, and Catherine Holmes, Demetra and Charalambos Bakirtzis, Cécile Morrisson, Archie Dunn, Elizabeth Jeffreys, Costas Kaplanis, Anna Contadini, Rustam Shukurov, Charalambos Bouras and Jessica Rawson for assistance with copies of rare books and articles, unpublished texts and guidance about finding others. Maria Vassilaki made it possible for me to accompany the pilgrimage to St Catherine's Monastery on Mount Sinai organized by the Society for the Preservation of the Greek Heritage, and I thank her, Lydia and Costas Carras and Anna Lea. Finally, I am especially grateful to Kallirroe Linardou for her help in finding the illustrations, and to Lioba Theis and the staffs of the Barber Institute of Fine Arts, Birmingham, the Byzantine Collection at Dumbarton Oaks, the

Benaki Museum, Athens, and the Courtauld Institute of Art for their generous assistance.

More than ever, I acknowledge the constant support of those who lived with and campaigned for the book in all its stages: Anthony, Tamara and Portia.

Index